Masterplan

Judaism: its program, meanings, goals

Jerusalem Academy Publications

Masterplan

Judaism: its program, meanings, goals

ARYEH CARMELL

Published by
Jerusalem Academy Publications, 18 Blau St. Jerusalem
© 1991 by Aryeh Carmell

Library of Congress Cataloging-in-Publication Data
Carmell, Aryeh.
  Masterplan : Judaism, its program, meaning, goals / by Aryeh Carmell.
    p. 23 cm.
  Includes bibliographical references and index.
  ISBN 0-87306-574-3 (hardcover), 0-87306-581-6 (paperback)
  1. Commandments (Judaism) 2. Judaism—Essence, genius, nature.
I. Title.
BM520.7.C37 1991
296.3'85—dc20
                                      91-22593
                                        CIP

Distributed by
Philipp Feldheim Inc.   Feldheim Publishers Ltd.
200 Airport Executive Park   POB 35002
Spring Valley, NY 10977   Jerusalem, Israel

Typesetting: Astronel

Printed in Israel

10 9 8 7 6 5 4 3 2 1

מוקדש
לזכרם ולעילוי נשמתם
של הורי האהובים
אשר הנחוני בדרך אמת
לאור באור החיים

אבי מורי
ר' אברהם חיים ז"ל
ואמי מורתי
מרת רבקה ע"ה

יהי זכרם ברוך

Acknowledgments

I wish to express my sincere gratitude to all those who have been kind enough to offer advice during the various stages of the planning and writing of this book. I am grateful, first and foremost, to my dear wife מרת חי׳ גיטל תחי׳ for her constant encouragement throughout this project — as in so many others — and for reading through the manuscript and making many valuable suggerstions; to my son הרב יעקב מרדכי ישראל שליט״א for devoting so much time and energy to all aspects of this book; to my son הרב אברהם חיים שליט״א for his many acute and helpful suggestions; to my son-in-law Jay Steingroot (ר׳ יעקב בן גדלי׳ נ״י) for his valuable comments; and to my daughter-in-law מרת שרה תחי׳ for her superb and devoted work in producing an accurate text on the word-processor. My special thanks are reserved for my friend and colleague הרב יהודה לוי שליט״א (Professor Leo Levi) — in conversation with whom this work was first conceived — for taking much of his valuable time to read through the wholc manuscript with great care and for making many cogent and helpful criticisms, all of which were carefully considered and taken into account in the final version.

כולם יעמדו על הברכה
ותהי משכורתם שלמה
מאת ה׳ אלקי ישראל

A.C.

Contents

Contents

Contents

Introduction

What does Judaism mean to the average man-in-the-street? Nine times out of ten: Sabbath, Festivals, synagogue, dietary laws, circumcision, mourning rites.

But all these are merely a small part of what Judaism means. Judaism is a comprehensive scheme which covers all aspects of life; the individual and society, modes of behavior, personal relations, husband and wife, the tax system, ruler and ruled, professional integrity and business ethics, how to run a home, a community, a society, a state. In other words, it embodies the art of living in all its aspects.

The laws which govern all these matters are just as distinctive as those which regulate our diet or our synagogue service. All departments of Torah work together towards an all-embracing goal which may be summed up provisionally as: the creation of a just society inspired by a vision of man as the image of God.

> "'The ways of pleasantness and the paths of peace' — this is the whole Torah."
> (Talmud)

> "The dietary laws were given to refine the human being."
> (Midrash)

> "The ordinances of the Torah are...a means of ensuring mercy, kindness and peace in the world."
> (Maimonides)

But the Torah does not stop there. The idea is to establish a model society which the world will wish to emulate, thus bringing the benefits of Torah life to as large a proportion of humanity as possible. Whenever the special obligations of the Jewish people are mentioned, the Torah never fails to emphasize this wider, universal goal:

> "The whole world is Mine, but you shall be to Me a kingdom of priests and a holy nation...."
> (Exodus 19:5:6)

> "I shall make you a covenant-people, a light to the nations."
> (Isaiah 42:6)

> "And all the families of the earth will be blessed through you."
> (Genesis 12:3)

It is a fact that, as a non-Jewish historian has put it, "[the Jews] always knew that Jewish society was appointed to be a pilot-project for the entire human race."

It is in this context that we can begin to understand the significance of the commandments of the Torah and the comprehensive program which they embody.

THE CONCEPT OF A "MITZVA"

"Mitzva" (plural: mitzvot) means "commandment." In the Western world we are not familiar with the concept of doing something because it is a commandment. We behave in moral ways, if we do, because of the value system to which our upbringing and society happen to have conditioned us. When challanged we often find it very difficult to defend the system. This mode of behavior is unreliable because it is based on vague general concepts without formal or rational basis. There could be no better illustration of the instability of this type of system than the Nazi experience. In a few years we saw a nation which prided itself on its high level of culture have its morality turned on its head, with disastrous results.

Throughout history great thinkers — Plato, Spinoza,

Kant, Marx — have produced splendid ethical systems suggesting that we curb our egotism in various ways for the good of the community. Insofar as they were tried, they all failed abysmally. First, they lacked credible authority. Second, they failed to deal with the brute facts of the human being as he really is. They failed to provide a detailed program which would nurture the growth of the individual from a self-contained being to a person prepared and motivate to give up his self-interest for an ideal beyond himself. Everyone agreed that the system was wonderful — for everyone else.

Both these shortcomings are overcome by the mitzva system of Judaism.

The concept of "mitzva" introduces a new motive into our lives: we act in certain ways not because we happen to feel it is right, but because we realize that this is how God wants us to act. This introduces a higher dimension into our lives. In fact it involves a revolutionary change in our attitude to ourselves, the world and our fellow beings. (How this relates to the "Kantian ethic" is discussed in the Notes.)

Furthermore mitzvot work on many levels. They give us general guidance on principles. They also provide very detailed and specific instructions regarding both interpersonal relationships and modes of relating to God — the spiritual reality that is beyond ourselves. The latter include many significant symbolic acts designed to restructure our personality on both the conscious and unconscious levels.

"THE IMAGE OF GOD"

We can become aware of this higher dimension of our lives because we are "created in the image of God." What does this mean? It means that we are created with free will, and thus with the capacity to change ourselves from selfish to unselfish, from being interested only in "taking" to being interested also in "giving" — in being a blessing to those with whom we come in contact in our day-to-day activities. It is this capacity for giving which is meant by the image of God, since God is the "Giver" par excellence.

It is pathetic to see "liberals" and humanists attempting to solve the problems of mankind on an atheistic basis. The great illusion of the twentieth century has been the idea that all human problems can be solved at one fell swoop by some grandiose project of political or social engineering, without relating to the hidden depths of the human personality.

The most prolonged and extensive of these experiments, Marxist-Leninism, by the admission of its own proponents, has turned out to be the most abject failure. An atheistic ideology which tyrannized the minds and lives of countless human beings and subjected them to ruthless oppression and terror for the best part of the 20th century is now seen to have been misconceived from the start. It robbed human beings of their freedom, value and dignity, and, ironically, failed to provide even a minimum standard of material existence. Human beings simply cannot function as cogs in a machine.

A TURNING POINT?

But what is the alternative?

The Western world, with the United States of America in the lead, has gone to the opposite extreme. Rampant individualism, while providing the material means for affluent living for most of the population, is making it more and more difficult to enjoy this affluence in reasonable security. When libertarianism is taken to extremes and "each man does what is right in his own eyes," human dignity and value again suffer, and liberty for most people is actually diminished. In common with the other ethical systems we referred to above, this system, too, with all its vaunted ideals, fails to be realized in practice, for the simple reason that it ignores the need for restructuring the human personality. If pluralism is taken to such extremes that there are no agreed standards of right and wrong, there can be no stable society. As Lord Justice Devlin remarked, "If men and women try to create a society in which there is no fundamental agreement about good and evil, they will fail." Where there is no sense of higher values, there drug abuse, crime and pollution will proliferate to intolerable proportions.

One cannot help thinking that the liberal atheistic philosophies which have dominated western thinking for so long may also be due for drastic revision. We are now able to see that they are ultimately as self-defeating as Marxism.

One senses a certain openness in certain quarters; a certain willingness to consider alternatives previously rejected out of hand.

We are at a turning point in human history. It may be an opportune moment to consider what the concept of "mitzva" has to offer to the questing spirit of man — and primarily Jewish man.

RELEVANCE OVER THE MILLENNIA

This book is based on the predicate that the Torah, although promulgated thousands of years ago, is still relevant at the present day.

True, it comes to us dressed in the garb of the 2nd millennium B.C.E. Its cases often involve cows and donkeys, ploughshares and millstones. It assumes the existence of customs and conventions belonging to that faraway world. But if one can bring oneself to look beyond the outward garb and see the reality within, the Torah is seen to be as relevant now as it was then. Its principles and prescriptions, translated into the language and concepts of today, can be applied successfully to contemporary human societies and contemporary human problems. The reason is that the Torah is less concerned with the outer trappings of life than with the abiding questions of human-human relations and human-Divine relations on both the conscious and subconscious levels. And above all it is concerned with the subtle connecting links between all these — human and divine, conscious and subconscious. It is a culture and a civilization which, while it gave birth, directly or indirectly, to all the liberal ideas which have molded the modern world, is also capable of pointing beyond them to something higher and more sublime.

This is what we mean when we say the Torah is eternal. It is also something of what we mean when we say the Torah is of Divine origin. This means that it is derived from a spiritual source incomparably higher than even the greatest human mind — the One Who created that mind.

When we compare the world of three millennia ago and the world we live in today, there is no doubt that it is as if we were living on a different planet.

To imagine that some people from *that* world could out of their own mind string together some stories and devise some laws and principles which would retain their significance through millennia and speak so directly and cogently to us here today, is simply incredible. We are therefore right not to believe this but to hold firmly to our faith that the Torah derives its power and significance from a higher source — God.

SCHEME OF THE MITZVOT

The Torah contains traditionally 613 mitzvot, taking positive and negative mitzvot together. On many occasions the

Torah insists that they form a coherent whole. However the overall scheme is not immediately apparent from the written Torah.

During the course of history attempts have been made to classify the mitzvot in various ways. In the Mishna, the authoritative recension of the Oral Law by Rabbi Judah the Prince in the second century C.E., the mitzvot in their entirety are grouped into six classes, or Orders, with sixty sub-divisions, or Tractates. They are arranged according to subject matter, so that we have one Order dealing with the laws relating to agriculture in the Land of Israel, one dealing with Sabbaths and Festivals, one with civil legislation and so on. The Talmud follows this classification.

A thousand years later, Maimonides made a more detailed classification of the entire Oral Law into fourteen main groups. A couple of centuries after Maimonides, Rabbi Jacob ben Asher (known as the author of the "*Tur*") confined his presentation to mitzvot which apply at the present day (i.e., excluding the laws of the Temple service and related topics). He reduced the main groupings to four, of which the first ("The Way of Life") follows the Jew from the moment he wakes in the morning until he retires at night, and then throughout the year, with its Sabbaths and Festivals, days of joy and mourning. The other three classes comprise, first, dietary laws and other regulatory provisions, then civil law and finally marriage law.

In the present work we follow, in principle if not in detail, the innovative classification of Rabbi Samson Raphael Hirsch in his *Horeb*, where the mitzvot are grouped according to *function*.

Accordingly we shall present the mitzvot of the Torah which are applicable at the present day in the following five categories:

GROUP ONE: Justice Towards Other People
  Laws which form the basis of social legislation.

GROUP TWO: Justice Towards the Environment
  Mitzvot regulating our use and enjoyment of the environment.

GROUP THREE: Love and Concern for Other People
  Mitzvot fostering enhanced awareness of the needs of other people.

GROUP FOUR: Enrichment of the Environment
  Mitzvot which fill our environment with God-oriented activities.

GROUP FIVE: The Inner Life
  Mitzvot addressed to our heart and mind, expressing an intimate relationship with God.

Even at this preliminary stage we can see the emergent pattern in this classification. The first two groups seek to achieve just relations, first with other people and then with the total environment. Group 3 aims to raise our relations with other people from relations of justice to those of love and concern. Group 4 seeks similarly to ensure our progress from just relations with the environment to spiritual enrichment of that environment.

Finally, Group 5 comprises the spiritual qualities which underlie all the mitzvot and in a sense form their end-product and goal. (See Notes.)

One of the aims of this book is to demonstrate how all these different mitzva-types are interdependent and how they are designed to work together towards the final goal. Precisely what this goal is — whether it is the perfection of the individual or the perfection of society or some other purpose — may emerge from the explanations of mitzvot offered in the course of this work. The epilogue will attempt to draw these ideas together and, if possible, to arrive at some degree of clarity on this profound issue.

WHO WAS SAMSON RAPHAEL HIRSCH?

We mentioned that in principle we follow Rabbi Samson Raphael Hirsch in his classification of the mitzvot. We follow him also, in most cases, in his presentation and interpretation of those mitzvot. We do this because we believe that it is his voice, above all others, which has the most to say to our day and age.

Who was Samson Raphael Hirsch? When European emancipation began to offer Jews entrée into the social, intellectual and economic life of the early nineteenth century, the previously ghetto-bound Jews and Jewesses found the experience intoxicating. Traditional Judaism with its restrictions was seen as an impediment to progress. It seemed to them dark and lifeless, belonging to the ghetto they had left behind them. All the lights beckoned on the other side.

The young Rav Hirsch, born in Hamburg in 1808, *knew* that they were making a terrible mistake. He saw that Torah was a program for living with ideals much more elevated and profound than those of the Western world. Far from impeding progress, it stood for the ultimate progress of all mankind. Far from being outmoded, many of its commandments comprised symbols which stood for the most powerful ideas ever presented to man. The people of Israel were the chosen instrument through which these ideals were to be realized.

While still a young man he proceeded to communicate his vision to his German-speaking co-religionists. He succeeded in inspiring a significant number of young people to be completely Torah-observant while still participating fully in the emancipated society of 19th-century Germany. He was the founder of a movement which still flourishes in many parts of the world today, particularly in the U.S.

Introduction

His first major work was *Horeb*, which he addressed to "the thinking young Jews and Jewesses" of his time. It is on Hirsch's presentation in *Horeb* of the plan of the mitzvot and the meaning and goals of Jewish life that the present work is largely based.

TORAH SYMBOLISM

The reader will find that symbolism plays a prominent part in a proper understanding of the mitzvot. In Group Two — Justice for the Environment — many mitzvot are brilliantly illuminated by this approach, for which we are eternally indebted to the genius of Rav Hirsch. Group Four — Enrichment of the Environment — comprises mitzvot expressly stated in the Torah to be symbolic in nature, and we shall find symbols playing their part in other areas too.

It should not surprise us that the Torah makes extensive use of symbolic objects and activities. Man has been called the symbol-making animal. Our lives are governed by symbols, from handshakes to traffic lights. Some modern psychologists have discovered that symbols retain their significance in the human unconscious over very long periods of time. Since the Torah's message was meant to be projected over thousands of years it is only to be expected that much use is made of symbols.

The Torah speaks so much in symbols also because symbols influence our mind at the deepest level. Symbols are not time bound. They reverberate through the corridors of the mind with infinite gradations of meaning. Even if we are not conscious of their meaning, they have an impact on our unconscious and so influence the springs of action.

KABBALA

We have followed Rav Hirsch in omitting references to kabbalistic (mystical) interpretations. In fact, however, it will be found that the symbolic explanations given of certain mitzvot often have their counterpart in the Zohar and other mystical works. This too is not surprising when it is remembered that Kabbala itself is essentially an exploration of the internal world of the unconscious mind and especially of the non-ego layers of the human psyche.

"REASONS" FOR MITZVOT

In *Horeb*, Hirsch usually presents his interpretations of mitzvot as if they were established facts, however original and innovative they may be. This is because of his unique methodology.

Some commentators make an approximate guess at what the mitzva seems to mean, often on the basis of some preconceived ideas of their own, and then proceed to "attach" this to the mitzva in question. If certain halachic details of the mitzva do not fit the explanation, they tend to ignore this or attempt to explain it away. Hirsch strongly opposed this method. He believed that the mitzva must first be analyzed in all its halachic detail, and the meaning developed on the basis of the data thus obtained. This is the method adopted in science, where a theory should ideally be consistent with all the facts. We just substitute the legal facts of halacha for the physical facts of science. Hirsch called this "understanding Torah from its own sources." Aggadic and midrashic sources are an important element in his research, since they provide indications of how the purpose and function of the mitzva was understood by the Sages of the Torah.

A case in point is the Torah's prohibition of work on Shabbat. Taken superficially the motive seems to be merely the desire to establish Shabbat as a weekly day of rest. But the halachic details of the Shabbat laws are not at all consistent with this assumption. We find that hard physical labor in certain instances is not necessarily a desecration of Shabbat. The principles which define which kind of activity constitutes an actual desecration of the sanctity of Shabbat do not seem to be related to physical labor at all. What criterion is being used? This is not at all obvious.

Superficial thinkers ignore this problem. Hirsch refused to ignore it. By dint of brilliant analytic reasoning he deduced the principles from the halachic data and derived an original interpretation which makes all the intricate details of the Shabbat laws perfectly comprehensible. (See chapter 41.)

Nevertheless one should be aware that in many instances the explanations are in fact theories and should be taken as such. Moreover, various explanations have been suggested for many mitzvot, but in this book we have followed Rav Hirsch in giving one reason only.

In any case it should be pointed out that loyal Jews have never made their commitment to Torah and mitzvot dependent on whether or not they understood the reason for any particular mitzva. The Torah expects a Jew to accept its mitzvot as Divine commandments. Explanations are only sought to deepen our understanding, never for justification. Even if no satisfactory explanation is immediately forthcoming, we have faith in God and in the wisdom of our Sages that there *is* an explanation and we hope that one day we shall be privileged to understand it.

WHY ARE MITZVOT SO COMPLICATED?

The question is often asked: "Why are mitzvot so complicated?"

This reminds one of the question raised regarding the DNA molecule and other complex life-mechanisms, by the famous physicist Professor Freeman Dyson: "Why is life so complicated?" In view of the variety and complexity of the various particles and forces of physics he might just as well have asked: "Why is *matter* so complicated?"

The fact is that we live in an extremely complex world and we ourselves — even physically speaking — are extremely complex beings. Furthermore, the brain of every human being contains many more than ten billion (10,000,000,000!) neurons and these are in constant interaction throughout our lives. Our brain indeed is the most complex structure in the known universe. We have been given such an enormously complex instrument because *we* — the people who use this instrument — are faced with very complex tasks in our interactions with our environment, which includes other human beings and also God, the Source of our being. It is understandable therefore that simple instructions like "the greatest good of the greatest number" are completely inadequate to enable us to live as human beings and Jews, with our multiple spiritual challenges. (In chapter 64(5), when discussing the mitzva of Torah study, we shall suggest a further reason for this complexity.)

THE NATURE OF THIS WORK

We have been asked: "Is this book a new translation of Rabbi S.R. Hirsch's *Horeb*, or is it an original work?"

The answer is that it is neither. It is certainly not a new translation of *Horeb*, as anyone at all familiar with that work will see at once. But neither is it an original work, since it is based so extensively, both in structure and in content, on that pioneering achievement. Nevertheless it contains a good deal of original material, as an inspection of the sources will show.

As we have already said, the division of the mitzvot into groups and the allocation of the mitzvot within these groups, as well as the attempts to understand their meaning, are based to a very large extent on *Horeb*, supplemented by Rav Hirsch's later writings.

Hirsch's great work, which made such a tremendous impact in its time, was written over 150 years ago. It spoke to the spirit of its time. What we really need is a 20th-century Hirsch who can speak to the spirit of *our* time. Failing this, we have tried to imagine what Hirsch might have said had he been writing in our time rather than in 1837. Besides changing the order of sections we have introduced many changes which are sure to infuriate loyal Hirschians. Our aim, however, has been not to present Hirsch, but to present Torah to our generation — an aim of which we may be sure Hirsch himself would have heartily approved.

In the majority of cases we have retained Hirsch's original ideas, but wherever this seemed appropriate we have modified, adapted, and re-written the original and we have sometimes adopted ideas from other sources. Above all we have abbreviated. This book is approximately one-half the size of *Horeb*.

Most chapters of this book contain a section headed HALACHA. Halacha comprises the practical details of a mitzva as recorded in Mishna and Talmud (the "Oral Law") and established by Torah authorities from the earliest time to the present day. (See "Torah through the Ages" in the Appendix.)

In *Horeb*, Hirsch included a considerable amount of halachic detail. In the present volume this has been drastically curtailed. Hirsch's youthful readers had little knowledge of Hebrew and at that time there was little or no halachic material in German. Apart from its other important functions, *Horeb* was in fact used for a long time also as a text book of halacha. Today much halacha is available in English and other languages. We have therefore concentrated on the main aim — the presentation of Torah as a coherent and meaningful scheme. The Bibliography lists books available in English which treat the topics referred to at greater length.

All sources have been indicated in the Notes. So as not to clutter up the text with supralinear numbers, we have given the sources at the end by the page number and quotation method.

We have made good use of the late Dayan Dr. I. Grunfeld's excellent English translation of *Horeb* (published by Soncino Press) and grateful acknowledgment is made for the help this has afforded, though the original German edition has been constantly consulted. In the great majority of cases Hirsch's ideas have been presented in the present author's own words. Where the wording of Dayan Grunfeld's translation has been adopted verbatim, or with minor modifications, this has been indicated in the Notes.

We have done something that Hirsch never did. In appropriate places we have added stories, episodes and parables illustrating the aspect of the mitzva under discussion. It is hoped that this will illuminate the real-life application of the principle behind the mitzvot.

CONTEMPORARY CHALLENGES

Due account has been taken of the changes in Jewish life brought about by the existence of a Jewish state in which about a third of the Jews of the world reside. This presents a challenge on many levels, not least in relation to the social legislation of the Torah. The Torah's great vision of a just and caring society as a model to the nations has become extremely relevant in our present situation, and we have given due prominence to this fact. In fact it was this consideration that led us to place the Torah's social legislation and environmental concerns at the head of the book, as explained at length in the note to p. xv of this Introduction.

Another contemporary challenge which this book is

designed to meet is the ongoing influx of hundreds of thousands of Jews from Soviet Russia into Israel — Jews who have for generations been forcibly alienated from any form of Jewish knowledge. Perhaps an even greater challenge is presented by a large proportion of the Israeli population, who for different reasons, have unfortunately been estranged from Torah and fed false and distorted ideas of what Torah is and what its goals are. It is sincerely hoped that the publication of this book may go some little way to enlighten those who wish to know about the true nature and purposes of Torah and mitzvot. For these reasons Hebrew and Russian editions are planned to follow closely on this English edition.

We pray to Almighty God that He may grant that His work prospers in our hands.

A.C.
Jerusalem 5751

GROUP ONE:
JUSTICE TOWARDS OTHER PEOPLE

Mitzvot dealing with social justice in all its aspects

This first group comprises those mitzvot which aim at ensuring justice in all human relations. They define our obligations to respect human rights, to deal justly and honestly in all our transactions, to remove potential dangers from the environment and to refrain from hurting people in more subtle ways.

1. The Just Society
Establishment of a system of justice

2. Respect for Human Life
Prohibition of murder

3. Respect for the Person
Prohibition of assault / Injury

4. Protecting Human Rights
Liberty / Privacy / Self-incrimination

5. Justice in Employee-Employer Relations
Fair wages / Withholding payment / Employee's obligations

6. Respect for Other People's Property
Prohibition of theft / Pressuring people to sell

7. Justice in Property Transfers
Honesty in buying and selling / Loans and claims / Employment / Custodians

8. Safety of the Environment
Mitzva of roof-parapet / Prevention of accidents / Dealing with pollution

9. Honest Speech
Falsehood / Flattery / Hypocrisy

10. Justice for the Weak and Vulnerable
Oppression / Vexation / Humiliation / Hurting someone's feelings / Abuse of weakness

11. Respect for a Person's Reputation
The evil tongue / Slander / Tale-bearing / Respecting confidence

1

1. The Just Society

ESTABLISHMENT OF A SYSTEM OF JUSTICE

Justice, justice is what you shall pursue! — DEUTERONOMY 16:20

You shall appoint judges and officers of the law in all your cities...and they shall judge the people fairly.
— DEUTERONOMY 16:18

I have chosen him [Abraham] so that he will command his children and household after him to keep the way of God, to establish charity and justice. — GENESIS 18:19

Let justice roll down like water and charity like a mighty stream. — AMOS 5:24

Seek out justice, put right the wrong, grant justice to the orphan, stand up for the widow...[Then] if your sins are as scarlet they shall be white as snow. — ISAIAH 1:18

You shall not bear false witness against your neighbor.
— EXODUS 20:18; DEUTERONOMY 5:17

(1) Establishing the just society

The Torah of God recognizes that no society can exist in the long term unless it is governed by a system of social justice. The precept of social justice applies also to non-Jewish societies. It is one of the Seven Noachide Commandments addressed to all human beings without distinction.

The Torah was given to a nation — the Jewish nation — and not to individuals. Its primary purpose was not to "save the individual's soul" but to bring into existence that extreme rarity in human affairs — the *just society*. It was intended that all the facets and institutions of this society would be pervaded and sanctified by the spirit of justice and love which is the hallmark of the Torah.

God promised that through the Torah we would become

2

"a holy nation." This means a dedicated nation — dedicated to just and fair relationships between man and man, between man and woman, citizen and alien, strong and weak.

(2) Law courts (batei din)

But meanwhile we have to deal with the reality — fallible human beings. Law courts (*batei din*) and officers of the law are necessary to settle disputes, to enforce justice and prevent the exploitation of the weak by the strong and of the poor by the rich.

The *bet din* of the Torah also has an educative function. The Sanhedrin or supreme court, composed of the greatest Torah Sages of the generation, is empowered to make ordinances to assist people to keep the laws of the Torah. This is the source of the *takkanot derabbanan*, "rabbinical decrees," which we shall meet frequently in the course of this work. The approval of the Sanhedrin must be obtained for all decisions affecting the national welfare; particularly the decision to go to war. The Sanhedrin appoints the judiciary and is also the final court of appeal.

But, above all, the role of the judge in the eyes of the Torah is "to redress the grievances of those who are abandoned and alone, to protect the dignity of the poor and to save the oppressed from the hands of his oppressor."

(3) Witness and judgment

"You shall not bear false witness against your neighbor" is one of the Ten Commandments. In court the fate of another may depend on our words. Therefore nowhere is good faith and truth more sacred than here.

In Torah law the two witnesses who establish the truth in civil or criminal proceedings must stand completely independent of the case. They must not be related to each other, nor to the litigants or accused, nor to the judges, nor may they have any interest in the outcome. Theirs is a public function; they represent the people of Israel.

If any substantial wrongdoing is proved against them, they are disqualified as witnesses. On the other hand if they are honest, God-fearing Jews, their evidence is accepted, so long as there is no contradiction between them. The judge is not to evaluate their credibility on the basis of status. If they are honest people, their evidence is given full credence. Any Jew has equal status before the court, be he street cleaner or professor.

Among the duties of the judge is to hold himself completely aloof from the parties and the case. He must ignore the status of the parties and not be more polite to one than to the other, nor intimidate anyone by his manner. He must not listen to one without listening to the other and must fearlessly speak out the truth as he sees it, regardless of consequences. The very existence of the world depends on justice. Our Sages have said: "One who judges according to the truth is a partner with God in the act of creation."

(4) Kindness to the cruel is cruelty to the kind

The Torah of love is also a Torah of justice. Indeed it has to be. There can be no love without justice. A society which does not bring its evildoers to justice is no society in which love can flourish.

This is how Torah deals with the liberal dilemma. Thinking that kindness to all is an absolute good, western liberals oppose stern measures for the suppression of violence. The result is they often show more consideration for the criminal than for his victim. The Torah teaches us that kindness which encourages crime is bad and violence used against evildoers is good. The Sages say: "He who is kind to the cruel will end up being cruel to the kind."

Violence is needed to put an end to violence. But who will

4

decide whether the ends are truly just or merely self-seeking? For this crucial decision the Torah refers us to the Sanhedrin of Israel, the distillation of Torah wisdom. Their decisions alone can be relied on to transcend personal or political considerations and to reflect nothing but Torah truth.

(5) The long term solution

But in the long term the problem of violence will not be solved by more violence, however justly applied.

It can be solved only by adopting the whole program envisaged by the Torah for the individual and society, as described in this book. Active participation in this program engenders more positive ways of thinking and behaving and enhances people's images of themselves and others, making them less prone to violence.

It is a fact that in Torah observant communities crimes of violence are very rare. Also, work among the prison population of Israel has shown that, while generally over 50% of released prisoners soon return to a life of crime, among those who have become Torah observant and have been absorbed by the Torah community the rate is only 10%.

◆ *Halacha*

◇ *If one lives in an unjust and corrupt society and has no hope of influencing it in the right direction he must leave the society as soon as possible and settle in a society which is closer to the Torah's ideals.*

◇ *The taking of bribes — not only in money but in favor, services, courtesy — even with the stated intention of giving a fair judgment, disqualifies the judge.*

◇ *Paid testimony is not lawful testimony.*

◇ *One may not withhold evidence which could help a fellowman in his case. [See chapter 35(3).]*

5

A BASKET OF FRUIT

Rabbi Yishmael had a tenant-farmer with whom he shared the crops. Every Friday morning the farmer used to bring the Rabbi a basket of fruit; from the Rabbi's share, not his own. One week he brought the fruit early Thursday morning instead of Friday. He explained that he had a case that day in the *bet din* and he was on his way to town. "Who is going to try the case?" asked Rabbi Yishmael. "You are," he replied. "Oh, no, I'm not," said the Rabbi. "Bringing the fruit one day earlier is a special favor. Someone else will have to be the judge." During the case Rabbi Yishmael listened in the corridor. He caught himself thinking of ways in which the farmer could make a better case. "Aha!" he said. "That's the effect of accepting a favor. What would have happened if I *had* tried the case? Don't believe anyone who tells you he can accept a favor and remain unbiased."

2. Respect for Human Life

PROHIBITION OF MURDER

You shall not murder. — EXODUS 20:13

*From the hand of man, from the hand of every man's
brother, I shall demand the life of man. Whoever sheds man's
blood, by man shall his blood be shed; for God made man in
His image.* — GENESIS 9:5

(1) God's image

"God made man in His image." This concept is central to
the Torah scheme. It means that just as God has revealed
Himself to us as spiritual and the source of life, goodness
and love, so the human being is essentially spiritual and
capable of promoting life, goodness and love.

To sever a human being's link with life is therefore the
crime of crimes. Since life is infinitely precious, to shorten
a life even by a moment is an act of murder. The hand of the
murderer drives God's presence from the world. "He who
kills a man destroys a whole world" (Mishna *Sanhedrin*
4:5).

(2) The humanist paradox

We live in the era of humanism. Much lip-service is paid to
the value of life. Yet when we look around us we see that in
truth human life is held very cheap. Some very "idealistic"
people are prepared to murder hundreds of innocent
human beings just to prove a point, or to gain publicity for
their cause. Others, while not condoning it, profess to
"understand" their behavior. To "understand" evil is to be
a party to it in one's heart.

Man as a species produced at random by a mindless

7

universe is of no special significance.

Man created by God for a sublime purpose is of infinite significance.

♦ *Halacha*

◇ *One may not directly or indirectly endanger a person's life. A reckless driver is a potential murderer in the eyes of the Torah.*

◇ *"From a man's brother I shall demand the life of man." Even if he thinks he is acting as a brother and takes a life out of a mistaken feeling of mercy, his act is still murder. No human being can presume that someone's life is worthless — even that human being himself.*

◇ *Even one who is completely comatose is considered alive, so long as respiration can function autonomously, and to terminate his life is murder.*

◇ *It is not permissible to remove any organ from a dying person for transplantation, even if the recipient's life might thereby be saved. In a case of brain-stem death with the heart still beating, no definitive consensus of halachic authorities has yet been reached regarding the point at which such a person is held to be dead. A competent halachic authority should therefore be consulted in each case.*

◇ *Killing in self-defense is permitted but to kill someone else — who is not threatening you — to save your own life is murder.*

◇ *One may — and should — kill someone who is intent on murder or the violation of another's chastity if there is no other way to prevent this.*

◇ *The waging of war is permitted in self-defense. If there is a manifest threat of attack a pre-emptive strike is permitted.*

◇ *After the 39th day of pregnancy, abortion is normally permitted only when the mother's life is in danger.*

3. Respect for the Person

PROHIBITION OF ASSAULT AND INJURY

Two Hebrews were quarrelling. [Moses] said to the guilty one [the rasha], *why do you strike your neighbor?* — EXODUS 2:13

If in a fight a man strikes another with a stone or with his fist, and the blow is not fatal but he has to take to his bed...he shall compensate him for loss of work and pay for medical treatment. — EXODUS 21:18-19

(1) Assault

The Torah calls someone who is prepared to strike his friend a *rasha*, an evil person. It seems hardly worthwhile earning such an epithet for a momentary gratification of one's temper.

The Torah's principle of justice is violated whenever one treats another person in a way which denies the image of God within him and hurts him physically or mentally. Robbing a person of his self-respect is a serious crime in the eyes of the Torah. (See chapter 10(2).)

♦ *Halacha*
◊ *Striking someone else is permitted in self-defense or to save someone else from attack or injury.*
◊ *A parent is legally permitted to discipline his child and a teacher his pupil, but if corporal punishment is used, this should be minimal and of symbolic nature only.*

4. Protecting Human Rights

LIBERTY / PRIVACY / SELF-INCRIMINATION

*Whoever kidnaps anyone and sells him [into slavery] shall be
put to death.* — EXODUS 21:16

*They are My servants whom I brought out of Egypt; they
shall not be sold as slaves.* — LEVITICUS 25:42

*If a [non-Jewish] slave escapes to you [the Jewish nation]
from his master, you shall not give him up to his master. He
shall dwell with you...wherever he chooses. You are not to
oppress him.* — DEUTERONOMY 23:16

*If you are your neighbor's creditor...you shall not enter his
house to take his pledge (Deuteronomy 24:10). This applies
even to the bailiff of the court.* — TB BAVA METZIA 13a

Disturbance of privacy is a civil wrong. — TB BAVA BATRA 3a

It is forbidden to read someone else's private correspondence.
— ORDINANCES OF RABBENU GERSHOM, 10th cent.

No one can incriminate himself. — TB SANHEDRIN 9b

(1) Liberty

Thousands of years ago, in a world in which slavery was
an entrenched practice and an essential element in the
economy, the Torah introduced the first pointers to a more
humane society.

Illegally depriving a fellow Jew of his liberty was a
capital crime. Between Jews, slavery was made illegal.
Moreover, over 3,000 years ago the Torah raised the banner
of freedom for the slaves of the world. Abrogating the
worldwide convention of those times that fugitive slaves
were to be handed back to their masters, the Torah provides that any fugitive slave, from any country, who
reaches the boundaries of the Holy Land is automatically
freed and can apply for residence rights. If he is prepared to

renounce idolatry and observe the laws of human decency (the Seven Noachide Commands) residence rights will be granted.

(2) Searches and seizures

The Torah protects the privacy of the home by refusing entry to the court officials for the purpose of searching and seizing goods as pledge for a debt. The debt must be satisfied, but which goods shall be provided must be the debtor's own choice. This is the foundation of the rights of privacy written into most modern constitutions.

(3) Privacy

If a neighboring homeowner can see into my windows he must, under certain conditions, share the expense of erecting protective fencing.

The privacy of personal correspondence is guaranteed by an ordinance first promulgated in the 10th century. A natural extension of this would protect the citizen against phone-tapping, release of personal computer-data, etc., even by a government authority, except in a case of suspected criminal activity.

(4) Self-incrimination

Most democratic legal systems provide that a defendant cannot be compelled by a court or tribunal to give an answer which might incriminate him. In the United States making use of this right is called "citing the Fifth Amendment." The trouble with this is that it cannot fail to raise suspicions that the defendant has something to hide. In Torah law the right need not be claimed. Any statement by which the speaker incriminates himself is automatically excluded from the record and no attention may be paid to it by the court. This also protects a defendant against attempts by the police to extract a confession from him, since any confession will not be accepted as evidence by the court. (This is an example of what we have called the Torah's "on-off" switch; i.e., a principle either applies or not; its application does not depend on the discretion of an individual. So here: the operation of the principle does not depend on whether the defendant claims it or not. See also chapter 22(3).)

5. Justice in Employee-Employer Relations

FAIR WAGES / WITHHOLDING PAYMENT / EMPLOYEE'S OBLIGATIONS / WORK ETHIC

For these sins I will not forgive [Israel]...for trampling the head of the poor into the earth and treating the humble with injustice...exploiting the poor while taking from him the fullness of his produce. — AMOS 2:7; 5:11

Do not withhold the wages of a hired worker...whether he is one of your brothers or a stranger... You must pay him on the same day...for he is poor and his soul yearns for the money. Do not cause him to cry out against you to God; it will be counted against you as a sin. — DEUTERONOMY 24:14-15

[Jacob said to Laban:]...I have served you for twenty years; your ewes and she-goats never miscarried...I was consumed by the heat in the daytime and by the frost at night; I had little sleep. — GENESIS 31:38-40

(1) Fair wages

When fixing wages and hours of work, the Torah obliges the employer to consider his employees as human beings, as "children of Abraham, Isaac and Jacob," and not as "hands" or "work units." Marxism considered any employment of one man by another as exploitation — as evil. Yet in practice Marxist "humanism" robbed all men of their human status and reduced them to slaves of the state, that is, of the Politburo and the secret police. Marxism placed "man" at the center of its ideology, and failed. In Torah, it is not the concept "man" which is at the basis of its humanism; it is *"man as the image of God."* And the other man receives his sacred status only when he is seen as the creature of God. It has been well said that the love of

13

God reveals itself in the employer's negotiations about the wages and working hours of his employees.

THE DIGNITY OF A LABORER

When the son of Rabbi Johanan ben Mathia arranged with laborers that his father would give a meal in addition to their wage, Rabbi Johanan was aghast. "What, you said 'a meal' without telling them what would be served? There's no limit to what they may be entitled to! After all, they're the children of Abraham, Isaac and Jacob!" He sent his son running back to tell them, before they started work, that his father intended to give them only bread and vegetables (the normal meal) and to get their consent to this.

One can easily imagine the surprised reaction of the laborers to the message the breathless youth brought them. But can one measure the educative effect of this little episode on the son, and on us who read of it, throughout the generations?

♦ *Halacha*
◇ *According to the Torah, workers are entitled to form a union to bargain with employers collectively and to withhold work when circumstances require this.*

(2) Paying wages without delay

The Torah considers it a serious crime to withhold or delay payment of an employee's wages. If a doubt arises whether or not wages have been paid, the employer must remove the doubt, even if this means (according to his story) that he is paying the wages twice.

The Mishna states that when workmen line up at the end of the day to receive their wages and a dispute arises and one workman says, "I did not receive my wage," and the

14

employer says, "I paid you with the others," the workman can take an oath, and get the money. Why? What proof is there that he was not paid? Oaths are almost always taken to avoid paying; very rarely to obtain money. The Sages of the Torah say that it is more likely that the employer, who has many things on his mind, would have made a mistake than that the employee would try to get paid twice. This goes against the general rule that in cases of doubt, the person claiming the money loses the case unless he brings witnesses to support his claim.

The Torah stands up for the interests of the employee. It even recommends the employer in some cases to go well beyond the strict requirement of the law in order to protect the employee's interests.

THE PATHS OF THE JUST

Rabba bar Rav Huna employed porters to transport his wine barrels from the harbor to his warehouse. On the way, through lack of care, they broke the barrels, causing Rabba considerable loss. In part compensation for the loss he confiscated the clothes they had deposited with him.

They took Rabba to the *bet din*, claiming return of their clothes. The judge was Rav, who said to Rabba: "Give them back their clothes."

"Is that the law?"

"Yes!" said Rav. "The verse says, 'You should follow the ways of good men.'"

The porters then said to Rav:

"We worked all day, we are hungry, and we received no wages."

"Go and pay them their wages," said Rav.

"Is that the law?" protested Rabba.

"Yes! Don't you know the end of that verse? 'And keep to the paths of the just.'"

15

(3) Deductions from agreed wage

A contractor, who receives a price for a job, is in the same position as a salaried employee. He is just as entitled to receive prompt payment and payment without deductions.

Often disputes arise at the conclusion of a job because of vagueness regarding price and quality. The saintly Ḥafetz Ḥayim advised that, to avoid the possibility of the very serious offense of withholding due payment, detailed specifications and price should be agreed upon before work is begun.

AVOIDING TROUBLE

Mr. Sherman urgently needed some work done in his home. He called in Yankel, whom he knew slightly, and told him what he wanted. Yankel agreed to finish the job within a week. "O.K.," said Mr. Sherman, "go ahead. I know I can rely on you to do a good job at a reasonable price." When the job was completed and Yankel presented his bill, Mr. Sherman was very dissatisfied. "This is not at all the quality of work I expected," he said. "The bill is much too high. I will pay you only two-thirds of the amount." When Yankel protested Mr. Sherman said, "If you don't accept what I offer I will pay you nothing and you can sue me for the whole amount." Knowing that this would mean great delay and high costs, Yankel reluctantly agreed, although this meant he had made no profit on the deal. Mr. Sherman went to synagogue for the evening service, satisfied that he had acted with complete fairness.

But had he? His decision to dock one-third of the charge was his own subjective judgment. If there was any overcharge maybe it was closer to ten percent. In that case Mr. Sherman was guilty of withholding 23% of a worker's just wage, exacting work without paying for it, and exerting undue pressure to force a worker to accept less than what was due to him — all crimes against the justice of the Torah. And all this could have been avoided if only they had agreed beforehand on the standard of work required and the amount to be paid instead of relying on vague expressions of goodwill!

(4) Employee's obligation

God's Torah is just. It imposes strict standards on the employer regarding fair wages and working conditions. It imposes equally strict standards on the employee, as regards quality of work and honest time-keeping. Unless the employer's consent is obtained, private telephone conversations in working time constitute theft of the boss's time. In fact one must not engage in any other activity during working hours. One must be prepared to give of one's best. If one has to perform intellectual work, one must keep oneself mentally alert and have enough sleep. If one is engaged in physical labor, one must likewise not impair one's strength by working elsewhere after hours or by not eating enough.

Our father Jacob was the only one of the three Fathers who spent a good deal of his life as an employee. (Abraham and Isaac were sheep owners; we do not find them working for others.) In the quotation at the beginning of this chapter he describes the kind of devoted service he gave to his employer, Laban, over a period of twenty years. We must recall that the work of the second seven of these twenty years was extorted from him by Laban by a trick. Nevertheless his sense of honesty compelled him to give a degree of service during that time equal to that given during the time he worked of his own free choice. We may begin to understand how Jacob earned the title "the man of truth."

We may equally say that the love of God reveals itself in the quality of service an employee gives to his employer.

WHEN THERE IS NO TIME FOR CONVERSATION

Abba Ḥilkiya, a Sage of the first century C.E. in Eretz Yisrael, was famous for his special closeness to God. Two rabbis were sent to him from Jerusalem to ask him to intercede with God regarding the drought which was afflicting the Holy Land. They went to his home, but he was not there. "He is at work," said his wife.

They went out to the fields and found him digging in one of the fields. They greeted him, but he did not respond. The rabbis waited until he went home at the end of the day. They asked him, "Why did the master not respond to us when we greeted him?"

"I am a day laborer," he answered. "My time is not my own. If I had allowed myself to be drawn into conversation, this would have been theft of the employer's time."

6. Respect for Other People's Property

PROHIBITION OF THEFT/PRESSURING PEOPLE TO SELL

You shall not steal. — EXODUS 20:13

You shall not oppress your neighbor [withhold payment due to him], nor may you rob. The wages of a hired worker shall not remain with you till morning. — LEVITICUS 19:13

You shall not covet your neighbor's house...nor anything that belongs to your neighbor. — EXODUS 20:14

(1) Respecting property

God's primary gift to man is his mind, through which he knows God, knows the world and becomes aware of the task which lies before him.

The second gift is his body, which is the instrument by which he brings the world closer to God.

The third gift is the property he acquires, which provides him with the means of living in the world and carrying out his holy task.

The Torah therefore commands us to respect property as something holy. First our own property, which may not be wantonly destroyed (see chapter 14), but above all our neighbor's property, which God has given him for his own use and which we may on no account misappropriate for ourselves.

Just as it is God's command that we may not kill or injure anyone but must respect the human body for the Divine spirit that is in it, so is it His command that we respect the other person's property out of respect for the human being who owns it.

One who steals does not sin merely against human convention but against the God Who allocated this property for the use of that human being. Human society must be ruled not by cunning or by force but by ideals and by right. Stealing reduces man to the level of the beast.

(2) Withholding payment

Even where no dishonesty is involved, it is forbidden to unjustly withhold payment due for goods bought, work done or rent accrued. This too is stealing. See chapter 5(3).

(3) Undue pressure

A person who has designs on his neighbor's property and by applying pressure of various kinds induces his neighbor to sell it to him against his better judgment, even though he pays the full price, has transgressed the commandment: "You shall not covet...."

(4) Another person's property is sacred

Misappropriating your brother's property is like taking that which is sacred to God. Anyone who does not hold someone else's property sacred is a thief at heart, and when the opportunity arises is very likely to be a thief in practice.

THE SILVER CUP

The yeshiva was disturbed. The Rosh Yeshiva's landlord had a silver cup and it had been stolen. The yeshiva students were constantly in and out of the house and there were strong suspicions that one of them had taken it. But which of those hundreds of eager students would be likely to do such a thing?

A visiting rabbi was standing by the wash basins as the students lined up to wash their hands before the meal. He noticed that one of the students wiped his hands on his neighbor's clothes. He immediately pointed him out to the Rosh Yeshiva. "I suggest that you investigate that boy," he said. "I have a tradition that one who is careless with his neighbor's property is likely to be a thief." After being questioned in private the student confessed and the cup was recovered.

◆ *Halacha*

◇ *Borrowing an object without the owner's consent counts as stealing.*

◇ *It is immaterial from whom you steal, pilfer or withhold, whether it is a Jew or a non-Jew, adult or minor, individual or corporation. The sin persists until the article is restored or compensation paid.*

◇ *Tax evasion, smuggling or similar offenses against legitimate tax authorities are in no way better than theft.*

◇ *Buying goods which you have reason to suspect are stolen is a grave offense. Buying stolen property is much worse than the theft itself, because it finances a hundred thefts.*

◇ *Regarding lost property, see chapter 35(2).*

◇ *If coats, etc. have been exchanged at a party, the fact that the other person may have taken your coat by mistake does not entitle you to wear his without permission.*

7. Justice in Property Transfers

HONESTY IN BUYING AND SELLING/LOANS AND CLAIMS/CUSTODIANS

If you sell anything to your neighbor or buy anything from him, you shall not wrong one another...you shall stand in awe of God; I God am your God.
— LEVITICUS 25:14,17

You shall commit no dishonesty in judgment, in measure, in weight or in volume. You shall have honest scales and honest weights...I God am your God Who brought you out of the land of Egypt.
— LEVITICUS 19:35-37

For all who do such things, all who act dishonestly, are an abomination to God your God.
— DEUTERONOMY 25:16

The first question a person is asked when he stands before the Heavenly Throne is, "Were you honest in your business affairs?"
— TB SHABBAT 30

(1) Being true to one's commitment

The laws which follow form the subject matter of some of the most acute argumentation in the Talmud. Within the confines of this volume one can discuss only some of the principles involved and we shall try to select those which can be applied to everyday situations.

The principle of justice on which they all rest is this:

Be true to your commitments as a human being and a Jew. If you have undertaken to give your goods or services to another, do exactly what your neighbor has a right to expect. He must know that he can rely implicitly on you and your word without being disappointed.

(2) Spiritual dimension

It will be noted that all the Torah verses at the head of this chapter make reference to God. Only someone who has a

22

spiritual dimension to his life, who sees himself as standing in the presence of God, will have the moral strength to withstand the many temptations which beset one in the world of business, often involving dishonest acts which no human being will ever know of.

(3) Buying and selling

"You shall do no wrong in buying and selling." "Wrong" may take many forms. One party must not take advantage of the other's ignorance to sell or buy above or below the proper value. If this occurs, in certain circumstances the injured party may rescind the contract. Descriptions must be accurate and defects may not be disguised.

The Torah counts all dishonesty as stealing. Dishonesty against a corporation or a government is the same as dishonesty against an individual. It is self-deception to think otherwise. Corporations and governments are organizational devices; they are fictions. The reality is the real people who own the shares, the real citizens who elect the government. If I swindle the tax authorities I cause a real loss to the other taxpayers who will have to pay more to make up for it.

Scrupulous attention must be given to accuracy in weights and measures. Talmudic law provides that an inspector of weights and measures must be present in every marketplace.

One is sometimes tempted to back out of a bargain. If an act of legal acquisition has already taken place, the *bet din* will enforce the contract. But Torah morality goes far beyond the letter of the law. If a confirmatory act has taken place, falling short of a legal act of acquisition but sufficient to entitle the other party to expect that the bargain would go through, the court cannot enforce the bargain. However they will apply moral pressure. They will summon the parties and read out this declaration:

"He Who punished the generation of the Flood and the generation of the Dispersion, the citizens of Sodom and the Egyptians at the Red Sea — He will punish the one who does not stand by his word."

(4) Keeping faith

If nothing more than a word has been given, the *bet din* will not intervene. But the Talmud makes it clear that a man who does not stand by his word is not "a man of faith." the Hebrew word *emuna* has two meanings: faith, and faithfulness. Abraham, the man of faith in God, has the strength of character to refuse the riches of Sodom (Genesis 14:22-23).

There is a still higher level. There are some who feel themselves bound to keep a bargain if they have only agreed to the price *in their mind*, without a word being uttered. These are the moral élite of Israel.

TRUTH IN THE HEART

Psalm 15 speaks of the person who "speaks truth in his heart." Where do we find an example of this?

Rav Safra (a Talmudic Sage in 4th-century Babylonia) had been negotiating to sell some land. The offer he had received, 12,000 dinars, did not seem sufficient, and negotiations were broken off. Some days later the prospective purchaser (a non-Jew) approached Rav Safra in synagogue with an increased offer of 14,000 dinars. Rav Safra, who was standing silent in prayer, could not reply. Misconstruing his silence as refusal, the purchaser increased his offer to 15,000, 16,000 and eventually to 18,000 dinars. At that point Rav Safra completed his prayers and turned to his friend with an apology. "I am so sorry I couldn't answer you. I was in the middle of my prayers. I will accept your offer of 15,000." "But, but...," said the other, "I offered you 18,000." "I know," replied Rav Safra, "but when you said '15,000' I felt this was the price I could accept. I can't back out of what my mind accepted just because you happened to offer me more."

(5) Who is a man of faith?

Do not be misled by people who tell you they know "very religious" people who are dishonest in business. Don't be taken in by the outward show. A person who keeps the mitzvot because he is sincerely trying to do God's will, will keep the mitzvot relating to honesty too. If he does not, this means that he keeps only those that come easy to him. It is a mistake to call him "very religious." If in certain circumstances it should turn out that keeping Shabbat (for example) becomes very difficult for him, he will find ways to get around this too, provided he can hide it from other people. The man of faith keeps faith with others. One who does not keep faith with others is not a man of faith.

WHAT MAKES HIM TICK?

Reb Berel was known as a very religious man. He was a popular member of his synagogue and was seen to fulfill all his religious duties punctiliously. There were rumors that he did not treat his employees so well, but nobody knew this for sure. One Shabbat he was honored by having a great rabbi as his guest. The whole congregation would come to his house that Friday night. He was looking around to see that everything was ready. To his horror he realized that he had forgotten to switch the lights on. The rabbi and all his friends would come and the house would be in complete darkness! It was dark outside, Shabbat was definitely in. But he was alone in the house. Nobody would know. How could he stand such humiliation?

Knowingly desecrating the Sabbath, he switched on the lights.

Was he "very religious"? Only so long as he was not presented with a test. Going to synagogue daily, being generous with his friends, presented no test. On the contrary, it earned him the applause of his peers. And this is what made him tick — not the sincere wish to obey his Creator. In the privacy of his factory, in the privacy of his home, his own interests ruled.

The "very religious" person who is dishonest in business does not exist.

(6) Loans and claims

The obligation to repay a loan is a mitzva — a religious obligation. It derives from the pronouncement "You shall not withhold payment." (See above, chapter 6.)

If a person makes a firm claim against you and you cannot recall whether you owe him money or not, in the absence of clear evidence the court will release you from obligation. However, Torah morality requires you to pay him. To be right before God you must avoid all doubt that you might be keeping someone else's money.

Say you carelessly took someone's coat after a meeting and you do not know to whom it belongs. Five people who were at the meeting claim the coat, each insisting that it is his. In the absence of evidence you can deposit the coat with the court and leave them to sort the matter out between themselves. You can stop there if you like. Nobody is going to compel you to go further. Torah morality, however, suggests that you should compensate each one of them for the value of the coat. To be right with God you must ensure that the rightful owner shall not lose because of your negligence.

(7) Custodians

If someone entrusts you with his property for safekeeping you must look after it to the best of your ability. "Your friend's property should be as dear to you as your own." This is Torah justice. The question of legal liability, if for some reason you were unable to return it, depends basically on two factors: (1) What kind of custodian are you? Are you voluntary or paid? If you are entitled to use the object do you pay for the use or not? (2) How did the loss occur? Through negligence, through theft or loss without negligence; or through circumstances beyond your control? The following pattern emerges:

Table 1

TYPE OF CUSTODIAN	A LOSS DUE TO NEGLIGENCE	B THEFT OR LOSS WITHOUT NEGLIGENCE	C LOSS DUE TO CIRCUMSTANCES BEYOND CONTROL
UNPAID CUSTODIAN	LIABLE	EXEMPT	EXEMPT
PAID CUSTODIAN OR HIRER	LIABLE	LIABLE	EXEMPT
BORROWER	LIABLE	LIABLE	LIABLE

If we leave out of account column A, negligence, in which all are understandably liable, we can see the following rationale:

THE UNPAID CUSTODIAN gives on two counts: (1) he gives his services to guard the object and (2) he gives them free of charge, taking neither payment nor use. Consequently less liability is imposed on him and he is exempt in both columns B and C.

THE PAID CUSTODIAN gives one and takes one: he gives his services but he takes payment for them. The hirer similarly takes one and gives one: he takes the use and pays for it. They are therefore liable in one case, B, and exempt in one case, C.

THE BORROWER takes all and gives nothing. He is therefore liable in both cases, B and C. (The only case in which a borrower is exempt is when the object fails under normal use, through no fault of the borrower, e.g., he borrows a car and it breaks down while being driven normally.)

In all cases where the custodian is exempt he may be required to take a solemn oath (a) that he was not negligent; (b) that he did not take the object himself. An unpaid custodian who would like to do his friend a favor but wishes to avoid any claim being made against him in case he is unable to return the valuables, may accept the task on condition that he accepts no liability whatsoever.

8. Safety of the Environment

MITZVA OF ROOF-PARAPET/PREVENTION OF
ACCIDENTS/DEALING WITH PHYSICAL POLLUTION

*When you build a new house you shall make a parapet for
your roof, so that you do not bring blood-guilt on your house
should anyone fall from it.* — DEUTERONOMY 22:8

*If a man digs a pit or opens a pit and fails to cover it [he is
liable for the consequences] ... (Exodus 21:33-34). This
includes any object left in the public domain in circumstances
where it might cause harm to others.* — MISHNA, BAVA KAMA CH.3

*Morality is measured by how one disposes of one's broken
glass or other dangerous objects. The highest degree of
morality would lead one to bury them so deep that they could
never cause harm to anyone.* — BASED ON TB BAVA KAMMA 30a

(1) Responsibility

A person is responsible for all the material things in his
possession and in his use. Even without the verdict of
a court, and even if no claim is made, he must pay compensation for any harm they do to another's person or property
as a result of his negligence.

(2) Safety

The mitzva of the parapet cited at the beginning of this
chapter is generalized by the Oral Law to include taking
the utmost care with anything in your domain which is
potentially dangerous to human life or limb. This includes
wells or holes in the ground without adequate guard;
broken staircases, rickety ladders, poison, weapons or
objects left at the edge of the roof which might be blown
down in a normal gust of wind.

In a word, you are responsible for *the safety of your
environment*. Think! Think of the possible consequences of

29

what you do or leave undone. Water or other liquids carelessly poured into the road can be potential killers, causing cars to skid. Factories which pour dangerous effluents into the rivers or allow them to seep into the soil are infringing this mitzva. The Torah does not allow responsible human beings to hide behind the fiction of a corporation.

If any person or firm persistently infringes these laws, he or it may be forcibly restrained by the *bet din*. In the last resort the *bet din* has the power to confiscate the property of the offender, under the principle of *hefker bet din hefker* — "the court has the power to confiscate the property of offenders against the public interest" (TB *Yevamot* 89b). This ultimate power of enforcement vested in the *bet din* of the Torah is rooted in the Torah principle that there is no absolute ownership of property. All property is held conditionally and ownership rights can be exercised only so long as they tend to the benefit and not the detriment of the public.

This principle is particularly important in view of the often manifest inability of governments and courts to enforce anti-pollution laws, especially against powerful multinational conglomerates.

(3) A blessing to all

We are given all that we have, all the riches of this world, by God, He wants us to be, with all our belongings, a blessing to the world. We must be on our guard that these riches do not become a curse.

Remember: the Talmud judges a person's morality level by how he disposes of his broken glass or any potentially dangerous object.

♦ *Halacha*
◇ *Any activity resulting in smoke, dust, noise, noxious smells or vibration must be sited where it cannot interfere*

with the public enjoyment of the environment.

WE ARE THE PUBLIC

Mr. Schwartz was clearing one of his fields of stones. Finding it too much trouble to transport them to the quarry on the other side of the highway, he dumped them on the public footpath which ran by his farm. A *hassid* (a sensitive person) who happened to be passing and saw this happening said: "Fool! Whoever heard of taking stones from land that is *not* yours and putting them on land which *is* yours." The landowner laughed at him uncomprehendingly.

Years passed. Mr. Schwartz sold his farm and became a commercial traveler. Many years later he came back to the place where he used to live, but at first failed to recognize it. Hastening along a footpath to get to the town before dusk, he crashed into the pile of stones he had placed there himself long before. Picking himself up he said ruefully, "I see now the *hassid* was right." When we injure the environment we act against our own interests.

9. Honest Speech

FALSEHOOD / FLATTERY / HYPOCRISY

Keep far from falsehood. — EXODUS 23:7

God's signature is truth. — TB SHABBAT 55a

*The remnants of Israel do no injustice, speak no falsehood,
and have no dishonesty in their mouths.* — ZEFANIA 3:13

(1) Faculty of truth

The Creator has endowed the human mind with the faculty
of mirroring the reality of things in all their relations, and
of communicating this knowledge to others. On the basis
of this knowledge we deal with people and things and
attempt to apply to them the dictates of justice. This representation of reality in the mind is truth. Truth, therefore, is
a precondition of justice.

All this implies that we can rely on our brother for that
great spiritual good — the truth.

But one who communicates a false image of reality turns
God's supreme blessing into a curse. Lies give birth to
injustice — and misery. By stealing from another something precious — truth — and so indirectly the most precious thing — justice — the liar also kills himself
spiritually. He dims in himself the Divine spark which
alone makes him a human being created for the benefit of
his fellow-man.

(2) Fear the lie

Every lie, even one that seems to you to be trivial, is a
betrayal of the other person and undermines one's integrity. We should beware of any deviation from the truth as
we know it. We have all felt how our soul revolts against
the false word our lips attempt to utter. In any case, we

surely felt it when we lied for the first time. This inner rebellion is a warning not to ruin our humanity. It warns us that God created us to be truthful, just as His Torah calls on us to be truthful. We cannot calculate the harm a lie can do — to others and to ourselves. It is better not to lie even for fun. And even if telling the truth would draw upon us anger and punishment, we should fear the lie more than the worst punishment.

(3) A sense of honesty

The habit of lying can destroy the whole of life's purity. Most sins are accompanied by the resolve to lie one's way out of the consequences if discovered. Therefore if we train ourselves to become incapable of deviating from the truth, this will serve us as a shield against many sins. Conversely, the more we are at home with lying, the easier will be our path to every other evil.

And we who are educators of the young should consider it our most important task to train our charges to be truthful above all else. Woe to those so-called educators who overlook, or even encourage, cheating in examinations. Whatever imaginary benefit that is supposed to accrue from this is utterly worthless compared to the loss of that most precious asset — a sense of honesty and truth.

THE POWER OF THE TRUTH

A Jew who was a confirmed burglar came to the Rebbe after Yom Kippur. "Rebbe," he said, "I want to take a few steps in the direction of Judaism. Nothing too difficult, you understand. Don't tell me to stop burgling; it's my livelihood. But some little thing that will give me some credit 'up there,' you know."

"My son," said the Rebbe, "I want you to undertake just one thing. Make up your mind to tell the

33

truth and only the truth — at all times and in all circumstances."

"I promise," said the thief.

That night, when on the prowl, he met an acquaintance called Berel. "Where are you going so late at night?" asked Berel. The thief was just going to reply, "Oh, just to see an old friend" when he remembered his vow. "Well, to tell you the truth, Berel," he replied, "I'm going to do a job over at the Metropol." Berel raised his eyebrows and walked on. A little later the same thing happened with Shmerel. The thief thought to himself, "I can't do this job. I've got two witnesses against me." He went home. Soon he was weaned from a life of crime and became a normal member of society. And all because of the truth.

(4) Flattery and hypocrisy

A lie about the personality of the person to whom it is told, giving him a better opinion of himself than he really deserves, is flattery. A lie concerning our own personality is hypocrisy. Nowhere is truth more necessary than in knowing oneself. Flattery undertaken to obtain some advantage, to ingratiate oneself into the other person's favor for gain is despicable. Better to forfeit all imagined advantage and retain our self-respect.

We tend to give our heart to anyone who seems to have a special affection for us. A person who deliberately misleads us about his feelings towards us, by insincere words or acts intended to create that impression, has in effect "stolen our heart." This is the type of hypocrisy designated by our Sages as *genevat da'at* — "stealing the mind." For instance, you may not shower invitations and other offers on a friend if you know he will not accept them. If you open a new bottle when your friend comes in, but were going to open it anyway, you must not give the impression that you are doing it specially for him. Many other examples will spring to the mind of the thoughtful reader. As we mentioned above, in the realm of honesty nothing is trivial.

(5) Requirements of courtesy

A warning. Our Sages were aware that social intercourse would be impossible if everyone told the brutal truth all the time. In certain contexts making people happy takes precedence over precise truth. One may — indeed should — compliment the housewife on her cooking even though its flavor leaves a good deal to be desired. In one's own mind the compliment may refer more to the good lady's efforts and desire to please rather than to the actual result. The Torah recognizes the requirements of courtesy.

(6) When not to tell the truth

One may not tell the truth to someone who will make unlawful use of it or where the truth would harm anyone else. This would apply for example to a murderer asking you about his intended victim, or a thief about the whereabouts of some property, or a person who would be unduly disturbed if told about the death of a close relative. Similarly, I am allowed to deviate from the strict truth where truth would arouse discord between man and man, or where I can restore peace, that blessing of all blessings, where it has departed.

10. Justice for the Weak and Vulnerable

OPPRESSION / VEXATION / HUMILIATION / HURTING SOMEONE'S
FEELINGS / ABUSE OF WEAKNESS

*You shall not vex a stranger or oppress him, for you were
strangers in the land of Egypt. You shall not ill-treat a widow
or an orphan...If they cry out to Me I shall hear their cry and
My anger will flare against you...* — EXODUS 22:20-23

*The stranger who lives among you must be treated as one
born among you; you shall love him as yourself, for you were
strangers in Egypt.* — LEVITICUS 19:33-34

*You shall not hurt one another but you shall hold your God
in awe; I GOD am your God (Leviticus 25:17). — This refers to
hurting by words.* — TB *BAVA METZIA* 58b

*Do not put an obstacle before the blind, but hold your God in
awe; I GOD am your God.* — LEVITICUS 19:14

*Jeroboam [ben Nevat] who not only sinned but caused Israel
to sin.* — I KINGS 14:16

(1) Freedom from oppression

The prohibitions against oppression and vexation are
directed against hindering and harassing a person in his
legitimate pursuits. They are also directed against all
forms of discrimination and persecution. The liberal ideas
which dominate western societies and are now beginning
to penetrate the Eastern bloc too, have their roots in these
commandments of the Torah.

Vexation and harassment cry out to high heaven when
they are perpetrated against the hapless and defenseless
— the stranger, the widow and the orphan. And not only
these — all the underprivileged of society, the poor, every

dependent person, everyone who is unhappy or suffering, they are all under the special protection of the Almighty, Who entrusts them to our care.

(2) Watch your words

But do not think that you can sin only by deeds, that you can satisfy the law if you merely refrain from afflicting and oppressing your neighbor by your actions. The fleeting word, with which you can do so much good, can inflict more injury, destroy happiness more surely, than violent acts.

God has endowed the human being with a sensitive soul, capable of vibrating to the most sublime emotions — gratitude and serenity, ecstasy and love. By the same token it can easily be wounded by a malicious, scornful or thoughtless word.

To the young readers of this book, for whom God's gift is still pure, whose hearts have not yet hardened: Listen to the message of the Torah of Israel, watch your words, so that no one is wounded by them. Above all watch them in your dealings with the unfortunate, the underprivileged, who are the first to feel the slightest suggestion of scorn; indeed they often feel one where none is intended. We who are the heirs of the Torah, Prophets and Sages of Israel — let us try and bring back into Jewish life some of that sensitivity that they cultivated and nurtured. Those who speak glibly of "building our society on the ideals of the prophets" — have they any idea of what these ideals really involve? Do they think these are satisfied by government welfare payments to the poor? Why do they think that our "welfare state" witnesses such an alarming increase in battered babies, child abuse, beaten wives, rape and all the rest? Where the spiritual dimension of life is denied, the image of God in man fades, human sensitivity is crushed and justice is no more. As will be seen in the course of this book, the Torah's plan for a truly just society can be realized only if all the aspects of Torah are developed simultaneously.

(3) Taking advantage of weakness

Besides the literal meaning, "the blind" in the verse quoted above ("You shall not put an obstacle before the blind") includes, according to our Sages, someone who is ignorant on certain matters and comes to you for advice. You are commanded to give him honest advice, leaving completely out of account your own interests in the matter.

It also includes the morally blind. You may not help anyone to do a sin, whether he is intent on doing it out of ignorance, moral weakness or malice. If you cannot change his mind, you may on no account facilitate his act in any way. Do not provide him with an opportunity to commit the sin. Even if he can obtain the means elsewhere, you should not be the one to provide it. Do not say, "It's not my fault; he doesn't have to do it if he doesn't want to." It is your sin, because you gave him the opportunity.

♦ *Halacha*

◊ *One may not support or promote any wrongdoing.*

◊ *One may not publish or sell any material which could influence people in the direction of sensuality and vice.*

◊ *One may not sell anything containing prohibited or harmful matter.*

◊ *One should not sell weapons, etc., to anyone who has not official authority to use such things. In general one is not to sell anything which one has reason to believe might be used for an evil purpose.*

38

◇ *It is advisable not to make a loan to anyone without written acknowledgment or a witness, not even to one's best friend or the most honest person: he might forget it, and this could lead to dispute and dissension.*

◇ *A father may not strike his grown-up son; this would be "putting an obstacle before the blind." The son might be tempted to strike back.*

11. Respect for a Person's Reputation

THE EVIL TONGUE / SLANDER / TALEBEARING / RESPECTING CONFIDENCE

You shall not go around as a talebearer among your people.

— LEVITICUS 19:16

You shall not accept an evil report. — EXODUS 23:1

Cursed be he who strikes his neighbor in secret (Deuteronomy 27:24). — This refers to the slanderer. — TARGUM YONATAN

To the wicked one God has said, Why do you recite My laws and mouth the words of My covenant?...Since you hate morality...You lend your mouth to evil and your tongue is joined to deceit. When you sit down — you speak against your brother, you find fault with your own mother's son...

— PSALMS 50:16-19

Slander is equivalent to the three cardinal sins: idolatry, immorality and bloodshed. — TB ARACHIN 15b

Slander kills three: the one who speaks, the one who listens, and the one who is spoken about. — MIDRASH RABBA DEVARIM 5:10

Who is the man who desires life...? Guard your tongue from evil. — PSALMS 34:13-14

What can be so wrong with a little gossip? What if in the course of conversation we do sometimes touch on someone else's faults, foibles and weaknesses? How can this be such a terrible crime?

I will ask another question. What is so attractive about character assassination? Why do we enjoy it so much? Is it the perverse thrill of evil for evil's sake? Or is it that small minds delight in dragging someone else down to their own level?

Let us be clear about one thing. Destroying a person's

good name is never a trivial thing. The precious gift of speech is given to us for spreading blessing in this world — and we are using it to bring a curse. Our soul, our personality, is capable of so much improvement — and we are warping it by dwelling on our neighbor's faults.

Still worse when you make it your business to tell Mr. A. the hateful things Mr. B. has said about him. Then you stamp yourself as the enemy of human happiness, an enemy of God's universe. You can become the curse of your community. You have killed unity and peace, trust and love, and leave in your wake hatred and discord, strife, vengeance, disaster and crime.

Is it really an excuse to say you did not mean any harm, you slandered only out of thoughtlessness, for fun, without bad intentions?

In our generation, largely owing to the efforts of the 20th century Sage and saint Rabbi Yisrael Meir Hacohen (the "Ḥafetz Ḥaim"), certain circles in Torah Jewry, worldwide, have begun to treat this mitzva with the seriousness it deserves. If you, the reader, wish to find what it is like to live with one's tongue under control, join one of these circles.

The secret is (i) To resolve to take seriously what our Torah and Sages have told us. (ii) To be so occupied with learning and doing that we have no time left for idle gossip. (iii) To be too aware of one's own imperfections to venture to pass judgment on someone else.

◆ *Halacha*

◇ *The evil tongue (*lashon ha-ra*) does not apply to a person's moral failings alone. It can apply just as well to blanket condemnation of the quality of the goods or services that he provides, or it might relate to his health or abilities.*

◇ Lashon ha-ra *applies even when the information that is exchanged is true.*

◇ *A person who listens to* lashon ha-ra *without saying a word is as guilty as the one who talks.*

◇ *If you know something about your friend's private affairs you may not pass it on to anyone else (even "in confidence") without your friend's permission.*

◇ *Realistic as always, the Torah recognizes that there are circumstances in which it may be necessary to supply derogatory information. For example, a person may ask you for information regarding a prospective marriage partner, or business partner. Here your concern must be to save your friend from making an injudicious decision. But the information supplied must be known to you at first hand and may be accompanied by no exaggeration or unnecessary comment. If you do not know it at first hand, you may not accept it as a fact, but you may indicate to the enquirer that he should make further enquiries before committing himself.*

GROUP TWO:

JUSTICE FOR THE ENVIRONMENT

Mitzvot regulating our relations with the total environment

We have seen something of the Torah's distinctive concepts of justice and honesty in human relations. Now we shall investigate the Torah's plans for just and proper relationships with the environment. The Torah will stretch our minds by including in its concept of the environment, besides the land, plants, animals and food sources, also our bodies, our property, our words and our sexuality.

21. Respect for One's Words
Vows / Promises / Charitable commitments

22. Respect for Our Sexuality
Oasis of sanity / Sex education / Standing by our children

23. Regulating our Sexual Relations
Incest / Adultery / Homosexuality / Period of separation

24. Function of the Dietary Laws

25. The Kinds of Animals Fit for Our Food
Ruminants / No birds of prey / Fish with scales

26. The Condition of the Animal
Treyfa / Flesh from living animal

27. *Shehita*
The Torah's Painless Method of Slaughter

28. Parts Excluded from Our Diet
Blood / Some fats / Sciatic nerve

29. Dealing with Moral Pollution
Holiness in the camp / Sexual stimuli / Purity of speech

12. Building Up Eretz Yisrael

WHY THE TORAH NEEDS ERETZ YISRAEL/THE MITZVA
OF LIVING IN ERETZ YISRAEL

*I have given to you [Abraham] and to your descendants after
you...the whole land of Canaan as a possession forever, and
I shall be your God.* — GENESIS 17:8

*And you shall inherit the land and dwell in it, for I have
given you the land as a possession.* — NUMBERS 33:53

*He gave them the lands of the nations...
So that they should keep His statutes
And guard His teachings. Selah.* — PSALMS 105:44-45

*God has given you His Torah. If you do not carry out the civil
laws, He will take His Torah away from you. Why? Because
He gave you the Torah only so that you should carry out the
civil laws.* — MIDRASH RABBA, SHEMOT, 30:23

The mitzva *of living in Eretz Yisrael is equivalent to all the
other* mitzvot *put together.* — SIFRE, EYKEV, END

(1) A Land for the Torah

God gave the Torah to a nation, not to an individual or
individuals. And that nation was to live in a specially selected land where they were to develop a Torah
civilization, a just and caring society which would be the
wonder of the world. In this land all aspects of the national
life were to be transformed and sanctified by the commandments of the Torah — the government, the judiciary,
the police and the army, the agriculture, the commerce and
the industry. We have already seen that only an intense
spiritual commitment can ensure that social relationships
will reach a stable level of justice and love.

In most countries the laws in force were largely designed
to protect the vested interests of the powerful landowners.

45

In such a state any movement to improve the laws would have had little chance of success. It would have been seen as a threat to the interests of the rulers, and forcibly suppressed. An ideal social system could only be established by a *nation*, whose members were imbued with a determination to set up such a system and who saw it as a task bestowed on them by God, the Source of all justice and love. This was to be the overriding national commitment.

The practical and symbolical "holiness" mitzvot (as we shall see) are designed to keep this commitment always at the highest possible level. All facets of life are thus intertwined and work together towards one supreme goal.

The land selected was strategically situated for propagating the message of this ideal state — at the junction of three great continents and with a coastline to the sea to ensure that the message could spread still further afield. Israel was to be a "kingdom of priests and a holy nation." Priests? No, not religious functionaries. They were to be agriculturists, businessmen, professionals, but the way they ran their state and their commerce was to be exemplary. They were to be "priests" in the sense that they would represent the spirit of God in the world — in practice. And "a holy nation." Holy? Does that sound to you cold, withdrawn, other-worldly? This would be a great mistake. "Holy" in the Torah sense means dedicated — dedicated to justice, integrity and *giving*. We have to create the environment in which Torah can flourish.

TAKING UP THE CHALLENGE

This was the plan. But human failings prevented it from being realized. We lost our land — twice. We went into long exile, doing our best to keep Torah ideals alive in foreign environments. More often than not we succeeded. But sometimes the alien environment overwhelmed the

Jewish soul and many lost the sense of mission that had buoyed us up over the centuries.

In our time Jewish sovereignty has returned to our land — after an interval of 2,000 years. This is a significant event in our history. We are called upon to take up the challenge. We have been given the opportunity of re-creating the Torah environment in this land, of rebuilding the Torah state as envisaged so long ago, of again being a "light unto the nations." And this is the only place where it can be done. Jews who live outside Eretz Yisrael cannot take part personally in this great enterprise. Some of them may have very high standards of Torah learning and practice, but the Torah and mitzvot they practice so assiduously have no chance of fulfilling their true function — to mold a Jewish society in accordance with Torah principles. They occupy a niche in an alien environment. This is why our Sages say that mitzvot practiced outside Eretz Yisrael can never be truly authentic.

But in Eretz Yisrael too we face an alien environment. So many, through factors beyond their control, have become estranged from the Torah vision. But there is one great difference. The situation in Eretz Yisrael is one *which may well be within our power to change.* Maybe if more of us, world-wide, were to understand the challenge a Jewish Eretz Yisrael presents to us we could change the face of this land. And maybe...maybe...if one succeeded in this tremendous task, our enemies' hostility might eventually change to grudging respect...Who knows?

We are privileged to live in an age of the breaking of idols. Ideologies, such as communism, which held the bodies and souls of hundreds of millions of human beings in an iron grip for generations, have been overthrown. This is a challenge to us to replace them by ideals which have an incomparably sounder basis and have stood the test of time.

(2) Town planning in the Torah

The Torah is also concerned with the beauty and amenity of Eretz Yisrael — the land of the Torah environment. The Sages of the Torah stress the importance of cleanliness, beauty and "naturalness" of environment for a balanced development of the Torah personality. The enjoyment of the beauties of nature, the contemplation of flower-clad meadows, lofty mountains and majestically flowing rivers, are essential to spiritual development.

Consistent with this we read in the Torah something which is probably the earliest recorded example of town planning legislation. The forty-eight cities which are allocated to the tribe of Levi are to have a belt of land 1000

Figure 1

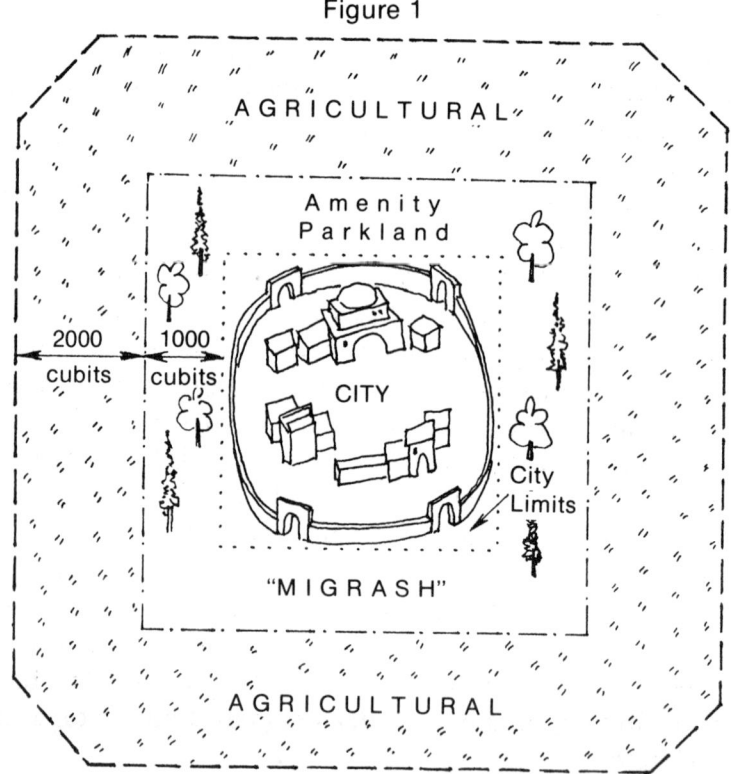

cubits wide all around the city reserved as a *migrash* (open space). In addition there are to be an additional 2000 cubits all around for agricultural use. The function of the *migrash* is to be "an amenity to the city, no building and no planting of vineyards, etc. is to be allowed there." We recognize in this the 20th-century town planning concept of the "Green Belt," whose purpose is to allow city people to enjoy the fresh air of the countryside.

The Oral Law tells us that these regulations applied not only to the Levitical cities but, by analogy, to all the cities of Israel.

Here we have, 3,500 years ago, an unparalleled awareness of the importance of the physical environment which we would do well to take to heart.

◆ *Halacha*

◇ *The mitzva of living in Eretz Yisrael does not depend on the coming of* Mashiaḥ. *It applies at all times.*

◇ *However, one cannot be said to be truly "living" in a place unless two conditions are present: (i) the availability of high-level Torah learning; (ii) the means of earning a livelihood. The first is certainly present in ample measure at the present day (though there have been times in history when this was not the case). The second often presents problems. In case of doubt a Torah authority in Eretz Yisrael should be consulted.*

13. Respecting the Environment

VALUING OUR POSSESSIONS AS GIFTS OF GOD

When you besiege a city...you shall not destroy its [fruit] trees just to swing an ax on them. You eat of them, do not cut them down; for man's life depends on the trees of the field...
— DEUTERONOMY 22:19

God took Adam and showed him the Garden of Eden. "Look," He said, "how beautiful, how excellent is My world! And all I have created is for you. Do not destroy it, for if you do, it will not repair itself."
— KOHELET RABBA 7:13

Do not pour away the water of your well; other people may need it.
— TB YEVAMOT 44a

Whoever in his rage tears his clothes, breaks his crockery, or throws his money away, should be in your eyes as one who worships idols.
— TB SHABBAT 105b

(1) The environment in war

Even in war, the Jewish army must have regard for the environment, and think of the long-term needs of humanity. The Oral Law derives two things from this passage. One: Senseless destruction — "just to swing an ax" — is always forbidden. Two: If you have to cut down trees be wise in your choice: when you have timber trees at your disposal do not cut down fruit-trees; they have a higher purpose to fulfill.

In general terms, God is teaching us here that He has entrusted to us the world and its riches to use for His purposes which require the preservation of the world as a human habitat. If we abuse them, if we destroy them, if we ruin them — we lose our right to them. Human beings will respect the environment only when they realize that they are not its absolute owners. They have it on trust from God, Who expects us to use it for the good of mankind, in fulfillment of the Divine plan.

(2) The urge to destroy

Why do our Sages say that one who destroys his property in his rage is like an idol-worshiper? "Because," they say, "this is the way of passion — today it says: 'Do this,' tomorrow it says: 'Do that,' until he becomes its slave; from then on, it is an easy path even to idolatry." But in fact he is already serving the most powerful idol in his inward self — anger, pride and above all his own ego, which regards itself as the master of all things.

(3) The purpose of property

The miser, who denies himself and others the benefit of his possessions, is also a destroyer. What he keeps buried and unused in his coffers or numbered bank account is destroyed for all mankind. The vice of avarice regards things as if *possession* was their whole purpose, while God has told us that everything is there for *use*, for wholesome human ends. In the holy language of the Torah there is no word for "having," for mere possession. The expression we translate by "I have" appears there as "*yesh li*" — literally, "it is there for me." It is there for me — not for my selfish advantage but so that I can convert it into as many mitzva-fulfillments as possible.

◆ *Halacha*
◊ *Wasting food or other goods counts as destruction.*
◊ *Even fuel is to be used in the most efficient manner possible.*
◊ *It is permitted to cut down a fruit tree which is doing harm to other more valuable plants or to a building, or if its wood is more valuable than the fruit it produces.*

14. Restraint in the Enjoyment of the Fruit of Young Trees

A LESSON IN TORAH ECOLOGY

When you come into the Land and plant any tree for food, you shall apply a restriction (orla) to its fruit. For three years it shall remain restricted for you; it may not be eaten. In the fourth year all its fruit shall be holy, for praising God.

— LEVITICUS 19:23-24

(1) Universal significance

The verse refers to trees planted in the Land of Israel, but the Oral Torah tells us that the restriction applies, to a limited extent, to fruit trees everywhere. A Jew may not consume the fruit produced by any fruit tree in the first three years after it has been planted, whether planted by Jew or non-Jew.

The significance of this law must therefore be universal. We, the people of Israel, are called on to show the world that human beings are not the masters of the earth. The earth is entrusted into our care by its true owner, God, and we are expected to use it prudently and to take its riches with forethought and restraint.

We planted the tree for the fruit. But we wait three years before we enjoy that fruit. For that period we give up our property rights at God's command. By this restraint we practice the self-control which is so necessary for keeping all enjoyment within the limits of morality. We learn to free our sensual enjoyment from the chains of animal greed and bring it into the sphere of true human happiness. Happiness does not lie in self-gratification but in enjoyment which remembers God and serves God.

The universal lesson is this: The planet is not ours to plunder and rape without concern for others in the present or the future. This is the lesson in basic ecology which was implanted in our midst by this mitzva of the Torah so many centuries ago. "Don't grab," it tells us. "Be patient. It will taste better if you wait for it. Instant gratification is not the way — neither for you nor for the future of the planet."

THE OLD MAN AND HIS TREES

An old man was planting carob trees in Eretz Yisrael. This is a tree which does not produce its first fruit for many years.

A king was passing and asked him his age.

"Eighty-five," he replied.

"And do you expect to live long enough to enjoy the fruit of these trees?" he asked.

The old man looked up at him. His eyes twinkled in his wrinkled, wizened face.

"Maybe not," he said, "But when I came into the world I found carob trees. I want my sons to find carob trees after I am gone."

With the revival of agriculture in Israel in our time it is possible to see this mitzva being observed in practice. In any Torah-observant kibbutz or settlement you will see plantations of young trees placed away from the rest and marked with "Year so-and-so." So mitzvot come into their own again after millennia.

(2) Enjoyment which is holiness

When the Temple was standing in Jerusalem, the fruit of the fourth year had to be brought to Jerusalem and enjoyed there in the precincts of the Holy City together with the

poor, widows, orphans and other underprivileged people.
The purpose of this was, as the verse says, to praise God for
His bounty. The best way to say thank you to God is to
enjoy the fruits He has given you, and to enjoy them "in
holiness"; that is, by joining the poor, the stranger, the
widow and the orphan in your enjoyment — by making
others happy as well as yourself and your immediate
family. This is what holiness means in the Torah (Deuteronomy 16:11).

One could if one wished redeem the crop with money and
spend the money in Jerusalem on foodstuffs for enjoyment
in the same way (Deuteronomy 14:24-27).

♦ *Halacha*

◇ *The law of* orla *applies only to trees planted specifically
for food. Fruit trees planted as a hedge or for other
purposes are exempt.*

◇ *Bushes whose stem remains from year to year count as
fruit trees.*

◇ *If trees are transplanted the* orla *years start again,
unless sufficient earth was attached to the roots to enable
the tree to grow.*

◇ *No benefit whatsoever may be derived from fruit which
grows during the first three years.*

◇ *Nowadays since there is no Temple the fourth-year crop
need only be redeemed for a small amount and then
enjoyed without restriction.*

15. Respecting Divine Order in the World

SEPARATION OF KINDS IN ANIMAL
HUSBANDRY/AGRICULTURE/WORKING WITH
ANIMALS/CLOTHING

The earth produced vegetation that developed seed according
to its kind. — GENESIS 1:12

*And God created every living creature...*according to its
kind...*and God saw that it was good.* — GENESIS 1:21

And you shall be to Me a special kind *of people.* — EXODUS 19:5

*You shall keep My statutes. You shall not breed your cattle
with different kinds. You shall not sow your field with
different kinds, nor shall a garment of different kinds —*
shaatnez — *be worn by you.* — LEVITICUS 19:19

*You shall not sow your vineyard with different kinds of
seed... You shall not plow with an ox and an ass together, nor
may you wear* shaatnez — *wool and linen together.*
— DEUTERONOMY 22:9-11

(1) A special kind

Every living being in creation has the great law *l'mino* —
"after its kind" — imprinted on it. We, the people of the
Torah, are called upon to respect living things in all their
wondrous variety of form and function and not attempt to
improve on the work of the Creator by creating new
species. Among mankind too, every nation is made "after
its kind" and has its distinctive function to perform in
God's plan. Israel, which is called upon to be *am segula*, a
"special kind" of people, was chosen to lead the world
towards its true destiny, and the Torah is the law which
qualifies it for this task. These laws concerning order in the
living world have a symbolic function.

The orderliness which these laws establish in our environment may serve above all to remind us of the Torah's moral order which should govern all aspects of our lives. We, the Jewish people, should remain true to the laws which determine our specific function in the universe.

(2) Application

The *l'mino* laws operate in four different aspects of the environment:
- Animal husbandry
- Agriculture
- Use of animals for work
- Clothing

We will briefly discuss each one of these.

(3) Animal husbandry

Cross-breeding. The Torah prohibits any attempt at cross-breeding with different species or "kinds" of animal or bird. What constitutes a "kind" and what a mere variety is defined in the Oral Law. Even animals which show some anatomical similarities and, if forced, copulate fruitfully, such as wolf-hound and wolf, goat and deer, chamois and sheep, etc., are different "kinds" and may not be paired. What is prohibited is the act of forcible copulation.

(4) Agriculture

a. *Tree-grafting.* Trees of diverse kinds as defined in the Oral Law may not be grafted on to one another. However, the fruit of such grafting is permitted.

b. *Close planting of different food plants.* In the Land of Israel different kinds of grain, legume or vegetable may not be sown or planted so close together that they take nourishment from the same place or in such a way that

56

they seem to the eye to be planted in confusion. In the ideal Land of Israel one would only have to walk among fields and vegetable gardens to see at once that it was the land of the Torah.

c. *Close planting of grapevine and grains.* The ban on the planting of grapevines and grain together is the most serious of these laws, since the resulting mixture must be burnt. The grapes and grains which have grown together may not be eaten and no benefit may be derived from them. (As a protective measure the Rabbis extended the prohibition to all legumes and vegetables planted with the vine.)

The reason for the special severity of this law undoubtedly resides in the fact that the grapes produce wine, which, if abused, can be the source of much moral confusion, leading to lapses and excesses unworthy of human beings.

THE PROPER USE OF WINE

The Torah does not prohibit the enjoyment of wine. This is not the Torah's way. The Torah wants us to enjoy the good things of this world, but in moderation, so that our enjoyment shall be complete, and truly human. And this enjoyment is not to be an end in itself but a means to an enhanced relationship with God; the pleasure and joy derived from wine should heighten our gratitude to God for all His bounties. Thus our physical enjoyment itself is sanctified.

Perhaps it is this thought that is conveyed to us by the mitzva of separating growing grain from vineyards. From grain we get bread, the staff of life. From the grapevine we get wine, which has its special function in life, as we have noted. By insisting that we carefully separate the grape from the grain at their first emergence into the world, perhaps the Torah is hinting to us that we should not confuse their functions. Wine should not be thought of as a mainstay of life (as is unfortunately the case with alcoholics), nor should bread be associated in our minds with the "pleasure principle" of wine. Food should not be consumed merely for enjoyment, without thought of its true function — to build up our health and strength for the service of God. By this mitzva, the very environment of Eretz Yisrael may help to convey this message to its inhabitants.

For many centuries the land was not in our hands and this mitzva was in abeyance. Now it is again being observed. But over the ages the message of healthy moderation was conveyed by many mitzvot and became ingrained in the character of the Torah observant Jew.

The Rabbis have helped us to use wine for its true purposes by associating it with the performance of many mitzvot. Wherever joy is to be expressed, the Rabbis put in our hands a brimming cup of wine. We welcome Sabbaths and Festivals with wine (see chapter 65(2)), wine is needed at weddings, circumcisions and redemptions of firstborn, and so many other joyous occasions, when we feel particularly close to God. The low incidence of alcoholism in Torah observant communities has long been noted by sociologists, and some have attributed it to the training these practices have given us in the proper use of wine.

(5) Use of animals for work

Even in this area the Torah wants us to bear in mind the incompatibility of different species. The Oral Law tells us that the "plowing with an ox and an ass" of the verse is only an example. The prohibition extends to *any* work carried out by *any* two animals of diverse kinds, e.g., it is forbidden to ride in a carriage drawn by a horse and a donkey together.

(6) Clothing

The Torah's concern that we separate different "kinds" in our everyday life extends also to the sphere of clothing. The instinct which leads human beings to wear clothes is one of the things that distinguish man from the animals. (See also chapter 57.) Jewish clothing must carry the further imprint of "separation" — this time not a separation of species but of kingdoms. In the world of clothing linen represents the plant kingdom, and wool — the animal kingdom. In our clothes these two may not be mingled, bringing to mind the higher function of Jewish clothing.

Plant life has two elements: nutrition and reproduction. Animal life adds to these: perception, feelings and locomotion. The human being possesses all these and adds to them: understanding, free will, morality and spiritual potential.

In the animal the "higher" elements of perception, feelings and locomotion are used entirely in the service of the vegetative goals — the instinctive urges for food and reproduction. In man, and particularly in the Jew, the vegetative aspect is to be subordinate to the animal elements, and the animal elements to the freely deciding human mind, which should use them both for the spiritual goals laid down by the Torah.

The animal is a self-contained, self-serving system in which the "vegetative" function (symbolized by linen) and the animal function (symbolized by wool) are intimately interlaced and intertwined. The animal has no other goals but to satisfy the drives for food and sex. It is thus well symbolized by *shaatnez* — "wool and linen together." In man, mind and will power are not merely to serve the vegetative ends of food and sex. These aspects of our human nature are not, God forbid, to be denied, but controlled and guided by the human spirit for the higher goals of the holy Torah. The "linen" and the "woolen" must be kept strictly separate in our clothing.

It is highly significant that where the clothing is itself "holy," i.e., worn as part of a mitzva (e.g., the holy vestments of the Kohanim in the Temple service and in certain circumstances the mitzva of *tzitzit*), wool and linen *are* combined. It is only when the "mitzva" element — the dedication to our higher purpose — is absent, that separation of the "woolen" (animal function) and "linen" (vegetable function) becomes necessary. Where "mitzva" is present, "animal" and "vegetable" may be joyously combined in the service of that higher function. How these instincts can be used in the service of our highest ideals, see chapter 22(1), regarding sex, and chapter 24(1), regarding eating and drinking.

♦ *Halacha*

◇ *From the principles enunciated above it is clear that the Torah requires us to approach genetic engineering with great caution. This is a matter for decision by halachic authorities.*

◇ *Even a single thread of linen in a woolen garment, or vice versa, is shaatnez.*

◇ *In modern manufacture there are numerous places in a garment in which mixtures of wool and linen might be introduced. Garments should therefore be submitted to a "shaatnez laboratory" for examination.*

◇ *Even garments made from 100% polyester fiber need examination since wool and linen trimmings are often introduced.*

16. Respecting Motherhood in the Animal Kingdom

NOT SLAUGHTERING MOTHER AND YOUNG ON ONE DAY / NOT TAKING THE MOTHER BIRD WITH CHICKS / SEPARATING MEAT AND MILK

You shall not slaughter an ox or a sheep and its young on the same day. — LEVITICUS 22:28

If you happen to come across a bird's nest...with the mother bird sitting on the chicks or the eggs, you shall not take the mother bird with the young. You must send away the mother, and only then may you take the young ones, so that it may go well with you and your days will be prolonged.
— DEUTERONOMY 22:6-7

You shall not boil a kid in its mother's milk.
— EXODUS 23:19; 25:26; DEUTERONOMY 14:21

(1) Motherhood

Animal life is by its very nature egoistic. Motherhood is one point at which altruism intrudes into the self-contained world of nature. A mother gives up part of herself for the existence of another being and devotes care and concern for its well-being. In the animal we can see this as the first approach to that willingness to sacrifice oneself for others which is the highest attainment of human character. The Torah permits us to take our food from the animal realm, but only after many safeguards. (See chapter 24.) One of these is that at this moment we are to impress on our minds the supreme value of motherhood and all that it stands for. We must not be so eager to take the animal for our food that we trample on our own feelings of respect for that value wherever we find it. The Torah introduces this idea in the following three areas.

(2) Not slaughtering mother and young on one day

This law applies only to domestic animals permissible as food (cattle, sheep and goats) and only to slaughtering by *shehita* (see chapter 27). This is understandable, because it is at the moment we are taking this animal into our diet that the Torah wants us to be aware that an animal is not "just meat." It is a living being and we must respect in it those qualities which in some sense are a reflection of human qualities. Even if the animal knows nothing of it, it would be heartless *of us* to slaughter mother and young on one day. When our Father Jacob wanted to express the extreme cruelty of Esau he said "...he will strike me down — mother with children" (Genesis 32:11).

The educative power of mitzvot can protect the Jewish soul from such inhuman tendencies — so long as the mitzvot are practiced.

(3) Sending away the mother bird

The oral tradition tells us that this mitzva is governed by the following special conditions:

1. The bird must be of a species permitted to us for food (see chapter 25).
2. The bird and eggs must belong to free creation (*hefker*); they must be no one's property.
3. The prohibition is to appropriate the mother bird *while it is sitting on the eggs.*
4. If one wants the eggs or chicks, one must first take the mother bird and let it fly freely from one's hand. As soon as it has flown away, the eggs or chicks may be taken.
5. Once the mother bird has flown away, it too may be appropriated, as well as the eggs or chicks.

At first sight these details seem incomprehensible, especially the last. But we have probably learned by now not to be satisfied with superficial understanding when dealing with the mitzvot of God's Torah. In the context of this group of mitzvot the meaning unfolds as follows:

When taking from God's creation for your human needs, think of its wildlife. Say you find in the wild a bird sitting in its nest, tending its eggs or chicks. If it flies away at your approach there is no problem. If its mother instinct is stronger than its fear and it continues to fulfill its motherly function despite your approach, you are not to exploit its loyalty to its young by taking it together with its chicks. Do not appropriate it at the moment of its service to its species. Once this moment is past and it has again become part of free creation there is nothing more to prevent you from taking it.

The Talmud calls this "the easiest of mitzvot." But its message is of universal significance, especially in our time.

(4) Separating meat and milk

The Oral Law teaches us that the "kid" and the "mother's milk" in the verse are only examples; the Torah's prohibition extends to any meat of cattle, sheep and goats and any milk of these species. The reason for the Torah's choice of these particular words will be discussed a little later. (Rabbinical legislation includes also venison and fowl in the prohibition, since these are commonly referred to as "meat" and to permit them would cause confusion.)

This mitzva contains a threefold prohibition: (a) the act of boiling meat and milk together is itself forbidden; (b) it is forbidden to eat the mixture; and (c) no other benefit may be derived from it.

This law and its ramifications have laid their imprint on the Jewish kitchen and the Jewish table perhaps more than any other dietary law. There must be some great lesson that the Torah wants to teach us. What can it be?

The significance must certainly lie in the expression "kid in its mother's milk." It would almost seem that the Torah is trying to arouse our pity. But since the Oral Law tells us that the intention is to prohibit boiling *any* meat of a *kosher* beast in *any* milk of the same, we must ask why the Torah chooses to express it in that way. It would seem that the Torah wants us to look beneath the surface of things and become aware of their inner significance. We should be able to see the "kid" in the flesh of the adult animal and "mother's milk" in the milk carton we buy at the supermarket. We should be aware that when it produces milk, the animal diverts part of its resources away from its selfish needs to meet the needs of emergent new life. This too, is one of the points at which altruism intrudes into the natural universe. It is this point of unselfishness that the Torah wishes us to respect. This is the Torah's message: The milk that was created by God to nurture the new generation may not be used to boil for our own pleasure the flesh that "milk" was created to nourish. In the eyes of the Torah to do this would be perverse, it would be an unacceptable reversal of function.

When we take flesh into our diet we have to beware of such greediness. In such ways the Torah endeavors to train us to see the full significance of what we do. It subtly instills into our lives a respect for unselfishness as the highest value.

We can now understand how this law comes to appear three times in the Torah, each time as the conclusion and climax of a great chapter of laws. First and foremost it comes as the climax of the first and greatest compendium of the Torah's social legislation — *Parashat Mishpatim* (Exodus 21:1 to 23:19). Most of these social mitzvot, as we have seen in the first section of this book, are based on the principles of human rights and brotherly love, and cannot depend on legal enforcement. God did not appoint police or court officials to be the guardians of His law; He preferred to entrust it to the God-fearing conscience of His people. He requires not mere legality, or outward conformity. Loyal, faithful adherence to the spirit of the law is to form the character of Jewish citizens. His "policemen" are the mitzvot, the spiritual and mental heralds of what is right, which accompany every Jew into the innermost sphere of his home life.

Sensitivity, sensitivity! This is what the Torah is trying to teach us. Do not see only what meets the eye. Look beyond appearances. Use your imagination and see the truth as the Torah sees it. The Torah comes to heighten our sensitivity to the world around us and the living creatures it contains.

WHERE ARE THE POLICE?

Rabbi Levi Yitzhak, the hassidic rebbe of Berdichev in 19th-century Russia, often acted as a defending attorney for the people of Israel before God. Once on Erev Pesach he gave his attendant a large cardboard box and asked him to go around to the Jews of Berdichev and bring back whatever leavened bread he could get. He returned with an empty box. It was past midday and the Jews had already burnt all their *hametz*. (See chapter 45.)

Then he gave him another cardboard box and asked him to go to the same Jews and see if he could get a few pounds of contraband tobacco. He succeeded in this task in a short time.

The Rebbe took the full box and the empty box and laid them in front of the Holy Ark.

"Lord of the universe," he said, "the Czar of

Russia decreed that anyone who deals in contraband tobacco shall go to prison or be exiled to
Siberia. He has police, gendarmes and a great
army to see his commands are carried out. And
see the result! But You, God, decreed over 3,000
years ago that Jews shall own no *hametz* on
Pesah. You have no police, no army, no Siberia,
but see how Jews carry out Your commands! It can
only be that Your Jews love You and *like* to do Your
mitzvot."

17. Respect for the Feelings and Instincts of Animals

RELIEF OF SUFFERING/PHYSICAL AND MENTAL/CASTRATION

If you see your enemy's donkey lying down under its load and you would like to ignore it — you shall surely join him in helping it up.
— EXODUS 23:5

You shall not muzzle the ox which does the threshing.
— DEUTERONOMY 25:4

Castration of any animal is prohibited.
— TB HAGIGA 14b

(1) Animals are a trust

God has delivered animals into our power only for fulfilling humane and wise purposes. As soon as we go beyond this and become insensitive to the physical or mental pain of animals we become tyrants and torturers. It makes no difference whether this is out of thoughtlessness, self-interest, to satisfy a whim or, God forbid, for the satisfaction of crude sadistic desire.

It is forbidden to overload or overwork the animals entrusted to our care by God. What constitutes over-working is to a large extent a question for the individual conscience.

Animals are a responsibility and we must be sensitive to their needs. Our animals must be fed before we sit down to our own meal.

A CASE WITH HORSES

Rabbi Israel of Rizhyn (a ḥassidic master in 19th-century Poland) ran his court in regal style. It was his custom to be driven around the countryside every weekday in a carriage drawn by two fine

67

horses. When they reached a hill the Rabbi would stop the carriage, alight, and walk beside the carriage to the top of the hill, where he would resume his drive. "But Rebbe," his followers protested, "is this really necesary? These horses lead a wonderful life. They are well fed, well groomed, free in the paddock by day, warm in the stable by night. Their sole duty is to draw your carriage for an hour a day. And if they were to pull you up a hill or two, would this be overworking?" "You may well be right," replied the Rabbi. "When after 120 years I stand before the Heavenly Tribunal, if these horses accuse me of overworking them I could advance the arguments you mention and I would probably be acquitted. But who wants to have a court case with horses?"

(2) Education to sensitivity

God's Torah teaches us to refrain from inflicting unnecessary pain on any animal. And not only physical pain; an animal can suffer mental pain too. It is mental torture for an animal to work with fruits or grain which it would dearly love to taste and to be forcibly prevented from enjoying them. The Torah forbids such insensitivity. "You shall not muzzle the ox which does the threshing."

It is an important part of Torah education to train children to respect animals as sensitive beings which should not be unnecessarily deprived of the joys of life. Do not forget that the child who crudely delights in the suffering of an injured beetle or the anxiety of a harassed animal will soon be numb towards human pain too.

(3) Respect for instincts

We are not to use our power over the animal world to eradicate powers and instincts which God has implanted in His creation. We are not allowed to castrate any animal by surgical intervention.

It goes without saying that these procedures may not be carried out on human beings. See chapter 20 — "Regard for One's Own Body" — for the Torah's concern for every aspect of our bodily nature, and chapter 22 — "Respect for Our Sexuality" — for the high esteem in which the Torah holds our sexual instinct and its sublime purpose in creation. When we read of medieval popes who sanctioned the castration of boys for the sake of a special timbre in the soprano voice (hence the musical term *castrato*), we note the contempt for sexuality in other civilizations. The Jewish soul shudders.

(4) Factory farming

It seems doubtful from all that has been said whether the Torah would sanction "factory farming," which treats animals as machines, with apparent insensitivity to their natural needs and instincts. This is a matter for decision by halachic authorities.

18. Respect for the Human Being after Death

BURIAL/HONORING THE DEAD/MOURNING

You shall surely bury him the same day. — DEUTERONOMY 21:23

And he [Joseph] observed for his father a mourning period of seven days. — GENESIS 50:10

(1) Dignity of human life

The body is the Divinely designed instrument for carrying out God's will on earth; it is a sanctuary. On death, it is a desolate sanctuary, but a sanctuary, nevertheless, and must be treated with due reverence.

A society which tolerates disrespect for human remains betrays disrespect for the value and dignity of human life in general. The Torah prescribes reverent burial of the dead particularly in connection with the corpse of a criminal who has been executed for his crime. This is to teach us that however low a man may have sunk, his body once was the instrument serving the sublime spirit of man. We honor him not so much for what he was but for what he might have been.

(2) Return to the earth

The Torah instructs us to dispose of the body by returning it to the earth from which it ultimately came. "For you are dust and to dust you shall return" (Genesis 3:19). It should be given back to the earth so that it may ultimately serve new life formation in the economy of the universe.

♦ *Halacha*
◇ *No benefit may be derived from a corpse.*

70

◊ *It is offensive to the dignity of the human being to allow the corpse to remain unburied longer than necessary. As soon as death is ascertained, burial should not be delayed unless the delay is necessary for a worthy funeral.*

◊ *It is forbidden to mutilate a dead body. However, in certain circumstances transplantation from a corpse may be permissible, e.g., skin from a corpse to save the life of a badly burned patient, kidneys for transplantation into a seriously ill patient, a cornea into a blind person; but a competent halachic authority must first be consulted in each case.*

◊ *Scientific experiments, even if they may at some future time save human lives, do not override the prohibition of mutilation or showing disrespect to the dead. A society which accepts the dehumanization of the dead body in the name of science will come eventually to dehumanize the living human being. (This has already happened.)*

(3) Mourning

To see a human being breathe his last is like seeing a Scroll of Law burn before one's eyes. That tremendous spiritual potential is no more. Respect for our common humanity requires that we do not go about our business as if nothing has happened.

When the person who has died is a parent or other close relative (spouse, sibling or child) a period of mourning is required. It is clear that the seven days of mourning (*shiv'a*), the custom of rending one's garment, neglect of personal appearance, etc. are of very ancient origin and were observed by the family of Abraham long before the Torah was given. They have the status of a rabbinic ordinance (except for the first day, when they are mandated by the Torah).

THE FOUR STAGES

The Rabbis divide mourning into four successive stages.

1. The first is that between death and burial. This is when the mourner's energies must be directed towards ensuring proper arrangements for the funeral. This is the overriding mitzva of the moment, and the Rabbis therefore free him from all positive commandments. He may not put on *tefillin* (see chapter 55) or pray or make any benediction, nor may he eat meat or drink wine during this period. At this time he is called *onen* (from a word meaning "grief") and his state is *aninut*.

At this stage no attempt should be made to comfort the mourner: the wound is too fresh. As the Rabbis say, "Do not attempt to console a person when his dead is still before him."

2. The second stage is the period of the *shiv'a*, the seven days following the burial. During this time the mourner emerges from his first shock and is prepared to talk about his loss and to accept comfort from friends and neighbors. He is now an *avel* ("mourner") and his state is *avelut*. He remains within the house, expressing his grief through the observances of *avelut*, wearing the torn garment, sitting close to the ground, not wearing leather shoes, refraining from shaving and grooming, and reciting *kaddish* when the services are held at the house. (See paragraph (5).) He may not engage in business nor listen to music or any entertainment. It is not distraction which is required but a sincere attempt to come to terms with the loss.

3. The third stage is the *shloshim*, that is, from the end of the *shiv'a* until the thirtieth day after the burial. (*Shloshim* means thirty.) The mourner may now leave his house and engage in his business or profession, but certain signs of mourning still continue, notably: no trimming of hair and no attendance at weddings, parties and entertainments. Out of respect for the dead, one's return to

normal life cannot be complete until this 30-day period is ended. This ends the mourning for all relatives except one's parents. Respect for one's parents demands the continuation of some mourning observance for a full year.

4. The fourth and final stage, after the loss of a parent, is thus from the end of the *shloshim* until the expiry of twelve months from the day of death. This relates chiefly to non-participation in weddings and entertainments. The hair may be trimmed after three months. A son says *kaddish* for his father or mother until a month before the end of this period.

THE PROCESS AND THE AIM

This carefully graduated process of mourning has a twofold purpose.

Firstly it leads the bereaved person from the first sense of tragic loss and bewilderment when he is alone with his grief to a structured environment in which he can eventually come to terms with his loss. It is comforting to know that even in a dire situation such as this there is a well-trodden path to follow. He is made aware that the community cares. He is given an opportunity to express, rather than repress, his grief. The wisdom of this course has been recognized by modern thinkers, one of whom writes:

> The discoveries of psychiatry...remind us that the ancient teachers of Judaism often had an intuitive wisdom about human nature and its needs which our sophisticated and liberal age has forgotten. Traditional Judaism...had the wisdom to devise almost all of the procedures for [dealing with] grief which the contemporary psychologist counsels.
>
> (J. L. Lieberman, *Peace of Mind*)

Secondly these observances ensure that the supreme value of the human personality is maintained. We talk a lot about grief, but we all know that in many cases the grief is more external than real. In our time people are often desensitized to emotion. Human dignity would be diminished if people were just to return to everyday life after a loss of this sort as if nothing had happened. Our age-old Jewish traditions ensure that the memory of the departed relative is duly honored.

(4) Comforting the mourner

Part of the mitzva of mourning is to sit and accept the condolences of relatives, friends and the general community. The traditional words of comfort to the bereaved are: "May the All-Present comfort you among all those who mourn for Zion and Jerusalem." We try to let him see his personal tragedy as part of the national tragedy — the millennial loss of our Sanctuary, the one-time focal point of our existence.

Israel continues, we tell him, in spite of grievous loss, and so will *he* continue. God has work for him yet.

The word we use for God, "*Hamakom*," which we have rendered by "the All-Present," actually means "The One in Whom the universe has its existence." God is not in the universe; it is truer to say that the universe is in God. The spirit is not a flickering flame which comes and goes in the darkness of a physical universe. On the contrary, the universe is bathed in an ocean of spirit to which the spirit of man returns when its journey is over.

This is why we say to the bereaved; *we* cannot comfort you. Only God as we know Him — the limitless sea of spirit in which we all have our being — only He can comfort you. Only He can assure you that the spirit of your loved one is not lost; the love of God nurtures and maintains it forever.

This is the only comfort we have, and it is the greatest comfort of all.

(5) Kaddish

The *kaddish* is not a prayer for the dead. There is no mention of death. On the contrary, it is an affirmation of life, a declaration of faith in the future. The bereaved person stands before the community of Israel and declares — in spite of the tragedy that has befallen him — that he remains confident that God's name will one day be recognized as great and holy throughout the entire world. And, he adds, this is not something for the dim and distant future; he wants it to be realized now, speedily and in our days. (See chapter 65(5).)

Here speaks the true spirit of Israel.

The Torah deals with mortality by transcending it.

19. Regard for One's Own Life

SUICIDE / SELF-INJURY / SELF-PRESERVATION / LIVING IN
THE WORLD / EARNING A LIVING

I will demand your own blood, concerning your own life.

— GENESIS 9:5

Take heed and guard your life well. — DEUTERONOMY 4:9

*You shall choose life (Deuteronomy 30:19). — This refers to
earning one's living by a craft or profession.* — TJ PE'AH 1:1

*Flay a carcass in the marketplace and stay independent, and
don't say "It's beneath my dignity."* — TB PESAH 113a

(1) Our life is not our own

One cannot say: "I am an ethical being. I will do no wrong
to anyone or anything. But my body is my own. I can do
with it what I like." The Torah teaches: Our body and our
life are not our own to dispose of as we see fit. Like the
world around us, they too have been given us by God for the
purpose of fulfilling His beneficent will for man. No one
has the right to injure oneself, to ruin oneself, to drug
oneself, to murder oneself. Not oneself, and certainly not
new life within oneself. We all have the duty to preserve
ourselves and all that is within us, because the world needs
us, God needs us. If human judges do not judge such cases,
nevertheless God judges! We have no more right against
our own life than we have right against our brother's. Like
every other part of the universe, we are servants of God,
framed in a physical body, to fulfill the mission of God on
earth.

However the world has shown itself to us, whether
friendly or unfriendly, kindly or cruel, it is the environment God has given us for our task in life; we must

treasure it. We should consider it a privilege to be alive. Maybe we blame it all on ourselves. We have made a mess of things. We have ruined our health, we have debased our moral stature. This may all be true, but it gives us no right to take our own life. If we are still alive this means that God thinks there is still some purpose in our existence. What did King David say? "My own father and mother may disown me, but God will gather me in" (Psalms 27:10).

I cannot say, I have no friends, no relatives, what does it matter to anyone if I take my life? No one is alone. The world still needs me. God still needs me. Anything I do affects everybody else. Every act, even in private, subtly changes the moral and spiritual atmosphere. If I realize the truth I will find that my mission in life is not over yet, not by a long run.

(2) Unnecessary risks

We may not go into danger unless our Torah duty requires this. We should not take unnecessary risks and rely on miracles to protect us; Providence does not protect carelessness or foolhardiness.

(3) Living in the world

The task the Torah imposes on us is to live in the world, live a normal life, and by living according to the Torah to be a blessing to all around us. This is implied by the whole Torah and every single word and mitzva in it. Do not say the world is evil, and I will flee it. One who renounces every bodily pleasure, avoids marriage, comfort and amenity, and lives a monk-like existence, is a sinner. Nothing is evil in the world if used wisely, in moderation, and in accordance with the ways of the Torah. If we are aware of our life's mission, all our physical activities can also become a service of God.

(4) Earning a living

"Living in the world," which the Torah demands, includes earning a living. A life of productive work combined with Torah study involves the whole personality and leaves no time or inclination for destructive pursuits.

If one runs one's business life in accordance with the principles laid down in the Torah this gives ample opportunity for "sanctifying God's name" and showing what human relationships can be like if guided by the mitzvot of the Torah. (See chapter 79.)

◆ *Halacha*

◇ *Preservation of life (*pikuaḥ nefesh*) takes precedence over all the commandments of the Torah, except idolatry, immorality and murder. (To avoid these cardinal sins one must be prepared to sacrifice one's life. What value has life if we betray our basic loyalty to God? See "Sanctifying God's Name" — chapter 79.)*

◇ *Although one is not strictly obliged to risk one's life to save another's (see chapter 3), this refers to a serious risk. Minor risks must be taken.*

◇ *It is a mitzva to risk one's life in a war for the defense of the people of Israel.*

20. Regard for One's Own Body

DISFIGUREMENT/TATTOOING/TONSURING (LEVELING THE HAIR
AT THE TEMPLES)

*You are the children of God your God. You shall not gash
yourselves nor shave your head...for the dead. For you are a
holy people to God your God, Who has chosen you to be His
special treasure...*   — DEUTERONOMY 14:1-2

*You shall not make scratches in your flesh for the dead, nor
tattoo any marks upon yourselves: I am God.*   — LEVITICUS 19:28

*You shall not round off the corners of your head nor shall you
destroy [by shaving] the corners of your beard.* — LEVITICUS 19:27

(1) Our marvelous body

In their pagan frenzy the priests of Baal "gashed
themselves as was their custom" (I Kings 18:28). In the
modern world too we are not unfamiliar with cults whose
members disfigure themselves in various bizarre ways.

As "children of God," as a people dedicated to showing
the world how life in this world can become a blessing, we
must treat our bodies with respect. The human body — the
most marvelous and complex system in the universe —
was designed by God for a high purpose. We must value it
and respect it for what it is. We may not mutilate it in any
way.

(2) Proper care of our body

Proper care of the body, its cleanliness, its attire, is a
mitzva.

On the other hand the Torah does not want us to go to the
opposite extreme and lavish exaggerated attention on our
bodies, their beautification and adornment. This would
not be treating the body as an instrument of the Divine

79

purpose but, on the contrary, as a pagan idol serving our baser, selfish concerns. Moderation in all things is the Torah's order of the day.

"DOING A MITZVA"

Hillel the Elder (1st century B.C.E.) was asked by his disciples where he was going. "I am going to do a mitzva," he replied. On further questioning he disclosed that he was going to the baths. "This is a mitzva?" they asked. "Look," he said, "the Romans appoint a man whose sole duty is to wash down the statues of their great men which stand in the foyers of their baths and theaters. He not only gets a good wage but he is on familiar terms with the great ones of the empire. Should our own bodies, given to us by God, be any less important?"

(3) How one cuts one's hair

Our awareness of the God-given nature of our bodies must extend even to the way we cut our hair. Every activity of life, even the seemingly trivial, thus receives sanctification.

When cutting the hair of our head we are not to remove the sideburns, which would level off the hairline all around the scalp. This would give the Jew a "tonsured" look, such as affected by pagan priests in the past and some other gentile priests still at the present day. The Torah wants us to be a "kingdom of priests" — but not to ape the appearance of that other type of priest. The priestly function of the Jewish nation lies just in showing how *ordinary* life can be sanctified. The significance of the sideburns is that they mark the division between the frontal lobe of the brain, which is concerned mainly with abstract thought and decision making, and the rest of the brain which is concerned with other functions. They mark off and emphasize the specifically human factors of intellect and morality, and their retention teaches that these human elements are to prevail in our lives. This hair at the temples graces the countenence of every human child — the emblem of its human calling. (This may go some way to explain the importance attached to the complete retention of these sideburns in certain Jewish circles, although the Torah forbids only their complete removal.)

In the adult human male the lower part of the face is covered by a beard. This hair discreetly veils the jaws and chin devoted primarily to eating and mastication. Eating and enjoyment are fine, but they should be treated with discretion and not allowed to dominate our lives. The Torah's command is even more discreet. It does not say that the beard must be retained. It says merely that it must not be "destroyed" i.e., shaven off level with the skin by a razor. It may be removed by scissors or by an electric shaver acting like a scissors, i.e., leaving a small fraction of the hair above the skin. This subtle hint, imprinted on our subconscious every time we shave, suffices for the Torah's purpose. (This idea may explain why in Jewish tradition the beard is considered an adornment, in accord with its biological function.)

21. Respect for One's Words

VOWS/PROMISES/CHARITABLE COMMITMENTS

When one makes a vow to God, or swears an oath...he shall not break his word. He shall do exactly as his mouth uttered.
— NUMBERS 30:3

If you make a vow to God, do not delay to make it good...If you do not vow, this is no sin. But whatever proceeds from your mouth you must keep; whatever you freely promised to God.
— DEUTERONOMY 23:22-24

(1) Promises to God

Just as we are responsible to God for the way we treat our bodies, so are we responsible to God for the way we treat our words. God demands from us that we value ourselves highly enough to give full value to our words, even where no one else is affected.

A promise to God is holy; to break a promise is an act of desecration. God does not need your gifts, but you need to give to God — that is, to the causes which He holds dear: support of the poor, support of Torah, the synagogue, the community.

The trouble with vows and promises is that it is easy to promise something when one is in the mood, but when the time comes to pay we find it more difficult than we thought. Delay is often fatal. One should give as soon as possible after the promise.

It is legitimate to make a vow when one is in trouble, if circumstances do not permit giving on the spot. Our Father Jacob made such a vow when setting out penniless on his journey into the unknown. "If you will bring me back safely to my father's house...I will build a house for God and I will give back a tenth of whatever You give me" (Genesis 28:20-22). Trouble is sent to test us and to pull out the best in us. At such a time it is right to stretch oneself to the utmost provided that one has steely determination to stand by one's promise when the time comes.

THE LADY AND THE BRIDGE

In the course of our history there have been Jewish businesswomen who often undertook arduous journeys in the course of their business.

In the 18th century there was one such lady whose travels took her to the edge of a frightening precipice. The only way to cross the ravine was by way of a plank bridge with one rope to hold on to. It looked extremely dangerous but seeing that there was no alternative she steeled herself for the ordeal. She was a deeply religious woman and before setting her foot on the planks she raised her eyes to heaven and said, "God! If you get me over this safely I'll give... I'll give...twenty long tallow candles to the synagogue."

Then she started walking, forcing herself not to look at the depths below. To her surprise she found the planks were firmly set and seemed perfectly stable. She started thinking to herself: "Twenty tallow candles? That's a lot of money...." The very next step she took, the planks started wobbling. "Hey, hey! Wait a minute!" she cried. "I haven't even said anything yet, and He's pushing already!"

We can admire the immediacy of the lady's awareness of God, but her experience also teaches us something about the vowing process.

(2) In battle with sin and as spurs to duty

In the past, if a Jew found that he had a moral weakness — for example, he was prone to overeating — he would make a vow to deny himself certain foods for a time. These foods then became forbidden to him just as if they had been forbidden by God in the Torah. In this way he hoped to train himself to be more moderate. Similarly, if he felt himself indolent in the fulfillment of certain mitzvot he could set himself certain tasks backed by a solemn vow. This might help him overcome his indolence.

In our time this tactic is very rarely used. Indeed, when making any promise, whether to give charity or to do any other mitzva or good deed, it is recommended that we add the words *"bli neder,"* i.e., "this promise is not intended to be a vow." We consider it an achievement if we are able to observe the commandments of the Torah, without involving ourselves in additional commitments of a voluntary nature.

ADAM'S DONATION

Adam was doomed to die on the same day that he ate the forbidden fruit, but God extended the time limit to one of *His* days, that is, a thousand years. Yet we find that Adam lived only 930 years. How come?

The Rabbis tell us in one of their parables that God showed Adam all the generations of his descendants — all the souls destined to live on the earth — and the years allotted to each one. God showed him one soul who would pass by the world stillborn. It had no years allotted to it. This was the soul of King David. Adam took pity on this soul and asked God whether it was possible to donate years. "Yes, it is possible," said God. "Then," said Adam, "I will donate 70 years of my life so that this soul may live." "Very well," said God. "Just sign this piece of paper confirming the arrangement." Adam did so.

Nine-hundred and thirty years passed, and God

said to Adam, "Well, Adam. Time's up. You have lived 930 years."

"Wait a minute," said Adam. "Didn't you say I could live a full day, that is a thousand years?"

"But didn't you donate 70 years to that poor little soul with no years?" asked God.

"Certainly not!" said Adam. "Whoever heard of anyone donating part of his own life to someone else?"

"If you don't remember," said God, "perhaps this piece of paper with your signature will remind you?"

We learn from this that what may appear from our present vantage point to be a very small sacrifice, may appear a very large sacrifice when it is due for payment.

22. Respect for Our Sexuality

OASIS OF SANITY / SEX EDUCATION / STANDING BY OUR CHILDREN

*No daughter of Israel shall be devoted to immorality, nor any
man of Israel...*
— DEUTERONOMY 23:18

*You shall not follow the practices of Egypt where you lived,
nor those of Canaan where you are going, nor shall you obey
their laws...It is My laws and My statutes that you shall
obey, which a man can practice and live by: I am God your
God.*
— LEVITICUS 18:3-5

Do not come near to wrongdoing.
— LEVITICUS 18:6

*A woman shall not wear anything pertaining to a man nor
shall a man wear a woman's garment...This is an
abomination to GOD.*
— DEUTERONOMY 22:5

(1) Biological purpose

God introduced sexual reproduction into the world of
living things to ensure unending variety. He also included
an instinct for home-building and nurturing the young. As
a bait He ensured that mating would be accompanied by
intense pleasure. (Without these biological incentives no
one would undertake the onerous task of producing and
rearing a family, with all the self-sacrifice and "giving"
involved. Even so, some people find it possible to allow
their instinct for "taking" to overcome their home-building
instincts, preferring to gratify more selfish desires.) The
human species is the only one that has devised means of
taking the bait without serving any purpose beyond its
own selfish ends. We are born with the potential and the
destiny to be givers. When we take without giving, or
without giving adequately, we feel shame. When we "take"
the extremely intense pleasure involved in sex without
"giving" to the ends for which sex was created, we feel

shame. This is the true source of the shame associated with sexual activity. If, God forbid, this sense of shame is lost, this means that one's human stature is dangerously diminished.

But if a young man and young woman sanctify their union by *huppa* and *kiddushin* (see chapter 33), found a fine Jewish home, and raise children who are sound in body and spirit, their marriage bond kept stable by the enjoyment of sex in accordance with Torah law (see chapters 33(3) and 23(2)), then sex has fulfilled its true function and is sanctified thereby. The taking is balanced by the giving, and husband and wife can achieve their full status as human beings and Jews.

Every union of the sexes which is not for this high purpose is a misuse of powers, a degradation of humanity, a taking with nothing given in return to the true goals of life.

This is why a union without *huppa* and *kiddushin* is immoral. And such immorality saps the spirit from a person. His better and nobler part dies out. Once pleasure becomes the goal — animal pleasure — the human being sinks to the level of the animal. But much worse: his deranged spirit, his misdirected intellect, which should be master and director of the animal within him, must now serve his baser desires. Once this most potent force in human life becomes the plaything of casual desire, sex becomes trivialized and diminished, and living becomes less and less worthwhile. Not so long ago we were assured that the relaxation of sexual restraints would usher in a new and happier age. Let us think: since then have general moral standards throughout the world improved or deteriorated? Has there been more or less violent crime, drug abuse, battered babies, broken families? Have happiness, security, a sense of the wonder of being alive kept pace with the improvement in material conditions?

(2) Oasis of sanity

The Torah wants the people of Israel to be an oasis of sanity in a deranged world. "You do not have to follow the norms of Egypt where you were or those of Canaan where you are going. You are to follow My norms," says God, "laws which will ensure that you maintain the true values of life." We are to be a holy nation. Holy means dedicated — dedicated to all that is true and good, dedicated to the good of others, to the value of life, to the beneficent purposes of God in this world.

Our mode of dress, our demeanor, the way we go about the world, should proclaim what we stand for. Our dress does not have to ape the fashions of those around us. If basically decent people affect styles worn only by prostitutes a generation ago, this does not mean that we have to admire them. We do not have to fall into all the traps laid by and for others.

The Torah requires a married woman to cover her hair in public. This is an act of modesty; it also serves to remind the woman of her married status.

The Torah wishes the sexes to be clearly distinguished by their mode of clothing. There need be no aping of one sex by the other. Each should take pride in his or her own nature and the dignity bestowed on them by God. It follows that "unisex" is out. (For a discussion of the function of sex differences in Torah thought, see "He called them 'Adam'" — chapter 78.)

(3) Making life easier

"Do not come close to wrongdoing." If we want to follow the path of the Torah and reserve the powers that are in us for good and wholesome ends, let us not make life more difficult by inviting temptation. The Torah and its Sages have laid down rules, which if followed make life much easier. Thus, two persons of opposite sex should not be alone in a place which is not accessible to or frequented by others, in a house or in the countryside (*yiḥud*). Since this is a law, the matter can be discussed quite openly, without fear of hurting the other person's feelings. The people involved may be personally completely above suspicion, but "the law's the law." (See chapter 4(4), "self-incrimination," for a similar solution in a different context.) Physical contact, embracing, kissing, lightheadedness, are forbidden. Avoid reading or seeing things which inflame the imagination. We should be too proud to sin — and give ourselves no time to sin. If we work hard and learn hard, lewdness can be kept at bay. As Maimonides said, "Thoughts of lust arise only in an empty mind."

(4) Stand at their side

Jewish parents should not forget how much the fate of their children depends on them. They should be aware of the temptations which constantly face their children and should assess the situation realistically. Be ready to stand by your children *before* they have been hurt. You should know that age 11 is not too early to merit your concern. Observe the schools, the playmates, the servants, the friends of the family. Stand by your children's side in their battle. Do not leave them on their own just when the battle is hardest. Explain to them what we stand for in the world, the task for which we have been chosen. Make them proud that the responsibility of carrying on the holy tradition of our people will be theirs.

And above all — be an example to them of purity in word and deed. Let them see how the spirit of Torah inspires *your* life. Then you are giving them the best weapon of all for victory in the battle of life. Remember that it was the vision of his father that saved Joseph in the hour of his greatest temptation.

23. Regulating Our Sexual Relations

INCEST / ADULTERY / HOMOSEXUALITY / PERIODS OF SEPARATION

No one shall approach anyone who is closely related to him...
— LEVITICUS 18:6

You shall not commit adultery. — EXODUS 20:13

You shall not lie with a male as with a woman.— LEVITICUS 18:22

You shall not approach a woman in her period of separation.
— LEVITICUS 18:19

(1) A mystery

Forbidden unions (*arayot*) — incest, adultery and the like — form one of the three cardinal sins for which a Jew is obliged to sacrifice his life rather than transgress. This gives us some idea of the gravity with which the Torah treats these laws.

We cannot expect to gain complete understanding of any of God's laws, still less these laws of *arayot*, which deal with the mysteries of sex and life. And even if we did understand them, we should not observe them for this reason, but because they are God's laws and our life's task is not to fulfill *our* will but God's will. However, as we become more familiar with the Torah's goals, certain underlying ideas may suggest themselves.

(2) Incest

We have seen above that the purpose of sex is to promote a stable home in which a happy and contented family can be reared. (This explains why sexual desire persists in a woman long after child-bearing age. Sex is needed to keep

90

the home atmosphere sweet and stable until the last child born is well into adulthood.) A stable, happy home is a universal requirement if children are to grow up bearing the moral ideals of humanity — the Torah of the nations of the world. It is all the more necessary as an environment in which children can flourish who will proudly bear the ideals of the Torah of Israel. To create and foster such an environment many things are necesary, and many of the mitzvot of the Torah are directed to this end, as we have already seen and shall still have occasion to note later in this book.

One absolutely essential element is that the parents must be, and must be seen to be, *givers*. Whatever they do for the children must be seen to be for love of the children and not for love of themselves. This creates the bond of love, gratitude and trust between children and their parents. It has been suggested that this may be one of the factors involved in the prohibition of incest. If there were any sexual connection betwen parent and child, the parent would be taking instead of giving and this delicate relationship would be destroyed. The home would cease to function as an environment for the development of sound human beings. (This may explain the instinctive aversion to incest in the human psyche.) The prohibition extends to other close relatives, both blood relations and relations by marriage, who may be subconsciously identified with the parents in the child's mind or with whom a sexual relationship would tend to disturb the home atmosphere.

(3) Adultery

Torah Jews have always prided themselves that they know who their fathers are. But this is not the only reason why the Torah is so determined to ban adultery from the midst of our people.

The marital bond is a very delicate one. It comprises elements which are physical, personal and emotional. It flowers into love and affection. Above all it can only operate on a basis of mutual trust and confidence. Once trust is broken the marriage withers and cannot fulfill its function in the Torah scheme — to form a tranquil, happy, moral environment for the development of a Torah family.

Adultery usually breaks up a marriage and this is crime enough. But it is no less a crime if the husband condones it. Adultery is a sin against the sanctity of marriage itself. It is a sin against God and His purposes for marriage and no human being can condone it.

(4) Homosexuality

A homosexual relationship between males is an abomination in the eyes of the Torah. It is not difficult to see why. By its very nature it subverts the Divine purposes of sex and marriage. In fact the more permanent and "life-enhancing" the liason purports to be and the greater the publicity given to it, the worse the offense in the Torah's eyes. Again the reason is not far to seek: the more plausibly it can be presented as an "alternative lifestyle," the greater the danger it poses to the Torah's concept of marriage.

So long as Jews were loyal to Torah, the healthy attitude to sex which it promulgates and the happiness of the Jewish home seem to have discouraged the growth of homosexuality. The Rabbis of the Talmud could state (in a halachic context), "The people of Israel are not suspected of homosexual practices." And if this can no longer be said so confidently in our time, there can be no doubt that it is the social and cultural milieu which is largely to blame.

Moral realities do not change. God sees further than we do. It would be presumptuous to assume that life could be "enhanced" by behavior concerning which the Creator of life states the contrary.

(5) "Consenting adults in private"

The Torah does not accept the argument that an act done in private affects no one but oneself. In chapter 19 we wrote that in the eyes of the Torah there are no private acts. I cannot indulge in drug abuse in private and say that my act affects no one else. Science now knows that in many complex systems small causes can have extremely unpredictable effects. It has even been said — only half in jest — that the flutter of a butterfly's wing in the English countryside may affect the weather in California a month later. (This is known as the "butterfly effect" and is dealt with in the recently developed theory of "Chaos.") How much more in the spiritual world are we all interconnected! And we are not talking about trivial acts. When we abuse our powers the consequences are potentially always grave.

(6) Period of separation

In the animal world we often find a periodicity in sexual activity, programmed and regulated by instinct. The sexual life of human beings is free of the restraints of instinct. Instead, the restraints have to be imposed by the freely choosing human will. The Torah introduces periodicity to Jewish conjugal life by confining sexual activity to the time outside the menstrual period.

The physiological basis of menstruation is that whenever the ovum completes its cycle without being fertilized, the womb lining sheds the proteins it had been storing for a possible fetus. The somewhat depressive effect — often unconscious — of this slight "loss" — a kind of "death" — is important enough in the eyes of the Torah to exclude the person for a short time from the Holy Temple, which should be entered only in a state of pure joy. And by the same token, the exclusion extends also to the sanctuary of Jewish marital relations.

93

Restoration is effected by complete immersion in a *mikveh*, a pool connected with natural rain- or spring-water (not conveyed by pipe, or other artificial means). Under the waters of the *mikveh* one is, for a moment, as if "out of this world." This breaks the contact with the world of impurity and failure, and marital relations may be resumed. The wife then comes to her husband "like a new bride."

Such are the subtleties of the Torah's depth psychology. The Torah thinks so highly of marital union that it makes observance of this mitzva a touchstone of allegiance to Torah life, on a par with the observance of Shabbat and Yom Kippur. It is possible for a Jewish community to exist without a synagogue. One can pray at home. But it is not possible for it to exist without a *mikveh*. In Nazi Germany, as in other dangerous periods of our history, Jewish women — Jewish heroines — braved the perils of the night in order to go to the *mikveh*. They knew that Jewish spiritual survival depended on them.

(See Bibliography for books in English on this subject.)

24. Function of the Dietary Laws

Do not defile yourselves [by eating food which is unsuitable for you]. You shall be holy, for I am holy. — LEVITICUS 11:43-44

(1) Refining the human being

To judge by the time and interest lavished on it by human beings, eating is one of mankind's most important activities.

Like most human activities eating is significant on various levels. Besides its physical function it also serves important social and psychological needs. It can also degenerate into a purely animal activity, serving nothing but selfish greediness.

Because of the prominent role it plays in human affairs the Torah lavishes much attention on it, surrounding it with mitzvot and regulations whose purpose is to refine and humanize the whole process.

It was in connection with one of the dietary laws that the Rabbis asked their famous rhetorical question:

> Does it really make any difference to God whether one slaughters an animal from the front or the back? Why then were the mitzvot given? Answer: *To refine human beings.*

This could have been said about many other mitzvot, as we have been at pains to elaborate in this book. The rhetorical question must not be taken literally however. Of course God, as a loving Father, is concerned about everything we do. The point is that we should not think we are doing God a favor by following the plan He has laid down for us. We

95

are doing *ourselves* a favor. This is the only way there is to
become truly human, to become sensitive, *giving* human
beings.

Only very superficial minds can be satisfied with the
suggestion that the reason underlying all these regulations is hygiene. The Torah clearly announces these laws
as part of its "holiness" program. It repeatedly says,
"These foods are *tamei* for you." "Do not make yourselves
tamei through them." *Tamei,* usually translated "unclean," comes from a root meaning "blocked," "obtuse." If
you absorb them into your system you may be well-fed in a
physical sense but your mind will become blunted as an
instrument of the spirit. Instead of being alert and eager to
follow all that is holy and good, your mind will become
apathetic and dull. Your spirit will be faced with a fiercer
battle and less well-equipped for the fight. You become
tamei, impure, less capable of your holy mission.

We are called upon to be *anshei kodesh,* "people of dedication," members of a great and dynamic movement
which has already had a tremendous influence on the
world and is destined to have a still greater impact in the
future. These laws are designed to keep us "in trim" for this
great task.

(2) Conditions for kashrut (fitness)

This explains why, when we turn to the animal world for
our food, the Torah's interest and concern become
especially intense. Many considerations come to the fore.
Before we can be sure that the meat we will be introducing
into our system is *kosher,* that is, precisely as the Torah
wants it to be, we have to be satisfied on all the following
questions:

1. Is the *kind* of animal, fowl or fish suitable for our
consumption?

2. Is the animal or bird in a fit *condition* to be used for our food?
3. How is the animal or bird to be *killed*?
4. What *parts* of the animal must be excluded from our diet?

There are mitzvot dealing with each of these questions and they will be discussed in the next four chapters.

ONE KOSHER MEAL

A young Rabbi took a position in a town in the U.S. with a very small Jewish community. Nearby was a university with many Jewish students. How to attract them to the community? He hit on the idea of making a "felafel evening." It was well advertised on campus, but when the time came not a single student turned up. By eleven o'clock he gave up and started putting the things away. Just then one student turned up. Overjoyed, he plied him with felafel and beer. When he'd finished he asked:

"What's all this about? What do you want from me?"

"You Jewish?" asked the Rabbi.

"Uh huh."

"Ever heard of kosher food?"

"Yeah, but I don't keep kosher."

"I understand," said the Rabbi. "But I want you to do me one favor. As soon as you can, just eat one kosher meal. That's all."

The student promised, and he was a man of his word. On the airplane going home he asked for a kosher meal but they didn't have one. In New York he asked for a cabbie to take him to a kosher restaurant. When he got there it was closed. It was a meat restaurant and he saw a notice saying

"Closed for the nine days." (See chapter 52.) While he was puzzling over this an Orthodox young man passed by.

"Can I help you?" he asked politely.

The student told him his problem.

"Come home with me," said the young man. "I'll give you a kosher meal." As a result the student became friendly with the young man and his family. It was not long before he became attracted to Torah Judaism and eventually became a fully observant Jew. See the power of one kosher meal!

25. The Kinds of Living Things Fit for Our Food

RUMINANTS / NO BIRDS OF PREY / FISH WITH SCALES

These are the animals which you may eat...whichever is...cloven-hoofed and chews the cud...
                                            — LEVITICUS 11:3

These are the birds you may not eat; the eagle, the vulture...
                                            — LEVITICUS 11:12

Of all that is in the water you may eat only that which has fins and scales.
                                            — LEVITICUS 11:9

You shall not make yourselves disgusting with all that swarms on the earth; do not defile yourselves with them... You shall be holy, for I am holy.
                                            — LEVITICUS 11:43-44

(1) Which living things?

For all practical purposes the Torah first of all restricts our intake from the world of living things to animals, birds and fish. In each case the Torah specifies the class or classes which are suitable or unsuitable for our diet.

(2) Animals

In the case of animals the Torah restricts us to one single family, the family of the ruminants. This includes all those domestic and wild animals which are cloven-hoofed and chew the cud; i.e., cattle, sheep, goats and also antelopes, gazelles, deer, buffaloes, etc. in all their various species and sub-species.

As the Rabbis point out, these characteristics stamp them as species which are preyed upon but do not prey on others. They are completely herbivorous. A further characteristic mentioned in the Talmud is that they have no incisor teeth in the upper jaw. Instead, they have a pad, which enables them to break off the grass or foliage more easily. In the wild they are vulnerable to predators when feeding. Their complicated digestive apparatus, which includes four stomachs, regurgitation and re-mastication (chewing the cud) is therefore designed for maximum food intake in the shortest possible time. They can then retire to the relative safety of the forest where they can masticate and digest their food at leisure. The cloven hoof is designed to give them extra spring for a quick getaway if threatened. Their whole structure emphasizes their non-aggressive nature.

If the Torah's purpose is to lead us away from an aggressive lifestyle to one more suited to our spiritual development, we think it is pretty clear why the Torah selected just this particular family for our sole meat intake.

(3) Birds

In this case the Torah permits all bird species for our food except twenty-four named species, all of which are birds of prey. In fact the main criterion of a forbidden species is that the bird is or acts like a bird of prey. Here again we think the intention is clear.

(4) Fish

The Torah forbids all sea-creatures except fish equipped with fins and scales. This ensures that our intake is limited to vertebrates with a body structure basically similar to our own.

(5) Examination

The exclusion from our diet of all insects requires careful examination of most fruits and vegetables to ensure that they are not infested by insects or their larvae.

26. The Condition of the Animal

TREYFA/FLESH FROM LIVING ANIMAL

You shall be men of dedication to Me; you shall not eat flesh torn in the field. You should rather throw it to the [sheep] dog.
— EXODUS 22:30

You shall not eat flesh which is still alive. — GENESIS 9:4

(1) Disease

If the animal is in a diseased condition, so that eating its meat could be harmful to our health, it is of course not to be eaten, under the heading of self-preservation; see chapter 20.

(2) Treyfa

Apart from this, the Torah wishes us to exclude from our diet the meat of any animal which is *treyfa*. In the Torah verse at the head of the chapter this means an animal torn by a wild beast. The Oral Law tells us this is only an example. The prohibition refers to any animal suffering from a lesion in a vital organ which will cause its death within a year. It makes no difference whether the lesion is caused by the claws of a wild animal or by bacterial invasion or otherwise.

"People of a holy calling" must take their food from the animal world by a freely willed human act. (See next chapter). A fatal wound takes the body of the animal away from its original purpose and designates it to serve as nourishment for the earth or for other animals. We free human beings are not to share our table with the blind forces of nature.

101

(3) Limb from living animal (Ever min ha-ḥai)

Any limb severed from an animal while it is still alive is prohibited for food. This restriction applies to all human beings, non-Jews as well as Jews. It is the only dietary law addressed to the non-Jewish world.

This mitzva stands for the basic guideline of all morality — don't grab, don't take things before their time. A person who is so insensitive, so impatient for instant gratification that he will take his food from the animal before it dies, forfeits his human dignity.

A further example of this principle in a less extreme form, addressed to the Jewish people only, is the mitzva of *orla* — to wait three years from the time of planting before enjoying the fruit of a tree (see chapter 15).

27. Shehita

THE TORAH'S PAINLESS METHOD OF SLAUGHTER

You shall slaughter it as I have commanded you.
— DEUTERONOMY 12:21

You shall not eat any animal that died of itself, for you are a holy people to God your God...   — DEUTERONOMY 14:21

(1) The act of shehita

No explicit regulations concerning the act of *shehita* are to be found in the written Torah. When the Torah says "... as I commanded you" (see quotation at head of this chapter), the reference is to the Oral Law, which was given forty years earlier than the Written Law.

The Oral Law contains very precise regulations regarding *shehita*. Their purpose is to ensure a quick and clean cut by an extremely sharp knife applied at the neck. This severs the windpipe and foodpipe and also the jugular vein. The sharp cut causes no pain and the flow of blood from the brain causes loss of consciousness in a matter of seconds.

There is also a symbolic element. The Torah insists that *shehita* shall be a freely willed and intended act of a member of the covenant of Israel, not the act of some blind mechanical force nor of someone whom the end result does not concern. When we take our food from the animal realm it is important that we emphasize our free human status.

(2) Success story

In chapter 24 we cited the very basic dictum of our Rabbis; "The mitzvot were given to refine human beings." It is certainly significant that they made this statement precisely in connection with the laws of *shehita*. It is just when we are engaged in taking the life of another living creature like ourselves that the refining influence of the mitzvot is most needed. When we see the type of people engaged in abattoir work in other cultures and compare them with the personality of the *shohet*, we can get some idea of what the Torah is aiming at, and can also gauge the measure of its success. First of all a *shohet* has to be a learned person. He has to be familiar with the intricacies of the laws of *shehita* and also those of *treyfa* and other related subjects. Then he has to be extremely proficient at his task. He has to develop a degree of sensitivity which makes it possible for him to detect the slightest flaw in a super-sharp knife-edge. The slightest defect would disqualify the *shehita*, since it would catch the animal's neck instead of making the clean and painless cut required. The whole community depends on his conscientiousness and skill for the *kashrut* (fitness) of the meat they eat. He is considered to be engaged in a holy calling and in many communities his status is second only to that of the Rabbi.

When we make the comparison with the average abattoir worker referred to above, we think we can consider this one of the Torah's "success stories."

THE SHOHET AND THE WIDOW

A very conscientious *shohet* once had a dream. In his dream he was dead and being judged by the Heavenly Tribunal. In his favor were cited his long years of service to the community and many other good deeds. But there was one thing against him. Once on the eve of a Festival, after he had finished his work and locked up, he was approached by a poor widow with a chicken to be slaughtered. "I'm sorry, madam," he said, "I have finished for Yom Tov. I can't start over again for you." The woman begged him to change his mind but to no avail. She went home disappointed. The Torah views any slight to a widow or orphan with the utmost gravity and the *shoḥet's* act was considered unforgivable. In his dream he was condemned to suffer for a period in Gehinnom for his sin. Then he woke up.

He searched his memory but failed to recall any such episode in his life. In the course of time he forgot the dream completely.

Years passed and the *shoḥet* was on the verge of retirement. On his last day of work, which was the eve of a Festival, he had just put everything away and had locked up for the last time, when a poor widow urgently asked him to slaughter her chicken. He refused and went home to prepare for Yom Tov. Something troubled him at the back of his mind but he did not know what it was.

While making *kiddush* that night at the festive table the memory of the long-forgotten dream returned to him. He dropped the kiddush cup and fell back in a dead faint. He quickly revived and gathered up his platter with its tastily cooked chickens, ran off with it to the widow's home and persuaded her to accept it in lieu of the chicken he had failed to slaughter. He died the next day, but we may hope that the Heavenly Tribunal judged him more leniently this time.

28. Parts Excluded from Our Diet

BLOOD / CERTAIN FATS / SCIATIC NERVE

You may not eat any blood...of bird or animal...For the personality is in the blood, and I have given it...on the altar to atone for your souls... That is why I say none of you shall eat blood. — LEVITICUS 7:26; 17:11-12

If anyone...hunts a wild animal or a bird which may be eaten and sheds its blood, he shall cover it with earth. Because...no blood may be eaten. — LEVITICUS 17:13

You shall not eat the separated fat (ḥelev)...of the [type of] animal which is brought as an offering to God.
— LEVITICUS 7:23,25

Even when we have the right species, the animal or bird is in the right condition, and has been properly slaughtered, there are still parts that are excluded from our diet. These are:

(1) Blood, in the case of animals and birds.
(2) Certain fats, in the case of domestic animals.
(3) The sciatic nerve, in the case of all animals.

(1) Blood

The blood of animals and birds must be rigorously excluded from our diet. The significance of this resides in the fact that blood is an extremely important element in all animal life. Besides bringing life-giving oxygen to all parts of the body it also contains the hormones which govern all the functions of the organism. It is understandable that the Torah considers this unsuitable for the diet of people whose task in life is to rise above the animal and achieve true human status.

Symbolically, too, animal blood represents the biological urges and vital forces — the *nefesh* — of the animal. This is why it was chosen to represent the *nefesh* (vital force) of human beings in the service of the Holy Temple. The dashing of the animal's blood on the altar symbolized in dramatic fashion the dedication of all our vital forces to the service of God in the world. This is another reason given by the Torah for the exclusion of animal blood from our diet. (See verse cited at beginning of this chapter.)

(2) "Covering the blood"

As an additional warning to our subconscious mind the Torah requires the blood of wild animals such as deer, etc. and birds (when slaughtered for food) to be covered with earth. This is the mitzva of "covering the blood" (*kissui hadam*). Deer, antelopes, etc., belong to the wild by virtue of their habitat, and birds by their essential nature. The lure of the wild is ever present in the subconscious of modern man. An additional reminder is required here that the soul of man must strive upwards while by contrast the lifeblood of animals must go to nourish the earth from which they came (Genesis 1:24).

(3) Helev (some parts of the fat)

The layers of fat encased in a special membrane and covering some of the internal organs of animals are called *helev* in Hebrew and must be removed from the animal before it is permitted for our food.

This fat represents the animals "capital reserve" and in a sense this is the organism's greatest achievement. This is why *helev* in Hebrew is a metaphor for the finest and best, as in "they shall eat the fat of the land" (Genesis 45:18). In the Temple service the *helev* of the animal was burnt on the altar as a sign that we offer God the finest of our achievements and our most heartfelt dreams.

This explains why the *helev* of animals of the type from which offerings are brought — i.e., cattle, sheep and goats — is prohibited as food.

The messages conveyed by these last two prohibitions — of blood and *helev* — are considered by the Torah extremely basic. To take these two items into our diet would be to take for ourselves what must be reserved for God. Such a deliberate and defiant infringement of the Torah therefore results in *karet* — being cut off spiritually from the congregation of Israel.

(4) Gid Ha-Nasheh (the sciatic nerve)

This is an unusual law. It is based on a strange episode in the life of our Father Jacob (Genesis 32:33). Having worked in faraway Padan Aram to establish his family, Jacob has returned to the borders of Eretz Yisrael and is bracing himself for the fateful meeting next day with his powerful brother Esau, who had once sworn to kill him. Left alone that night he is forced to wrestle with a mysterious "man," who turns out to be some kind of angelic being. Seeing that he cannot win, the being "touches" Jacob's hip joint just where the sciatic nerve traverses it, and dislocates it. Jacob still holds fast however and will not release him without being given a blessing. The blessing he gets is that his name will no longer be *Yaakov*, "the one who follows after," but *Yisrael*, "the one who is victorious with God." Therefore, the Torah says (as interpreted by the Oral Law), "the descendants of Israel are not allowed to eat the sciatic nerve," and this is one of the 365 negative commandments given at Sinai.

We cannot here delve into all the ramifications of this fascinating episode. It must be understood though that a fight with an angel can take place only on a spiritual plane. When the angel "touched on" the question of the sciatic nerve he was alluding to a common human failing — a failing that is integral to the human situation.

What is the function of the sciatic nerve? It conveys the impulses of sensation and motion between the spinal cord and the thigh, leg and foot. In the animal organism these impulses come from the lower brain and serve the instinctive urges for food and sex. In the human being these messages may be overridden by decisions of the higher centers of the brain, which has the power to set different goals. But only a firm decision of the spirit of man, backed up by willpower, can ensure that the message is effective. Otherwise the brain's higher directive will be ignored and the instincts will take over as usual. This is what we mean when we say "I wanted to go to A, but my feet took me somewhere else." This is the point of the human being's greatest strength — and also of his greatest weakness.

Jacob's adversary was pointing to this weak point of the Jewish people; they have high ideals but so often fail to carry them into practice. He was touching on the point of failure, where theory and practice are dislocated.

But the Jewish people are not to accept failure. If the sciatic nerve hints at failure, the Torah tells us to cut it out of our diet. By this we are to express our confidence that, with the help of God, we shall eventually deserve the (spiritual) victory-name of YISRAEL.

◆ *Halacha*
◇ *Before meat or fowl is cooked it must have the residual blood removed by salting. The meat should first be soaked in water for at least half an hour, then placed in a*

perforated vessel and salted generously with cooking salt on all sides to draw out the blood. It should remain in the salt for an hour (in urgent cases, eighteen minutes). The salt is then washed off and the meat is ready for cooking. This process is called "kashering."

◊ *Nowadays in many places it is possible to buy meat already "kashered" by the butcher.*

◊ *If an egg has a bloodspot in it - a sign of a developing chick - it may not be used.*

Table 2
FOOD FROM THE ANIMAL KINGDOM

	Domestic animals	Wild animals	Birds	Fish
Only certain species permitted	√	√	√	√
Not *treyfa* or *neveyla*	√	√	√	-
Requires *shehita*	√	√	√	-
Excluded parts: Blood	√	√	√	-
Certain fats (*helev*)	√	-	-	-
Sciatic nerve (*gid ha-nasheh*)	√	√	-	-
Mitzva of covering blood	-	√	√	-

√ = applicable

◊ *The removal from the carcass of internal blood vessels,* helev *and* gid ha-nasheh *(this removal is called "porging") is a matter of considerable expertise. If the hindquarters (to which most of the "porging" applies) are to be used, this is invariably done by the butcher or* shohet. *In many communities however it is the custom to exclude the hindquarters from the Jewish market.*

BLOODSPOT AND BLOOD LIBEL

In 14th-century Posen, near the boundary between Poland and the Duchy of Brandenburg, the population suffered greatly because of the wars that ravaged the countryside. The Jewish community, always vulnerabe, suffered worst of all. The army decided to billet soldiers on the householders of Posen, the Jewish community included.

The soldier billeted on the Jewish family Jochlein was a young officer who had been wounded in the fighting, named Gerhardt von Ebeling. As he grew stronger he had long conversations with the members of the family and discovered many interesting and surprising facts about those mysterious Jews, concerning whom so many horrible legends flourished among the Christian population.

One day the officer was sitting in the kitchen as Frau Jochlein was preparing supper. He saw her break an egg into a bowl and inspect it carefully.

"I'm afraid I'll have to throw this one away," she said.

"Why?" he asked. "It looks perfectly fresh to me."

"It's got a bloodspot," she said, and showed him a speck of blood on the yolk.

"So?" he queried. "For that you throw it away?"

"Our Torah forbids us to use anything with blood in it, even the smallest speck."

"How many eggs do you get a week for the family? Three or four?" he said. "And you're prepared to throw one away just because of a speck of blood? Remarkable! Is this just you, or...?"

"Every Jewish family would do the same," she assured him.

"And what if all four eggs had bloodspots?"

"Then we would throw them all away. We'd rather go without a meal than eat a speck of blood," she said.

"Amazing! Quite amazing!"

Twenty years passed. The Jewish community of Posen was in dire trouble. They were faced with a blood libel — that product of a diseased imagination which accused Jews of using the blood of a murdered Christian to prepare their *matzot* for Passover. The entire Jewish community was arrested and taken to jail. Their lives hung in the balance. The case was to be tried the following week by a visiting magistrate.

The whole community was taken into the great hall of the castle to face the magistrate who was flanked by police and officials. The magistrate allowed his eyes to roam over the unfortunate assembly. Then he looked at the list of prisoners in front of him.

"Is Family Jochlein here? Let them step forward!"

Herr and Frau Jochlein stood before him.

Addressing the city officials he said:

"You see that good lady? Many years ago I enjoyed her hospitality for months on end. I happen to know that no Jew would use anything with even a speck of blood in it, even if it meant going without a meal. The charge you bring against these people is ridiculous. Case dismissed!"

Then he turned to the amazed Jews:

"Go home, good people, and prepare your Passover as I saw Frau Jochlein do it," said Gerhardt von Ebeling. "And a happy Passover to you all!"

(5) Training for holiness

We have seen something of the seriousness with which the Torah treats the whole question of diet, especially when we are taking our food from the realm of living creatures who bear some outward resemblance to ourselves but whose status and function are so different to our own.

Only when all conditions outlined above have been fufilled is the meat that we eat *kosher*, i.e., fit for consumption by the people of the Torah. This is our "training" for holiness.

29. Dealing with Moral Pollution

HOLINESS IN THE CAMP/SEXUAL STIMULI/PURITY OF SPEECH

When you go out in a military camp against your enemy, you shall be on your guard against every evil thing...God your God goes in the midst of your camp...therefore your camp shall be holy, so that He does not see anything shameful among you and withdraw from you. — DEUTERONOMY 23:10-15

(1) Holiness in the army camp

As in the case of "Respecting the Environment" (chapter 13), the Torah makes known its requirement in this area in connection with the army of Israel. Army camps have never been known for their high standards of morality. This is precisely why the Torah emphasizes its standards of environmental purity in the military situation.

With the people of Israel everything is different. Even a military camp is a Divine abode. Using the equations of spiritual relativity, "God is in the camp" means that the minds of Jewish soldiers must remain aware of God and His purposes even in that unpromising situation. Whatever we learn about the Torah's requirement for the camp of war can be transferred *a fortiori* to the everyday situation in the environment of home and city.

We learn first that there should be in our environment no physical pollution. A place outside the camp had to be designated as a latrine. Every soldier had to carry a spade with his weapons, to be used for hygiene purposes. (Deuteronomy 23:12-13). Physical pollution, because it coarsens our sensibilities, is also moral pollution.

(2) Sexual stimuli

The military camp of Israel has in some respects the degree of holiness normally associated with the courtyard of the

114

Holy Temple. Any soldier who has become impure owing to an accidental flux of semen is excluded from it. (Deuteronomy 23:11-12). We learn from this that our environment should include no undue sexual stimuli. Stimulation of the senses by immodest clothing, for example, is a prime example of moral pollution. This type of pollution drives the holy presence from the minds and streets of Israel.

(3) Purity of speech

Even more important than protecting our physical eye from pollution is guarding our speech from pollution. Our speech is the function which mainly distinguishes man from animal. The spoken word is, or should be, something noble, spiritual, Divine. To defile human speech by obscene and unclean talk means to kill shame and modesty in man. What did the prophet of Israel, so many thousands of years ago, declare as the final degradation? "Every mouth speaks *nevala* (obscenity)" (Isaiah 9:16). The root *naval* expresses the withering and dying of an organism. In the moral sphere, the word *nevala* indicates the withering and dying of the spirit.

(4) During learning and prayer

If our everyday life should bear the stamp of man's nobler side, this is even more important during Torah learning, when we study the words of God (chapter 64), and during *tefilla* — prayer — (chapter 65), when we approach Him for assistance with our task in life. At these moments, when we "bring God into our camp," so to speak, we must make doubly sure that there are no polluting elements of any kind in our vicinity. During *tefilla* we must be properly clothed. Our body must be clean, as must be the place of prayer itself. Our head should be covered as a sign of modesty and submission to God. (See chapter 58.)

GROUP THREE:
LOVE AND CONCERN FOR OTHER PEOPLE

Mitzvot fostering acts of love and concern for other people

We have now gained some insight into the Torah's concept of justice in two contexts: just relations with the other person and just relations with the environment.

Now we move on to the enrichment mode. In human relations this means we move from justice to love, and we shall discover precisely what the Torah means by requiring from us "love and concern for other people."

30. Loving Your Neighbor

SENTIMENT OR ACTION / POSITIVE OR NEGATIVE / PARADOX OF THE MODERN WORLD

You shall love your neighbor as yourself: I am God (Leviticus 19:18). — This is a great principle in Torah life. — SIFRA AD LOC

A non-Jew once came before Hillel. "I am prepared to become a Jew," he said, "on condition that you tell me the whole Torah while I stand on one foot."

"Don't do to others what you wouldn't like to be done to you," replied Hillel. "This is the the whole Torah. The rest is commentary. Go and learn it." — TB SHABBAT 31a

(1) Can love be commanded?

Of course one cannot love on command. "Loving your neighbor," however, is not so much a matter of sentiment as of action. It means "behave with love towards your neighbor." This is a fundamental principle of Torah. We are to behave lovingly to everyone, whether we happen to like the person or not.

But matters will not rest there. Actions affect feelings. Once we have taken the trouble to help someone, we tend to look more favorably on that person. Feelings of interest and even affection are aroused. We have invested something of ourselves in that person and that alone makes us view him or her through different eyes. Sensing our feelings, the other person is likely to reciprocate them, starting a cycle of love and affection. "Love is increased in Israel," which is what the Torah wants.

THE MIDNIGHT RESCUE

It was past midnight. I was walking through the deserted city to my hotel on the other side of the river. The night was dark and foggy and I couldn't get a taxi. As I approached the bridge I noticed a shabby figure leaning over the parapet. A "down-and-out," I thought. Then he disappeared. I heard a splash. My God, I thought, he's done it. Suicide!

I ran back under the bridge, onto the embankment, and waded into the river, grabbing him as he came past, borne by the current. I dragged him up onto the embankment. He was quite a young guy. He was still breathing. A couple of people noticed and I shouted to them to get an ambulance. They managed to stop a taxi and between us we half dragged, half carried the man into the taxi. The driver was not too pleased about this, but we convinced him it was a matter of life and death. I got in and told him to drive to the nearest hospital emergency room. I waited until the man was admitted, gave my report, and got a taxi back to my hotel at last.

I had ruined a good suit and knew I would have a terrible cold in the morning. I could feel it coming on. But anyway I had saved a life. I had a hot bath and got into bed but it still worried me. Such a young man! Why had he done it?

The next morning, as soon as I was free, I bought a large bunch of grapes and set off for the hospital. I was determined to find out what was behind this matter. Maybe I could help.

Why was I so interested in the guy? In this great city there were at least half a dozen would-be suicides every night. Their plight did not touch me. Then it dawned on me. Of course. First you *give*, then you *care*. I had given quite a lot. I had risked my life and gotten a bad cold in the bargain. I had invested something of myself in that man. Now my love and care were aroused. That's how it goes. First we *give*, then we come to love.

(2) Why did Hillel present the negative?

Why did Hillel not tell the would-be proselyte that to love one's neighbor is the whole Torah? Why did he put it in the negative: "Don't do to others what you don't like yourself"?

For a beginner, "loving one's neighbor," even in the sense of "acting with love towards your neighbor," is too grandiose a project. One has difficulty in imagining what precisely it involves in practice. Therefore Hillel gave him — and us — a guideline to which we can always easily refer. What will benefit our neighbor, what will cause him pleasure or pain, joy or grief? No great research project is needed to establish this. We need only consult our own feelings. We have a handy reference book in our mind. You don't like someone to hang up on you on the telephone? Don't do it to someone else. You don't like to be spoken to brusquely, without a smile? Then you know what not to do to the other person. And so on. Innumerable examples spring to mind. Hillel has provided us with an entire guide-book to the mitzva of love. For all of us who are still beginners in true Torah living there is a great lesson here. We must train ourselves in stages and not try to run before we can walk. The negative criterion is easy to apply, and it opens our minds to the existence and rights of our neighbor — the beginning of all spiritual progress.

"THIS IS THE WHOLE TORAH"

Hillel did not tell the would-be proselyte that "love is all you need." He said, "The rest is commentary; go and study it." Concern for your neighbor's needs may be the text, but it is meaningless and unrealizable without the commentary, which is the rest of the Torah. That is, you will never reach the goal without committing yourself to the comprehensive program of practical mitzvot.

Hillel was stating in concise form the main thesis of this book — that *all* mitzvot of the Torah, both those "between man and man" and those "between man and God," are designed to refine our character and increase our sensitivity to all that is just and good.

(3) "Love your neighbor — I am God"

The great commentator Rashi (1040-1104 C.E.) rather daringly interprets the "neighbor" in this verse as referring to God Himself, Who after all is our Neighbor par excellence. The point is that the simple meaning, where "neighbor" means human neighbor, contains within itself the deeper meaning, in which the Neighbor refers to God. First we have to turn away from preoccupation with ourselves; we have to open our hearts to the needs and concerns of our human neighbor. Only then can we have any true concern for the requirements and purposes of our Divine Neighbor. Only when I am prepared to be weaned from self-centeredness can I enter into any meaningful relationship with God and be ready to co-operate in His plan for humanity.

(4) Amazing paradox

But the words "I am God" at the end of the verse also have a reverse connotation. It is only the recognition of God — the spiritual substratum of our lives — that provides the logical basis for caring for our fellow man.

The 20th century presents an amazing paradox. On the one hand there never was a time when there was so much concern for the sick, the young, the handicapped, the underprivileged, the environment. And the driving force in most of these improvements has come from secular quarters. On the other hand the number of human beings killed, maimed, tortured and made miserable in secular wars, persecutions and revolutions in our time is horrendous. It is only too clear that in our secular civilization human life is cheap. Medical advances have greatly increased the life expectancy of every man and woman in many countries, but the existence of nuclear weapons has drastically reduced the life expectancy of the whole human race in an unprecedented manner. The explanation of these anomalies is that when the "I am God" is missing and there is no awareness of the unique value of a human being as a spiritual being, the care and concern for people's welfare is only a matter of sentiment with no logical basis. It can therefore be easily overruled by power-mad demagogues.

31. Parents

HONOR AND RESPECT FOR THOSE TO WHOM WE
OWE OUR EXISTENCE

*Honor your father and your mother, so that your days on the
land...may be prolonged.* — EXODUS 20:12

*Each of you shall respect his mother and his father, and keep
My Sabbaths; I am God.* — LEVITICUS 19:3

(1) Three partners

Three partners co-operate in bringing every person into
existence — God, and the person's father and mother.

The person who realizes that life itself is the pearl
beyond all price will be filled with unbounded gratitude to
these three who have bestowed upon him this incom-
parable gift.

This is the basis for the mitzva of honoring one's
parents. This is why "God has equated their honor to His
own."

But this is only the beginning. They have also nurtured
you, cared for you, looked after your every need; they have
probably done far more than nature and custom require.
And much more, they have educated you in your moral
duties as a human being and a Jew and enabled you to
become a living link in the great traditions of our people.
For all this the Torah requires you to honor, respect and
obey them.

(2) Respect and honor defined

But this honor and esteem should not remain mere
sentiment; wherever we can we should give practical proof
of them, in word and deed. The Oral Law defines "respect"

in a practical way: Not to contradict them, to keep them from vexation and trouble and to give them as much joy as we can. We should not stand in the place which is reserved for them in a public gathering; nor sit in the place reserved for them at home. We should never call them by their personal name either in life or after death.

"Honor" is defined in practice in positive terms : To feed, clothe, tend and look after our parents; to wait on them as a willing attendant. We should always let them feel that we consider it a privilege to serve them. The Talmud condemns to hell the son who fed his parents on expensive food but made them feel their dependence.

We should rise before our father and mother when they enter the room and always speak respectfully of them and to them. We may never disturb the sleep of our parents, unless we know they would be displeased if we did not wake them.

THE HOW AND WHY OF A MITZVA

"One son fed his parents on fatted pheasants and went to hell. Another made his father work in a treadmill and went to heaven."

One son provided expensive meals for his parents. The menu often contained delicacies such as fattened pheasants.

One day the father said to the son: "Doesn't all this cost you a lot of money?"

The son replied: "Shovel it down, old man, and don't ask questions."

He went to hell.

Another son saw press gangs coming to conscript able-bodied men into the army. They exempted anyone who was engaged in productive work.

The son earned his living by working a treadmill.

He worked it himself and kept his father in comfort. When he saw the press gangs approaching he set his father to work the treadmill and allowed himself to be conscripted into the army.

He went to Heaven.

It only goes to show that it is *how* and *why* you do things that counts in the eyes of God.

THE RIGHTEOUS GENTILE

At the time the Temple was standing in Jerusalem a gentile lived in Ashkelon from whom we can learn how far honoring one's parents can go. His name was Dama ben Natina, and he was a dealer in precious stones.

The Sages needed rare gems for the *ephod* of the High Priest and were prepared to pay a very large sum for them. Dama owned the precise stones which they required, and at the price they were prepared to pay he would have made a profit of 600,000 dinars on the deal.

He was unable to supply their needs, however. The keys to the treasure chest were under the pillow of his sleeping father. He would not disturb his father and told the Sages he regretted he could not fulfill their order. They went elsewhere and Dama lost his profit of 600,000 dinars.

The following year a red heifer was born in his herd. This was a great rarity and was required for a certain mitzva connected with the Temple service. Again the Sages visited Dama, prepared to pay virtually any price for this unusual animal.

"I know I can ask whatever I like," said Dama, "but I shall ask you no more than 600,000 dinars, the amount I lost last year because I refused to wake my father."

The Talmud comments: If God so rewards a gentile who keeps the mitzva without being commanded, how much more will He reward a Jew who keeps the mitzva and *is* commanded!" (It is a principle of our Sages that a person who submits to the will of God and observes a mitzva because he is commanded to is greater than one who observes it of his own free will. The former has more inner resistance to overcome.)

(3) **If parents do wrong**

Even if your parents had never earned any title to your love and gratitude, and had never troubled themselves about you, nevertheless you would have to be respectful and obedient to them. Remember they gave you the gift of life, and remember that God requires this of you.

If you see your parents doing wrong, merely remark humbly, "The Torah says so-and-so," but not: "Parents, you acted wrongly."

If you are unfortunate enough to have parents who, through faulty upbringing or otherwise, transgress the laws of the Torah, you still owe them the Torah duty of honor and respect — and obedience. But what if they require you to transgress the Torah? What to do when duties conflict? God Himself has given the answer: "Respect your mother and father, but keep My Sabbaths." You owe great respect to your parents, but greater still to God.

If you are unfortunate enough to have to be disobedient to your parents in this way, then be all the more obedient to them in everything else, be all the more ready to meet their slightest wish in other things, so that they realize you are disobedient only because you have to obey God.

If you have learnt what it means to be a member of the

covenant of Israel and the spirit of Israel burns high within you, and God has subjected you to the hard trial of having parents who do not recognize that duty or that spirit, be strong and steadfast in this trial. Pray to God for strength and wisdom to fulfill all your duties, and stand firm.

32. Respect for Age and Wisdom

RISING BEFORE THE WISE AND THE ELDERLY

Rise up before gray hairs and honor the face of the elder, and stand in awe of your God; I am God. — LEVITICUS 19:32

A civilization of the mind

A civilization is known by its attitudes to youth and old age. One which values above all the body and the pleasures of the body will venerate youth and despise — and fear — old age. One which values the mind and the spirit will venerate the accumulated wisdom of years.

The Torah is a civilization of the mind. It does not deny or despise the body, but above all it values the mind and the spirit. The Torah Sage personifies the wisdom of the Torah. "How foolish," says the Talmud, "to stand up before the Sefer Torah when it is paraded in the synagogue, and not to stand up before the Sage!" The Sage is the living embodiment of that Torah.

We have to rise before everyone distinguished in Torah learning even if he is not old, and before every old man, even if he is not learned, because of the wisdom he has gained in the school of life. But even an old man and a wise man should rise before one who gives a shining example of good deeds and uprightness.

The act of standing up before someone we respect indicates symbolically our readiness to be of service to him.

When we see an outstanding Torah Sage of exceptional renown, the Rabbis have prescribed the following blessing: "Blessed are You, God, etc. Who has shared His wisdom with those who hold Him in awe."

When we see a truly outstanding non-Jewish scholar of world renown, the blessing we say is: "Blessed are You, God, etc. Who has given of His wisdom to flesh and blood."

(For "Blessings" see chapter 65(2).)

33. Jewish Marriage

And God blessed them... "Be fruitful and multiply and fill the earth"...
— GENESIS 1:28

When a man takes a wife and marries her... — DEUTERONOMY 24:1

Therefore a man leaves his father and mother and stays close to his wife, and they shall be one flesh.
— GENESIS 2:24

No man is complete without a wife.
— TB YEVAMOT 63a

A man without a wife is without blessing, without protection, without Torah.
— TB YEVAMOT 62b

A man should love his wife as himself and honor her more than himself.
— TB IBID.

Children's children are the crown of the old, and the glory of children are their parents.
— PROVERBS 17:6

(1) Marriage is giving

In some cultures marriage is a strategy for *taking* — for "getting the most out of life." In Torah it is an institution for *giving* — for putting the most *into* life. A Torah home is one in which Torah learning, good sense and hospitality are freely dispensed. Its warmth spreads outwards and many a young Jew and Jewess have found their first taste of Judaism within its walls.

(2) The aim

The living discipline of Torah marriage is an ideal environment in which to rear healthy children, mentally and morally stable, conscious of their mission and destiny as budding members of the community of Israel. Here obedience is not demanded at the whim of the parents but as part of Torah obedience, which applies to the parents equally with the children. In a home where children see

130

their parents willingly give up their own pleasures to fulfill the will of God, there will be no generation gap. The main purpose of Torah marriage is to produce such children, who will willingly carry on the great traditions of Torah to another generation.

(3) Functions of sexuality

As we saw in the chapter on sexuality in the previous section (chapter 22), human sexuality achieves its purpose in the innermost sanctum of the Torah home. Besides its obvious biological function in procreation, sexuality continually nourishes the love and affection between husband and wife, and thus provides a surety for a stable marriage. This stability is the rock on which the Torah home stands, with all its beneficent results on the children and the environment. When we think of the enormous effort, both physical and mental, which the successful rearing of Torah children demands from parents, and the incalculable benefits to Israel and the world that can flow from such a family, we understand why *this* use of sexuality is considered by the Torah to be holy. It is holy because it gives more than it takes.

We noted that God in His wisdom allowed sexual desire and attraction to last long beyond child-bearing age, as a factor in keeping the family center stable during the adolescence and early adulthood of the children. A stable family center has much to contribute to the healthy growth of these young Torah families growing up in the environment of the nuclear family.

(4) A true partner

The selection of a partner for Torah marriage must take into account, above all else, suitability for the achievement of Torah aims. If one is willing to be guided by the Torah in the direction of true, lasting happiness and true fulfillment, one must reject the barren, thoughtless maxims of the world. Physical beauty, wealth, intellectual brilliance, are *not* the foundations for a happy and lasting marriage, as a little investigation will show. If we truly want success in our married life, we must look for richness of heart, beauty of character, good sense and a loving and affectionate nature as the qualities of our life's companion.

A good family — *yihus* — is important only if it shows itself in the nurturing and production of *these* qualities. On the other hand, if you see a family in which disputes and quarreling, insolence and evil talk are common, in which hard-heartedness, hate and uncharitableness hold sway — steer clear. According to the view of our Sages, even the Jewish descent of such a family is doubtful.

(5) Intermarriage

It goes without saying that marriage to a non-Jew would be a betrayal of all that Jewish marriage stands for.

The prohibition ceases only when the non-Jew has been accepted into the faith-community of Israel by a *bet din* fully convinced of his or her sincere determination to adhere to the Torah in its entirety.

♦ *Halacha*

◊ *There are two steps in the process of getting married: One, a man and a women join together for the tasks of life; the other, they begin to accomplish that purpose by founding the marital home. Corresponding to these two aspects are the two steps by which a marriage is concluded,* kiddushin, *consecration, and* nissuin, *"taking up" the wife into the joint home. The first is signified by the gift of the ring; the second is symbolized by the* huppa — *the bridal canopy, and* yihud — *bridegroom and bride having a meal together in a room on their own. Written documentation of the duties the husband has undertaken with regard to his wife is also necessary; this is the* ketuba.

◇ *Since every marriage is not merely a private matter but something which affects the whole community, the marriage should take place in the presence of a* minyan *(a quorum of ten) and is not valid unless it has been witnessed by two independent members of the community, who have been designated for this purpose.*

◇ *Blessings are recited under the* ḥuppa *declaring in moving terms the spiritual grandeur of the moment and invoking God's blessing for the attainment of the joys and high aims of Torah marriage.*

34. Parenthood and Education

The law which Moses commanded us is an inheritance of the community of Jacob.
— DEUTERONOMY 33:4

Make them known to your children and your children's children.
— DEUTERONOMY 4:9

You shall teach them to your children, talking of them when you sit at home and when you walk in the way and when you go to bed and when you get up.
— DEUTERONOMY 11:19-21

Train the child according to his way; even when he grows old he will not depart from it.
— PROVERBS 22:6

(1) Education for blessing

Our highest vocation — the one which every page, every law of the Torah proclaims — is: Be a blessing! These were the words addressed to our Father Abraham at the start of his great journey and they are still addressed to us today.

One who is aware of this vocation will welcome every opportunity to *give*, to be a blesssing to others. When we become parents this opportunity presents itself in its highest and holiest form.

Here is a little creature which has just awakened into being. It has nothing. It can do nothing. But it is "ours." It is only through our love that it will survive, that it will become whatever it is destined to be in life. What a responsibility! But what an opportunity!

We must realize all the holiness, the blissfulness, the loftiness of this opportunity. We must feel how the name "parent" — "Jewish parent" — consecrates us as priest and priestess in holiness and joy. If only we prove fully worthy of this name! The child is not there for us; we are there for the child. (This is the lesson that the obligation to redeem the first-born should impress on our mind — see chapter 61.) We will think of nothing but what we can do for this child. If the chance of doing this supreme service to a human being is not the height of our happiness, if giving is not incomparably more blessed to us than receiving, then we should never have been parents at all!

(2) Purpose of parenthood

So in this frame of mind we come before God and ask to what end has He placed so sacred an object as a human soul in our hands. His voice comes back to us from Sinai: the Torah which Moses commanded us — this is the inheritance which we as parents are to transmit to our child in the community of Jacob. This is the purpose of our parenthood.

Every man and woman of Israel exists for this purpose — to realize the Torah in our lives and in the world. For this one purpose we are to bring up our child; this is the purpose for which it was given to us. By entrusting us with this child God has declared His confidence that we are qualified to carry out this task. He has given us and will continue to give us the qualities and strength we need to make a success of it. Out of all people, out of all generations, *we* are the ones whom this particular baby needs. This child, this human being, this Jewish soul, could have no better parents.

We commit treason, treason against all that is most holy, if we neglect this task. In our daily life there are not only certain hours, certain places, certain words that are holy. If we understand what being Jewish means we will know that every one of our thoughts, feelings, enjoyments, words and deeds bears the stamp of God if it contributes in some way to the blessing we are to be in the world. The training of our child for a life thus permeated with holiness must also be one of the foremost tasks in our life.

35. Saving One's Neighbor from Danger and Loss

RESCUE / RETURNING LOST PROPERTY / GIVING EVIDENCE

Do not stand idly by the blood of your neighbor; I am God.
— LEVITICUS 19:16

You shall not see your brother's ox or his sheep wandering on the road and ignore them; you shall bring them back to your brother...
— DEUTERONOMY 22:1

If you meet your enemy's donkey lying down under its burden, though you wish to avoid helping him — you certainly shall help him.
— EXODUS 23:5

(1) Your brother's keeper

Your mission — to be a blessing — is not confined to your own home or to the members of your household. Far from it. Every Jew is your brother. Do not stand idly by when your brother's life is at stake. The whole world descends from one Adam, say the Sages, to teach us that if one preserves one soul alive it is as if he has preserved a whole world.

One may offer part of one's body (e.g., kidney or bone-marrow) for transplantation into a seriously ill patient, and this is considered a most meritorious act, provided that according to expert medical opinion the procedure carries only a small risk for the donor, and he (or she) will not suffer permanent harm. However, competent halachic authority must first be consulted.

If you see someone drowning or attacked by thugs, or otherwise in trouble, and you have the power to help him or to summon help — the Torah places the responsibility squarely on your shoulders. If you hear others planning to

136

do him an injury, you must warn him. If you are able to divert an assailant from his murderous purpose by money or otherwise, you must do so. Do not say, "It's none of my business," or "better not get involved." In Torah society my neighbor's trouble *is* my business.

(2) Lost property

In the opening section of this book we learnt that it is a requirement of justice to ensure that no damage is caused to someone else's property by our action or our negligence. (See chapter 8.) In this present section we learn that we are commanded to go out of our way to protect his property and save it from any damage that threatens it, whatever the source of that danger. In fact, God requires us to treat our neighbor's property just as if it were our own. We are members of one covenant, co-workers in the great project that God has laid before us, and brotherly love requires us to be as concerned about our brother's welfare as we are with our own.

If one finds property lying in a public place in such a way that it has obviously been lost or forgotten by its owner, we have to take it and restore it to its rightful owner. If we do not know who the owner is, we must advertise the kind of article that has been found and the date, and restore it to the claimant who can identify the object by giving its distinguishing marks. If no one claims it, we must keep it indefinitely. If it is perishable, we must take it to the *bet din*, who will arrange for it to be sold and the proceeds put on deposit until the owner is found.

If however there are no distinguishing marks at all, it is assumed that the owner will have despaired of ever getting it back. Consequently his ownership rights in the object cease and you may keep it.

AN UNUSUAL LAW

This law of the Torah, as elucidated by the Sages of the Talmud, seems strange. It differs from common practice on two counts. First: Even if there are distinguishing marks, common practice allows the finder to claim it as his own if the owner has not come forward within a reasonable time, while in such a case the halacha requires us to treat it as the owner's property indefinitely. Second: even if there are no distinguishing marks, secular law does not permit the finder to keep it until a reasonable time has elapsed, while the Torah permits us to appropriate it straight away. This calls for explanation.

The reason for the differences is that secular law is concerned only with arranging human affairs to the mutual convenience of the people concerned, while the Torah uses its laws to teach us basic truths. The basic truth about property is that it does not "belong" to us in any real sense; it is merely made available to us to use in furthering the aims of God in the world. (For this reason the Holy Language contains no verb "to have," as we have explained in chapter 13(3).) My link with any object which I am said to "own" persists only as long as two conditions are fulfilled: (a) it is in my possession, and (b) it is in my mind, i.e., I have not given it up as lost. As soon as both these links are broken: (a) it is no longer in my possession because I left it unattended in some public place, and (b) it is no longer in my mind since I have despaired of ever finding it; it is in the eyes of the Torah ownerless and may be taken by anyone. On the other hand if there *are* distinguishing marks, the link with the owner persists and we are obliged to keep it available for him irrespective of the time that has elapsed. This is an example of how the Torah gets its message across by means of its laws.

Such is the law. But if I happen to know the owner who has despaired of his lost property and therefore no longer owns it, and I also know that the loss affects him very much, it is a mitzva of love to return it to him all the same. The Torah has made its point about the nature of ownership, and the mitzva of love has made its point about helping somebody in trouble.

(3) Obligation to give evidence

At the beginning of the book (chapter 1(3)) we learnt of the grievous sin of giving false evidence in a court of law. Here we discover the duty of giving true evidence whenever this can help our brother. It may not always be easy. One may prefer "not to get involved." But the duty of love, the need to be a blessing, the necessity of helping your brother in his hour of need, take precedence. This mitzva applies in cases where my brother's money is at stake and my evidence can help him win his case. All the more so where a criminal charge is involved. But as explained above, I can testify only on the basis of my personal observation. I may not state as a fact what I know only from hearsay, even though I may have heard it from the most trustworthy of men.

(4) Readiness to help

Be ready to help your brother whenever he is in trouble. Do not wait to be asked. If his car has broken down and he is stranded, it is your business as much as his. This is the mitzva of love.

(5) Basic guidelines

It is not an empty command of "love" which the Torah places on us, but an active readiness to come to our brother's aid whenever his life, property or happiness are endangered. By following this guideline we will be following the Torah's basic guideline: be a blessing to all.

Does he deserve it? Would he do the same for me? Such

questions do not arise among brothers. Will he remember my good deed? Will he be grateful for it? Such questions are unworthy. Even if he is your enemy, even if he is one who has made you miserable, the Torah commands your practical aid. This is the teaching of love.

EXTRAORDINARY!

I was driving along a somewhat deserted country road when I saw old Harry working on his car. He obviously had a flat tire. He had a jack in his hands and was trying to insert it into the side of the car, without success. He never was any good with mechanical things; they always got the better of him.

Now I never did like old Harry. Couldn't stand him in fact. Always avoided him like the plague. Hadn't spoken to him for years. He had been very nasty to me sometime ago. I decided to drive past pretending I hadn't noticed. After all, he had gotten himself into this mess. It was nothing to do with me.

Then I remembered. We had just learnt it last week. "You shall not see your enemy's ass crouching under its burden and pretend you haven't seen it." This was it. I couldn't just drive past. "I don't have to speak to him," I told myself. "I'll just change his tire and drive off."

I parked my car a little way up the road and walked back. Without saying anything I took the jack from his hands and started adjusting it to fit into the leverage point. I couldn't keep it up however. Changing a tire goes better as a cooperative enterprise. I soon had to speak to him to get things moving. Eventually we did the job together, more or less. Anyway, I worked and he helped.

When it was finished, he was extremely grateful.

He got out a cold drink and two plastic cups from his picnic case and we drank together. His gratitude seemed to me very sincere. "Perhaps he's not such a bad guy after all," I thought to myself.

"I don't know how to thank you," he said again.

"That's quite all right, Harry," I said. "Any time."

I walked back to my car. Before I got in I turned around. "All the best," I called out. "Be well!"

"Extraordinary thing, this Torah," I thought to myself. "It tells you to help your enemy, and then it turns out you haven't got an enemy. Extraordinary!"

36. Support of One's Neighbor in His Undertakings

LOANS/PROHIBITION OF INTEREST

If you lend money to any of My people, to the poor who are with you, you shall not behave towards him like a creditor; nor may you take interest from him. — EXODUS 22:24

If your brother has become poor and his means fail...you shall uphold him...a foreign resident too — and enable him to make a livelihood with you. You shall not give him your money on interest. Be in awe of your God, so that your brother may make his livelihood with you. — LEVITICUS 25:35-37

If there is a needy man among you...you shall open your hand to him and lend him sufficient for his need...

— DEUTERONOMY 15:7-8

(1) Loans

Just as our strength and abilities must be ready to help our brother Jew so must our wealth. Whatever God has given us in excess of our reasonable needs is to be held in trust for those in need. Hence we have the mitzva to be ready with financial aid to enable someone to overcome his temporary difficulties, earn his livelihood and retain his independence.

For this reason the duty to lend has precedence over the duty to give, because by making a loan you preserve the recipient's independence.

◆ *Halacha*

◇ *A relative has precedence over someone else; the poor of one's town over those of another.*

◇ *However much it is our duty to lend to one in need, it would be wrong to lend, even to the most honest person, without witness, bond or some other proof. We must not be the cause of a wrong being committed, either by intent or mistake, and of litigation arising from it.*

◇ *If there is reason to doubt the borrower's ability to repay, one may require a security or guarantee.*

◇ *We may not press our debtor if we know he is not in a position to pay. In such circumstances we must avoid meeting him; he would feel embarrassed to see a creditor he is not able to satisfy. (NOTE: In other societies the debtor avoids the creditor: in Torah society it is the other way around!)*

◇ *We have already mentioned the Torah's concern to protect the debtor's privacy, in chapter 4.*

(2) No interest on loans

No Jew may accept from another Jew any interest on a loan, nor may a Jew pay another Jew any interest on a loan. The Torah calls upon our "awe of God" as a warrant for this law, because this law will be kept only by those who realize that their surplus wealth was given them by God primarily for the purpose of helping others. To insist on payment for this act of brotherly love is not only unworthy in the eyes of the Torah, it is also a denial of this basic principle. Also interest tends to accumulate and get out of hand, and the borrower eventually finds that he must pay more than the original debt in interest. This is why the verb used in the Torah for taking interest also means "to bite."

◆ *Halacha*

◇ *The taking and giving of interest is prohibited whether the borrower is rich or poor.*

◇ *Interest is defined as any recompense for leaving one's money temporarily in someone else's hands as a loan or by granting credit. If it arises from a loan, it is prohibited* d'oraita *(by Biblical law)*, if from buying or selling on credit, d'rabbanan *(by rabbinical decree)*.

◇ *As long as our brother Jew has any of our money in his hands we must not receive from him any advantage even remotely connected with the loan; not even favor, word or benefit.*

◇ *One who advances money for a joint business venture is allowed to share in the profits under certain conditions, since he also shares the risk. This principle (known as iska) has been applied by rabbinical authorities since the 16th century to facilitate credit among Jews, and it is on this principle that banks operate in Israel today without infringing the laws discussed in this section.*

(3) Equity

The Torah cannot provide specific rules for every possible case that might arise during the course of time. It lays down general guidelines which the Sages of the Torah then apply in individual cases as they arise.

One of the most basic of these is "Do what is right and good in the eyes of God" (Deuteronomy 6:18). This means: apply the principles of justice and love which pervade the whole Torah to any case in which we have no specific ruling.

We see, for example, how the Torah is concerned to protect the rights and dignity of the debtor. (See chapter 4(2) and paragraph (1) above.) If a debtor has had his land seized by his creditor (by order of the court) in satisfaction of the debt, and the debtor afterwards finds the money, what is the time limit by which he must redeem his land or forfeit it to the creditor? Applying the above principle the Rabbis decided that there is *no* time limit. Unless it has been sold to someone else the debtor can always redeem it. The creditor gets his money back and the debtor has got his land back. This is what is "right and good" in the eyes of God.

Again, acting on the same principle, the Rabbis do not allow a landowner to stand on his rights if a little flexibility would enable his neighbor to gain an advantage at no cost to the former. Such inflexibility, say our Sages, is reminiscent of the Sodomites, who were notorious for standing on their rights and who refused to do favors on principle.

NO SODOMITES HERE!

ABC Bakers were a firm of bakers who also owned a large flour mill. The capacity of the flour mill was too large for their needs so they leased it on long-term contract to M.M. Millers. The contract stated that instead of paying rent, M.M. Millers would mill 20 tons of grain a year for ABC.

ABC grew prosperous and wished to expand. They bought a new bakery complex which included a modern mill. They were now able to provide for all their needs themselves and no longer needed the 20 tons supplied by M.M. They therefore proposed to M.M. that they should negotiate a monetary rent instead of the milling services provided for in the contract. M.M. refused and insisted on adhering to the letter of the contract.

Talmudic law decides: If M.M. have plenty of customers and will suffer no loss by milling the 20 tons for other people instead of for ABC, they must agree to the change and cannot insist on the letter of the contract.

Reason: Only Sodomites refuse to do a favor to a colleague even when no monetary loss is involved.

37. Charity and Good Deeds

THE NEED FOR CHARITY / HOW TO GIVE
CHARITY / HOSPITALITY / VISITING THE SICK / COMFORTING
MOURNERS

To keep the way of God, doing charity and justice.

— GENESIS 18:19

Do not harden your heart or close your hand against your needy brother. Open your hand wide to him...Do not feel bad about giving to him...it will be a source of blessing to you.

— DEUTERONOMY 14:7-9

And Abraham waited upon them [the three unknown travelers] under the tree while they ate...

— GENESIS 18:8

Follow the ways of God: clothe those who lack clothing...as He did (Genesis 3:21); visit the sick...as He did (Genesis 18:1); comfort the mourners...as He did (Genesis 25:11); bury the dead...as He did (Deuteronomy 34:6).

— TB SOTA 14a

(1) The need for charity

Long before the welfare state was thought of, Maimonides (12th century) testified that he had never seen or heard of a Jewish community which did not have an organization geared to providing for the needs of the underprivileged. And even today, not all cases of need are looked after by government welfare agencies — not by a long shot. There are still plenty of opportunities for personal charity even in the modern welfare state. The extent of charitable donations in the Torah community is much higher than in other Jewish groups, both on a per capita basis and in absolute terms. This is because the Torah community takes seriously the Torah's "held in trust" theory of wealth. (See chapter 36(1).) The word *tsedaka* stands for charity in the Torah. *Tsedaka* comes from the root *tsedek*, justice. It is not your condescending piety which leads you to give to the needy; it is only *just* that you give to those whom God

Himself has commended to your care. Nobody becomes poor through *tsedaka*, God has promised.

Nevertheless the Torah does not base its laws on miracles, and in normal circumstances it is not permitted to give away more than 20% of one's income. Giving away so much that one would become a burden on others is in effect "taking," not "giving."

The custom is to give to *tsedaka* 10% of one's net income. (This is modeled on the obligation of the farmer, in Torah law, to give one tenth of his produce to the Levite. See chapter 63.) If one accedes to wealth, one should give 10% of the capital on acquisition.

Table 3

PRIORITIES IN TSEDAKA

Charitable Causes In Order of Importance

1. Rescuing captives and hostages.
2. Relief of starving and destitute people.
3. Helping community to build a *mikveh*. (See chapter 23(6).)
4. Helping provide Torah education at all levels.
5. Helping to build and maintain a hospital.
6. Helping to build and maintain a synagogue.
7. Provision of dowries for orphaned brides.

Relief of Poverty — Order of Precedence

1. Support of one's parents and relatives.
2. Poor of one's own community.
3. Poor of one's own city.
4. Poor of other cities.
5. Non-Jewish poor.
6. For those living in the Diaspora, the poor of the Holy Land have preference over those living elsewhere, but only as regards their minimum basic needs.

Within each category the priorities are:

1. A woman precedes a man.
2. A learned man precedes an unlearned.
3. Same level of learning — the order of precedence is: Kohen, Levi, Yisrael.

THE QUALITY OF A MITZVA

The quality of every mitzva resides in the way it is done. In the case of *tsedaka* the quality is determined by the extent to which the self-respect of the recipient is preserved. On this basis there are eight degrees of *tsedaka*, in this order:

1. The highest level is when, through gifts, loans or business partnership, we enable the recipient to maintain or regain independence and earn his own livelihood.
2. Giving in such a way that the giver does not know the recipient and the recipient does not know the giver. Almost at this level is giving to public charities, if their administrator is known to be reliable and prudent.
3. When the giver knows to whom he gives but the poor person does not know from whom he receives.
4. When the poor person knows the giver but the latter does not know him.
5. Giving without being asked.
6. Giving a proper amount after being asked.
7. Giving less than proper with sympathy.
8. Giving with a sad heart.

BETTER GET BURNT THAN EMBARRASS YOUR FRIEND

The Talmudic Sage Mar Ukba (Babylonia, 3rd century C.E.) was in the habit of leaving four dinars every day at the home of a poor person of his town. So that the poor man should not discover the identity of his benefactor Mar Ukba used to hide the money in a hole in the doorstep of the man's house. Try as he would, the poor man could not find out who was leaving the money. Mar Ukba was always too quick for him.

One day Mar Ukba was delayed in the Bet

Hamedrash and his wife came to meet him. They went together to leave their daily donation. The poor man noticed two people bending over his doorstep and looked through the window to see who they were. Mar Ukba and his wife ran away. The poor man ran after them. To avoid discovery Mar Ukba and his wife ran into a baker's oven whose floor was extremely hot. Mar Ukba's feet began to blister but his wife suffered no harm. "Stand on my feet till he goes away," suggested his wife.

Mar Ukba was somewhat concerned that the mitzva of lovingkindness seemed to protect his wife more than himself. "You see," said his wife, "your charity consists of money. The poor man can't eat money. He has to go and exchange it for food. I sit the poor man down at the kitchen table and give him a nourishing plate of hot soup. My charity is more direct, and that counts more in God's eyes."

(2) How to give charity

In other societies charity has a bad name. It is connected with a cold, condescending attitude. Not so in Torah society. The Torah commands us to give whatever we give with a friendly mien, with a good and cheerful heart, with feeling and with kindly, consoling words. If we give in a surly manner, our face is taking back what our hand has given. In a classic epigram the Rabbis said: "Better to give a smile without milk than to give milk without a smile."

If you cannot accede to the request of the needy, do not turn him away angrily. At least give him encouragement, show him your goodwill and that it grieves you not to be able to help him. Never turn a destitute person away empty-handed, even if it is only a slice of bread that you can give him.

If you can persuade others to do good you have a double mitzva. You are helping the needy and you are encouraging a charitable lifestyle in others.

◆ *Halacha*

◇ *It is good to give alms before or during the Daily Prayers. (See chapter 65.) This is to emphasize that one cannot face God without first caring for one's brother.*

◇ *It is customary to vow to give* tsedaka *on being called up to the Reading of the Torah (see chapter 65(9)). This honors the Torah. (But see chapter 21.)*

◇ *It is an accepted custom to give* tsedaka *in memory of departed parents. If their memory spurs us on to good works we are enabling them to continue their good influence even after their passing, and this benefits them in the spiritual world.*

(3) Good deeds (gemilut ḥassadim)

In the Torah's scale of values *gemilut ḥassadim* — practical help — stands much higher than *tsedaka* — financial and material charity. In *tsedaka* we give away our worldly goods; in *gemilut ḥassadim* we devote to God — by caring for His people — all the best and noblest that we have. Our mind, our word, our strength, our deeds, our entire personality are involved for the good of our brothers. In *tsedaka* we offer only the means. In *gemilut ḥassadim* we ourselves create the joy, the peace, the health, the happiness, the welfare of our neighbor. We utilize our own God-given talents to advise the widow, educate the orphan, comfort the suffering, tend the sick, bury the dead, reconcile those who are at variance, heal the injured heart and dry the tears of the despairing.

If man's highest aspiration in life is to emulate His Creator, then this is the way to do it. (See chapter 74.)

(4) Visiting the sick

Visiting the sick has three practical purposes: (i) to see that he is receiving proper medical attention; (ii) to ensure that he is being properly nursed and has everything he needs; (iii) to pray for him.

BETWEEN LIFE AND DEATH

It is recorded of the great *tanna* Rabbi Akiva (2nd century C.E.) that he heard one of his pupils was sick. He visited him and found him lying in a dark and dirty room in an unmade bed with none of his needs attended to. None of his fellow students had found the time to visit him. Rabbi Akiva drew the curtains, let in the fresh air and sunlight, swept the floor, made the bed, washed the dishes and prepared some fresh food. "Rabbi," he said, "I felt I was close to death, but you have revived me." Rabbi Akiva called all his students together and gave them a lecture on the subject "Making the difference between life and death."

(5) Attending to the dead

In the traditional Torah community the preparation of the dead for burial and the burial itself was, and in many places still is, carried out by volunteers, who form themselves into a society known as the *Hevra Kadisha* ("the holy company"). Each member holds himself in readiness to take his turn to participate when called upon. Membership in this society is considered a great privilege, granted only to those considered worthy of the honor.

(6) Consoling the bereaved

Modern man is uncomfortable in the face of death. For once he is forced to face the ultimate and it unnerves him.

The Torah community, with its robust faith and the good sense bestowed on it by the Torah, shows the mourner that he is not alone. The entire community is with him in his sorrow. We link his personal tragedy with the national tragedy and say "May the Ever-Present God comfort you among all the mourners of Zion." We assure him that God alone can comfort him, because only God ensures that death is not final. As the Psalmist says: "For God, death itself has many outcomes" (Psalms 68:21).

We can try to melt the bitter sorrow in silent dedication to God's will. But we should *not* say, "What can one do, one must resign oneself," for that is not consolation but blasphemy; it is the murmuring of the helpless caught in the toils of fate, not the recognition of the blessed wisdom of God, sensed if not understood.

Mourning by the bereaved and what it teaches us has been fully discussed in chapter 18 (3) - (5).

(7) Peace-making

The crown of good deeds is the making of peace where dissension and strife reign. There, even the greatest blessing becomes a curse and an instrument of disaster. If we can bring together souls that are hostile, hearts that hate each other, and teach, cajole, persuade them to live together as brothers; if we can restore the peace that has fled from husband and wife, parents and children, brothers and sisters, families, houses, cities — then we can be sure that God values our efforts as the supreme achievement of *gemilut hassadim*, of which we will enjoy the fruits in this world while the full reward awaits us in the world to come. (See also chapter 39(3).)

(8) True riches

It is not the fleeting riches of this world that stand by a man in the hour of his greatest need. The riches we should strive for are: to enrich our mind with experience, our heart with love, our tongue with eloquence, our arm with strength, to enable us to become a support and inspiration to others. *Tsedaka* requires material means; it cannot be exercised by all. But *gemilut hassadim* is accessible to all; it requires only an honest mind, a loving heart and a helping hand.

If we have acquired these riches during our journey through life, then we can consider — and God will consider — our life a success.

38. Forgiving Wrongs Done to Us

NOT TO TAKE VENGEANCE OR BEAR A GRUDGE

You shall not take vengeance or nurse a grudge against the members of your nation.

— LEVITICUS 19:18

(1) Three options

Say you ask your friend for a favor and he refuses you. A week or two later he comes to you and asks you for a similar favor. There are three options before you. You can say "No. You didn't do it for me, why should I do it for you?" This the Torah calls taking vengeance. You can say, "All right, I agree. I am not like you. You wouldn't do it for me, but I will do it for you." This the Torah calls bearing a grudge. (You could not resist using the occasion to remind him of the "wrong" he did you.) The third option is to grant his request with good grace. What he did or did not do for you is forgotten. It is irrelevant to the need to help your neighbor whenever necessary. This is the attitude which the Torah requires in its adherents.

WHY THREE DAYS?

A great Rabbi held office in London for many years. He was not appreciated and was made to suffer humiliation and worse by those who should have known better. Not long before his retirement a member of the community came to see him before Yom Kippur. (See chapter 42(3).)

"Rabbi," he said, "Some years ago I did you a great wrong. I am sorry. I want you to forgive me."

"What was it you did? I can't remember anything so terrible."

"Never mind what it was. You didn't know I was behind it. I'd prefer not to tell you. Just forgive me."

"You will have to tell me," said the Rabbi, "or I will not be able to forgive you."

The man refused but the Rabbi insisted. Reluctantly, hesitantly, the other told the whole story. The Rabbi was silent for several minutes.

"So it was you who did that," he said at last. "You can't imagine what harm you did, what anguish you caused me."

"Well, Rebbe," he said. "I've said I'm sorry. Now please forgive me."

"I'll have to see about that," said the Rabbi. "Come back in three days and I'll give you an answer."

Why did the Rabbi make him wait three days? Was it to make him suffer? That was hardly the Rabbi's mode of behavior. No, the Rabbi estimated that he would need three days to work on himself sufficiently so that he would be *willing to forgive* such a grievous wrong. As he said afterwards: "To say 'I forgive you' is easy; if you want me *really* to forgive you, then that takes time."

(2) Why vengeance is wrong

What if our neighbor has caused us real hurt? What if he has damaged our health, wealth, honor, or peace of mind?

The Torah does not condemn the harsh retort spoken in the heat of the moment, even the blow given for the assailant's blow. The Torah was given to ordinary human beings and does not expect superhuman restraint. But revenge is something else again. Revenge nurses the grudge silently, long after the event. Revenge plans its moves cunningly, with malice aforethought. And when the blow strikes — the gloating...the savoring of the brother's hurt...These are not emotions which should be nurtured in the Jewish heart. They are unworthy of one who is the bearer of the Torah of love.

If our highest goal is to emulate God, let us learn from Him to forgive injustice, to return good for evil. If we were to judge ourselves as we judge our neighbor we would have to admit that our account with God is greatly in debit and we are the recipients of much mercy and undeserved love. Let us be to our brother what God is to each of us. (On "Emulating God" see chapter 74.)

Our Sages say: "He who suffers wrong and does no wrong in return, who receives insults and does not return them, does his duty for the love of God and rejoices over suffering, regarding it as an education and a test, of him it is said, 'And those who love Him are like the sun when it goes forth in its might.'" Just as the sun breaks through the clouds with its healing power, so do those who love God break through the clouds of hate and envy, conquering through the light of love that possesses them. If the training program of the Torah has notched up one such success it was worthwhile.

PRESCRIPTION FOR CONQUERING RESENTMENT

Rabbi Yisrael Salanter, the founder of the *mussar* movement in 19th-century Lithuania, used to say that the best way to overcome resentment is to go out of one's way to shower favors on the one who has offended you. And of course he acted on this principle.

Rabbi Yisrael made a point of not showing outwardly that he was "anyone special." He always traveled alone, dressed in the manner of an ordinary businessman. Once on a train journey to Vilna, a self-important young Jewish man was offensive to him and caused him a good deal of annoyance during the journey. Rabbi Yisrael of course took no notice.

When the train drew into Vilna station and the young man saw crowds waiting to greet his traveling companion, he realized his mistake.

The next morning he presented himself at Rabbi Yisrael's lodgings and abjectly begged forgiveness for his bad behavior. Rabbi Yisrael promptly forgave him and enquired about his business in Vilna. It turned out that he had come to seek authorization as a *shohet* for which he would have to pass a strict practical and theoretical examination. Rabbi Yisrael asked his son-in-law Rabbi Eliahu Eliezer to have a few words with him. After a short time the son-in-law came back.

"He'll never pass," he said. "He's well below standard."

On the same day Rabbi Yisrael arranged at his own expense for the young man to receive special coaching from a first-class *shohet*. After three months the son-in-law tested him again and this time found him competent, and in fact he soon passed his examinations with ease.

Rabbi Yisrael concluded the case by obtaining a position for him in an important community.

By this exercise in beneficence Rabbi Yisrael succeeded in banishing from his mind any lingering subconscious resentment he might have still harbored.

The rule is: "Kind deeds banish hard feelings."

(Compare chapter 30(1) and the story in 35(5).)

39. Teaching and Guidance

TEACHING TORAH/GUIDANCE IN MITZVOT/"BRINGING IT
INTO THE OPEN"

*The Torah which Moses commanded us is an inheritance for
the whole community of Jacob.* — DEUTERONOMY 33:4

*You shall not hate your brother in your heart. You shall
correct your neighbor but not in such a way as to bear a sin
on his account.* — LEVITICUS 19:17

(1) Teaching Torah

If we have to share our material possessions with those in
need, how much more must we share our spiritual possessions, our knowledge of Torah, our experience of life!

There is no higher or holier goal in life than to impart the
wisdom of Torah to those who are in need of it. If we know
more than our neighbor and he is willing to learn, we
should teach him what we know. If we are proficient in
many departments of Torah, we should not say "My time is
precious." There is nothing more precious than imparting
God's Torah to His people.

When lighting the Menorah in the Temple, the Kohen
had to hold the fire against the wick until the flame went
up by itself. Similarly the teacher's highest task is to enable the student to learn by himself, so that the teacher
becomes redundant. Yet it is good for the student always to
have a master, for there are things in Torah which cannot
be learnt from books but only from the living word and
example of one who loves Torah in all its depth.

(2) Guidance in mitzvot

Life is higher than knowledge and actions are the fruit of
wisdom. So helping our neighbor to fulfill the Torah is

greater than learning *about* Torah. Again, if it is our duty to save his life and his worldly goods when they are in danger, we certainly cannot remain indifferent when we see him struggling with his passion and his error, in danger of losing what is much more precious than his life. If your brother is going astray, you must not say: what does it matter to me? God did not give the Torah to the Orthodox alone but to the whole community of Israel. If you can, show him the right way, remind him of his dignity as a human being and a Jew, awaken the better nature within him and help him on to the right path. But remember, the impression he gets about Torah may well rest on how you behave. Be kind and gentle with him. Show him that you are not interested in gaining adherents for your "party" but are genuinely concerned that he should have a happier, more fulfilling life, both in a physical and spiritual sense. Be careful not to put him to shame, so that you do not "bear a sin on his account."

(3) "Bringing it into the open"

What if the fault you see in your neighbor is something that he has done to you personally? It seems from all the evidence that he deliberately injured your interests, he slandered you, he caused you to lose your job. Not being one of these exceptional people we mentioned in chapter 38(2)(end), you are not able just to forget about it and go on to the next thing. Here the Torah gives us some extremely important guidance. "Do not hate your neighbor in your heart." Do not nurse your resentment. Carry out the specific positive command which follows: "Correct your neighbor," that is, make clear to him the hurt he has caused. "But not in such a way as to bear a sin." Take him aside quietly, discuss the matter without excitement, without raising your voice. You may be surprised to find that the facts are not at all as you thought. You may find that there was a misunderstanding either on his side or yours, and that he never intended to harm you at all. Or when he hears your side of the story he may be contrite and willing to make amends.

If only everyone who feels injured, insulted, offended by someone would fulfill this mitzva and explain to the other person exactly how he feels. If only he would ask him in the privacy of his home whether he realizes the hurt he caused and why he thought he was justified in doing this. Both may be surprised at the beneficial results of this frank and friendly exchange. But no, the demon of discord prefers to let the sore fester in the dark. He prefers that the offended and the offender never speak to each other, never come to an understanding. He wants each to avoid the other until they become strangers, enemies, letting imagined slight feed upon slight until they find real reasons for enmity, and the feud is passed on, maybe even unto their grandchildren — the feud which a few minutes' conversation could perhaps have nipped in the bud. And all because they listen to the words of the dark angel instead of the words of the living God, Who tells us not to nurse our petty resentments but bring them into the open and watch them wither in the wholesome light of day.

40. Duties towards the Community

Whoever occupies himself unselfishly with the affairs of the community will find that the merit of his forefathers will support him. — MISHNA AVOT 2:2

You shall seek out from among the people able men, God-fearing men, men of truth, who hate unjust gain, and place them over them [as judges]. — EXODUS 18:21

(1) The community

In chapter 1 of this work we introduced the basic require-ment of the Torah — justice and sound administration at the national level. But the Torah nation is made up of communities, both in Israel and in the Diaspora. Every individual is duty bound to support his community, finan-cially and actively.

The individual is weak and mortal; the community is strong and immortal. Time and effort expended on strengthening the community is therefore an investment in the future of *Klal Yisrael* (the collectivity of Israel).

(2) Goals and organization

A Torah community is based on three things: on truth, on justice and on peace. It must be true to its purpose as a Torah community. It must be just to its members and its members must be just to it, contributing to its upkeep according to their means. Above all it must be at peace with itself, or it is not a community. Its goals are also threefold: *Torah, avoda* (Divine Service) and *gemilut has-sadim* (good deeds). All the communal institutions are cen-tered on these three things.

(i) *Torah.* Torah is Israel's soul and Israel's life. Torah is

161

the thing sacred to all for which Israel came into being and which it will carry throughout the changing ages. First, therefore, the community must provide opportunities for Torah learning. (See chapter 64.) There must be a *Bet Midrash*, a house of study, where people can come at all hours and study on their own or in groups. There must be schools and a *yeshiva* for the children and youth.

The community must also create the establishments and institutions which are necessary for the observance of the Torah as a whole by all its members. It must establish a *bet din*, a court of law to decide disputes in accordance with Torah legislation. It must establish a *mikveh* (see chapter 23(6)), *shehita* (chapter 27), supervision of *kashrut* (fitness) of all food products (chapters 24-28) and clothing (chapter 15(6)), and in Eretz Yisrael supervision of separation of *teruma* and *ma'aser* (chapter 63). If this is not attended to by the central government, there should also be supervision of weights and measures and business practices in stores and markets.

(ii) *Avoda*. The meaning and importance of communal religious services are explained in the fifth section of this book, "The Inner Life" (chapter 65). Because religious service is such a mighty pillar of life in general and communal services help also to draw people into brotherly unity, the community must — next in importance to Torah — provide facilities for *avoda*. The members should encourage each other to provide a *Bet Knesset* (a synagogue), *sifrei Torah* — Torah scrolls for public reading, a *hazzan* to lead the prayers, prayer books and all the other appurtenances needed for communal prayer.

(iii) *Gemilut hassadim*. The mitzva of practical loving-kindness was discussed above in chapter 37, where we also cited Maimonides' statement that he had never seen or heard of a Jewish community which did not provide assistance for the poor. In well-organized communities, voluntary societies look after all the departments of *gemilut hassadim* described in that chapter.

(3) Communal council

The affairs of the community are run by a democratically elected council which is empowered to impose communal taxes and has a great deal of discretion in formulating and implementing policy.

(4) The crown of the community

We have not yet mentioned the most important, the most essential of all aspects of the community, without whom a community can never truly be a Torah community. We mean — the *Rav*, the rabbinical authority who stands at the center of the whole communal organization. It is the *Rav* who has the ultimate responsibility for the proper working of all the communal activities. All the decisions of the communal council are valid only if they have the approval of the *Rav*. All halachic questions are brought to him for decision and he is *ex officio* also head of the *bet din*. In earlier times he was also head of the *yeshiva*.

But the *Rav* is much more than all this. He is the living example of Torah life. From him the spirit and wisdom of Torah radiate downwards throughout all the levels of the community. Through him even those farthest from a life of Torah still feel part of the community. Even those who attend synagogue perhaps only on Rosh Hashana and Yom Kippur (see chapter 42), feel privileged that they have in some way made contact with him. They feel the warmth of his personality, they see the Torah shining from his eyes, and renew their resolve to remain part of the Torah community. However far away they may be in the practice of Torah, they still identify with the community; they rejoice in its joys and mourn with it in its losses. This very fact keeps them from sinking below a certain moral level. And so every level of the community is strengthened and encouraged to maintain and improve its Torah standards.

(5) The Jewish State

We have already pointed out in this book that the Torah's goals can be realized only in a Torah State. (See chapter 12.) In our time, after 2,000 years, we have again been granted an independent State. Unfortunately it is very far from being a Torah State, but it is certainly a turning-point in Jewish history. With all its frailties, imperfections and dangers, it is a challenge and an opportunity. Torah Jews must consider it as a first step towards a glorious future. We must work to correct its errors and strengthen its positive features. We must look at it as potentially "the Torah State in the making" and work with all our strength to that end.

This is perhaps the highest of all "precepts of love." It is an expression of love for the whole community of Israel and its high purpose in the world.

GROUP FOUR:
ENRICHMENT OF THE ENVIRONMENT

Mitzvot which fill our environment with God-oriented activities

We have concluded our study of the precepts of love, but the Torah's plan is by no means completed. How do we *maintain* that high level of love and concern which the Torah demands?

Answer: by a wide-ranging program of practical and symbolic activities and observances which enrich the environment, increasing our awareness of God and of ourselves as "in the image of God."

The Torah begins by building into our lives uniquely powerful symbolic structures which instill God-awareness in the spheres of: time (Sabbath and Festivals), our bodies, clothing, home, family and other aspects of the environment. Only by enhancing our vision of God's image in ourselves and others will we be inspired to maintain loving relationships with all around us and so bring God's plan into fruition.

[TIME]

[THE BODY]

54. Circumcision

55. Tefillin

56. Washing the Hands

[CLOTHING]

57. Tzitzit

58. Covering the Head

[THE HOME]

59. Mezuza

60. Immersion of Vessels

[THE FAMILY]

61. Redemption of First-born

[THE LAND AND ITS PRODUCE]

62. Shevi'it (The Seventh Year)

63. Teruma, Ma'aser, Ḥalla
(Rules Relating to Agricultural Produce)

41. Observance of Shabbat

And God blessed the seventh day and sanctified it because on that day He rested from all His work which God had created to go on developing.　　— GENESIS 2:3

Six days you shall labor and do all your work but the seventh day is a Sabbath to God ... you shall engage in no productive activity...　　— EXODUS 20:9

So that your manservant and maidservant shall rest as well as you. Remember you were servants in Egypt...therefore God commanded you to keep the Sabbath.— DEUTERONOMY 5:14-14

And on the seventh day you shall cease your activities, so that your ox and ass may rest and the son of your maidservant and the stranger may be refreshed.

— EXODUS 23:12

You shall keep My Sabbaths as a sign between us throughout your generations, so that you may know that I am God Who sanctifies you.　　— EXODUS 31:13

Thus says God: Take care...not to carry any burden on the Sabbath day...through the gates of Jerusalem and not to take any burden out of your houses on the Sabbath...but to sanctify the Sabbath as I commanded your fathers...[if you comply with this] then this city will be inhabited forever.

— JEREMIAH 17:21,22,25

(1) The need for Sabbath

God created heaven and earth and all that they contained — galaxies, stars and the multitude of living things that people our planet. All these are programmed to follow the law of their nature. Only man is free to create his own programs.

The earth and its host of beings is given over to man to administer in accordance with God's beneficent purposes. But what guarantee is there that man will not use his freedom to work against God's plans and so bring disaster on the world and on himself?

THE SABBATH OF CREATION

The Sabbath is introduced at the beginning of the Torah as the culmination of the creation narrative. If, as the Maharal of Prague tells us, the six days of creation symbolize the physical world which exists in the three dimensions and six directions of space, then the seventh represents the spiritual dimension, the dimension of mind, which gives meaning to the whole. Using poetic license, the Torah tells us that God Himself, Who creates by word alone without work or effort, still in a sense needs to "stand back" from His creation to consider its spiritual purpose and import, and by this very act brings sanctity and blessing into the world. The seventh day henceforth symbolizes the need for man to remind himself continuously of the purpose for which he was put in the world; that is, to administer it in such a way as to be a blessing to all.

THE SABBATH OF MANKIND

There are indications in our sources that the symbol of the Sabbath day of rest was once the legacy of all mankind. But the arrogant men of Babylon spurned the teaching of the Sabbath and their vaunted civilization degenerated into dissension and strife, idolatry and superstition. In ancient Babylon, it seems, there was still a memory of the seventh day called *sabbatu*, but it had lost its sublime significance and had become a day of bad omen when it was considered unlucky to engage in any activity.

(2) The Sabbath of Israel

So the true Sabbath was given to Israel, the nation through which the realization of God's sovereignty and man's stewardship was to be restored to the world. The Sabbath day became the symbol of the spiritual purpose of the world and of Israel's special task in the realization of this purpose. No other culture, no other civilization, in the whole course of human history, has ever produced an institution like this.

THE SABBATH SYMBOL

How is the Sabbath to become such a symbol? How is it to become an education and a sanctification for our true task in life? "The seventh day is to be a Sabbath to God your God." How? "On it you shall not do any kind of work." This is much more than a mere day of rest. It is an all-embracing symbolic statement.

How does man show his domination over the earth? By fashioning all the things in his environment to suit his own purposes — the earth for his habitation, plants and animals for his food and clothing, metals and plastics for his industry, coal and oil and the atom itself for his energy. With his science and his technology he can transform everything into an instrument for his own service.

How wonderful this is! What tremendous power resides in the mind of man! But wherever we see a great concentration of power, we must ask: how is this power regulated? Uncontrolled power leads to disaster. As we have learnt while studying other mitzvot, the control envisaged by the Torah is a self-imposed control. It consists in replacing selfish, materialist goals by unselfish, spiritual goals, revealed to us by the world's Creator. This ensures that the way we administer the world will be beneficent rather than disastrous.

It is our task as Jews to keep this option open. We do it by maintaining the symbol of the Sabbath. On this day, at the behest of the Torah, we are to refrain from all productive activity. For this one day we relinquish our domination over the world and its resources. This is why the Hebrew name of this day is *Shabbat,* which does not mean "rest" but "cessation of activity." On this day we, so to speak, restore the world to God, and thus proclaim — to ourselves and to others — that our life in this world has higher, spiritual aims.

(3) Definition of melacha

Refraining from work on Shabbat is thus a "sign," as the Torah puts it: an expressive symbol for all time. The bearer of the symbol — the "work" that we refrain from on Shabbat — is very carefully circumscribed in Jewish law. *Melacha,* as this type of work is called, certainly does not mean physical exertion. It refers to carrying out an intelligent purpose by practical skill — production, creation, transport, transforming an object for human purposes; all, as we saw, activities which bespeak man's domination of the physical world. A person can have tired himself out the whole day, but so long as he has not *produced* something of significance, or effected some significant change in an object, he has not done a *melacha.* On the other hand if one has brought about such a change, without the slightest exertion, then he has desecrated the Shabbat. In fact the less exertion needed, the more the act proclaims man's successful domination of his environment, and this is just the type of act that we have to relinquish on Shabbat to God.

The laws concerning the prohibition of *melacha* on Shabbat, which are the realization in practice of the above concept, have as their scope practically all the productive activities of man. To qualify as a *melacha* an act must be deliberate, it must aim at, and achieve, some significant, constructive purpose, and be done with reasonable skill. It is an important principle of the Shabbat laws that an act done in an unusual manner or for purely destructive purposes is not a *melacha*. A little reflection will show how all these principles fit into the concept of the prohibition of *melacha* which we developed above.

(4) Concept of melacha in practice

The Rabbis grouped the *melachot* prohibited on Shabbat into 39 categories, derived from the types of activity employed in the construction of the *Mishkan* — the desert sanctuary and its appurtenances described in Exodus 25-28, 30-31, 35-40. (The sanctuary in time is modeled on the sanctuary in space.) Whether an activity is a *melacha* or not is decided by the Rabbis by relating it to one of these categories. We can give only a few examples here. (Those interested in a more detailed treatment should refer to the Bibliography.)

Thus, picking a fruit or a flower is a *melacha*, since one of the categories of *melacha* is "severing plants from their place of growth." Another category is "changing the physical state of an object by the application of heat." Under this heading we find the *melachot*: baking, cooking, boiling water, driving an automobile, melting metals, etc. "Furtherance of plant growth" includes planting seeds, pruning trees and watering the lawn. Knitting comes under the heading of "weaving," and fixing a loose tile under the heading of "building activities."

Most *melachot* involve making some material change in our physical environment. By doing them we demonstrate our control over the world. But there is one, which we earlier called "transport," which involves not so much physical as social categories. It is "taking an object from the private to the public domain and vice versa." The most usual form of this is carrying between the house and the street, or from house to house by way of the street. This activity belongs to the sphere of human society. By refraining from this activity on Shabbat, in the ways defined by our Rabbis, we bring the holiness of Shabbat into the realm of our social activities.

(5) The riches of Shabbat

The main thrust of the Sabbath legislation is this proclamation of the sovereignty of God and the stewardship of man. But this very far-reaching principle brings many rich and varied effects in its train.

SOCIAL ASPECTS

An important aspect of the Shabbat laws is their effect on employer-employee relations in particular and social relationships in general. The opportunity given by the Shabbat to employees to rest one day in seven is emphasized in the Ten Commandments (Deuteronomy 5:14). The Torah does not fail to mention also the beasts of burden who work for us patiently all the week; to them too Shabbat gives rest and refreshment (Exodus 23:14). The Torah is not referring only to the obvious fact that if there is no work the servant and the animal rest. The point goes much deeper. Shabbat brings home to us our duty to administer the world and all that is in it in accordance with the beneficent purpose of the Creator. Shabbat also brings us into a close and intimate relationship with God. It is only from this vantage point that we can appreciate the image of God in our neighbor and see God's creature in the animal.

SANCTUARY OF TIME

Shabbat as the sanctuary of time has proved more durable than the sanctuary of space — the Temple in Jerusalem. It has always been, and still is, a summons to the ennoblement of life. If during the six working days people forget the true source of their power, the Shabbat comes to direct them once more towards their Creator. One can hardly imagine a greater enrichment of the environment than Shabbat in all its aspects. It has proved its power over the millennia. "The Sabbath has guarded Israel more than Israel has guarded the Sabbath."

COVENANT OF BLESSING

Shabbat is also a permanent reminder of the covenant — a living demonstration of the unique relationship between God and the Jewish people. Jews throughout the ages have felt that Shabbat gave them a unique spiritual power, enabling them to rise above the adversities of everyday life.

This is the blessing of Shabbat. If we renew our covenant with God every Shabbat, and rededicate ourselves to His purposes, then every Shabbat God will give us renewed enlightenment, enthusiasm and strength for the fulfillment of this great task. We will experience the elevated state of life which is the blessing of Shabbat. This is what our Sages mean when they say that every Jew gains an "extra soul" (*neshama yetera*) on Shabbat.

THE DISTURBED SABBATH

Jakob de Vries was a gem merchant in 18th-century Amsterdam. He had good relations with all his customers and particularly with his main customer, the local Duke. Jakob was a Torah observant Jew and it was well-known that he could never be induced to do business, or even to talk about business, on the Sabbath.

One Sabbath morning Jakob was sitting with his family over *kiddush* when a ducal herald accompanied by two army sergeants appeared at the door. "A message from his Grace the Duke for Mijnheer Jakob de Vries." Jakob read the message and his face grew pale. It requested him politely, but firmly, to appear before the Duke within an hour with a selection of his choicest gems, since the Duke had urgent business to transact. A very large profit for the merchant would be forth-coming.

"My humblest respects to the Duke," said Jakob to the herald. "Tell him that there is nothing I would like more than to oblige him, but he knows that I never do business on the Jewish Sabbath. As soon as Sabbath is out I shall be glad to do his bidding."

But the Duke would not take no for an answer. Within the hour another delegation arrived, more numerous than the first. "The Duke's business brooks no delay," they said. Jakob again politely refused.

Throughout the day more and more messages came from the ducal palace, more and more threatening in tone. "Jakob de Vries should know that if he disobeys this command the Duke will break off all business relations with him and revoke his license to sell jewels in the whole province."

Beads of perspiration stood out on his forehead but Jakob de Vries stood firm. "Tell the Duke," he said, "that I am loyal to him but I owe a higher loyalty to my God."

After the termination of the Sabbath — and Jakob curtailed none of the ceremonies and songs with which observant Jews say farewell to the Holy Sabbath — he hastened to the palace, not know-ing what to expect there.

To his amazement, as soon as he entered the great hall the Duke rose from his throne and clasped him in a warm embrace.

"Thank you, my friend," said the Duke. "You

174

were great! And what's more you have added 10,000 guilders to my coffers. You see, I had a guest here today, the Duke of Brabant, and I told him about your loyalty to your Jewish laws. He laughed and said that no Jew could resist making a big profit, and he bet me 10,000 guilders that a combination of monetary incentives and threats would surely break your resolve. I had faith in you and bet 10,000 guilders that you would stand firm. Thank you for living up to my expectations!"

(6) Shabbat and earning a living

Israel is the only modern state to have declared Shabbat to be its official day of rest. This means that in Israel for the average person there is little or no conflict between earning a living and complete Shabbat observance.

In the Diaspora however this conflict is often very acute, and may pose a great test of faith, as illustrated by the incident recounted above. One of the functions of the institution of Shabbat is to teach us that God is the ultimate power to whom we must look for our livelihood. (See chapter 75: "Faith in God.") Jews who live among the nations must often summon up great courage, determination and trust in God to remain loyal to the Shabbat.

(7) Shabbat on the national level

Shabbat was given to Israel as a nation. In previous times, when Israel was sovereign in its land, Shabbat was observed nationally as a matter of course. The Torah's provision that the laws of Shabbat are set aside in all cases of danger to life make it feasible for a completely halachic Shabbat to be observed nationally in a modern state with due provision for all essential services. Much thought has been given to this question in rabbinic circles in the past 50 or 60 years and if in the event of an overwhelming national consensus in favor of introducing Shabbat legislation throughout the country, this could be done without significant damage to the economy or security interests. Such a step, when introduced, would be of inestimable benefit to Israel and the world.

(8) Shabbat and the modern world

If Shabbat did not exist it would have to be invented for our time. The headlong rush of modern life, the sense of purposelessness, the inability to be still, to be alone with oneself even for a moment, the all-pervasive mechanization and the resulting dangers of de-personalization and de-humanization — all call for the institution of Shabbat. Shabbat *forces* us to assert our independence. We are no longer the slaves of the machine; the television has lost its power, the peremptory ringing of the telephone goes unanswered. *We* are in control, and we have time to stand back and think for once about ends rather than means. Shabbat brings parents and children together as a family; it gives us back our humanity, our true personality. In a time of shattered illusions, when mankind is groping for permanent guidelines, the world may yet come to see that its ultimate salvation lies in the direction of the Shabbat of the Torah.

For the Torah's ideas on how to use the leisure time gained on Sabbaths and Festivals — see chapter 44(2).

42. Yom Kippur and Rosh Hashana

On the tenth day of this seventh month [Tishrei] *is the Day of Atonement. It is a summons to holiness, and you shall afflict yourselves...and do no work at all on that day. For it is the day of atonement, to atone for you for all your sins before God.* — LEVITICUS 23:26-27

On this day He will atone for you and cleanse you; you will be clean of all your sins before God. — LEVITICUS 16:30

Rabbi Akiva said: Happy are you, Israel! Before whom do you cleanse yourselves and who cleanses you? Your Father in heaven. — MISHNA, END YOMA

...For all your sins before God. Yom Kippur atones for sins committed against God but not for sins committed against your neighbor. For these you need first your neighbor's forgiveness. — MISHNA, IBID.

On the first day of the seventh month you shall have a day of rest, a remembrance of shofar-blowing, a summons to holiness. — LEVITICUS 23:24

(1) The nature of atonement

THE HAIRY AND THE BALD

Two men were standing near a threshing floor, one hairy and one bald. A gust of wind covered the two men with chaff. The bald man simply wiped the chaff off his head with his hand. The hairy one found the chaff so entangled in his hair that it was virtually impossible to get rid of it. Similarly: the people of Israel sin during the year, but are able to get rid of their sins by the cleansing action of Yom Kippur. Esau, "the hairy one," finds it impossible to get rid of his sins and becomes more and more enmeshed in them as the years go by (Midrash).

177

The secret of Israel's ability to cleanse themselves from sin on Yom Kippur is the fact that their heart was not in the sin in the first place. However far the Jew may have drifted from Torah, deep down, in his heart of hearts, he would be only too happy to lead a full Torah life. If he has sinned, this is because of the pervasive influence of the environment and its temptations. Yom Kippur gives him the opportunity to rediscover his true identity and reassert his loyalty to God and the Torah. Once he has done this he will mentally reject his sins which can then be shaken off like dust — like the chaff in the parable which could be wiped off with one's hands. They were not truly part of his personality in the first place.

The secret of Yom Kippur is that it gives us an opportunity to reaffirm our allegiance to God on the deepest level of our being.

(2) Abstaining from productive activity and food

Yom Kippur is a Sabbath too. Exactly as on Shabbat we have to refrain from all productive activity — all *melacha*. This time not as a declaration that "the earth is the Lord's and the fullness thereof" but as a confession of our own unworthiness. We have abused the power He gave us to manage the world for His purposes and we have misused it for our own selfish ends. For this one day, therefore, we are to lay no hand on anything in the world to transform it for our human purposes.

Yom Kippur also teaches us that, as a result of our sins, we have in justice no further right to continue our existence and to gratify our senses — we must abstain from food and drink and from certain other enjoyments and conveniences. Only the shofar blast at the conclusion of the Day signals the completion of our atonement and renews our license to continue the world's work and our own sustenance.

In addition, this temporary abstinence trains us in the all-important faculty of self-control.

(3) Earning one's atonement

We have to make these ideas our own by our own personal contrition and repentance. Above all we must make amends to our neighbor for any wrong done to him. No atonement can be obtained from God for such wrongs unless we have first obtained forgiveness from our neighbor. (See source at head of this chapter.)

(4) Erev Yom Kippur — the eve of atonement

Perhaps to guard against a wrong conception of Yom Kippur — namely, that physical deprivation alone can atone for our sins — the Torah tells us to eat and drink well on the eve of Yom Kippur, and the Rabbis have declared that this eating and drinking is as meritorious as fasting on Yom Kippur.

Apart from this, eating and drinking on Yom Kippur eve has three functions:

1. To strengthen our bodies for the impending fast;
2. To give a festive welcome to Yom Kippur, since we are unable to do this on the Day itself as on other Festivals (see chapter 44);
3. To celebrate the anticipated atonement of our sins.

(5) Rosh Hashana — New Year's Day

The first day of the month of Tishrei, which is the Jewish New Year, is decreed by the Torah as a Festival — a day of spiritual arousal and of blowing the shofar (see chapter 48). (For calendrical reasons this Festival is universally observed on the first *two* days of the month. Why this is so, and why the Torah calls Tishrei the seventh month, will be explained in chapter 53 — "The Calendar.")

DAY OF JUDGMENT

Rosh Hashana ("the birthday of the world") is also the Day of Judgment for the whole of mankind. Every human being is responsible to his Maker for the way he has carried out his allotted task. On this day every person's deeds are reviewed by God and decisions are made accordingly.

Three themes dominate this day:

KINGSHIP: we acknowledge God's rule over the world.
REMEMBRANCE: we recognize that God is aware of all our deeds.
SHOFAR TONES: by this symbolic sound we drive home these truths, deep into our hearts.

The significance of *shofar* will be dealt with in greater detail in chapter 48.

The judgment of Rosh Hashana is only provisional however. Repentance can completely change the spiritual atmosphere. This is why Rosh Hashana is followed by Yom Kippur, the great day of repentance and atonement we have discussed above. The ten days from Rosh Hashana to Yom Kippur are known as the Ten Days of Penitence and they provide an opportunity to prepare for true repentance.

The work prohibited on Rosh Hashana is the same kind of work as prohibited on all other Festivals. Cooking and other such activities required for the celebration of the Festival are permitted. (See next chapter, paragraph (4).)

◆ *Halacha*

◇ *The fast of Yom Kippur lasts from before sunset on the 9th of Tishrei until after nightfall on the 10th.*

◇ *No refreshment whatsoever may be taken during this period, not even a sip of water.*

◇ *In addition washing, annointing, wearing leather shoes and having marital relations are forbidden during this period.*

◇ *Children should be introduced to the fast by degrees after their ninth year. A girl after the 12th year and a boy after the 13th year are obliged to keep the fast, as well as all other mitzvot.*

◇ *Sick people and women in confinement are not allowed to fast if any danger to their life is involved.*

43. The Pattern of the Festivals

These are the appointed times of God...which you shall proclaim in their due time...On the fifteenth day of the [first] month [Nissan] is the Festival of matzot, for seven days...On the first day...and on the seventh day...you shall do no laborious work. [See paragraph (4).]
— LEVITICUS 23:4-8

And you shall count...seven full weeks...and on the fiftieth day you shall proclaim a summons to holiness; no laborious work may be done. It is a statute forever...throughout your generations.
— LEVITICUS 23:15,21

On the fifteenth day of this seventh month [Tishrei] is the Festival of Succot to God. On the first day...you shall do no laborious work...On the eighth day...there shall be a day of assembly.
— LEVITICUS 23:34-36

No work at all may be done on those days, except that relating to the preparation of food — that alone may be done by you. (See paragraph (4).)
— EXODUS 12:16

(1) Mo'adim — appointed times

Just as *Ohel Mo'ed* — the "Tent of Meeting" — denoted the desert Sanctuary which was the meeting place between God and Israel, so the Mo'ed of time — the "Festival" — is a meeting-point in time for Israel to encounter its God throughout all ages. The Mo'adim interrupt the ordinary activities of our life and summon us to reflect on those ideas which lie at the root of our relationship with God. They are called *mikra kodesh*, a summons to holiness — to dedication. If used properly they can give us new spirit, power and consecration for our task. (Mo'ed is also called "Yom Tov": or "Happy Day.")

Shabbat and Yom Kippur are also in a sense Mo'adim. We discussed them separately in the preceding chapters because of their fundamental significance, expressed by

182

the exceptional prohibition of all productive activity on these days. We also discussed Rosh Hashana in this connection since it is the herald and harbinger of Yom Kippur. This leaves Pesaḥ, Shavuot and Succot, the Festivals of pilgrimage to Jerusalem. But as we shall see in a moment, according to the Oral Law there are in certain respects not three, but four Festivals.

(2) The four Mo'adim

Each of the Mo'adim has two aspects. On the one hand they perpetuate the mighty acts by which God was manifested at the creation of our nation. On the other hand they are correlated with the seasons of the year.

The Oral Law teaches us that what is called the eighth day of Succot is actually a Festival in its own right — Shemini Atzeret ("the Assembly of the Eighth"). This stands in a similar relation to the seven days of Succot as Shavuot stands to the seven days of Pesaḥ. The difference is only that Shemini Atzeret follows immediately after Succot while Shavuot is linked to Pesaḥ by the counting of the Omer. (See chapter 47.) Again, Pesaḥ and Succot each have their distinctive practical mitzvot (see chapters 45-46 and 49-50), while Shavuot and Shemini Atzeret have no practical mitzvot; they are purely spiritual in character.

Pesaḥ, which perpetuates the redemption from Egypt, represents the creation by God of the physical aspect of the nation of Israel. This corresponds to the springtime when nature breaks free from the bonds of winter and awakens to new life.

Shavuot, the Festival of the First Fruits — the summer ripening of those tender shoots of spring — relives the historic event of the giving of the Torah on Mount Sinai — in a spiritual sense, the "first fruits" of the Exodus.

Succot, which commemorates the miraculous preservation of Israel's national body during the desert wanderings (and throughout history), mirrors the safe ingathering of the summer harvest into the barn.

Shemini Atzeret celebrates the less obvious but equally momentous preservation of the spirit of Israel — the holy orah — throughout the generations. This is symbolized y the onset of winter whose rain and frost preserve and ourish the underground seed for next year's harvest.

Table 4
SCHEME OF THE MO'ADIM

1.

SHABBAT

Consecration of life

2.	3.
PESAḤ	SHAVUOT
Seven days	One day
Physical creation of Israel	Spiritual creation of Israel
(Exodus)	(Giving of Torah)

4.	5.
SUCCOT	SHEMINI ATZERET
Seven days	One day
hysical survival of Israel	Spiritual survival of Israel
(Sojourn in desert)	(Preservation of Torah)

6.　　　　7.

ROSH HASHANA and YOM KIPPUR

Renewal of life

Interesting parallels emerge. The number seven stands for the physical world. Pesaḥ and Succot which relate to the physical aspect of Israel each have *seven* days and distinctive practical mitzvot. Shavuot and Shemini Atzeret are one-day festivals (in the Torah) and are linked to the number *eight*, since they relate to the spiritual aspect of Israel, the Torah, which derives from a realm above creation. There is one important difference which is not

184

shown in the diagram. As mentioned above, Shemini Atzeret follows immediately after the seven days of Succot while Shavuot is separated from Pesaḥ by the seven-times-seven days of the Omer. The significance of this will be discussed in the chapter on Counting the Omer — chapter 47(2).

(3) What the festivals teach

Pesaḥ teaches that God rules over nature and the nations, over life and death. God is Israel's Creator; to Him we owe our very existence as a nation. As "God's nation" we are pledged to devote our personal and national existence to furthering His purposes in the world for the ultimate good of all mankind.

It should evoke in us feelings of loyalty and devotion to the One God and to the life and destiny He has allotted to us. This leads to *ahava* — the love of God. (See chapter 73.)

Shavuot teaches that God created nature and mankind for a sublime purpose and that He revealed that purpose through the Torah He gave to His people. He has chosen human action as the agent for carrying out His will, and we, the nation of Israel, are privileged to be the bearers of His purpose. It awakens in us the resolve to cling to His Torah more than to our very life. This leads to *yir'ah* — awe and reverence for the Almighty God. (See chapter 72.)

Succot conveys the lesson that in spite of all the mighty achievements of man, it is ultimately God Who sustains nature and to whom we owe our day-to-day existence, on the individual, national and world level. (For the symbolism of Succa, see chapter 49.) In particular Israel was not only created by God but continues to exist through Him. Only God guarantees our preservation in the happy as well as in the darkest hours of life. We should resolve: in times of success to see God as the source of our success, and in times of need to see Him as our sustainer; to preserve a modest sobriety in good fortune, and courage and confidence in the face of misfortune. The motto is *emuna* — faith and trust in God. (See chapter 75.)

Shemini Atzeret reminds us that God keeps His spirit eternally alive in Israel; He rejuvenates again and again the forces of spiritual and intellectual progress in our national life — a fact amply demonstrated in our time by the amazing regeneration of Torah life and learning after the Holocaust. We should resolve to continue learning and teaching Torah with joy, even if many scorn it; to cultivate the light of Torah with confidence even if many announce its extinction. We know that God, from Whom the stream of Torah flows, will ensure its continuation until its ultimate purpose is attained. This leads to *simha* — joy in God.

In complete accordance with these ideas it has been the custom throughout the House of Israel for a thousand years to celebrate — in conjunction with Shemini Atzeret — "Simhat Torah," the Rejoicing of the Law, on which the annual Torah reading is concluded and recommenced amidst expressions of exuberant joy and festivity. In Israel this is celebrated on Shemini Atzeret itself; in the Diaspora on the additional day which is the the second day of Shemini Atzeret (see paragraph (5) and chapter 53(4)). This symbolizes the unending chain of Torah study.

(4) Work forbidden and allowed on Yom Tov

The common factor of all these days is that they interrupt our everyday life in order to make us contemplate the truths lying at the base of our existence. They consecrate us and endow us with spiritual strength to resume our everyday life on a higher level. This is what makes them into Mo'adim — joyful meeting points with God.

The prohibition of work on all these days arises from this general Mo'ed character. The activity which the Torah calls m'lechet avoda — "laborious work" — is work which transforms the objects around us in order to continue our everyday life in a workaday fashion. This must stop. But where the Mo'ed itself requires some activity for its celebration — particularly for the preparation of food to be enjoyed on the Mo'ed — there is no prohibition. Work in the honor of the Festival is raised to Divine service by the Festival. (See next chapter.)

On Shabbat and Yom Kippur, on the other hand, the essential message of the day is conveyed and realized by cessation from all productive activity. This is why the infringement of this prohibition on Shabbat is considered equivalent to idolatry and on Yom Kippur as a flagrant denial of the sanctity of the Day. Here refraining from work is an end, not a means.

In the case of the Mo'adim however the prohibition from work is a means to interrupt our everyday life and make room for us to absorb the message of the Mo'ed. For this reason its infringement, while serious enough, is not invested with the same gravity as working on Shabbat and Yom Kippur, and work which contributes to the enjoyment of the Yom Tov is permitted.

(5) Second day Yom Tov

In the Diaspora (i.e., wherever Jews live outside Eretz Yisrael) each Yom Tov is observed for two days. This means that the Yom Tov prescribed by the Torah for the first day of Pesaḥ is observed on the first and second days, and that prescribed for the seventh day is kept on the seventh and eighth days, and similarly for the other Festivals. Pesaḥ thus has eight days, Shavuot two, and Succot nine. The reason for this is explained in chapter 53(4).

◆ *Halacha*

◇ *The work permitted on Yom Tov is only such work required for the preparation of food for immediate consumption on Yom Tov, and which could not have been done, or is not usually done, on the day before.*

◇ *This includes all kinds of cooking, kindling fire (but by rabbinical decree only from a flame already burning from before Yom Tov), and carrying; but* not *"farming" activities, such as picking fruit from a tree, milling etc.*

44. Celebration of Shabbat and Yom Tov

*"You shall proclaim these festivals as a summons to
holiness." How? By eating and drinking and wearing fresh
clothes.* — SIFRA ON LEVITICUS 23:35

*You shall rejoice on your festivals: you, your son, daughter,
manservant and maidservant, the Levite, the stranger, the
orphan and the widow within your gates.* — DEUTERONOMY 16:14

*If you make the four of My family rejoice [the Levite, the
stranger, the orphan and the widow] I will make the four of
your family rejoice, says God.* — MIDRASH TANHUMA RE'EY NO. 18

*If you turn away your foot, because of the Sabbath,
From pursuing your business on My holy day,
and call the Sabbath "a delight"
and the holy day of God — "honored,"
and honor it by not going on your usual ways,
not pursuing your business, nor speaking of it —
Then you shall delight in God
and I will make you ride on the high places of the earth...
For the mouth of God has spoken it.* — ISAIAH 58:13-14

(1) Celebration and observance

The *celebration* of Shabbat and Yom Tov and their *observance* are two very different concepts which are often con-
fused. As we saw in chapter 41, Shabbat in particular is
observed by ceasing all creative activity in the physical
world. This observance is symbolic. It brings home to us
that God is the Creator and it is He Who sets the goals of
our existence in this world. This symbol and this idea are
the very essence of Shabbat.

But this unique mode of observance, while absolutely
essential to the Torah concept of Shabbat, is still not the
whole story. The Torah wants us to *enjoy* the experience of

devoting a full day to God's holy purposes, and has therefore ordained that we celebrate and honor the day in ways
which are typical of the Torah outlook on life.

(2) How to honor Shabbat and Yom Tov

We honor the coming of Sabbath and Festivals by showing
that we regard them as a sanctuary of body, mind and
spirit. "They are a summons to holiness" says the Torah.
"How do we express their holiness?" ask the Rabbis. And
the answer: "By good food and wine, fresh clothing, a clean
house, a spotless white tablecloth and plenty of light." We
have already seen that to be holy in the eyes of the Torah
does not mean to be sad and gloomy but to be merry, lively
and happy. Holiness means dedication, and if a festive
meal contributes to our sense of dedication to the goals of
our wonderful Torah, then that meal is itself an aspect of
holiness.

Moreover the festive meal on Sabbaths and Festivals is
holy because it helps cement the family relationship. The
wife is honored as the queen of the household, the children
get the attention they deserve and crave, their faces glow-
ing in the warmth of the Sabbath and Festival atmosphere, to which they too contribute by words of Torah and
songs of praise. Meals such as these sow the seeds of a
spiritually productive future.

There is one other way by which we can tell that our
eating and drinking are aspects of holiness and not plain
gluttony, and this applies especially to Festivals. If we
have invited other people to enjoy our meal with us, then
our meal is certainly a mitzva. If the people we invite are in
need — not necessarily in physical need, but in need of
cheering up, encouragement, companionship — then we
have turned our enjoyment from taking into giving. We
have given happiness to someone else, and *that* is holiness
in the eyes of God.

A DIFFERENT PERSON

We show that we value Sabbath and Festivals by our appearance, our smiling face, our bearing. A famous Rabbi now in Israel relates that when he was a freshman at the great Mirrer Yeshiva in Poland before the War, he was convinced for the first couple of weeks that the Rabbi who entered the synagogue on Shabbat was not the same person as the one who sat in the same seat during the week. The glow of Shabbat so changed his face, his bearing, his whole personality, that the mind could not accept the fact that it was the same person.

♦ *Halacha*

◊ *Before the entry of every Sabbath and Festival, including Yom Kippur, it is a rabbinical command to light candles in the home, in addition to the normal lighting. These symbolize the joy and peace ushered in by the holy day.*

◊ *This privilege and duty is primarily that of the housewife.*

(3) Reserving one's energies

The need to refrain on Shabbat from *melacha* (productive activity, however effortless), which is so integral to the whole concept of Shabbat, has been discussed at length in chapter 41. The similar but not identical prohibition on Yom Tov has been discussed in the preceding chapter. There are still many types of activity which could in theory be undertaken on these days, for example, shifting furniture from one part of the house to another, which would involve no *melacha* whatsoever. We *honor* Shabbat however by refraining *in addition* from physical effort and from all "weekday" activity. The avoidance of "work" in the normal sense, which is so often wrongly considered to be what the Torah means by its prohibition of *melacha* on

Shabbat, here comes into its own. We should not tire ourselves on Shabbat and Yom Tov but reserve our energies
for the mental and spiritual tasks of the day.

These tasks include Divine Service with the community,
listening to the majestic words of the Torah reading, the
resonant voice of the Prophets of Israel (see chapter 65(9)).
They include imbibing the spirit of the Sabbath or Festival
by studying the relevant portions of Torah, both with our
families and in the communal setting. We should discuss
them at our festival meals, give our children a chance to
repeat what they have learnt during the week. In a Torah
community Shabbat is certainly not a day of laziness. The
mind and spirit are kept very busy.

In all these ways we invoke and foster the peace of mind
which is the heritage of Shabbat and the joy which is the
portion of Yom Tov.

(4) Kiddush and havdala

Our Sages tell us that it is not enough to welcome Shabbat
and Yom Tov in silence. It is necessary to gather one's
friends and family around one and to proclaim the day's
sanctity and purpose in words. This is the ceremony of
kiddush, or sanctification, when in noble words we address
the sanctity of the day and declare our allegiance to God
Who chose us to carry out His purposes. To add to the
impressiveness of the occasion this declaration is made by
the head of the family over a brimming cup of wine and is
followed by the festive meal.

At the conclusion of Shabbat and Yom Tov, after the
Evening Service, a *havdala* ("separation") blessing is pro-
nounced in the home, also over a cup of wine (or other
beverage), but not necessarily followed by a meal. By
ancient custom this ceremony is preceded, at the conclusion of Shabbat, by blessings over some fragrant spices (to

"restore our soul" at the departure of the holy Shabbat —
see chapter 41(5), "Covenant of Blessing") — and on a
newly lighted flame (to signify our re-entry into the world
of productive activity).

(5) Ḥol ha-moed (the intermediate days of Festivals)

The Torah designates seven days for Pesaḥ and eight days
for Succot (i.e., Succot plus Shemini Atzeret) but only the
first and last days carry a prohibition of labor. These
"intermediate days" are holy in one respect since they are
part of the Festival; in another respect they are "ordinary"
days, since the prohibition of labor does not apply. Hence
their name *ḥol ha-moed* — the "ordinary" days of the
Festival. Our Sages have ruled that wherever possible they
should be distinguished from other days by refraining
from one's usual working activity. One must not engage in
work involving great physical effort, except to prevent
serious financial loss. Activities which serve the purposes
of the Mo'ed and assist its proper celebration are permitted.

(6) Social aspects

"You shall eat, drink and enjoy yourselves in the holy city
where God's name rests, and you will learn to revere God
all your days."

We see that in the Torah's eyes reverence for God is a
function of enjoyment. Nowhere does this principle come
to the fore in greater measure than in the Festivals of the
Torah. The home, the city, the whole nation is in a festive
mood. People are happy and are glad to make other people
happy. The Torah environment ensures that enjoyment
will not remain a stultifying selfish enjoyment but a cata-
lyst for caring about the happiness of others. "Where God's

name rests" means where Torah is studied in depth and its wisdom is made available to all who seek it.

In chapter 64(4) we shall discuss the beneficent influence of Torah study on all levels of the community. Festivals lend themselves to the spread of Torah learning on a national scale. "Festivals were given to Israel so that they can eat and drink and occupy themselves with Torah." In a Torah State the leisure time of Festivals presents an opportunity to raise the intellectual and spiritual level of the population, and greater Torah knowledge makes for better living.

EXPENSES OF THE WEDDING

The Rabbis tell us that all expenses incurred in honoring Shabbat and Yom Tov will be refunded by God. But this applies only when the good food and wine are purchased to honor the Festival and not merely for the person's own pleasure. How can one tell? If we invite "God's family" to enjoy and celebrate with us, this shows we are doing it to honor God and His festival. (Who are "God's family"? The underprivileged, the widow, the orphan, the young person estranged from Judaism through no fault of his own.) If we confine the celebration strictly to ourselves and our immediate family, then we are not honoring God but our own belly.

The Maggid of Dubnow, the famous weaver of parables (18th century) relates:

There was once a well-to-do Jew, two of whose sons, David and Ephraim, lived in a distant city. David was a reasonably prosperous businessman, but Ephraim had great difficulty in maintaining his large family and lived in the town's poorest neighborhood.

David received a letter from his father informing him that his youngest brother was to be married

194

three months hence. The whole family was invited and he was to spare no expense in preparing for the wedding. All expenses incurred in honoring the wedding would gladly be refunded by the father. "Please convey this message also to your brother Ephraim," the letter concluded. "I know the mail is not so reliable where he lives, so I leave it to you to tell him that everything I have written to you also applies to him."

There was great excitement in David's home. The dressmakers were called for the girls, tailors for the boys. "Spare no expense," said the father. "Grandfather is paying for everything." The months sped by and at last the day came when dressed in all their finery they got into the carriages which were to take them to the wedding. They were about to start when David smacked his forehead. "Oh, Uncle Ephraim!" he cried. "We forgot all about Uncle Ephraim!" He directed the coachman to the other side of the town to pick up Uncle Ephraim and his family.

"How can we go like this?" they asked. "We only have these old clothes. We have nothing to wear."

"Never mind," said David. "It can't be helped now. Dad will be disappointed if you don't come. You must come just as you are."

Willy-nilly, they crowded into the carriages and set off together for the wedding.

It can be imagined that the appearance of Ephraim and his family was somewhat of a disgrace, but all was forgotten in the joy of the wedding celebration, in which all the townspeople joined. After a few days David approached his father.

"I would like to stay a little longer," he said, "but I have to get back to my office, you know."

"I quite understand," said the father. "Well, I guess it's good-bye then."

195

"Isn't there something we have to settle first?" said David.

"Settle? I don't know what you mean."

After much hesitation David produced the bills for the expenses he had incurred.

"That's nothing to do with me," said his father. "Why should I pay your tailor's bills?"

"But father, you wrote..."

"I wrote nothing of the kind," said his father. "I wrote I would pay for expenses incurred in honoring the wedding. If you had wanted to honor the wedding you would have seen to it that your brother Ephraim and his family were also suitably dressed. This shows me you were not thinking about me or the wedding but only about yourselves."

Similarly with Yom Tov, said the Maggid of Dubnow. We can tell your true motive by seeing whom you have around your festive table.

45. Ḥametz on Pesaḥ

Remember this day — the day you went out of Egypt, the house of slavery — for God brought you out of here by His power; that is why no ḥametz may be eaten. — EXODUS 13:3

Seven days you shall eat unleavened bread; by the first day you shall clear away all ḥametz from your house...
— EXODUS 12:15

They baked the dough they had taken with them from Egypt as unleavened cakes (matzot) — it had not had time to become leavened (ḥametz) - because they were driven out of Egypt and had no time to wait. Also they had laid in no provisions for themselves. — EXODUS 12:39

(1) Symbolism of ḥametz and matza

As soon as flour is kneaded together with water, enzymes begin working on the sugars in the wheat kernel, which ferment and release carbon dioxide. This causes the dough to rise and become "leavened" — in Hebrew, *ḥametz*. If the dough is kneaded, rolled out and baked in a hot oven within a few minutes, the process is stopped and the resulting bread is "unleavened" — *matza*.

Matza is therefore bread for people who are in a hurry, people whose time is not their own — it is the bread of servitude. *Ḥametz* on the other hand is bread for people of leisure, people who have time to wait for the greatly improved taste and texture of leavened bread — it is the bread of freedom and independence.

At the very time when we celebrate our release from Egyptian bondage to freedom and independence — our emergence as a nation on the world arena — the Torah of God requires us to banish the bread of freedom from our homes and tables for the full period of the Festival. It even makes this a criterion of our allegiance to God, for our very membership in the faith-community of Israel. If we deliberately flout this law we are "cut off" from the people of Israel. Why?

It is extremely important for us, the people of Israel, to remember that we did not emerge into nationhood, as other nations, by our own efforts, but by an act of Divine power which has resounded down the ages. Even at the moment of gaining independence we were not our own masters — we did not even have time to bake our bread.

The extraordinary events which surrounded our Exodus from Egypt stamped us for all time as a nation not like other nations — a nation with a mission. Our very existence in the world bears witness that behind and beyond the power politics the world is run by a Higher Power. To eat hametz during the week of Pesah would be a denial of God's presence in history — and in particular, our history — and a betrayal of our mission in the world.

In our time, after 2,000 years of wandering, we have regained our independence in our ancient homeland. The extraordinary events surrounding this achievement — in fact the very achievement itself — should lead us to see the hand of God still guiding us from behind the scenes, as in the past. Here, too, the inflated self-importance of hametz is out of place. The humility of matza is more appropriate. God uses the courage, determination and self-sacrifice of human beings to achieve His sublime purposes, irrespective of the intentions and purposes of the people concerned. In the end it will be His purposes that will prevail.

(2) The threefold prohibition

Hametz on Pesah belongs to the small group of substances which, besides being forbidden as food, may also not be used in any way, nor may any enjoyment or benefit, physical or economic, be gained from them. (We have already met three of these: fruit of the first three years [chap.14];

grapes and wheat which have grown together [chap. 15(4)(c)]; and meat and milk which have been boiled together [chap. 16(3)].)

Ḥametz is unique however in that it is also banned from the *ownership* of a Jew during Pesaḥ. It is thus subject to a threefold prohibition.

> 1. It may not be used as food — for the furtherance of our life.
> 2. It may not be used for enjoyment or benefit — for the furtherance of our well-being.
> 3. It may not be in our ownership — to increase our economic prosperity.

It will be noted that these things are what every human being yearns for in this world: life, well-being and economic prosperity. It is precisely to realize these aims that nations and states are usually established. In the private and public life of the people of Israel, however, *hametz* is banned during Pesaḥ from each of these areas. This is to remind us symbolically that *our* life, well-being and affluence are not based on the principle of *hametz* — the inflated ego which says "my strength and the might of my own hand have brought me this wealth." People who believe *this* pursue these aims at all costs, as if they were ends in themselves. We who know that we owe everything to God consider them not as ends but as means to the achievement of our primary goal — the furtherance of His beneficent purposes in the world.

◆ *Halacha*

◇ Ḥametz *can come in various forms, e.g.: bread, cake, crackers, wafers, breakfast cereals, beer (containing malt), whiskey (made from barley). Also there are many products in which* ḥametz *may be an ingredient.*

◇ Ḥametz *is unusual in that it is permitted throughout the*

199

year and prohibited only during Pesaḥ, so special care is taken to avoid its use by mistake.

◇ *It is necessary to make a thorough search of all places where ḥametz might have been brought: house, workplace, store, car, etc.*

◇ *On the night of 13th-14th of Nissan a final search is undertaken in the presence of the whole family, by the light of a candle, which also has symbolic significance. (It stands for the light of conscience searching out the innermost recesses of the mind.)*

◇ *No ḥametz may be eaten after approximately 9:00 a.m. on the morning of Erev Pesaḥ (14th Nissan). (The precise time depends on location and can be ascertained from a Jewish calendar.) Any remaining ḥametz is ceremonially burnt later on in the morning.*

◇ *As mentioned previously it is not only forbidden to eat ḥametz during Pesaḥ, it is also forbidden to derive any benefit from it, e.g., by selling it, using it for industrial purposes, etc.*

◇ *Since one may not own ḥametz on Pesaḥ one must either destroy what he owns (bi'ur), or relinquish ownership (bittul), or sell it to a non-Jew. Ḥametz which has been in Jewish ownership during Pesaḥ may not be used after Pesaḥ.*

46. Matza, Maror and Haggada

*In the first month, on the fourteenth day of the month, in the
evening, you shall eat* matzot.   — EXODUS 12:18

*You shall tell your child on that day: It is because of what
God did for me when I went out of Egypt.*   — EXODUS 12:8

*They shall take a lamb for each family...and eat the meat on
that night, roasted on the fire with unleavened bread and
bitter herbs.*   — EXODUS 12:3,8

*Everyone should consider himself as having personally taken
part in the Exodus from Egypt.*   — MISHNA PESAHIM 10:5

(1) The family celebration

When the Holy Temple was standing every Jewish family
renewed the covenant with the Almighty in Jerusalem on
the first night of Pesah by means of the Paschal lamb —
the *Korban Pesah*, which was roasted and eaten with *matzot* and bitter herbs (*maror*), amid songs of praise, discussion and story-telling. The lamb (which had to be roasted
whole, and eaten in one house, without a bone being
broken) symbolized the unity of the House of Israel, which
accepts the *maror*: the bitterness of exile and persecution,
and the *matza*: the humble bread of the servitude-
redemption process, as coming equally from the hand of
God (see chapter 45(1)).

We no longer have the roast lamb offering, but we still
joyfully fulfill the command of eating *matza* and *maror* as
the focal point of our celebration. As befits a family celebration, the children have a central role. They ask the
questions, which the father answers, following the order
(*Seder*) laid down in the *Haggada* — the little book which
has probably run through more editions than any other
book known to mankind, telling in simple terms the story

of the oppression and the Exodus. The recital is, and should be, interrupted many times by impromptu questions and answers on the part of the participants — particularly the children. The purpose is to help us relive those historic events and to feel it was indeed we who went out of Egypt.

The proceedings are punctuated by four ceremonial cups of wine, two before the festive meal and two after it. These mirror the four Divine acts referred to in the Torah (Exodus 6:6-7):

1. Rescue from oppression
2. Release from bondage
3. Grant of nationhood
4. Adoption as the people of God.

(2) The child is the focal point

Nothing was further from the Torah's intention than that we should train our children to think of Jewish life as a set of mechanical usages and customs. It is the *spirit* of Torah which we must nurture in the hearts and minds of our children. Seder night presents the golden opportunity for this. This is the night appointed by God for the dedication of our sons and daughters to our people's task, for filling their hearts with pride in their destiny. If our own hearts are permeated by the message of Pesaḥ, *matza* and *maror*, then we stand a chance of getting the message across to our children. The child's probing eyes look at you, his parents, and ask:

"What does this service mean to *you*?"

The Jewish future may depend on the answer to this question.

TELLING THE STORY

It is told of Rabbi Israel Baal Shem Tov (founder of the ḥassidic movement in 18th-century Russia) that on special occasions he would take his closest disciples to a secret place deep in the forest, and recite some mystic words, and the holy fire would come. His successor, the Maggid of Mezeritch, used to say: We no longer know the place in the forest, but we know the words, and when we say them the holy fire comes. Reb Bunim, in the third generation, said: We do not know the place, and we no longer know the words, but we tell the story — and the holy fire comes.

We also only tell the story, but if our heart is in it, the holy fire can still come.

47. Counting the Omer

*From the day after the day of rest, from the day
you bring the omer offering [i.e., from the second
day of Pesaḥ]...you shall count seven complete
weeks. Until the day after the seventh week you
shall count — fifty days...And that day you shall
proclaim as a call to holiness...it is the Festival
of the First Fruits.* — LEVITICUS 23:15,16,21

*You shall eat no bread or grain...[of the new
crop] until you have brought the offering of your
God. This is an everlasting law throughout your
generations wherever you may live.*

— LEVITICUS 23:14

(1) The omer offering

Barley ripens early in the Land of Israel. Already by Pesaḥ
the grain is ready for harvesting. But before we take any of
the new harvest for ourselves we have to present some
before the altar of God — and so we did, each year, when
the Holy Temple stood in Jerusalem. The amount to give
was the measure of one *omer* — symbolically, one day's
food supply for a human being. Hence the name, "the *omer*
offering."

We are not allowed to partake of the new grain harvest
until the offering has been brought, or if there is no offering, until this day is over. This is the (temporary) prohibition of *hadash* (the "new" [harvest]). God wants us to enjoy
the new grain harvest to the full. But every enjoyment is
enriched if it is subject to restraint. We are to learn that
God comes first. By bringing the first *omer* to God we
recognize that our sustenance comes from Him and we
dedicate to Him the life He sustains.

From this *omer*, which is brought on the 16th of Nissan,
we count forward, day by day and week by week, until, on

the fiftieth day, we reach the Festival of Shavuot, which celebrates both the giving of the Torah on Mount Sinai, and the ripening of the wheat harvest and the first summer fruits.

(2) The significance of counting

The counting means that we realize that the attainment of physical independence on Pesaḥ was only a beginning. It was a gift. Now we have to justify it by working forward to be worthy of receiving the Torah on Shavuot.

And more. The *omer* on Pesach was from the barley harvest. The offering on Shavuot was of wheat. Barley is mainly food for animals. Wheat is food for human beings. The Torah hints to us that physical independence by itself still leaves man — from the Torah perspective — on the animal level. The counting of the forty-nine days signifies a sevenfold refining process and marks our progress to full human status with our acceptance of the Torah at Sinai, seven weeks after the Exodus.

If "seven," the symbol of creation, represents the fullness of this world, "eight" refers to that which is above creation — the spiritual world from which Torah comes. "Fifty," which is the code number for Shavuot, could be called a "super eight," since it comes after a sevenfold seven. To be worthy of celebrating the *creation* of the Torah on Shavuot (see chapter 43(2)) we must first follow the hard preparatory path of forty-nine steps. This is why Shavuot is separated from the first day of Pesaḥ by forty-nine days. Torah can be *acquired* only by prolonged effort. Shemini Atzeret, however, comes immediately after the seven days of Succot; there is no preparatory period. This is because the *preservation* of Torah in Israel is something that depends more on God than on our own efforts. We have seen this happen in the miraculous regeneration of Torah life after the Holocaust; see above 43(3).

(3) A tinge of mourning

The joy of this period is somewhat marred by events which occurred long ago but whose memory is still with us. In Eretz Yisrael in the 2nd century C.E. many of the disciples of Rabbi Akiva died during this period in a mysterious epidemic. They were to have been the bearers of Torah in that generation. Our Sages attribute their deaths to certain character-failings which might have been overlooked in others but not in the transmitters of Torah. They failed to treat each other with the respect due to colleagues in Torah study. The lesson for our day is obvious.

Nearly a thousand years later, in the Jewish communities of the Rhineland, in this same period of preparation for Torah, many of Israel's finest sons and daughters gave their lives for that same Torah. They fell victims to the blind madness of the Crusaders (1096 C.E.).

As a result this period continues to bear a tinge of public mourning. Weddings are not celebrated, and hair is not trimmed. This is to remind us, the bearers of Torah, that our interpersonal behavior must be in accord with that great privilege. It should imbue us too with resolve to carry forward loyally that holy task for which our martyrs gave their lives. This is especially relevant in our time, when, not so long ago, millions of our fellow Jews were fiendishly murdered by "civilized" Europeans for no other reason than that they were Jews — the people of the Torah.

48. Sounding the Shofar

*The first of the seventh month shall be...a memorial pro-
claimed with the blowing of horns, a summons to holiness.*
— LEVITICUS 23:24

The message of the shofar

There can hardly be a greater contrast than the way we
and the nations around us celebrate a New Year.

The significance of Rosh Hashana was briefly discussed
in chapter 42(5). This significance is emphasized and
enhanced by the potent symbol of the *shofar* (ram's horn).
The rough, unmelodious blast of the shofar echoes the wild
cry from the heart, from the subconscious depths, which is
deeper than words and does not need words. It echoes that
cry, and also awakens it — the subconscious awareness that
we have to give account for our actions before the heavenly
throne.

The shofar speaks to us in three modes, and this is the
basic pattern of all our shofar blowing: 1. *tekia* — plain
note; 2. *terua* — broken note; 3. *tekia* — plain note. This is
their message:

> 1. First *tekia*: awakens us from our everyday slumber
> and summons us to become aware of our Creator and
> the duties He has imposed upon us.
> 2. *Terua*: Sounds the alarm and "shakes us up" men-
> tally and emotionally, when we realize how far we
> have fallen short of the standards set for us.
> 3. Final *tekia*: calls us to draw the necessary conclu-
> sions and advance with confidence to a better life.

The Torah's symbolism remains forever relevant
because it touches the deepest levels of the human heart.
Even today police cars, ambulances and air raid sirens use

an "up and down" *terua* sound to indicate urgency, danger and alarm, while "all clear" is indicated by an unbroken *tekia* sound.

The three stages of this basic pattern correspond to the three stages of repentance. These are:

1. *Viddui* — confession: admitting the truth to oneself. This corresponds to the first *tekia*.
2. *Ḥarata* — remorse: feeling deep contrition for the wrongs committed. This corresponds to *terua*.
3. *Kabbala al he-atid* — firm resolve to put things right and remain loyal to one's duty in the future. This corresponds to the final *tekia*.

This is the message conveyed by the shofar tones in all their variety of mode and context.

49. Living in the Succa

Beginning on the fifteenth day of the seventh month you
shall keep the Festival of Succot for seven days — for
God...For seven days you shall live in succot *(booths). All*
your generations shall know that I made the people of Israel
dwell in booths when I brought them out of Egypt...

— LEVITICUS 23:34,43

You shall keep the Festival of Succot for seven days, at the
time when you take home the produce of your threshing floor
and your wine press.   — DEUTERONOMY 16:13

(1) On the personal level

When our granaries are full and winter holds no terrors,
when our home is secure and our needs well provided for —
that is the time the Torah tells us to leave our comfortable
homes and spend seven days in a temporary booth. For a
full cycle of days we are to live under a flimsy roof of leaves
and fronds. By this dramatic change in lifestyle we are to
bring home to ourselves, consciously and subconsciously,
that it is God's power and presence that sustains us. We are
to see the hand of God in all that befalls us. If we absorb its
message, the Succa will give us the strength to withstand
the temptations of prosperity as well as the tests and trials
of misfortune.

After making legitimate use of all our opportunities,
after using our mental and physical powers to the utmost
and investing hard work, determination and initiative, we
must still know deep down in our being that — as Moses
our Teacher put it — "it is not our own power that has
brought us this wealth" (Deuteronomy 8:17-18). Not our
own power? But I thought we just said...? "Yes," he goes
on, "but it is God Who gave you the powers, the talents, the
ideas, in the first place, so that you should carry out His

209

purposes." In other words, it is not because you have the talents that you have the wealth, but because God wished you to have wealth that He gave you the talents. This attitude of mind, which sees the world right side up, is called *emuna* — faith in God (see chapter 75). It is the intended end-product of the Succa experience.

(2) On the national level

Succot as a Festival celebrates God's protective, preserving care for the Jewish people as symbolized by our miraculous 40-year sojourn in the Desert of Sinai at the start of our national existence. It has been manifested for all to see in our miraculous survival — of all the peoples of the ancient world — during our millennia-long wanderings in the "desert of the nations."

During the course of this immense journey through history our nation has suffered many grievous blows, culminating in the Holocaust in our time. Yet we still survive — living testimony to the hidden power of God.

Even when human beings think they are "taking charge of their own destiny," they will eventually discover that in fact their destiny has taken charge of them. The Divine plan has a way of realizing itself through the very people who deny it or think they are frustrating it.

(3) On the world level

We move into the Succa also as citizens of the world.

When the nations of the world once realize that the goals they have been pursuing so avidly and for so long are self-defeating, they too will move into the Succa. More and more people will begin to contemplate a Copernican revolution of the spirit and come to substitute spiritual goals for self-centered material goals. Then at long last mankind will be on the right path towards realizing its true potential.

We are merely the forerunners of that great and longed-for movement envisaged so long ago by the Prophets and Sages of Israel.

50. The Four Species

And you shall take for yourselves on the first day the fruit of the tree [called] "beautiful," fronds of palm trees, myrtle boughs and willows of the brook, and rejoice before God your God for seven days.

— LEVITICUS 23:40

(1) The four species

Tradition tells us that the "fruit of the tree called 'beautiful'" is the *etrog*, or citron. Besides the beauty of its form, its fragrance permeates even the wood of the tree itself. The date palm also produces fruit, but it has no fragrance. The part to be taken is the *lulav*, the young, unopened frond. The Torah loves to show us, in its symbols, the freshness and high potential of youth. The myrtle has fragrance but no fruit, while the willow has neither. Being the tallest and most prominent of the four, the *lulav* has given its name to the whole; we usually refer to this mitzva as the mitzva of *lulav*.

The Sages also tell us that the requirement of beauty applies to all four. Each must display the natural beauty of its kind; defects, imperfections and discolorations may disqualify it for the mitzva.

We are "to take them *for ourselves* on the first day"; they must be our own personal acquisition — one that we need not be ashamed to hold before the presence of God; not borrowed and not gained by dishonest means. They symbolize our legitimate ownership of the good things of the world.

After asking us to reject reliance on our material might by moving out to the Succa (chapter 49), the Torah puts into our hands the plants which symbolize the variegated bounties of God's world and tells us to "rejoice with them in the presence of God." The Torah does not want us to

Table 5

THE VARIEGATED BOUNTIES OF THE ENVIRONMENT

	BEAUTY	FRUIT	FRAGRANCE
Citron (*Etrog*)	√	√	√
Date Palm (*Lulav*)	√	√	-
Myrtle (*Hadass*)	√	-	√
Willow (*Arava*)	√	-	-

renounce the good things of this world. On the contrary, we are to value the environment in which He has placed us (see chapter 13). We should value it for its beauty as much as for its utility. We should take pleasure even in the beauty of the humble willow.

We can rejoice in it so long as we hold it "in the presence of God"; that is, if we use it in accordance with the laws He has laid down. Happy is the one who has nothing to be ashamed of in the way he has used God's world.

(2) Succa and lulav

The Succa teaches us not to place too high a value on our worldly goods; the *lulav*, to value them at their true worth.

The lesson of the Succa is that the acquisition of material goods is not the sole aim of life; the *lulav* teaches us to use all that God has given us as instruments for our true goal. And so it brings us *simḥa*, joy; because joy is the result of using all one's potential for good.

(3) National significance

The four species also bear a national and historical significance. Maimonides linked these species with the national joy at our emergence from the parched desert into a land of fruit trees and rivers. To keep this memory fresh we are to take the most beautiful and fragrant of the fruit of the land, and plants whose very leaves have fragrance (the myrtle) and beauty (the willow). Pursuing this line of thought, we might add that the myrtle (whose name *avot* means "thicket") may represent the thickets on the banks of the river Jordan, the *lulav* the date-palms for which Jericho is famous, the willows remind us of the wadis and brooks of the Land of Israel, while the *etrog* symbolizes the bounty of the Land. These plants thus symbolize our emergence from the desert, our crossing the Jordan and our settlement in the fertile Land of Israel. The species thus represent not only our personal possessions but also the national and historical possessions of the people of Israel. We are to rejoice in these resources and at the same time resolve as a nation to use them for the Divine purposes. When that happy day arrives we will at last as a united nation be able to "rejoice before God" — as a nation which has at last found its way back to its true destiny.

◆ *Halacha*

◇ *It is customary to go to considerable lengths to ensure that the four species that one takes on Succot are as perfect and as beautiful as possible.*

◇ *One should take: 1 etrog, 1 lulav, 3 myrtle (hadass) twigs and 2 willow (arava) twigs.*

◇ *The* lulav, hadass *and* arava *are bound together and held in the right hand and the* etrog *in the left. (It will be seen from Table 8 that the qualities of the* etrog *balance the qualities of the other three together.)*

◇ *The four species are held during Hallel (chapter 65(8)) and during the procession around the reading desk on which the Sefer Torah is held. (To make a circuit around an object expresses the choice of that object as the center of* one's aims and endeavors. To go around the Torah with our etrog and lulav represents our determination to use all the means at our disposal for Torah.) At certain points in the service they are pointed in the six directions — front, right, back, left, up, down — and shaken slightly in each direction. (This is the Ashkenazi custom. Others follow a different order.) This symbolizes our awareness that God is everywhere and that His gifts flow in on us everywhere and at all times.

◇ The requirement that the species shall be one's own property and not borrowed applies only on the first day.

51. Purim and Ḥanukka

*These days are remembered and celebrated in every
generation and in every family, in every province and in
every city. The days of Purim will never disappear from
among the Jews and their memory will never cease from their
descendants.*
— ESTHER 9:28

*Remember the days of old...
Ask your father and he will relate it to you,
Your elders — they will tell you.
When the Most High allots nations their inheritance...
He sets the boundaries of the peoples
According to the number of the Children of Israel.*
— DEUTERONOMY 32:7-8

(1) Rabbinical Festivals

The destruction of the First Temple by the Babylonians
ended an era. We lost our Sanctuary, our land and our
independence, but we have not ceased to be the people of
God, and His protective care still encompasses us. Though
we are often ravaged by enemies both within and without,
God, the Lord of history, prevents our foes from destroying
us either physically or spiritually.

The Sages of old selected two such acts of Divine salvation for national commemoration. Exercising the powers
given them by the Torah (see chapter 1), they introduced
two rabbinic Festivals alongside the Festivals of the
Torah, each with laws and customs appropriate to the
event being celebrated. These are Purim, on the 14th or
15th of Adar, and Ḥanukka, for eight days from the 25th of
Kislev. Each of them has considerable relevance to our
situation at the present day.

(2) Purim

In the Persian Empire of old a strong anti-Jewish movement threatened the physical survival of the entire Jewish people. A "Final Solution" to the Jewish problem was decreed in essentially the same terms as the one put into operation by the Nazis some 2,500 years later. By the heroic efforts of Mordechai and Esther and a mass rejection by the Jewish people of assimilationist tendencies, accompanied by a return to Torah commitment, the disaster was averted. The Festival of Purim was instituted to give thanks to God for this deliverance, no less miraculous for being clothed in the "natural" guise of palace intrigues. The Book of Esther contains a full account of these events.

(3) Ḥanukka

Several centuries later, when most of the known world was ruled by the Greeks, the Jews in Eretz Yisrael faced a completely new challenge. Unlike previous conquerors, the Greeks brought with them a system of thought: philosophy, art, humanistic ideals and the cult of the body beautiful. Many young Jews, particularly from the upper classes, were attracted to the new Hellenistic lifestyle and began to look on the eternal Torah as outdated and oppressive. The Jewish Hellenists took over the Holy Temple and "modernized" the Temple service. When they met opposition from the populace they enlisted the help of the Syrian-Greek government of Antiochus IV to compel all Jews to fall into line. The observance of Torah laws which emphasized the uniqueness of the Jewish people, such as Shabbat and circumcision, was punishable by death. It was then that the first individuals in history sacrificed their lives for their religion.

Eventually the banner of revolt was raised by the priest

Mattityahu the Hasmonean, his son Judah Maccabi and others. Judah, who proved to be a brave and resourceful general, carried on guerilla warfare in the Judean mountains for years. Having defeated the much stronger forces sent against him by Antiochus, he re-entered Jerusalem in 165 B.C.E. His first act was to rededicate the Temple and re-light the great Menorah in the Sanctuary. The Festival of Hanukka — which means Dedication — was instituted to render thanks to God for this great salvation. We note how God makes use of the self-sacrifice of His faithful ones in order to conserve the Torah of Israel for all time. The miracle of the single flask of pure oil which burned for eight days instead of one, hints at the unquenchable spirit of Israel. (For the significance of "eight" — see Shemini Atzeret, chapter 43(2).)

(4) Completing the scheme

These two events, which we celebrate on Purim and Hanukka, are typical of God's saving power throughout our history up to the present day. Purim typifies the miracle of our physical survival, Hanukka the miracle of spiritual survival, in conditions of exile and political bondage.

In our time we can truly say with the Psalmist:

God has caused me grievous suffering,
But to Death He has not delivered me. (Psalms 118:18)

We can now complete the scheme of Festivals given in Table 4. (See Table 6.)

◆ *Halacha*
◇ Purim. *The mitzvot of the day are:*
Spiritual: Hearing the public reading of The Scroll of Esther night and morning; inserting thanksgiving "for the miracles" in Daily Prayers (65(6)) and in Blessing after Meals (65(7)). No Hallel(65(8)) is said because the miracle

Table 6
SCHEME OF THE MO'ADIM COMPLETED

PHYSICAL	SPIRITUAL
PESAḤ Physical creation of Israel (Exodus)	SHAVUOT Spiritual creation of Israel (Giving of Torah)
SUCCOT Physical survival of Israel (Desert sojourn)	SHEMINI ATZERET Spiritual survival of Israel (Preservation of Torah)
PURIM *Physical survival in times* *of exile and bondage*	*ḤANUKKA* *Spiritual survival in times* *of exile and bondage*

took place outside Eretz Yisrael.

Physical: Edible gifts to friends, alms to poor, festive meal at end of day. (A Torah Festival engenders its own holiness, so the festive meal can coincide with the start of the Festival and partake of the holiness of the day. On a rabbinic Festival [Purim] we need to build up sanctity by observing the mitzvot of the night and succeeding day so that the festive meal may be invested with their spiritual energy. This may be why the Purim meal is eaten towards the end of the Festival.)

◊ *Purim is observed on the 15th of Adar in Jerusalem: the 14th of Adar almost everywhere else.*

◊ *Ḥanukka. Hallel is said in the morning service as well as thanksgiving "for the miracles." Candles or oil lamps are lit each evening, increasing by one each day.*

◊ *There is no obligation to have a festive meal, since the festival celebrates a spiritual victory only. However it is customary to commemorate the holiday with some degree of feasting.*

52. Fast Days

Thus says the God of Hosts: The fast of the fourth month (Tammuz 17), the fast of the fifth month (Av 9), the fast of the seventh month (Tishrei 3) and the fast of the tenth month (Tevet 10) shall become days of gladness and joy and happy festivals — provided you love truth and peace. — ZECHARIA 8:19

(1) The fasts ordained by the prophets

At the time of the destruction of the First Temple there were still prophets in Israel. These prophets, having witnessed the dire results of national disobedience to the Torah, which they had been warning against for so long, ordained four fasts during the year, corresponding to the four stages of the catastrophe. Their purpose: to help us keep in mind the lessons of our history.

(2) The events commemorated

After so many years of prophetic exhortation, the siege of Jerusalem by the Babylonians should have acted as an "early warning" of impending disaster. Had we responded, the final catastrophe might have been averted. But the only response was a futile decision to defend the city to the last.

The final collapse and downfall occurred three years later in the searing heat of Tammuz and Av. (The Festivals of the Torah fall in the equable weather of spring and fall, while the main fasts fall in the extreme heat of mid-summer. We should learn from this to avoid extremes.)

Gedalia, a righteous man, a follower of the prophet Jeremiah, accepted the post of governor of Judea subject to the Babylonian conqueror. He was murdered on Rosh Hashana by a Jew, a member of the royal family, for nationalistic motives. The assassin was apparently a member of the war party which refused to accept defeat by the Babylonians, and were prepared to sacrifice the remnant of Jews remaining in Eretz Yisrael for the sake of their ultra-nationalistic delusions. As a result of this futile

Table 7
PATTERN OF THE FAST DAYS

FAST	EVENT	SIGNIFICANCE
10 Tevet	Jerusalem besieged (589 BCE)	Early warning
17 Tammuz	Walls of Jerusalem breached (586 BCE)	Beginning of disaster
9 Av	First and Second Temples destroyed (586 BCE and 70 CE)	Final fury
3 Tishrei	Assassination of Gedalia ben Ahikam (586 BCE)	Extinction of the remnant

act of rebellion, the remnant of Jews left in Eretz Yisrael dispersed, leaving the country desolate. This was the final blow. The fixing of this fast on a par with the others teaches us, say the Rabbis, that the death of the righteous is as grievous a blow to Israel as the destruction of the Temple. We might add that refusal to heed the words of the prophets, even after the catastrophe they predicted had occurred, only completes the work of the enemy.

(3) The purpose of fasting

Just as the Torah's joyous Festivals provide us with opportunities to reflect on and absorb the great truths of our special relationship with God, so the Fast Days encourage

221

us to reflect on the failings which brought upon us these national disasters.

According to our Sages, the First Temple was destroyed because of the sins of idolatry, immorality and bloodshed; the Second Temple because of the more subtle character defects of quarrelsomeness, causeless hatred and love of money. If you want to know which are worse, say our Sages, compare the lengths of the respective exiles. The Babylonian exile lasted only 70 years, while *our* exile is still not completed after more than 1900 years. The reason is that a person who falls into open and obvious crimes, such as idolatry, etc., is that much closer to repentance. Hidden and inward sins, like causeless hatred, are much harder to track down and eradicate and therefore further from repentance; hence the longer exile.

Fasting is a sign of contrition, and helps us to reflect on what we can do to correct these failings which are still with us to the present day. It is also an exercise in self-control, a factor which is essential to any plan for self-improvement.

(4) Minor fasts

The Fast of Esther on the 13th of Adar is of post-Talmudic origin. It commemorates the fast of the Jews before their battle with the anti-Semitic hordes of Persia as described in the scroll of Esther (see chapter 51(2)).

The Fast of the First-born on Erev Pesaḥ has its origin in custom. It is customary to set it aside by participating in a mitzva meal, e.g., the meal at the completion of a tractate of the Talmud (*siyum*).

♦ *Halacha*
◇ *The Fast of the ninth of Av (*Tish'a Be'Av) *is the most stringent of these fasts, and must be observed from evening to evening, and with restrictions on washing, etc.*

exactly as on Yom Kippur (see chapter 42).

◊ *During the "Three Weeks" from the 17th of Tammuz to the 9th of Av certain aspects of mourning are customary: no music, no weddings, no trimming of hair. During the "Nine Days," the 1st — the 9th of Av, one may not partake of meat or wine, except on Shabbat, and no laundry may be done (unless essential). (Sephardim keep these restrictions only in the week in which Tish'a Be'Av falls.)*

◊ *The other fasts are kept only from dawn to dusk and there are no restrictions other than abstention from eating and drinking.*

53. The Calendar

LUNAR/SOLAR CALENDAR/ROSH HODESH (NEW MOON)

This month [Nissan, the month of Spring] shall be the beginning of the months; it shall be the first of the months of the year.
— EXODUS 12:2

Observe the month of Spring and keep the Pesah...for it was in the month of Spring that God brought you out of Egypt — in the night.
— DEUTERONOMY 16:1

You shall celebrate the Feast of Weeks at the beginning of the wheat harvest and the Feast of Ingathering at the turn of the year.
— EXODUS 34:22

(1) Lunar and solar calendars

The calendar of the Torah is basically a lunar one. The months referred to in the Torah are always lunar months. The Torah wants us to be aware of the waxing and waning of the moon, which mirror the ups and downs of Israel's spiritual life and its constant power of self-renewal.

On the other hand the Torah insists that its Festivals shall be attuned also to the rhythms of the solar year. Pesah must always fall in the spring and Succot in the fall.

Since the solar year is almost eleven days longer than twelve lunar months, some adjustment must be made to keep the two calendars in step. This is achieved by inserting an extra month, Adar I, (between Shevat and Adar II) seven times in each nineteen-year cycle. These leap years thus have thirteen months. (See Table 8.) This adjustment, which is correct to less than half a day per century, ensures that the first day of Pesah never falls before the vernal equinox and the first day of Succot never before the autumnal equinox.

It is remarkable that this calendar, which was planned

and put into operation in the 4th century C.E., has been operating for over 1600 years without needing adjustment.

(2) Two new years

We celebrate our New Year in the fall — on the first of Tishrei. This is when the year changes from 5751 to 5752 and so on. However the Torah tells us to count our months from Nissan — the month of our liberation from Egypt, in the spring. God is telling us that the Exodus from Egypt marked a new epoch. In Nissan the world is full of promise. Plants are putting out their first shoots, birds are building nests, the vigor of spring is in our veins. It was in this month that the people of Israel marched into history, bearing the promise of the world's salvation. By counting the months from Nissan the Torah reminds us continually of this optimistic beginning. On this scale Tishrei is the seventh month. If Nissan is the month of promise, Tishrei is the month of judgment. This is the turn of the agricultural year. The harvest is already in; we can judge its quality. It is also the time for judging our spiritual harvest.

(3) Concern for the housewife

Besides the main goal of ensuring the incidence of Pesah in the spring, the calendar also has other constraints. One of these is to ensure that Yom Kippur should never fall immediately before or after Shabbat. On neither of these days is it permitted to prepare food, and the Rabbis considered it too onerous on the housewife to have to go forty-eight hours without being able to prepare fresh food for the family.

(4) Two days Yom Tov

Before the 4th century C.E. the beginning of each new month (known as *Rosh Ḥodesh*) and thus the Festivals, were fixed on the basis of eye-witness evidence. This provided an opportunity for the people of Israel to participate personally in fixing the time of their "rendezvous" with the Almighty. Though God had fixed the *date* in the month, e.g., the 15th day of Tishrei for the start of Succot, it was

---

Table 8
THE JEWISH CALENDAR

---

1. THE MONTHS OF THE YEAR
The lunar months which comprise the Jewish year are as follows:

SEASON	MONTH	DAYS	SEASON	MONTH	DAYS
FALL	Tishrei	30[1]	SPRING	Nissan	30
	Marḥeshvan	29 or 30[2]		Iyar	29
	Kislev	29 or 30[2]		Sivan	30
WINTER	Tevet	29	SUMMER	Tammuz	29
	Shevat	30		Av	30
	Adar	29[3]		Ellul	29

[1] In a normal year the number of days in the month alternate between 30 and 29. This is because the length of a lunar month is (approx.) 29.5 days.

[2] In some years, according to a fixed scheme, the length of these two months varies as indicated. This is to take care of the fact that the lunar month is slightly longer than 29.5 days (see below).

[3] In a leap year an extra month, Adar 1, is inserted here. We then have: Adar 1 — 30 days; Adar 2 — 29 days.

2. RECONCILIATION OF LUNAR AND SOLAR CYCLES
As stated in the text, this is effected by having 7 leap years in each cycle of 19 years. The precise figures are as follows:

Solar year = 365.242 days. Lunar month = 29.5306 days.
12 lunar months = 12 × 29.5306 = 354.367 days.
Deficit = 365.242 — 354.367 = 10.875 days.
In 19 years this deficit = 19 × 10.875 = *206.63* days
Seven intercalated months of 29.53 days each = *206.71* days.

3. THE 19-YEAR CYCLE AND HOW TO KNOW IN ADVANCE WHICH YEARS ARE LEAP YEARS
Standard pattern of 19-year cycle (leap years in bold):

1 2 **3** 4 5 **6** 7 8 9 **11** 12 13 **14** 15 16 **17** 18 **19**

Since 302 × 19 = 5738, it follows that the current cycle (cycle 303) extends from 5739 to 5757. According to the standard pattern therefore the leap years in the cycle are:
5739 5740 **5741** 5742 5743 **5744** 5745 **5746** 5747 5748 **5749** 5750 5751 **5752** 5753 5754 **5755** 5756 **5757**

Israel who fixed the *day* from which the fifteen days were counted. This was not done until the evidence of eye-witnesses had been accepted by the Sanhedrin. Jews who lived in the Diaspora, far from Eretz Yisrael, not knowing the precise day of *Rosh Hodesh*, had to observe two days of Yom Tov to be on the safe side. To commemorate this, Diaspora Jews to this day keep two days Yom Tov. In Eretz Yisrael this applies only on Rosh Hashana which falls on *Rosh Hodesh* itself. (See chapters 42(5) and 43(5).)

(5) Rosh Hodesh and the natural environment

For the city dweller the waxing and waning of the moon seems largely irrelevant. For the Torah Jew, however, this is not so. The Torah directs our attention to the moment when the new moon reappears and declares that day a semi-holiday — *Rosh Hodesh* — on which partial Hallel is said and special praises sung to the Almighty. (See chapter 65(8).)

The Torah wishes us to be attuned to the rhythms of our natural environment.

Symbolically too, as we mentioned above, the renewal of the moon has significance for our spiritual development. It reminds us that even after one has sunk to the very border of oblivion, regeneration is still possible. That subconscious feeling of optimism — "a new month is starting, a new beginning can be made" — is extremely valuable in the eyes of the Torah.

In many cities in Israel, soon after the beginning of the Jewish month, one may see little knots of people in the forecourt of a synagogue or in the street, dancing sedately in a tight circle, and singing praises to God for the gift of the new moon. They are concluding the service of *birkat levana* — the Blessing over the new Moon. This is how Torah Jews keep themselves aware of the beauty that is found in the natural environment.

54. Circumcision (Brit Mila)

I am God Almighty: walk before Me and be whole...
I will establish My covenant with you [Abraham] and your
descendants after you forever: that I will be your God [and
theirs]. And I will give them...all the Land of Canaan as an
everlasting possession...
And you shall keep My Covenant, and your descendants after
you throughout their generations...Every male among you shall
be circumcised...when he is eight days old. This is the sign of the
covenant.
— GENESIS 17:1,7-12

(1) Being whole

Being whole does not mean being perfect. Nobody is perfect. It means being single-minded — wholehearted. If one
is tired of being pulled this way and that by his inner urges
and ardently desires to have a single aim and pursue it
with all his heart — then he is a candidate for a covenant
with God.

The people of Israel are the people of the covenant. We
have undertaken to lead the world in single-hearted devotion to God's purposes. Our national purpose is to further
God's universal purpose.

As may be seen from the verses which head this chapter,
it was for this purpose that we were given Eretz Yisrael —
to show how every aspect of a society and a civilization can
be built up on this wholesome basis.

In the course of exile many of our people have lost this
sense of purpose and are driven hither and thither on the
currents of Western civilization. However admirable and
even glorious, this civilization may be in many respects, in
others it falls absurdly short of the standards set by the
Torah. Yet however estranged they may have become from
the *content* of the covenant — through circumstances we

228

understand, though deplore — they have shown very few signs of giving up the *sign* of the covenant, except where this has been virtually a physical impossibility, such as in Soviet Russia. It seems that God's words to Abraham, "a covenant with you and your children after you forever" still reverberate throughout the generations.

(2) The sign of the covenant

As we noted in chapters 22-23, the sexual drive is one of the most potent in human affairs. Wrongly directed, it has the power to wreck individuals, families and whole societies. Used positively, in accordance with the Torah's guidelines, it is the great builder of families and societies.

It can be readily understood why the Torah places the seal of its covenant on the male sexual organ. The proper use of this power is the key to Torah civilization.

The mitzva of *mila* — circumcision — is to remove the foreskin, which is called in the Torah *"orla."* We met this term previously, in chapter 14, in connection with the young fruit tree whose fruit is *"orla"* — restricted — for the first three years.

Man is naturally selfish; a "taker" and not a "giver." We are created takers and our task is to to transform ourselves into givers. In man's natural state, without the benefit of Torah, it is only natural that the power of sex, that most potent of drives, will be directed to the limited ends of self-gratification. That is why the male sexual organ is, in nature, covered by an *orla*. Left to itself its use is restricted, hemmed in, limited — for selfish ends only.

In Jewish life we are to rid ourselves of this limitation. We are to use our sexual urge for the infinitely wider and greater ends of the Torah — the founding and cementing of a Jewish marriage and a Jewish family, which is a stake in eternity.

This is the symbolism of circumcision.

(3) Living life to the full

When the Torah was given we were warned not to copy the sexual mores of the surrounding cultures. We now live in a time when very similar warnings need to be given. In the so-called civilized world in which we live, the number of divorces and broken homes is growing by leaps and bounds. One would think that civilization would lead to happiness and satisfaction, but we see this is not the case. Circumcision bids us stand back and consider how ludicrous this is. It teaches us that permissiveness — that is, selfishness — in sex, actually restricts our lives and our happiness, while Torah goals for sex open up for us infinite horizons of creative giving.

We were given this land of Israel to build a Torah civilization, to show the world how life can be lived to the full, not to copy the world's failures.

(4) The eighth day

Mila is performed on the eighth day after birth. We have already referred to the significance of the eighth day (chapter 47(2)).

The number eight in Torah symbolism always alludes to the spiritual world which is above and beyond the mundane. Control over these very powerful instincts can be achieved only with the aid of that realm which is above nature and from which the Torah itself derives.

Circumcision is performed in infancy. No conscious decision is present; none is needed. The very fact that this baby has been born into the Jewish nation means that he has the potential for a positive, unselfish Jewish life. The seal of the covenant on his flesh pledges him to use all his powers for the holy ends of his Creator, for good and for giving in the widest sense.

(5) Capacity for change

The mitzva of circumcision which involves making a change in our bodies hints at a very basic principle of Torah — that we are here to change ourselves morally and spiritually. We are born with many diverse powers, qualities and tendencies, but our time here has been wasted if we have not even tried to change them to conform to the purposes for which we were created. The *brit mila* symbolizes this capacity for change.

GOD'S WORKS AND MAN'S WORKS

The Romans strongly objected to circumcision. "This is the body that the gods have given you," they said. "It is impious to change it."

Tyrannus Rufus, the Roman governor of Judea in the 2nd century C.E., once tried to lay a trap for Rabbi Akiva on this point.

"Which would you say were better, Rabbi," he asked innocently, "God's works or man's works?"

Seeing through the trick Rabbi Akiva replied immediately: "Man's works."

Somewhat taken aback Rufus asked, "But Rabbi, how can you say such a thing? Surely God's works are much greater?"

Excusing himself, Rabbi Akiva went out and returned in a moment holding in one hand some ears of grain and in the other a cream cake.

"Well, which do you want, Your Excellency?" teased Rabbi Akiva. "These [the ears] are God's work and this [the cake] is man's!"

"I wanted to ask you," said Rufus, "if your God likes people to be circumcised why doesn't He arrange for them to be born circumcised in the first place?"

"I knew that's what you wanted to ask me," said Rabbi Akiva. "I've already given you the answer. God creates us in an unfinished state, like the ears of grain, so that we can work on ourselves in this world. 'Mitzvot were given to Israel so that we can refine our characters.'"

♦ *Halacha*

◇ *If the 8th day falls on Shabbat or a Festival the* brit milah *is performed on the Shabbat or the Festival.*

◇ *If the baby is not completely healthy, the* brit *is postponed until he is. A postponed* brit *is never performed on Shabbat.*

◇ *It is the father's duty to procure a* mohel *(accredited practitioner of circumcision) to carry out the circumcision.*

◇ *If this has not been done, the duty devolves upon the person himself, as soon as he is liable to mitzvot (at age 13).*

55. Tefillin

You shall tell your son...it was for this that God acted for me when I went out of Egypt. It shall be a sign for you above your forearm and a memorial between your eyes, so that the Torah of God shall be in your mouth... — EXODUS 12:8-9

These words... shall be on your heart, and you shall teach them to your children...and bind them as a sign above your forearm and as ornaments between your eyes.
— DEUTERONOMY 6:6-8

Keep My mitzvot and live,
[Guard] My Torah like the apple of your eye.
Bind them on your fingers,
Write them on the tablet of your heart. — PROVERBS 7:2-3

(1) Binding Torah to oneself

"To bind Torah to oneself" in the Hebrew idiom is a metaphor for absorbing it and identifying with it completely. In this mitzva we are asked to act out this metaphor in real life. We are to take selected passages from the Torah which have been carefully handwritten on parchment, pack them into leather receptacles of a cubical shape, and strap them to our arm and head and wear them during the morning service. (Originally the mitzva was to wear them all day, so that the spirit of Torah could guide all our everyday occupations. In later generations for various reasons it was not found possible to do this.) Each of these is called a *tefilla* (plural: *tefillin*) from the Hebrew root *pallal*, "think," because while wearing them we must think of them continually. (*Tefilla* also means "prayer" — see chapter 65.)

Each of the regulations regarding *tefillin* has great symbolic significance. We shall try to elucidate some of them in this section.

(2) The four parshiyot (Torah passages)

The four sections which are inserted in the *tefillin* are the four passages in which the mitzva of *tefillin* occurs in the Torah. These are:

> 1. *Kadesh* ("sanctify...") (Exodus 13:1-10). The first-born is dedicated to God. Remember the Exodus!
> 2. *Ve-haya ki yeviacha* ("when He brings you...") (Exodus 13:11-16). Pharaoh misused his power. We will use ours for mitzvot.
> 3. *Shema'* ("Listen, Israel...") (Deuteronomy 6:4-9). One God means total commitment. (See chapter 43.)
> 4. *Vehaya im shamo'a* ("If you listen...") (Deuteronomy 11:13-21). Our national destiny depends on how we carry out this task.

In these four *parshiyot*, therefore, we are binding to ourselves the whole Torah in miniature.

(3) Head and arm

The Oral Law teaches us that the "hand" *tefilla* is to be bound to the left arm at the biceps (the muscle that controls our hand, i.e., our action), while the *tefillin* "between the eyes" are to be positioned just above the forehead (opposite the frontal lobe of the brain which controls vision, and seems to be involved in decision making). The point seems pretty clear: the Torah is to control both our decision making (head) and the way we carry out our decisions in practice (arm).

If the head *tefillin* (*shel rosh*) represent theory and the hand *tefillin* (*shel yad*) represent practice, we can understand why we must always put on the *shel yad* before the *shel rosh* and take off the *shel rosh* before the *shel yad*. In Torah Judaism practice takes precedence over theory. We do first even if we understand only later. We know from experience that the Torah way is good, even if we don't yet understand how it works. The head *tefilla* has four compartments (visible from the outside — see figure 1). One *parasha* is inserted in each. The arm *tefilla* has only one compartment in which all four *parshiyot* are inserted, written on one parchment. In thought we have to analyze; to direct our mind to each of the basic ideas of the *parshiyot* separately. But as motive power for our action they must all work as one.

The Torah chooses the "weaker" arm as the vehicle for its lesson so that the act of binding may be done by the stronger hand.

(4) The battim (receptacles or "houses" for the parshiyot)

(a) *Material.* The *battim* (singular: *bayit*) are made of leather from the skin of an animal permitted to be used for food, generally lamb or calf. The material of the *tefillin* must in principle be "edible." The hint is that we have to "absorb" the message of the *tefillin* into our system: make it part of our constitution. The same applies to the straps, to the parchment on which the *parshiyot* are written and the sinews which are used to sew up the *battim* and tie up the *parshiyot*: they must all be from *kosher* animals (see chapter 25).

Intention plays a great part in everything that has to do with *tefillin*. The very leather from which they are made must be tanned for the express purpose of the mitzva of *tefillin*. Symbols must be *deliberate* and not haphazard.

(b) *Shape.* Like the altar in the Holy Temple, the *tefillin* must be precisely square. The rectangular form represents human creative ability. (We rarely or never find rectangles in the non-human organic world; there the circular form is the rule.)

Again like the altar, the *tefillin* are provided with a base. This means that our commitment to God must be firmly based on a rational appreciation of the goals of Torah.

Molded on each side of the *bayit* of the head tefillin is the letter *shin*, which is the initial letter of God's name *Shaddai* — the Almighty. The *shin* on the left has four arms instead of the usual three. The three arms of the *shin* hint at Abraham, Isaac and Jacob, the three Fathers of our nation, who started us on our historic journey. The fourth arm hints at David, whose descendant, the Mashiaḥ, will complete the process. The *tefillin*, as it were, mediate between the promise and the fulfillment of our destiny.

Figure 2
TEFILLIN

HEAD TEFILLIN

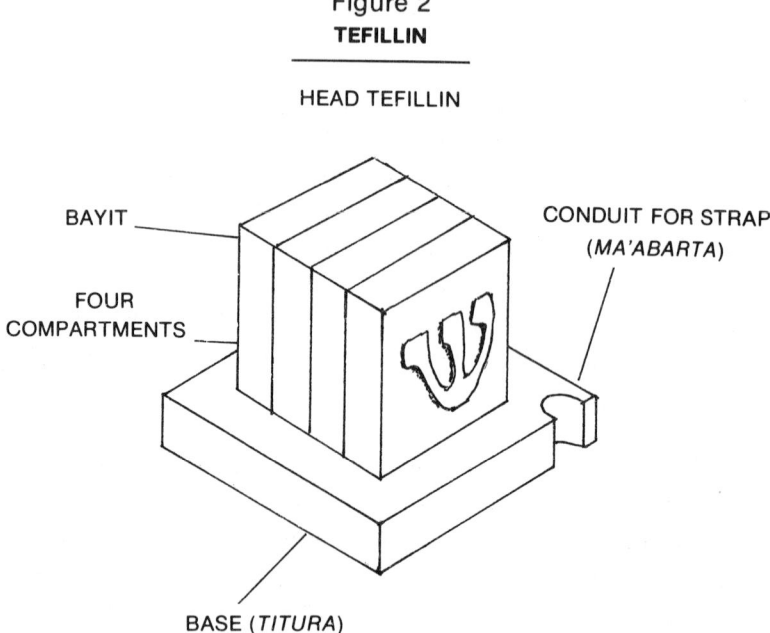

BASE (*TITURA*)

(c) *Straps.* Binding the *tefillin* to ourselves symbolizes our attachment to God. It tells us that the only way to bind oneself to the Almighty is to bind oneself to the mitzvot of the Torah.

(d) *Blackness*. The straps of the *tefillin* must be black on the outside and the *battim* themselves should also be black. It is thought that the meaning resides in the fact that black absorbs all the light that falls on it. *Tefillin* must absorb the lights of the world, convert them into Torah, and convey them to the wearer's mind and body. But this absorbing need not be a merely passive process.

ABSORBING AND RADIATING

Elia Meir Flesch, a captain in the Israeli Air Force, was the innovative genius behind many electro-optical devices which enriched the facilities of Israeli Intelligence. He was utterly devoted to his duties and equally devoted to Torah learning. A *daf ha-yomi* fan, determined to complete the Talmud at the rate of one folio per day (see chapter 65(9)(end)), he studied avidly with the aid of cassettes during the two hours he spent daily traveling to and from his laboratory. An overdose of radiation incurred during his duties ended his life in 1989 at a tragically young age. At the *shiva* a young rabbi well-known in Jerusalem presented himself as a pupil of the deceased. "But Elia Meir never taught in a yeshiva," said his widow. "We always traveled in the same bus," said the visitor. "His absolute devotion to his learning and his beaming face when he finished his *daf*, inspired me to do the same. He was absorbing Torah, but he was radiating Torah at the same time."

56. Washing the Hands

*"You shall sanctify yourselves and become holy" (Leviticus
20:7). — This refers to the washing of the hands.*

— TB BERACHOT 53b

The symbolic washing of the hands is one of the rabbinical
commandments.

(1) A life of service

Each morning before commencing his service in the Temple, each Kohen had to let water run over his hands and
feet. This symbolic washing is a requirement of the Torah
and without it the Kohen's service is invalid (Exodus 30:19-
20).

Every Jew is engaged in Divine service throughout his
everyday life, and the Rabbis ordained symbolic hand-
washing on various occasions in order to remind us of this
fact. On other occasions washing the hands is required for
hygienic reasons. The main occasions are these:

For symbolic reasons:

1. On getting up in the morning.
2. After attending a funeral or visiting a cemetery.
3. After union with spouse.

In these cases one should pour water three times over
each hand alternately. The Rabbis hint that a psychological factor is involved here. It may be that a certain degree
of disorientation is present and the orderly pouring of
water in the way described helps one to reassert conscious
control.

4. Before eating a main meal (i.e., with bread).

The Rabbis say that a Jew's table is like the altar in God's Temple and his eating is like the Temple service. The symbolic washing raises our eating into the realm of truly Jewish activity and dedicates it to the pure purposes of the One God. See paragraph (3).

In cases 1. and 4. the washing is accompanied by a *beracha*. (See chapter 65(2)-(3).)

For hygienic reasons:

1. After going to the toilet. (This is followed by a blessing in which we thank God for the wonders of the human body.)
2. After touching any part of the body which is usually covered.
3. After cutting one's hair or paring one's nails.

In these cases normal cleansing is sufficient.

♦ *Halacha*

◊ *Washing one's hands for a meal with bread has special requirements. The Rabbis compared our meal to the partaking of holy food by the Kohanim and special preparation and cleansing is required.*

◊ *The water must be poured on the hands from a vessel, once on each hand.*

◊ *The washing should extend to the wrist, and if possible a full measure — at least a cupful — should be poured over each hand. If water is scarce, one third of a cup is sufficient for* both *hands.*

AT WHOSE COST?

Rabbi Yisrael Salanter, the founder of the *mussar* (ethical) movement in 19th-century Lithuania, was once staying with some of his students at the house of a friend. They were surprised to see that when he washed his hands for the meal Rabbi Yisrael used the smallest quantity of water permissible rather than the "full measure" recommended. When they queried this, he replied, "You apparently don't see what I see."

"What don't we see?"

"Who brings the water supply into this house? I noticed that it's brought in by a 12-year-old girl. She fills the pails from the pump in the courtyard and carries them in on her own. So the more water we use for our mitzva, the more work we make for that poor child. I prefer to do mitzvot at my own expense, not when it's going to be at the expense of someone else."

(2) A note on Torah symbolism

It should be noted that the requirements for washing the hands are the direct opposite of the requirements for immersion in a *mikveh*. For washing the hands the water must reach the hands by an act of pouring from a vessel. In the case of *mikveh*, however, as we saw in chapter 23(6), the water must reach the pool naturally, not by pipe, vessel or any artificial means whatsoever. The reason is not far to seek. Immersion in the *mikveh* takes us "out of this world." For a brief moment we sink, as it were, beneath the primeval waters of creation and emerge "newly created" and pure. In the washing of the hands, however, the emphasis is on our human conscious decision to dedicate our eating to the service of God. This demands an act which belongs to the realm of human activity and human personality. The water must therefore be poured directly from a vessel and by human effort.

(3) The concept of a Torah meal

In Torah life, the meal is the first step to the ennoblement of man. This is why the table becomes an altar. If we eat only for pleasure, to tickle our palate or to fill our stomach, then our eating is not yet purely human. And so it is with every human function, if the allurement of pleasure alone attracts us.

If however we eat only so much as we need, with the intention of strengthening ourselves for a life pleasing to God, then our eating is truly human and part of our divine service. And so with every "animal" function, if we perform it with such an attitude, and in such a manner. The symbolic act of washing our hands for a meal encourages this attitude.

57. Tzitzit

*They shall put fringes at the corners of their garments...and
with the fringe of each corner they shall put a thread of
blue...So that you shall remember all the commandments of
GOD and do them, so that you will not go astray after your
heart and eyes...I am GOD Who brought you out of Egypt to
be your God.*
                                        — NUMBERS 15:37-41

You shall make cords...on the four corners of your clothing...
                                        — DEUTERONOMY 22:12

(1) Clothes and personality

We have all experienced the psychological effect of clothes.
We all know how clothes can make or break a mood. Above
all, clothes may help to make us conscious of our human
dignity and moral status.

THE PSYCHOLOGY OF CLOTHING

A Swiss girl met an African student in London and
married him. He turned out to be king of a tribe in
Malawi, and when they went home she found herself the queen. She noted that the women of the
tribe were listless and indifferent, almost animal-
like in their lethargy. They wore hardly any clothes.
She ordered bales of colorful print fabric. When
dressed in this, an amazing change came over the
women. They became lively, interested, cheerful
and active. Their humanity blossomed.

(2) Clothing that grows

The origin of clothing as described by the Torah was the
need to cover the shame of the first human beings, who had
failed in the task set them by the Almighty (Genesis 3:7-

242

11,21). The sense of shame is precious; it is the voice of God calling us to rise above our selfish, animal desires. One of the functions of clothing is to remind us of our higher human calling.

This applies to all human beings. Why does the Torah ask us, as Jews, to affix fringes (*tzitzit*) to the corners of our garment? The Torah itself gives us the answer. "So that we shall remember *all* the mitzvot with which God has entrusted us." How does it do this? It is reasonable to assume that just as *mila* on our bodies, *tefillin* on our head and arm, *mezuza* on our doorpost, are there to sanctify our body, head, arm and home and direct them to their proper purpose, so *tzitzit* are to sanctify our clothing in the same way. The word *tzitzit* also conveys the sense of growing, sprouting. *Tzitz* means "blossom." In other words, the Torah wants our clothing to blossom forth and bear spiritual fruit.

Clothes admonish every human being: Be human. You are much, much more than a cultured ape. Use your Divine gift of free will to rise to the heights of your moral potential.

The *tzitzit* on our clothes tell the Jews: Let the clothing you wear as a human being blossom into a full commitment to your additional calling as a Jew.

(3) Bound and free

If we examine the *tzitzit* more carefully we will see that they each consist of four threads which are inserted through a hole in the corner of the garment and doubled over to form eight. The two sets of four are knotted together and bound tightly by winding one of the threads around the other seven. (See figure 3.) The bound part should not exceed one-third of the whole, so that two-thirds of the *tzitzit* fall free.

We already know that "six" represents the physical

world and "seven" the spiritual dimension of mind and free will (chapter 41(1)). The number "eight," as we saw in connection with Shavuot and Shemini Atzeret, symbolizes that spiritual dimension which is higher than the human mind — the Divine source of the Torah (chapters 43(2) and 47(2). So the tight winding of the eighth thread around the other seven graphically illustrates the function of the mitzvot, which exercise their beneficent control over our physical and mental activities.

But two-thirds of the *tzitzit* hang free. The restrictions of the Torah serve to set us on the right path. There is much which is left to our individual decision. Within the guidelines laid down by the Torah we have free scope to develop our potentialities in the way that best suits us. The "free" is double the "bound."

Figure 3
TZITZIT

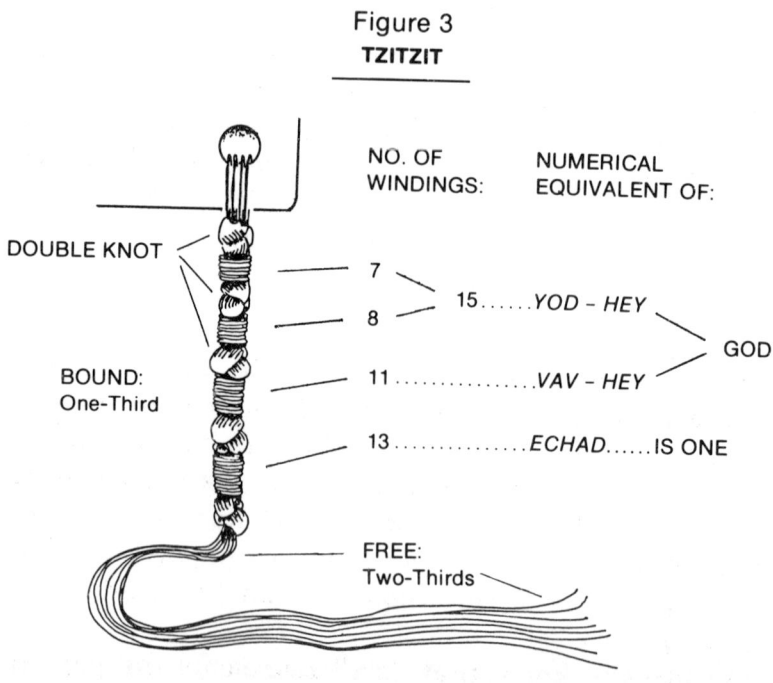

Table 9
THE SYSTEM OF GEMATRIA

Every Hebrew letter has a numerical value in accordance with its order in the aleph-bet. This system is called *gematria*.

The values are as follows:

1 : א	10 : י	100 : ק
2 : ב	20 : כ	200 : ר
3 : ג	30 : ל	300 : ש
4 : ד	40 : מ	400 : ת
5 : ה	50 : נ	
6 : ו	60 : ס	
7 : ז	70 : ע	
8 : ח	80 : פ	
9 : ט	90 : צ	

Note: 11 is written י״א; 12 — י״ב; 13 — י״ג; 21 — כ״א and so on.
However 15 is written ט״ו (9 + 6) and 16 — ט״ז (9 + 7) because the alternatives resemble the Divine Name.

(4) The sky-blue thread

The Torah requires that this eighth thread shall be dyed *techelet*. This is the blue dye that was used in the vestments of the High Priest (Exodus 28:31), and resembles the color of the oceans and the sky. Things at the limit of our horizon, such as a distant mountain range, also look blue. This color therefore aptly symbolizes the spiritual dimension at the very limits of our mind's reach and gives visual reinforcement to the significance of the "eighth."

During the course of time the art of producing *techelet* has been lost. The color could be simulated by other dyes but the Torah insists on *techelet* only. Great efforts are being presently made in Israel to rediscover *techelet*. But until its identity is definitely established we make do with eight white threads. However the very absence of *techelet* from our *tzitzit* proclaims that we can accomplish our Jewish mission only with authentic Torah and mitzvot and not with substitutes or simulations. The *tzitzit* with its eighth thread, whether having the *techelet* color or waiting for it, stamps us as "men of a holy calling" (see chapter 26) and as members of "the kingdom of priests and the holy nation" — our description at the giving of the Torah. (For some centuries now, a numerical system of windings conveys the idea that it is the One and Only God to whom our life is dedicated. See figure 3. This is based on the system of *gematria* — the numerical values of the Hebrew letters. See Table 9.)

(5) Four corners

We are commanded to place the *tzitzit* on the four corners of our garment, pointing to the "four corners of the earth." This may well serve to remind us that our Jewish calling is not for ourselves alone but for the benefit of all mankind.

58. Covering the Head

Rav Huna ...never went four cubits with his head uncovered.
He said, "The Divine Presence is above my head."
— TB KIDDUSHIN 31a

One should not go four cubits with one's head uncovered.
— SHULHAN ARUCH, ORAH HAYIM, 2:6

(1) A universal custom

Starting in Talmudic times as an act of exceptional piety, it has become an almost universal custom for men and boys loyal to Torah to cover their heads at all times, and particularly in holy places and under an open sky. In fact the symbol of the *kippa* (head-covering) above all else has become the outward sign of loyalty to Torah.

Perhaps the symbolism expresses this idea: Just as modesty demands that we cover up everything animal-like in our body before other people, so the most human part of our body — namely, our head — also has to be covered before God, as a sign of human modesty towards His Divine greatness. Be that as it may, the true sign of loyalty to God and His Torah will always be, not the symbol, but the actual behavior of those who bear the banner of Torah.

(2) Married women

Married women cover their hair in public for a different reason. This has been discussed earlier, in chapter 22(2).

59. Mezuza

And you shall write them [the words of the Torah] upon the doorposts of your house and inside your gates.

— DEUTERONOMY 6:9; 11:21

(1) The mitzva

The heart of this mitzva is a little parchment scroll on which a scribe has carefully written two passages of the Torah. This scroll is to be affixed to the doorpost of the entrance of every Jewish house and of every room in the house. "House" includes workplace, store, garage and any building or room devoted to human activity.

The two passages are those in which the mitzva of *mezuza* appears:

1. *Shema*: the unity of God and our total commitment to His purposes;

2. *Vehaya im shamoa'*: the destiny of Israel depends on its loyalty to the Torah.

These are identical with two of the passages in *tefillin* — see chapter 55(2).

(2) The symbolism

The symbolism here is clear enough. We are to hallow our homes and workplaces as places where God is ever present and where His purposes are pursued.

Shema' on the doorpost of the Jewish house proclaims that this home will be filled with the spirit of dedication to God and that in it the young generation will be brought up to honor the Torah and keep its mitzvot. At the entrance to factory and store it declares that the work done here and the human relations fostered here will be in accordance with the precepts and principles of the Torah.

Vehaya im shamoa' teaches us to be aware that all that happens to us in our homes and work comes from God and is related to our spiritual endeavors. Good fortune will not turn our heads, misfortune will not sway us. Whatever the circumstances, our task remains the same.

Mezuza proclaims that the Temple of the Torah is wherever Jewish people live or work.

(3) The encounter

This mitzva ensures that whenever we enter or leave our house we encounter God's name. This should prompt us to think of His love and to realize that everything in the world is temporary except the service of God, which, being spiritual, lasts forever and in all eternity.

60. Immersion of Vessels

[Vessels of] gold, silver, copper, iron, tin or lead [taken from Midian] — if they have been used with fire, they shall be cleansed by fire; but in addition they must by purified by [immersion in] water...
— NUMBERS 31:22-23

When one acquires from a non-Jew vessels previously used for cooking or for use with hot food, one must first purge them of all remaining traces of non-*kosher* food. This is done by bringing them in contact with fire or boiling water, and the process is known as "kashering."

In addition, before vessels of non-Jewish manufacture or ownership can be used, they require immersion in a *mikveh* (see chapter 23(6)). This is a symbolic act marking their entry into a higher function — to serve the needs of a Jewish family.

This mitzva of immersion primarily applies only to *metal* vessels. (Glass, because of its similarity in some respects to metal, was included in the requirement by the Rabbis at an early date. Later, by custom, glazed porcelain was added.)

We may ask why *metal* vessels were particularly singled out for this requirement. The answer may lie in the fact that the working of metals represented a landmark in the advance of human technology. A metal food vessel therefore may be said to represent advanced technology in the service of man's physical appetite. In the Torah environment, however, the goals are incomparably higher. Both the physical requirements and the technology that serves them are there to serve the goals of the Torah — the sanctification of *all* aspects of life. It may be understood therefore that a symbolic act of "purification" is required before such vessels can enter the service of a Jewish family.

◆ *Halacha*

◇ *The law of immersion applies only to vessels and utensils used in the preparation and consumption of food.*

◇ *The law applies equally to vessels bought second-hand from a non-Jew and to new vessels of non-Jewish manufacture.*

◇ *Metal and glass require immersion, with a* beracha. *Glazed porcelain requires immersion, but no* beracha *is said. Other materials, such as wood or plastic, do not require immersion.*

61. Redemption of the First-born

Sanctify to Me all the first-born...among the children of Israel...They belong to Me. — EXODUS 13:1

All the first-born of your sons you shall redeem. — EXODUS 34:20

(1) Origins

One of the first commandments given to Israel at the time of the Exodus was the sanctification of the first-born.

We had just seen mighty Egypt brought to its knees by the sudden death of its finest and best — its first-born. Our first-born were spared, not because of anything that Israel had done to deserve it but because of the promise of the future. When Israel becomes the nation of God and receives from His hands their own land and state, they pledge not to use their power for injustice and oppression like the Egyptians but to further the loving purposes of God.

(2) The mitzva

Every time a Jewish family is blessed with a first-born son to carry its name into the future, this promise is remembered. The father must "redeem" his son by giving to a *Kohen* — as God's representative — five shekels weight (about 2.5 ounces) of fine silver, or its equivalent.

By this act we remember that the first-born of every Jewish family should have been a Kohen. Because of a certain unfortunate event in our history (see Exodus 32), the priesthood was restricted to one family of the tribe of Levi — the descendants of Aaron. But the potential of priesthood remains, at least in theory, in the first-born of every family, and the symbolic act of redemption brings this home to us.

By this act, too, the whole family is sanctified. The father and mother undertake to regard their son — and any further sons and daughters entrusted to them — as sacred charges, to be brought up not for selfish or materialistic ends but to be worthy sons and daughters of Israel.

Numbers in mitzvot are always meaningful. Why "five" shekels? In the number symbolism of Torah "ten" stands for perfection and "five" — the striving for perfection. The five shekels prescribed for this redemption clearly articulate the aim of every Jewish individual and every Jewish family. None of us can *be* perfect, but each of us can *strive* for perfection. This in fact summarizes the goal of the whole Torah.

◆ *Halacha*

◇ *The time for this mitzva is when the baby is 30 days old.*

◇ *If the mitzva was not done it may be done at any later time. If the father is not there it may be done by the son himself after he is* bar mitzva *(13 years old).*

◇ *It is customary to have a festive meal at the time of the redemption.*

62. Shevi'it (The Seventh Year)

You shall not pervert justice...Keep far from falsehood...Do not oppress a stranger: you know the feelings of a stranger: you were yourselves strangers in Egypt. You shall sow your land and gather its harvest for six years; in the seventh year you shall leave it fallow and abandon your rights to it. The poor of your people shall enjoy it, and what they leave shall be eaten by the wild animals. The same applies to your vines and olive trees.
— EXODUS 23:6,7,9-11

When you enter the land which I am giving you, the land shall celebrate a Sabbath to God. You can sow your field for six years...But in the seventh year the earth shall have a Sabbath of rest for God...You shall not sow your field nor tend your vines...What grows during this Sabbath of the land shall be for you to enjoy...together with your servants and laborers. And also the animals...in your land shall be able to eat its produce.

If you say, what will we eat in the seventh year?...I will command my blessing in the sixth year and it will produce sufficient for three years.
— LEVITICUS 25:2-4,6-7,20-21

At the end of seven years...every creditor shall relinquish all claims to money owed to him by his brother; a moratorium (shemitta) has been declared by God.
— DEUTERONOMY 15:1-2

(1) An amazing law

In ancient times when Israel's main occupation was agriculture, this was certainly an amazing piece of legislation unparalleled in any other legislative system in history. The holiness of the land and its produce in the seventh year is expressed in three ways:

1. There may be no sowing or plowing, and other agricultural work is severely restricted.

2. The landowner must relinquish ownership for this

year. Access must be given on an equal basis to all who wish to take the produce. The landowner may take home only that which is required for the needs of himself and his family. Wild animals too must be given access to the land, provided they do not damage the trees.

3. The produce may be used for normal enjoyment only. It may not be used for medicinal or industrial purposes, nor may it be stored for trade or destroyed.

True heroism is shown by the landowner who is prepared to see his land lie fallow for a whole year and to stand in line with his laborer for a share in the produce. Heroism — and absolute faith in God and loyalty to His word.

By these laws God wants to give us a year-long practical lesson, once every seven years, to help us realize that "the earth and its fullness belong to God," and we are only His tenants. Our "ownership" is conditional on our using the earth for *His* goals, not our selfish ones. It is clear, therefore, why the Torah associates these laws with justice to the poor and consideration for the stranger. We are all "strangers" in God's world. The insistence that the animals of the wild are to be given access together with human beings emphasizes the importance of every species in the ecological scheme. It also reminds us of the need to have consideration for animals, too, of which we had several examples in the second section of this book.

THE ESSENCE OF HOLINESS

The fact that the "holiness" of the seventh year requires that it be enjoyed in the normal way, that is, by eating and drinking, and not sold for profit, tells us a great deal about the Torah's concept of holiness. The enjoyment of God's bounty in a spirit of thanksgiving and with the underprivileged seated as friends around the table — in the eyes of the Torah this is the essence of holiness.

(2) Shevi'it today

Jewish agriculture in Eretz Yisrael was virtually in abeyance for well over a thousand years, and the full observance of these laws was only a memory. With the revival of Jewish agriculture in modern times and the founding of agricultural settlements by Torah-observant Jews, the full observance of *shevi'it* again became a practical possibility. There is a small but growing band of stalwarts who sacrifice much to keep these laws to the letter. With every seventh year that has passed since the founding of the State, more and more agricultural settlements observe these laws and increasing numbers of individuals are careful to buy only such products as are guaranteed permitted during the year. They already form a significant part of the consumer market.

50,000 ORANGE TREES

Komemiut in the northern Negev is a religious settlement which from the first decided to observe the "Laws of the Land" and particularly the laws of the Seventh Year, in all their ramifications. In the early years of the State the ministry of Agriculture offered to provide an orchard of 50,000 orange saplings to every settlement capable of tending them. Komemiut qualified, and such an acquisition would have made an enormous difference to the struggling *moshav*. But the following year was *shevi'it*. The ministry official presented them with a contract which specified the work which would have to be done each year to nurture the saplings. The *halacha*, laid down more than 1700 years previously, provided that certain of these operations were not essential to the life of the trees and were not permitted during *shevi'it*. The minister of agriculture, impressed by the sincerity of Rabbi

256

Mendelson, the Rav of the *moshav*, agreed — over the protests of his own experts — to delete these clauses in the contract. To the amazement of all except Rav Mendelson the orchard flourished, and indeed turned out to be the best of all the eleven orchards that had been planted at the same time. The miracle of *shevi'it* still works today.

(3) Moratorium on loan payments

Loans were usually taken by the small farmer to tide him over the difficult part of the year and were repaid when the harvest came in. In the seventh year, when there is no harvest (see above, (1)), the Torah provides for all loans to be remitted. This law does not apply to loans registered with the *bet din*, as the court will use its discretion whether or not to insist on repayment.

Nowadays all loans are registered with a *bet din* by means of a document called *prozbul* (Greek: *pros boule* — "before the elders").

◆ *Halacha*
◊ *The observance of the law of* shevi'it *is now well organized in Israel, and it is possible to obtain fruit, vegetables and manufactured products with reliable certification that these laws were complied with.*
◊ *See Bibliography for books and pamphlets in English with details of the observance of this mitzva.*

63. Teruma, Ma'aser and Ḥalla (Separation of Gifts)

(1) In Temple times

The Jewish farmer is described in the Talmud as a man of faith. He places his seeds in the ground and trusts in God to bring them to fruition. But when he has an ample harvest in the barn he tends to feel somewhat differently. He looks back at all the hard work he put in during the year and tends to pride himself on his achievement. To guard against this natural human tendency to forget God when things go well, the Torah is quite lavish with reminders, which for the most part take the form of gifts of various kinds. We shall not be surprised to find that there are in fact *seven* mitzvot connected with the harvest. Each of these bring us into renewed contact with God.

First, *three* for the priest, the Kohen, who represents the highest degree of holiness. They come at the beginning, the middle and the end of the food production process:

1. *The first fruits (bikkurim)*. The fruits or grains we first notice ripening are marked, and later taken up to Jerusalem with much pomp and ceremony. We must keep fresh the excitement of seeing those first buds — the promise of future riches.

2. *The priest's gift (teruma)*. When the harvest is concluded, a first gift is set aside for the local Kohen, to be eaten by him and his family in holiness.

3. *The priest's cake (ḥalla)*. When preparing dough for baking her bread, the housewife sets aside a small cake for the Kohen.

258

Then *two* connected with the Levite, the teacher of Torah:

4. *The first tenth (ma'aser rishon).* When the produce is brought home, one tenth is given to the Levite, who gave up his share in the land in order to teach Torah and help in the Temple.

5. *The Levite's gift (terumat ma'aser).* The Levite in turn gives one-tenth of what he receives to the Kohen.

Finally, *two* for the Israelite:

6. *Second tenth (ma'aser sheni).* A second tenth is set aside from all one's produce to be taken to Jerusalem and enjoyed there by the farmer and his family: to be shared too with "God's family" — the poor, the orphan and the stranger. (See chapter 44(1).) It could also be redeemed for money which is then spent in Jerusalem for the same purposes. This applies in four years of the seven-year agricultural cycle (see Table 10).

7. *The tenth for the poor (ma'aser ani).* This applies in two other years of the seven-year cycle. Instead of taking it to Jerusalem, the second tenth is distributed to the local poor.

By means of these gifts the Torah keeps us continually in contact with God — in soul, in mind and in body, through Kohen, Levite and Israelite.

WHAT THEY TEACH

Taken as a whole, these mitzvot, in the fullness of their original form, teach us:

(a) To recognize God as the Prime Source of all our wealth, expressed as support for His Kohanim — 1,2 and 3.

(b) To think first of those who look after our spiritual

Table 10
THE SEVEN GIFTS

TO WHOM	AT WHAT STAGE	NAME OF GIFT	APPROX. PROPORTION	WHEN GIVEN	PURPOSE
KOHEN					
1. The Kohen	First ripening	*Bikkurim* (first fruits)	1.66%	Every year	Giving the first to God through His Kohanim.
2. The Kohen	Conclusion of harvest	*Teruma* (Priest's gift)	2%	Every year	
3. The Kohen	Preparation of bread	*Hallah* (First of dough)	4%	When baking	
LEVITE					
4. The Levite	When produce brought home	*Ma'aser Rishon* (first tenth)	10%	Every year	Support of Torah teachers
5. Levite to Kohen	On receipt of 4.	*Terumat Ma'aser* (gift from tithe)	10% of 10%	Every year	Levites' gift to God through Kohanim
ISRAELITE					
6. Yourself and family in Jerusalem	When produce brought home	*Ma'aser Sheni* (Second tenth)	9%	Every 1st, 2nd 4th, 5th year	Eating and enjoying in purity
7. The local poor	When produce brought home	*Ma'aser Ani* (Tenth for poor)	9%	Every 3rd, 6th year	Sharing with others

welfare — represented by the tribe of Levi — 4.

(c) To use "holy enjoyment" of our material goods as a means of coming closer to God in His holy city — 6.

(d) To care for our less fortunate brother — 7.

In the land of the Torah, seeds do not grow for the owner of the field alone. Every tree bears its fruits also for those who represent our spiritual calling.

(2) At the present day

Since we have no Temple and only a minority of our people live in the Holy Land, these laws apply today only by rabbinical decree, and for the most part only in symbolical form. (This is so that we shall be familiar with them when all Torah laws are restored with the coming of Mashiaḥ.) In their present form they are widely observed today in Israel by all sections of the Orthodox community.

◆ *Halacha*

◇ *The separation of* teruma, ma'aser, *etc. is now well organized in Israel, and it is possible to buy most fruit, vegetables and manufactured products with reliable certification that these laws were complied with.*

◇ *If these are not available, see Bibliography for books and pamphlets in English explaining how these* mitzvot *are to be observed.*

◇ *Fruits, etc. grown in the Holy Land and exported to other countries are also subject to these laws.*

◇ *Until all the separations have been made the produce is known as* tevel *(mixture) and may not be eaten.*

◇ *The housewife separates a small portion of dough as* ḥalla, *which is then burnt. This applies only if the dough is at least 1.25 kg. (2.75 lbs.) in weight. If it is 2kg. (4.5 lbs.), a blessing is said over the separation.*

GROUP FIVE:
THE INNER LIFE

Mitzvot addressed to our heart and mind

We have traversed the Torah's fourfold program: justice and enrichment in human relations and justice and enrichment for the environment. We now turn inwards.

The inner life envisaged by the Torah is now unfolded before us. In one sense this is the peak achievement of Torah life. In another, it is the springboard for a higher level of justice and enrichment in all our relationships.

64. Torah Study

THE MITZVA TO STUDY TORAH AT EVERY OPPORTUNITY

Listen, Israel, to the laws I tell you today, so that you may learn them and put them into practice. — DEUTERONOMY 5:1

These things which I command you today shall be upon your mind. — DEUTERONOMY 6:6

But the thing is very near to you, in your mouth and in your heart, to do it. — DEUTERONOMY 30:14

How I love your Torah! I speak of it all day. — PSALMS 119:97

Adopt a Torah teacher for yourself and acquire a colleague. — MISHNAH AVOT 1:6

We are told to "keep close to God." But how can one do this? The meaning is: Keep close to the Sages of the Torah. — SIFRE, DEUTERONOMY 11:22

(1) The necessity of Torah study

The first law of the Torah is: Learn Torah. The practice of Torah in all its aspects can flourish only in an atmosphere of knowledge, thought and mental stimulation. This mental stimulus, which is a basic tool of Torah civilization, is achieved by Torah study. Learning Torah is an essential element in the Torah environment.

> "Everyone is obliged to study the Torah, whether rich or poor, healthy or sick, young or advanced in age. Even the poor man who begs at the door; even the head of a family who works to provide a livelihood for himself and his dependents, must set aside fixed periods by day and night to study the Torah. How long must one go on studying? Until the day of one's death."
>
> MAIMONIDES

We do not think there ever has been a civilization like this, in which studying is a religious obligation at all levels of the population. Other civilizations have thought it best

265

to keep the populace in ignorance. But for the realization of the Torah's goals Torah study on the widest possible scale is essential.

(2) A mystery?

Learning Torah aims at more than the accumulation of knowledge. This is indeed important, but it is not everything. Learning Torah has incalculable effects on one's character too. Learning provides the incentive to live better — to perform better. It helps us to internalize Torah values. It has the power to change a person, a family, a society. The extraordinary effect of Torah learning is a fact of experience, but the mechanism by which it is achieved remains something of a mystery. (But see paragraph (4).)

THE FOREST

"Mitzva is a lamp but Torah is light itself" (Proverbs 6:23).

This is a parable of the human predicament.

A human being in this world resembles a traveler in a dense forest on a moonless night, without a flashlight. He can't see even two paces in front of him. His next step might plunge him into a deep pit or into thorns and brambles. He is in great danger of being attacked by wild animals or robbers. In addition he has not the faintest idea of where he is or in what direction he ought to be heading...

Suddenly he finds a flashlight. It works! He breathes a sigh of relief. At least he can now see where he is going. He won't fall into a pit or into thorns. But the wild animals and the bandits still pose a grave danger, and he still has no idea of where he ought to be heading.

Then at long last the sun rises. The animals go back to their lairs, the bandits to their caves. He is out of danger. But he still doesn't know whether he is heading in the right direction.

When he comes to a signpost his troubles are over.

— — — — —

The traveler is you and I — Everyman and Everywoman. If our journey through the world is without the guidance of Torah and mitzvot we travel in the dark. Our passions and prejudices obscure our vision and we cannot distinguish between right and wrong. We are in constant danger of falling into a pit, that is, making a wrong moral choice with dire consequences. Or we may fall prey to wild animals or bandits, that is, we may be swept away by sudden surges of passion with equally disastrous results.

The flashlight which saves us from the pitfalls of life stands for the mitzvot of the Torah. The training and discipline which a life of mitzvot provides can save us from being too strongly affected by the immorality of the world around us. But mitzvot without Torah knowledge provide only a partial remedy. One is not immune to the wild beasts and bandits. One can still be overwhelmed by sudden surges of passion. What is the solution?

Sunrise. The sun stands for the light of Torah knowledge in the mind. Torah in the mind elevates a person. The passion for Torah can displace other passions.

And what is the signpost? Opinions differ. Perhaps it is the fear of sin.

(3) Program of study

Torah is a vast subject — but not so vast that you cannot begin. Learn a little today, a little tomorrow, persevere.

Knowledge is cumulative. Torah is deep — but not so deep that it cannot be understood at *your* level. You may forget today what you learnt yesterday and seemingly have made no progress. But this is not true. The Torah you learned is in your subconscious, helping you on from beneath the surface.

Study the Five Books and discover the origin and mission of your people and the practical guidelines given by God for fulfillment of this mission. Study the Prophets of Israel and learn the triumphs and failures of your people in times long past and derive lessons for the present day. Let your spirit take fire from the spirit of the prophets, whose passionate demands for social justice have inspired mankind for millennia — and should inspire us too. Study the Writings — and attune yourself to the sweet harp-notes of the Psalms, which speak to the universal heart of man; absorb the noble wisdom of Proverbs and Job, the drama of Esther, the mysteries of Daniel. Learn them with the commentaries of the Sages of our people and discover the lessons which they derived from them.

Learn the Oral Law — the only authoritative guide on how the principles of the Torah are to be applied in practice. Learn Mishna for a comprehensive view of *halacha*. Study *Shulḥan Aruch* and the other codes and summaries of *halacha* which guide you in everyday life. (For an explanation of these terms see Appendix: "Torah through the ages.")

Graduate to *Gemara,* that compendium of Torah wisdom, and the brilliance and acumen of the great Talmudic masters. Accompany them to their Houses of Study, take part in their lively debates, walk with them through the teeming marketplaces of Babylonia, sit with them in the law courts. Live with them in their constant struggle to clarify the will of God and to apply it to all the realities of everyday life. This indeed is work for a lifetime. It has provided a challenge and a constant occupation for the best minds of our people for many centuries and it continues to do this to the present day.

THE MOUND, THE CAKE AND THE LEAKY PAIL

One person had a field with an enormous mound of earth on it. He looked at it again and again and came to the conclusion there was nothing to be done about it. The land was useless. He sold it. The purchaser said, "True, it's a lot of earth, but I can tackle it. I'll take a couple of pailfuls today, and a couple tomorrow, and eventually I'll clear it. Then I'll have a beautiful field."

Two people came into a large hall. They noticed there was a cake suspended from one of the rafters, high up near the ceiling. One said, "It's too high up. There's nothing to be done about it." The other said, "Well, someone must have put it there. If he found a way to put it there, I'll find a way to get it down." He got a large table, put a stepladder on the table, got a long pole, and took it down.

Two people were out of work. There was someone offering a good wage for filling a pail with water and taking it to a nearby field. The trouble was that the only pail supplied was leaky and most of the water leaked out before one got to the field. One said, "This is ridiculous. I'm not going to spend all day filling a leaky pail." The other one said, "They're paying good money for it, aren't they? What does it matter to me?"

The three parables refer to the three reasons beginners give for not learning Torah. The mound refers to the sheer amount that has to be learnt. The cake refers to the high level of the argument one finds in Torah. The leaky pail refers to the unfortunate fact that many people forget what they learn. The answers have already been given.

(4) An exciting pursuit

Studying the details of the mitzvot, tracing their sources, analyzing and discussing the principles which determine them, are certainly time-consuming occupations. They are meant to be. Our Teacher Moses recommended that we "keep them in mind and speak of them morning and evening, when traveling and when at home." It seems that he intended this to take up most of our spare time.

It is true that the mass of Torah legislation is extremely complex. As we pointed out in the Introduction, it matches the complexity of the human mind. But it is systematic and governed by identifiable principles. The consistent application of these principles and the reconciliation of apparent contradictions which arise in the course of study are the constant preoccupation of Torah students. The attempt to solve the logical problems involved is an exciting and absorbing task, as in any other science. This is the "high-level Torah study" to which frequent reference is made in this book.

There is an extremely subtle psychological motivation behind all this. As we have constantly stressed, the purpose of all mitzvot is the sanctification of life and the release of the full moral and spiritual potential of man. But one cannot talk about moral imperatives all the time. To dwell too much on this topic is counterproductive. The mind rebels against constant moral admonition. The Torah adopts the oblique method. Rather than dwelling constantly on morality, Torah Jews discuss mitzvot in all their variety and subtlety. By doing so they immerse themselves in the words of God, and this itself has a purifying effect. In addition, moral and spiritual ends are implicit in all mitzvot, though these are often not obvious on the surface. As a result one can delve into the logical subtleties of the halacha without being consciously aware of the moral demands that the mitzvot themselves imply. But the spirit of the mitzva is absorbed subconsciously, by osmosis, so to speak.

There is another point. Torah study is never conceived as the mere imparting of information, where one party is active and the other passive. On the contrary, questioning and debate are actively encouraged from the earliest stages. The hot debates which such Torah study often engenders is also a subtle psychological device for sublimating our natural aggressive drives. As our Sages remark:

> Father and son, teacher and student, who seem like enemies locked in combat in the House of Study, finally leave it arm in arm, the best of friends. (Talmud)

In addition, absorption in Torah learning can sublimate our sexual energies. The Rabbis say that Israel loves Torah with the same intensity that other nations love sex.

Here are some further examples of the Torah's inspired depth psychology!

(5) Learning for practice

We must study in order to practice. This is the fundamental principle of Torah. Torah reveals its true meaning only to those who learn it in order to discover a way of life. One can learn it for other motives — to sharpen the mind, to attain honor or a livelihood, or even for antiquarian interest. There is value in all these, but only because the contact with Torah may eventually lead one to learn it for its true purpose.

Procure yourself a teacher for Torah, even if you have to pay for the privilege. Acquire for yourself a good friend, with the same aims as yourself. Review together what you have learnt, so that you develop your own resources in Torah study.

But learn from no teacher, however knowledgeable he may be, whose way of life is open to reproach. The source of true wisdom is not to be found in him.

(6) Recreation

In a Torah life, time is divided between study and practice. Time is not our own to waste. Idleness is unthinkable. Is not life a continual task? There is so much to do. Do we not have to practice justice and love, preserve our stores of wisdom, train our minds to be constantly aware of God? And idleness leads to boredom and sin.

Recreation? Certainly. Recreation belongs to the duties we owe our mental and physical powers. To step out into God's fresh air and renew our covenant with earth and heaven and with the nature to which we belong — this is recreation. To step out of our loneliness into the circle of good people, or into the company of one good person, and in intimate exchange of thought, in conversation, to renew our covenant with society — that puts new life into mental and bodily faculties in need of refreshment. But to read, hear, or speak for recreation anything that does not promote our real life, that pollutes our imagination and our mind — this means to kill our better self for the sake of recreation.

(7) Environment of Torah

If we want to be a blessing in the world we must prepare ourselves for this task. And this is a preparation that lasts a lifetime. By learning Torah at every opportunity we create in our mind, in our home, in our society, an environ-

272

ment of Torah. This is the environment in which Torah personalities grow.

(8) Kollelim

In our orphaned generation many great Rabbis have seen the need for the largest possible number of young people to devote themselves full time to high-level Torah study, research and teaching. The aim is to do our utmost to reconstruct the world of Torah which was lost in the Holocaust. Wide sectors of the Torah public assist in maintaining these research institutes, which are known as Kollelim. Those hardy spirits who are prepared to forfeit prospects of economic security in order to take part in this great enterprise deserve our praise and admiration.

When these young people eventually go out "into life," either as Torah educators or in other spheres of activity, their influence is felt in society in many ways. Such individuals and groups of people are having considerable success in improving the Torah environment in many places in the world.

---

65. Prayer and the Synagogue

TURNING TO GOD IN THOUGHT AND WORD/BLESSINGS/THE
SYNAGOGUE/SILENT PRAYER/TORAH READINGS

---

*And to serve Him with all your heart and soul (Deuteronomy
11:13). What is the service of the heart? — Prayer.*

— TB TAANIT 2a

I call out to God...
Evening, morning and noontime;
I meditate, I groan —
And He hears my voice.

— PSALMS 55:17-18

*Daniel...had windows in his attic open towards Jerusalem,
and three times a day...he prayed and gave thanks
before his God.*

— DANIEL 6:11

You shall eat and be satisfied and bless God...
for the good land He has given to you. — DEUTERONOMY 8:10

*The Men of the Great Assembly ordained for Israel:
blessings, prayers, sanctifications (*kiddush) *and separations
(*havdala).

— TB BERACHOT 33a

(1) Prayer from the heart

Prayer is not so much a commandment as a privilege and
an opportunity. For reasons which will be touched on in
chapter 77(2) — ("The Need for Humility"), Torah Jews
who make progress in the life of the spirit find prayer to be
an essential element in that progress. Temporary
withdrawal from the whirl of life is necessary in order to
replenish, in the presence of God, one's spiritual power and
dedication to further service. It is a recharging of our spiritual batteries. Through prayer one allows the Divine will to
affect our inner self, to draw out the hidden potential for
spiritual progress. In addition, when we turn regularly to
God for our everyday needs we learn to recognize Him as
the true Source of our life and welfare. (See chapter 76.)

YOU ARE A FOOL!

Gershon Rosenstein, a scientist brought up as an atheist in the Soviet Union, a refusenik for fifteen years, reports on the first time he tried to pray, to probe the depths of his heart, without knowing what he might find. He reports that his scientific side then said: "Who do you think you're speaking to? You are a fool!" He overcame his hesitation and is eternally thankful when he considers what might have become of him had he yielded to that skeptical voice.

(2) Prayers and blessings

In First Temple times, the individual's own thoughts and deeply felt emotions produced the words of prayer. The Book of Psalms, which has been a source of inspiration to large sections of mankind for thousands of years, was produced in this way by men who were close to God.

In a later era, after the Babylonian exile, such spontaneity was no longer common. It became necessary to provide people with guidelines on the form and structure of prayers. Instead of the feelings producing the words, the words were to induce the feelings. The Men of the Great Assembly, early in the Second Temple period, embarked on a wide-ranging project to "bring Torah to the masses." The Torah already required us to bless God after enjoying the fruits of the land. One of their far-reaching innovations was to expand the concept of "blessing" (*beracha*) on a grand scale.

They brought God into our everyday lives on a continuous basis by introducing blessings to be said on many and various occasions. Among these are:

Blessings *before* enjoying the good things that are in this world.

275

Blessings before performing mitzvot.

Blessings of thanksgiving.

Blessings on certain sights and experiences (e.g., a thunderstorm, the ocean, the new moon, trees blossoming in spring).

Blessings as prayers. (See paragrah (6).)

They also introduced the blessings said at the entry and departure of Sabbaths and Festivals (*kiddush* and *havdala*), the Seven Blessings of the wedding ceremony, and many others, which may be found in the Daily Prayer Book (*siddur*).

By this unique institution, which has been functioning without interruption for 2,500 years, the Rabbis succeeded in bringing us into contact with the Almighty when engaged in our most mundane everyday activities. Every Jewish child knows that he cannot eat or drink anything without blessing the Divine Source of his enjoyment. We are taught that nothing in life is trivial. In all that we have, all that we experience, we are to see God. Even a glass of water calls for the tremendous declaration: "You are blessed, God…by whose word *everything* comes into existence." We are trained to realize constantly, in *practice*, the vision of the poet:

> To see infinity in a grain of sand,
> Eternity in an hour.

(3) Meaning of blessing God

Most blessings begin with the formula:

> "You are blessed (or, "May You be blessed"), God, our God, King of the Universe, Who creates [makes, gives] [the particular thing, experience, gift, etc. which is the subject of the *beracha*]."

When we call God "blessed" we mean we recognize that He is the source of all blessings. If we "bless" Him we mean that we hope that His plan for the creation may be fulfilled.

This, of course, involves our own co-operation. The blessing is therefore a commitment on our part to help bring about this much-desired goal.

(4) The synagogue

As part of their campaign to get Jews to identify themselves more intensely with Torah, the Sages at the beginning of the Second Temple period arranged that prayers should be said communally. Each community was to build a "House of Assembly" (*Bet Knesset*) where people would gather for prayer on Sabbaths and Festivals, and on weekdays too. The time of the services was co-ordinated with the times of the Daily Offering in the Temple in Jerusalem. The offerings in the Temple were also accompanied by verbal prayers and blessings, and many of these were also incorporated in the synagogue service.

Continuing and expanding a much older ordinance, readings from the Torah and prophets were included in the services and explained to the congregation. The congregation participates in these readings. Members are "called up" to the Torah, recite blessings which are responded to by the congregation, and either read (Sephardi rite) or have read for them (Ashkenazi) a part of the weekly Torah portion. On Shabbat and Yom Tov a selected portion is also read from the Prophets, bearing a message linked in some way to the weekly Torah portion. (See paragraph (9).) Children, too, were often taught in the synagogue. The Yiddish name "schul" (school) is certainly an apt description, since an important function of the synagogue has always been education.

The synagogue thus co-existed with the Holy Temple throughout the Second Commonwealth and served to forge a close attachment between Jews everywhere and the Jerusalem Temple — the heart of Torah life. After the Destruction, the synagogue has continued to bring the spirit of the

Holy Temple into every Jewish community. (In fact the Rabbis call the Synagogue "the Temple in miniature.") To express this thought, wherever Jews live they build their synagogues facing towards Jerusalem, and wherever on earth a Jew stands he faces Jerusalem in his prayers.

The Temple contained a "Women's Courtyard" (*Ezrat Nashim*). Similarly every synagogue, according to halacha, must provide separate seating for men and women, to avoid the distractions caused by the proximity of the opposite sex.

(5) Kaddish

There are certain prayers whose scope is so tremendous that they cannot be uttered by individuals but only in a *minyan* — a congregation of ten males representing the Jewish nation in its public manifestation.

One of these is *kaddish*, which, in sonorous Aramaic, opens with the request:

> May His great name be magnified and sanctified in the world He created according to His will, and may His Kingdom come... speedily and in our days!

To which the congregation fervently responds:

> Amen! May His great name be blessed in all eternity!

This prayer thus asks for no less than the final consummation of the object of all our striving — the spiritual redemption of all mankind! (See chapter 80.) It is this prayer which marks off every section of our synagogue service and forms its triumphant close. It is this prayer that marks the close of every public session of Torah study.

This is intended to make us constantly aware of the great principle which we have tried to emphasize throughout this book: the Torah is not primarily concerned with individual or parochial issues. Its ultimate purpose is Messianic. It looks continually and eagerly to the achievement of the final, universal goal.

This is the prayer that is recited by the mourner at the moment of greatest grief, and throughout the year of mourning and on each anniversary (*yahrtzeit*). This enables the mourner to transcend his individual tragedy and to submerge his grief in the knowledge that the community lives on and its great goal will one day be achieved. (See chapter 18.)

THE DREAM

About fifteen students of an American yeshiva accompanied their Rosh Yeshiva to the wedding of a fellow student in New York. On the way home, due to a blizzard their plane was directed to Washington D.C. While waiting for their connecting flight, they wished to *daven minha* (hold the afternoon prayer service) and they asked an airport official whether there was a room available for this purpose. It was the first time he had ever had such a request but he agreed. He showed them to an empty room on the first floor. As they were commencing the service another official, more senior than the first, entered the room.

"May I join you?" he asked. "I'm Jewish. I would like to say *kaddish* if I may."

He stood during the service without participating and at the end asked for assistance in saying *kaddish*.

Afterwards the Rosh Yeshiva took him aside and asked him the reason for his request. After some hesitation he revealed this remarkable story.

"My father died a few days ago," he commenced. "I left home a very young man and never had much contact with my father or with Judaism. But the night after he died he came to me in a dream and asked me:

279

'Why aren't you saying *kaddish* for me?'
'I just don't know what you have to do,' I replied.
'Can't you find a synagogue?' he asked.
'I don't know of one,' I answered in the dream.
'Well, if it can be arranged that a number of Orthodox Jews hold a prayer service in your airport in the next few days, will you join them and say *kaddish*?'
'Certainly,' I replied.
"So when I saw you all going into this room to say your prayers I kind of expected you, you understand!"

(6) The silent prayer

There is one prayer which is the climax of every service. It is the prayer in which the Jew faces his God and in silent words addresses Him in awe and adoration, and lays before Him his requests. The requests are not for himself alone, however; they are for all Israel. (There are however three places at which the individual can insert his or her private requests. See "Private prayer," below.)

This is the prayer which our Sages called simply *Tefilla* ("prayer"). It is sometimes referred to as *Amida* (because it is said standing), or most commonly *Shemoneh Essreh*, because on weekdays it consists of eighteen blessings (plus one added in the 1st century C.E.).

On Sabbaths and Festivals the number of blessings is reduced to seven. An Additional Prayer (*Mussaf*) is said, corresponding to the additional offering in the Temple on those days. The latter applies also on *Rosh Hodesh* (the New Moon — see chapter 53(5)).

In the service of the synagogue this silent prayer is repeated aloud by the reader, providing a kind of "heavenly echo" of our whispered words.

During this repetition there are three occasions when the

congregation participates:

1. *Kedusha* (sanctification), during the third blessing. Using the words of the angelic hosts as revealed to us by our prophets, we sanctify, bless, and acclaim the transcendence of Almighty God.

2. In the penultimate blessing, the blessing of Thanksgiving, the congregation joins its thanks to the words of the reader. Gratitude is such a basic principle in Torah Judaism that we cannot possibly remain silent when thanks to God are being expressed. (This is known as *modim de-rabbanan.*)

3. In the last blessing, the blessing of Peace, the Kohanim recite the Priestly Blessing. (See chapter 67.)

Table 11
THE STRUCTURE OF THE *SHEMONEH ESSREH*

INTRODUCTORY
1. God in history
2. God conquers death
3. God's holiness

SPIRITUAL NEEDS	PHYSICAL NEEDS
4. Knowledge	7. Deliverance
5. Repentance	8. Healing
6. Forgiveness	9. Blessing of produce

NATIONAL NEEDS	ULTIMATE CONCERNS
10. Reunion of nation	13. Restoration of Jerusalem
11. Social justice	14. Mashiaḥ
11a. Elimination of evildoers	
12. Reward of righteous	15. Acceptance of prayer

FINAL
16. Restoration of Divine Presence
17. Thanksgiving
18. Peace

PRIVATE PRAYER

The three places where a person may insert a prayer for his or her personal needs are:

281

1. In the blessing of *healing*, for a sick relative or friend.
2. In the blessing of *acceptance of prayer*.
3. Just before taking three steps backward at the conclusion of the prayer.

THE THREE SERVICES OF THE DAY

We face God in prayer at the three turnings of the day: morning, afternoon and nightfall.

The morning prayer (Shaharit). At the dawn of the new day we pledge ourselves, as part of the community of Israel, to be worthy of the tasks this new span of life presents to us.

The afternoon prayer (Minha). We turn to God in the midst of our active life.

The evening prayer (Ma'ariv, or Arvit). We dedicate the night to God for study of Torah and for repose of body and spirit and renewal of our powers for the tasks of a new day.

(7) Grace after meals (birkat ha-mazon)

As previously mentioned, we are asked in the Torah to bless God after enjoying His bounty. At the same time we promise that the strength gained from the food we have eaten will be used for His purposes. The Rabbis have laid down for us the form of this blessing.

As always, in their blessings the Rabbis look beyond the particular to the universal. They have put before us four blessings which reflect four different aspects of God's bounty. (See Table 12.)

(8) Hallel (songs of praise)

Hallel comprises the six psalms 113-118 which together form the national song of praise to God for deliverance from Egypt and from many other trials and dangers. It also refers to our future redemption.

It is said on the Festivals and on *Hanukka* and *Rosh Hodesh* (New Moon). It may also be said privately (without a blessing) by an individual to give thanks for some unusual or miraculous deliverance. Many people say it on the 5th of Iyar, the anniversary of the declaration of the State of Israel in 1948 and on the 28th of Iyar, the anniversary of the liberation of the Old City of Jerusalem in 1967.

Table 12
STRUCTURE OF BIRKAT HA-MAZON

FIRST BLESSING
HISTORICAL PERIOD: IN THE DESERT BEFORE WE HAD A LAND

We join our voice to the chorus of all God's creatures who thank Him for satisfying their needs.

SECOND BLESSING
HISTORICAL PERIOD: ENTRY INTO THE LAND

We thank God for the gift of the Land of Israel, mentioning at the same time the covenant of circumcision and the Torah, particularly the laws which govern our relations with the environment (see Group Two), which were given us primarily to observe in this land.

THIRD BLESSING
HISTORICAL PERIOD: BUILDING OF THE TEMPLE

Originally this was an expression of gratitude for the holy city of Jerusalem and the Temple. Now we ask for their restoration. We ask God also to support us in our present difficult situation so that we do not have to turn to human beings for help.

FOURTH BLESSING
HISTORICAL PERIOD: AFTER THE DESTRUCTION

We ask God to maintain us in the future as He did in the past, and recognize His saving hand during the long night of exile.

◆ *Halacha*
◇ *On* Rosh Hodesh, *Hallel is said by custom only and not by law. To mark this, certain paragraphs are omitted.*
◇ *The same applies on the intermediate and latter days of*

Pesah (see chapter 44(4)). On these days our joy cannot be complete because they are associated with the drowning of the Egyptians in the Red Sea.

◇ *On Rosh Hashana and Yom Kippur (chapter 42) Hallel is not said because these are times of judgment.*

◇ *On Purim (chapter 51(2)) Hallel is not said because the miracle occurred outside Eretz Yisrael.*

"GO AND SAY HALLEL!"

An 18-year old girl from a non-observant background was studying at a famous Torah seminary in the north of England and had become a fully observant and devoted Jewess. In spite of her efforts however her parents showed no interest in changing their lifestyle and refused to keep Shabbat or observe the mitzvot. As can be imagined this caused the girl much mental anguish and she prayed often that her parents might be helped to return to Torah.

One day she had a letter from her mother telling her that the previous Saturday she and the girl's father had been waiting for a bus to take them to a movie show. While they were waiting a feeling came over her that this was not the right thing to do. She told her husband and he replied that he felt the same way. They made their way home and from that time on had done their best to keep all the mitzvot.

She showed this letter to the principal, Mr. Kohn. "What shall I do?" she asked.

"Do?" he replied. "Go to your room and say Hallel!"

(9) Torah readings (Keriat ha-Torah)

The ceremonial reading from the Torah scroll is a prominent feature of the synagogue service, as we have seen.

This takes place on Sabbath, both morning and afternoon, and appropriate portions from the Torah are also read on Festivals as well as on Purim, Ḥanukka, Rosh Ḥodesh, Fast Days, and Monday and Thursday mornings each week.

For the Sabbath morning reading the Torah is divided into weekly portions, each called a *sidra*, or *parasha*, with an average length of about 100 verses.

There are 54 such *sidrot*, but in an ordinary year we have only 48 Sabbaths which do not coincide with a Festival. (When a Festival and a Sabbath coincide, the Festival portion is read instead of the Sabbath portion.) To take care of this, there are some Sabbaths on which two *sidrot* are read instead of one. All this is done in accordance with a pre-arranged plan, co-ordinated with the fixed calendar, and the pattern repeats itself in a nineteen-year cycle (see chapter 53). On Sabbath afternoon and Monday and Thursday morning, the portion read is the first section of the following week's *sidra*.

The annual reading begins with *Bereshit* (Genesis 1-6) on the first Sabbath after Succot and is concluded (and recommenced) with much pomp, ceremony and rejoicing on Shemini Atzeret (in Israel) or Simḥat Torah (in the Diaspora). (See chapter 43(3).)

A STROKE OF GENIUS

The idea of the weekly Torah portion and the annual Torah cycle was a stroke of genius consistent with the holy spirit which invested our Sages. Besides the public reading, they required that every person should study that portion of the Torah each week. This ensured, and ensures to this day, that Jews all over the world will be studying the same portion of the Torah at the same time. This encourages communal learning and cross-fertilization of ideas.

[By another brilliant stroke, a sage of our time succeeded in extending this idea to the whole Babylonian Talmud. This is the *daf ha-yomi* project, in which one folio page of the Talmud is studied by Jews all over the world on each day. The Talmud is completed in a seven-year cycle.]

READING FROM THE PROPHETS *(HAFTARA)*

As mentioned above, on Sabbaths and Festivals the Torah reading is complemented by a reading from the Prophets bearing a message related to the *sidra* of the week. The person who is called up for this is called the *maftir* (concluder) and the reading itself is called *haftara*. The last few verses of the *sidra* are re-read for (or by) the *maftir* to emphasize that all the words of the prophets are based on the Torah.

This ancient ordinance ensures that during the course of the year the congregation becomes familiar with all the main themes of the prophetic writings.

(10) Aleynu

Every synagogue service, morning, afternoon and evening, weekday, Sabbath and Festival, ends with the two-paragraph prayer called *Aleynu* — "Our Duty." This custom was introduced some six centuries ago, "in order to conclude the prayers on a high note."

It is in fact an excerpt from the Additional Service of Rosh Hashana — part of the "kingship" theme (see chapter 42(5)) — giving noble expression to the universalist goals of Judaism. It must be said standing.

It begins by declaring that it is *our* duty, above all others, to pay homage to the One and Only God Whose glory fills the whole universe, since we were given the privilege of knowing Him and being called to His service. But it does

Table 13
PEOPLE CALLED UP TO THE TORAH

SHABBAT	seven* (or more)
YOM KIPPUR	six*
YOM TOV	five*
ḤOL HA-MOED, ROSH ḤODESH	four
PURIM, ḤANUKKA, FAST DAYS,** SHABBAT AFTERNOON, MONDAYS & THURSDAYS	three

* Plus one for *maftir*

** On Fast Day afternoons the third person also reads the *haftara*.

not rest content with that. The second paragraph expresses our fervent wish that we do not remain alone on this lofty eminence but that God's glory be recognized and acknowledged by all mankind.

This is the "high note" on which all our prayers conclude. We are not to forget: this is the aim of all our striving.

66. The Shema

REMINDING OURSELVES OF THE BASICS OF TORAH LIFE

Listen, Israel! GOD is our God; GOD is One. And you shall love GOD your God with all your heart, with all your soul and with all your might. And these words...shall be upon your mind and you shall teach them to your children and speak of them...when you go to bed and when you get up.

— DEUTERONOMY 6:4-9

(1) The opening verse

The opening words of the Shema form a world of their own. They are the first prayer murmured by the little child and the last uttered by the dying. Throughout the ages they have been the defiant declaration of the Jewish martyrs, including our own heroes of the spirit before the doors of the gas chambers.

They are far from a cold, theoretical statement. On the contrary they are the rallying cry of the invincible Jewish spirit. They do not merely say God our God is one. They declare: "God Who is *our* God, now recognized by us alone, that same God will one day be recognized as the One and Only God by all mankind." It embodies the ultimate and universal mission of the people of Israel.

We can appreciate the Divine wisdom that selected, out of the 5,845 verses of the Torah, this one verse for inscription on the victory banner of Israel. The unity of God that it expresses is the foundation for many great and powerful ideas. The unity it declares forms a protest against all forms of polytheism under whatever guise they may come. It also forms the basis of the utter and comprehensive dedication of heart, life and means to the loving service of God, as expressed in the following verse. That is to say: "One God — one commitment."

288

The unity of God implies the brotherhood of man and also the unity of the cosmos (the foundation of modern science) and the unity of history and its Messianic goal. (See chapter 80.) To emphasize this latter point the Rabbis decreed that the first verse be followed (in a low tone) by the words: "Blessed be He Whose glorious kingdom is forever" — the proclamation of the ultimate triumph of justice on earth. This was a phrase frequently used during the service in the Holy Temple. (The low tone expresses our embarassment when we compare the final goal with the unfortunate reality.)

Giving these opening words of the Shema such a central position in the life and thought of Israel ensured that the sacred truths they enshrine became the heritage of the whole House of Israel.

(2) The three sections

The three sections that comprise the "Shema" in the wider sense are:

1. *Shema*. This is the passage which heads this chapter. It includes, as we have seen, the unity of God and our total commitment to Him in love. It indicates that the learning and teaching of Torah are ways by which this can be realized (see chapter 64) and also refers to the symbolic mitzvot of *tefillin* and *mezuza*, which dedicate our bodies (chapter 55) and our homes (chapter 59) to this end.

2. *Ve-haya im shamoa'* (Deuteronomy 11:13-21). This teaches that our prosperity in the Land of Israel is assured only on condition that we keep the Torah. Otherwise we are faced with exile. This section too ends with our obligation to transmit Torah to the next generation and with the mitzvot of *tefillin* and *mezuza*.

3. *Vayomer* (Numbers 15:37-41). This introduces us to the mitzva of *tzitzit* and to the dedication of our lives which

this symbolizes (see chapter 57). The section closes with a reminder of the Exodus from Egypt, which we must bring to mind every day of our lives.

PLACE IN THE SERVICE

The recital of the Shema was part of the Temple service and the Rabbis took it over to the synagogue.

Since the Torah requires us to "speak of them...when we lie down and when we get up," the Rabbis ordained the reading of the Shema both as part of the evening service and the morning service. It is given a place of prominence and is preceded by blessings thanking God for the physical gifts of day and night and the spiritual gift of Torah, and followed by an acknowledgment of the saving might of God, as seen in the Exodus and throughout our history.

67. The Priestly Blessing

REMNANT OF THE TEMPLE SERVICE

Tell Aaron and his sons,
This is how you shall bless the people of Israel:
Say to them:
May God bless you and keep you.
May God show you the light of His countenance
and give you grace.
May God raise His countenance towards you
and give you peace.
So they shall put My name on the people of Israel,
And I will bless them. — NUMBERS 6:22-27

(1) The blessing of peace

The priestly blessing was part of the morning service in the Holy Temple. The Rabbis took it over to the synagogue and incorporated it into in the last blessing of the Silent Prayer — the blessing of peace. (See Table 10.)

In Israel today the Kohanim ascend the platform and bless the congregation every day, in a manner reminiscent of Temple times. In the Diaspora, in Ashkenazi communities, this is done only on Festivals.

(2) "I will bless them"

To avoid the impression that this is some magical rite by which the blessing proceeds from the Kohanim to the congregation, the congregation's representative reads the blessing word by word to the Kohanim, who recite it after him. This emphasizes the fact that their spiritual power derives from the community of Israel itself. The Torah makes it clear that the Kohanim shall only "put My name upon the people" and it is "I — God — Who bless them." "Putting God's name on the people" means putting them

291

mentally and emotionally in contact with the bearer of that name — the Source of all blessing. Once that contact has been established the blessing follows. The blessing is proclaimed with uplifted arms, emphasizing this very point by pointing upwards to God.

(3) The content of the blessing

The threefold blessing of the Kohanim comprises:

1. That God bless us and preserve us, granting us health, strength and the provision of our material needs.

2. That God grant us the joy of His presence so that we learn to use our material blessings to fulfill His purposes. ("God's countenance" means our awareness of His presence.)

3. That God make us so intimately aware of the closeness of His presence that the clash between material and spiritual is eliminated from our lives and we are blessed with inner peace.

The ascending melody of this most sublime of blessings is emphasized by the very structure of the Hebrew text. See Table 14.

(4) Function of the blessing

Whenever a group of people is set apart from the ordinary folk, by reason of their superior knowledge or special function, there is a danger that a gulf will grow between the two sections. Ultimately this may lead to contempt on the one side and indifference or even hatred on the other. It may well be one of the functions of the Priestly Blessing to obviate these dangers. The Kohanim are commanded to present themselves before the people daily and to bless them in the name of God with that brief, but great and comprehensive blessing we discussed above.

By this God tells the Kohanim that they are there to further the welfare of the ordinary people and He tells the ordinary people to see in the Kohanim people who look upon them with love and concern.

There is a great lesson here for our time.

(5) The dignity of the priesthood

The priestly blessing, the last remaining vestige of the priestly function in the Temple, serves as a vivid reminder of the special status of the Kohen — chosen to represent Israel in the symbolism of the Temple service.

We recall that this Divine choice was made because of the special merits of Aaron, the ancestor of all the Kohanim. Aaron once made a grave mistake (see Exodus 32), but overcame it by repentance and humility. He devoted his life to making peace between husband and wife and between man and his neighbor; he loved people and brought them close to Torah. This is why his descendants

---

Table 14
THE PRIESTLY BLESSING

	FIRST VERSE		SECOND VERSE		THIRD VERSE		TOTAL
WORDS	3	+	5	+	7	=	15
LETTERS	15	+	20	+	25	=	60

It will be seen that the number of words amounts to 15, representing the first two letters of the Divine Name. It is also the *gematria* (numerical value) of *be'ahava* ("with love"). The number of letters is 60, representing the community of Israel: 24 divisions of the Priests, 24 divisions of the Levites, and 12 tribes of Israel, together adding up to 60.

were deemed worthy of officiating in the Holy Temple.

Although the Temple service is temporarily in abeyance, we still have to honor every Kohen by giving him precedence in all matters of sanctity. This is why he is the first to be called up to the reading of the Torah, followed by the Levite.

As an expression of his special sanctity, a Kohen must avoid all contact with a dead body (except in the case of the death of a close relative), and is also subject to certain special restrictions regarding whom he may marry. Defilement by contact with a corpse (known as *tum'at met*) excludes one from the Temple, which is devoted to life and not death. The continued application of this prohibition to the present day expresses our confidence that the Temple will regain its former glory one day soon, by the grace of God.

These laws have been looked upon as a badge of honor by Kohanim throughout the ages.

♦ *Halacha*

◇ *Contact with a corpse includes being under the same roof with one.*

◇ *Close relatives are: wife, parents, son, daughter and unmarried sister.*

◇ *Prohibited marriages for Kohanim include marriage to a divorcee or a proselyte.*

(6) The Temple precincts today

Since our miraculous victory in the Six Day War (1967) we have regained access to the one place on earth where every Jew feels closest to the Almighty — the *Kotel Ma'aravi* (the "Western Wall" of the ancient Temple compound). The Temple Mount itself may not be approached in our present state of impurity except for essential purposes such as guard duty.

68. Basic Attitudes

KNOWLEDGE AND LIFE / OUR RELATIONSHIP WITH GOD

You shall know today, and return it unto your heart, that GOD is the Power in heaven above and on earth below — there is no other! — DEUTERONOMY 4:39

I, GOD… brought you out of Egypt to be your God. — NUMBERS 15:41

(1) The threshold of life

Knowledge alone is not enough. Knowledge alone does not make us better people. The knowledge with which we have enriched our mind must be applied to *ourselves*. It must be transferred from the mind to the heart, the source of action. It must penetrate through the conscious to the unconscious layers of our mind; it must become part of ourselves. Only then will it become the springs of our action. Only then will it become our life.

So also, and much more, with the highest of all concepts — God. We may see God in all the stupendous works of nature, from the emergence of the galaxies to the genetic code. We may perceive God in history, in the downfall of tyrants and the miraculous survival of His people through the millennia. We may hear God speaking to us in the narratives of the Torah, the thunder of the Prophets, the music of the Holy Writings. But we may have grasped all this only with our mind, our intellect. This is not enough. So long as we do not receive God into our heart and embrace Him with all our being as *our* God, so long as this concept is a mere denizen of our brain, so long will this sovereign idea be without influence on our actual life.

Again, we may recognize in all created beings a great multitude of servants of the Divine purpose, without seeing and feeling *ourselves* as one of these. We may have recognized Israel's high vocation as God's instrument in history for the education of the human race, without feeling *ourselves* a part of that people. So long as this is so, our heritage is barren. The flower of real life does not spring from it.

That is why Israel's life history opens with the words: "I, GOD, Who brought you out of Egypt, the house of slaves — I am *your* God." The God of Being destined the human race for the fullest unfolding of its spiritual powers. That same God dedicated the people of Israel to be the instruments of His purpose. He now calls upon us, the nation, to be faithful to our history, even if all the world denies Him. And He calls upon *us* individually, to be loyal to this purpose, even if many in Israel deny it.

This is the threshold of Jewish life, the condition and basis of the whole Torah. In the previous sections of this book we have seen something of the loftiness of the Torah's ideals, and the wide-ranging program which seeks to ensure that they are put into practice. We can be proud that we have been entrusted with this tremendous task. To accept this challenge is to accept the sovereignty of God in our lives. The mitzva here is to be aware of the loftiness of this purpose and to value the privilege of being entrusted with its fulfillment. So we will ensure that the practical mitzvot will achieve their goal.

(2) What is the nature of God's demands?

Unthinking people tend to believe that God's demands on us are like those of a taskmaster who exploits his slaves to his own advantage. This is a ridiculous misunderstanding of the true position. The demands of God resemble those made by a good teacher on a brilliant pupil. He knows what the pupil can do and gives him tasks which will draw out the best in him. The teacher may say "Please do this work for me" but everyone knows that the pupil himself will benefit, not the teacher.

So the demands and responsibilities laid upon us by the sovereignty of God are never for God's benefit but only for our own. God's mitzvot are all love, His warnings are love, even His punishments are love. If we permit ourselves a metaphor, the only satisfaction God gets out of our keeping His Torah is the satisfaction of a father who sees his children taking the right direction in life.

69. Source of Our Obligation

ACCEPTANCE AT SINAI/"SINAI IN THE SOUL"

"...And you will be to Me
A kingdom of priests and a holy nation..."
And all the people answered together and said:
"We will do all that GOD has said." — EXODUS 19:6-8

I make this covenant...with those who are standing here
with us today before GOD our God, and with those who are
not here with us today (Deuteronomy 29:13,14). — This refers
to all future generations. — RASHI, FROM MIDRASH

(1) Acceptance at Sinai

Yes, Israel's acceptance of the Torah was unanimous.
From that time on Israel saw itself, and other people saw it,
as the people of God.

But how did that generation have the power to oblige all
future generations, thousands of years later, to follow the
same course? The Rabbis reply that the souls of all future
generations were present at Mount Sinai and accepted the
Torah.

(2) Sinai in the soul

What can we say to someone who tells us he has no recollec-
tion of accepting the Torah at Sinai? In the era of relativity
theory it should not be too difficult to show him that it
makes no difference whether we say his soul was at Sinai
or Sinai is in his soul. It is a fact that when a Jew has Torah
presented to him in a true light he often feels an affinity for
it in his heart. He may have known nothing about Torah
previously but he feels he has come home to something
which, deep down in his soul, he has been waiting for. This
is what we call "Sinai in the soul."

The rareness of this experience is due to the brainwashing we are subjected to in the various environments in which we live. In the communist part of the world the teaching is — or was until recently — that Judaism is nothing but capitalist money-grabbing. In the West, Judaism is projected as backward and useless in this so-called advanced age. In Israel the line taught in the schools and widely believed is that the distinctive mitzvot of the Torah were useful for preserving Jewish identity in the Diaspora but are no longer necessary in a Jewish state. Only when these distorting spectacles have been removed is it at all possible for the "Jewish spark" to ignite. It is hoped that the ideas presented in this book may make some small contribution to this process.

70. Unity of God

Listen, Israel: GOD *is our God,* GOD *is One! You shall therefore love* [Him] *with all your heart, with all your soul and with all your might.* — DEUTERONOMY 6:4-5

You have been shown, and you know, that GOD *is the Almighty God; there is no other power.* — DEUTERONOMY 4:35

(1) A unified view

The world presents us with a scene of enormous variety. We see creation, order, growth, destruction, disease and death. Here we see a call to existence, there a recall from existence; seed growing into blossom and fruit, fruit falling into decay and dust, dust and decay changing into new seed. We see amazing orderliness and complexity accompanied by apparent randomness and lack of control. We see a vast animal creation governed by instinct, and man released from compulsion and given freedom of choice.

Human history too is full of change and variety. We see men left to themselves as if without supervision. We see one people, among all others, created, guided, given the unique power of prophecy. We see war and peace, abundance and scarcity, life and death assigned to the peoples — nations set on the path of history and then fading into the sunset — and one nation suffering grievously but seemingly touched with the wand of eternity.

Our individual lives too are full of opposites. We see a continual giving and taking away. We see life and death, health and sickness, strength and weakness, pain and joy. We experience ourselves as a duality, with body and mind, good and evil, giving and taking, enduring and doing.

But however great the variety presented to us by nature and history and our own life, we must know that all this is the doing of One God, conforms to one design and is part of one all-wise plan. We must know too that the obscurity, the apparent randomness, are all part of the plan. In moments of tranquility, when we delve beneath the surface of our mind it is sometimes given to us to discern the pattern and purpose of our life, and the sweep and trend of world events. At these moments we sense the presence of the One God.

(2) A unified life

The most vital lesson is to realize that this One God is *our* God. Just as the whole universe is guided by one hand, and strives upwards towards One Being, so we must feel our own life, with all its ups and downs, to issue from one Source, to be guided by one hand, to flow towards one goal.

And One God demands total commitment. "I am One, therefore one love should dominate your life."

You love life? Good! But not for empty enjoyment, transient pleasure, but because life gives us the chance to give and do and be a blessing. This is to love God with all our life.

You love your wife, children, family, friends? Wonderful! But not for vague sentimental reasons; rather, because these are your partners in a great co-operative enterprise of building a living temple for God. This is to love God with all our heart.

You love your work, you are happy with your sense of achievement? Excellent! This brings us to love the Source of that achievement, the God Who endowed us with these powers, these talents, and enables us to direct them to His loving purposes.

Recognizing One God enables us to unify our life, to make all that we do part of one great goal, one great adventure.

71. Idolatry — Ancient and Modern

Nothing else shall be a god to you alongside My all-pervading dominion.
— EXODUS 20:3

Maybe you will look up to the sky and see the sun, the moon and the stars, all the hosts of heaven, and you will be tempted to worship them... The nations may be under the regime of the heavens, but you have been adopted by God Himself... to be the people of His inheritance to this very day.
— DEUTERONOMY 4:19-20

(1) The dangers of idolatry

Everywhere around us we see natural forces in their unceasing activity. We see "nature," in the eyes of man, raised to a power in its own right. We see men with their science and technology, their wisdom and foolishness, their power and weakness, fashioning, destroying and influencing for good and bad the fate and life of nations and the global environment. In ourselves we see the spiritual and the physical, we discern the same creative and destructive forces as in the world around us — the ability to be a blessing or a curse to everything that crosses our path.

But none of this exists by its own power or its own will. None of this is a god; all of it is created, and serves the purposes of the One all-powerful and ever-present God. In nature we see God's law, in the life of peoples God's providence, in ourselves powers implanted by God for positive purposes. As physical systems we are subject to the laws of nature imposed by God. As moral beings we enjoy a freedom which is the loving gift of God. With that freedom we are called upon to obey the higher law of the Torah. That much we have learned.

But what we have learned we have to absorb and put into

practice. In our lives we must recognize no power but God.

If there is any power in the world to which we give unlimited allegiance, then we are setting this up as an idol in place of God.

We are commanded by the Torah to live in the world and to make use of its powers — including our own powers — to the best advantage, knowing all the time that the sole source of these powers is God.

How would an outside observer tell whether our use of the powers of the world is legitimate or idolatrous? Very simple. If our economic activity is subject to the limits imposed on it by God's law — the laws of honesty and fair dealings discussed in Group One; the laws of Shabbat and Yom Tov in Group Four — then it is clear where our allegiance lies. If not, economics has become our god.

If our eating and drinking and our homes are dedicated to the Torah's goals — increasing human happiness and developing our spiritual potential — then it is clear where our allegiance lies. It is clear what we consider the ends of life and what the means. Otherwise we are in danger of falling into the idolatry of the affluent society, of whom it was said long ago:

> ...whose bellies are their god
> And the layout of their homes their religion.

Only if we recognize the One and Only God as the absolute in our lives and devote our energies to pursuing His ideals will we grow to our full stature as Jews and human beings.

(2) Modern nature worship, which is really self-worship

People who bestow on any part of the creation attributes which belong to God alone are committing idolatry. When people who should know better talk about "Nature" as far-sighted, all-wise, all-powerful — this is idolatry.

If you corner them they will admit that this is only fanciful talk. The idol they really believe in is Nature the blind god. They have convinced themselves that they have banished purpose from the universe. "We got here purely by accident," they proclaim. "Man was not planned. No one had him in mind." But, as a renowned Jewish thinker has so aptly put it, we are being asked to believe the frankly incredible. The proponents of this theory claim

> that this sturdy, lusty and vibrant child — the whole grand, incredible and wondrous process of teeming life — is but the offspring of two dead parents called respectively "natural selection" and "random mutations."

The originator of the theory once wrote: "When I think of the eye, I shudder." And well might he shudder! When one thinks of the tiny retina with its batteries of light detectors: 7 million cones for high-resolution of detail and color, and 120 million ultra-sensitive rods for the low levels of illumination, together with automatic focusing, image enhancement, movement detection and other sophisticated data processing mechanisms, one cannot help feeling revulsion at the idea that all this could have come about by blind chance. And one can say the same about any functioning organ in virtually any living organism.

What is the motive that leads men to ignore the evidence of their own senses and deny manifest purpose and an ordering principle in the universe? The driving motivation is man's desire for domination. This leads him to see even life itself as a machine which can then be brought under his power and control. In their egocentric way, men say that the only purpose that exists in the world is human purpose. It is confidently asserted that we are fast approaching the point where humanity will be in full control of its own destiny.

Evolution need no longer be a destiny imposed from without; it may be conceivably controlled by man, in accordance with his wisdom and his values.

THE NEW MYTHOLOGY

This is the new mythology. We may call it the idolatry of man. And like all idolatry, it is self-contradictory and absurd. Scientists see man as a speck of dust in a blind, meaningless universe, totally determined in all his aspects by outside forces. This is one side of the myth. Yet on the other hand, by virtue of his surging scientific knowledge, man is seen as capable of freely choosing to direct his destiny in accordance with his wise moral aims and purposes! Surely it is blatantly contradictory to assume that knowledge of the forces that totally determine his life will give him free and moral control over those very forces.

But the situation is much worse than that. Knowledge does not make man a better person. (See chapter 68(1).) On the contrary knowledge means power and power corrupts. A scientific culture can become demonic if its controllers have no absolute standards and rely completely on their own faulty and biased insights. The experience of our time tragically confirms this prediction. Our vaunted technology itself contains the seeds of doom. Exploited by evil men it has already wrought unimaginable destruction. Driven by greed and fear it proliferates unchecked. We are aware of its potential for global pollution and the dehumanization of man but are unable effectively to control its direction or goal. What price the grandiose dream of man's wisely controlling his cosmic destiny!

Hence the Torah's insistence that we reject at the outset all man-based idolatry and open our minds to the true source of our freedom — the free God Who stands above and beyond nature and Who gives us the purposes which lead us to true life.

72. Standing in Awe of God

AWARENESS OF GOD / WHERE THOUGHT CANNOT REACH

*[When they heard God's voice at Sinai]...the people were
greatly moved...They said to Moses, "Please transmit God's
message to us. We cannot stand God speaking to us directly
[anymore]. We feel we shall die if it continues..."*

— EXODUS 20:15-16

*God said, "Very good!...If only they would always feel like
this, to stand in such awe of Me and be so eager to keep My
commandments! It would be to their advantage."*

— DEUTERONOMY 5:25-26

*And now, Israel, what does God...ask of you? Only to stand
in awe of [Him]...to go in all His ways, to love Him...for
your own good.* — DEUTERONOMY 10:12-13

(1) Awe and awareness

If we take all that the Torah teaches us about God — His
greatness, His power, His majesty, His all-seeing eye, His
unceasing activity in nature and in human life — and
impress it on our mind, our feelings and our imagination,
we shall come close to what the Torah calls "awe." *Yirat
shamayim*, that central quality in Jewish life, does not
mean merely fear of what will happen to us if we do such-
and-such a thing. It means to be aware of God's ever-
present nearness; to realize one's responsibilities as a
human being and a Jew, and to be grateful too for the
confidence implied by one's being entrusted with furthering God's sublime purpose in the world.

If we have a vivid enough conception of even one aspect
of God's greatness and carry it about with us always, we
shall be unable to sin.

(2) Power

God is all-powerful. Heaven and earth exist minute to minute by His will. Eternity is for Him but an hour. How absurd it is for man, with his grain of power, his brief spell of time, to set himself up against the Omnipotent!

(3) Greatness

God's greatness extends to where man's thought grows dizzy. All existence serves the plan of His wisdom. He reaches His goal by ways which no human thought can dream of. How foolish must we be if we think we can impede the achievement of that goal!

(4) Omnipresence

God is everywhere. In the sublime words of the Psalmist (Psalms 139:7-10):

> Whither can I escape from Your spirit?
> Whither flee from Your presence?
> If I ascend to heaven — You are there;
> If I descend into death — there You are!
> Shall I take up the wings of the dawn,
> Dwell at the ends of the ocean?
> There too Your hand guides me,
> Your right hand holds me.

Go where we will, God's eye is everywhere, His hand is everywhere, above us, below us, around us, *in* us. Can we escape from ourselves — our higher self? Do we still want to sin?

We live in God's world. All that the earth contains, from the blood that flows through our veins to the air that we breathe, all is God's. Can we stretch out our hand to destroy, injure, waste, misuse, that which is not ours?

(5) Law

God is the lawgiver. We meet His law everywhere, in the blade of grass, in the orbiting satellite, in the economics of nations, in the stars which circle far above. That same God has revealed the law of our life in the Torah, for us to follow freely. Do we want to misuse that freedom to oppose God's will? Or shall we decide to use that freedom to fulfill the task that has been allotted to us? Then we range ourselves with that mighty host of God's creatures, from the greatest to the smallest, who, like us, are called upon to serve the purposes of the One and Only God.

(6) Knowledge

God is all-knowing. There is no darkness that can conceal us from Him. Our life, our acts, our very thoughts are open to His scrutiny. If this thought sends a shiver down our spine, that is as it should be. This is the essence of *yirat shamayim* — awe at being in the presence of such a God. Some men, great perhaps in intellect but deficient in understanding, have been unable to accept this idea. That their innermost secrets should be open to the inspection of an alien power is too much for them to bear. How wrong they are! God is not an alien power. It is in God that we live and have our being. Every experience, every thought, is given permanence in the mind of God with which our own higher self is in some sense continuous. We are important enough in the scheme of things for every act, word and thought of ours to be significant. Instead of crushing us, this fact elevates us and endows us with value as human beings and Jews.

But maybe this too is too much for us to take. We make ourselves small and say: "Man's life and actions are so puny, the earth itself is but a speck of dust in the cosmos, man is a mere nothing in God's vast universe. Can God, so holy and exalted, take an interest in mankind, in me? Can it really matter to Him how I act?" If we think so, we are hypocrites. When we first came into being, was it too little for Him to prepare, with loving foresight, the environment for our growth, our survival, our progress? Did He not equip us for life, provide for our every need? Do we not still perceive, in us and around us, the hand that provides for our moral and intellectual development? Can we then pretend to be astonished if that same God is also concerned about our actions?

(7) Justice

God is just. "Justice and right are the foundation of His rule." Everywhere we see cause and effect, premise and consequence, everything with its corresponding result, the impact corresponding to the force, the fruit to the seed. It would be foolish to think that only the seed of *our* thoughts, *our* words, *our* actions, *our* enjoyments have no fruit. Where we have sown evil do we think we can reap good? The way of repentance is always open (see chapter 42). But it would be foolish to think that we can build our life on opposition to His will. Let *yirat shamayim* guide us on the path of truth.

73. Loving God

HOW TO LOVE / HEART, SOUL AND MIGHT

You shall love GOD your God with all your heart, all your soul and all your might. — DEUTERONOMY 6:5

(1) Commanding love

How can one be commanded to love? Surely in matters of the heart there are no commands; one either loves or one does not. We raised this question once before — see chapter 30 (1).

We can now see that the assumption behind the question is wrong. We have the power to induce emotions and to inhibit emotions. The proper use of reflection and imagination can engender love.

One loves someone when just being with that person gives one a sense of fulfillment. For us God is not a mere abstract concept but the One Who breathes into us our life, Who supplies the power for our heartbeat, Who gives us our ideals and the means to achieve them. Whatever we are, we are only through God. He was already our benefactor thousands of years before we were born, since He has made us the heir to all those generations of Jewish living and learning.

If our life possesses value and significance it is only through our calling as a human being and Jew. We should therefore treasure and love God's Torah which reveals to us this calling and is the living source of its realization. Through His Torah we come to love God, whose love and concern enfolds us every day and hour and moment, protecting, warning, instructing and improving us always.

(2) All our heart

"To love God with all our heart" — that is, with mind and

310

heart, with intellect and feeling. If we follow the Torah's path, as laid down in the earlier sections of this book, we shall learn to refine our feelings and intellect, elevate our baser nature. We will love God for the serenity we then attain, and there is no purer love than the love of deep gratitude.

(3) Soul and might

"With all our soul and with all our might" — the life that has been lent to us, our physical powers, our health and bodily fitness, in the resources we have acquired, all that God has given us by way of money, property, honor, influence — *for* all these and *with* all these we love God. In all of them we see only the means and instruments for accomplishing what God in His Torah wants us to accomplish. That is how in our affluence we love God.

And if, God forbid, we lose all these — health, wealth, honor, influence — for this and with this too we are to love God. "Whatever measure He allots to you, give due thanks to Him." This may seem an impossibly hard task, but not if we realize that whatever befalls us in this world is not reward or punishment, but a task, a test sent by the loving hand of God. Affluence or hardship both show God's loving concern — to bring out the best in us, the best of which we are capable.

REB ZUSHA'S SURPRISE

A Hassidic Rebbe was once asked by a student to explain the statement of our Rabbis that "whatever measure God allots to us, good or bad, we must give due thanks to Him." "How is it possible," he asked, "for a human being to give thanks for something bad?" "The only person who can answer your question," said the Rebbe, "is Reb Zusha of Anapolia. You must go and see him." The student traveled

311

for hundreds of miles, through farmland and forest, and eventually found Reb Zusha in a broken down hut at the edge of a forest, in dire poverty, emaciated and racked with pain. The Sage greeted his visitor serenely. "What can I do for you, my friend?" The student explained his quest. "Why do you come to me?" asked Reb Zusha in amazement. "There must be some mistake. For an answer to this question you must go to someone who has experienced some bad in his lifetime. Nothing bad has ever happened to me. I am the wrong person to ask!" The student had his answer.

74. Emulating God

GOD AS OUR MODEL/PATIENCE, APPRECIATION, FORGIVENESS

God will establish you as a holy people...if you keep the commandments of God and walk in His ways.
— DEUTERONOMY 28:9

To love God your God, to walk in all His ways and to remain attached to Him (Deuteronomy 11:22). — The ways of God are...: "God is merciful and gracious, patient, abundant in love and truth; keeping in mind good deeds to the thousandth generation, forgiving iniquity, transgression and sin" (Exodus 34:6-7). Just as God is called merciful and gracious, so should you be merciful and gracious; just as God is called righteous and loving, so should you be righteous and loving.
— SIFRE, DEUTERONOMY 11:22

(1) No model but God

God gives us no human model to emulate. He sets Himself before us as a model and says: "Try to follow my example — and love!"

No other being but man has the ability to discern and recognize God. The purpose of this recognition is that we should imitate Him in action. This is why we were created in His image. Being in "God's image" gives us the capacity for love. (See Introduction.)

The one aspect of God which we can behold everywhere and always is His activity, and this activity is suffused with love. Creation itself is an act of love, the existence of every creature is love, the maintenance of the world is love, its ordering and advancement is love — love for the whole, for every individual, for us. Even what seems to us as severity, cruelty and indifference, will be seen, in the ultimate scheme, to be part of Divine love. Similarly, on our human scale, the goal of our striving should be love, love in action with all our powers, so that we may become a bless-

313

ing in our circle, wherever and however we can. (The mitzvot which embody this love have already been described in
the third section of this book, chapters 30-40, and in many
other contexts.)

This Divine model is constantly before us. There is
nowhere we can turn our glance or direct our thought
without meeting Him. Every paving stone on which we
tread, every creature we meet, every breath we draw, every
joy that delights us, every tear we shed, everything from
earth to heaven is His work, the fruit of His love, for the
well-being of His creation. His love is given freely and
without constraint, for no being has any claim on Him.

The ever-present and all-loving God calls on us to follow
Him according to our powers, to be His image in our own
sphere. But we must not fall into the trap of loving mankind at large and ignoring the actual person who stands at
our side or whom we meet in everyday life.

(2) Patience

God is patient. We too must be patient. God has no pleasure
in the punishment of the wicked; His pleasure is that he
should mend his ways and live. He has patience with the
weaknesses of human beings and gives them time to make
good and reform. We, who are ourselves frail and weak
human beings, should surely do no less. Why can't we have
patience with the weaknesses of our brother? Why must we
take offense at every real or imagined slight, instead of
learning forbearance from our God?

(3) Appreciation

God remembers a good deed to the thousandth generation;
so should we remember a kindness even to the children
and grandchildren of our benefactor. A sense of gratitude
is our most precious possession. We should nurture it and

always be eager to express gratitude and appreciation for good acts and good intentions. Words of gratitude and appreciation sweeten relationships between children and parents, husband and wife, employer and employee. Gratitude is the purest and profoundest motive for the service of our Creator. Let us make gratitude a way of life.

(4) Forgiveness

As God forgives wrongdoing and accepts the repentant sinner, so should we forgive wrongs done to us and be reconciled with the one who regrets his error. How can one just forgive and forget? It may take considerable mental and spiritual exercise. One may put oneself in the other person's shoes, imagine his motives and misunderstandings, judge him in the scale of merit. It may be hard work, but the prize is glittering — the ability to forgive.

(5) Conclusion

This is perhaps the most demanding and most challenging of all the mitzvot. It is breathtaking in its scope and in the trust it reveals in the moral powers of every Jew and Jewess. We can only hope that we may be found worthy of this trust.

75. Faith in God

FAITH AND TRUST/THE EMERGING PATTERN

Unshakable as a rock, His work is perfect,
God of faith, without injustice;
He above all is righteous and just.   — DEUTERONOMY 32:3-4

"God of faith?" ask the Rabbis. "In whom then does God have faith?" And they answer: "He had faith in man and created the world." He had faith in man that, despite all his failures and blunderings, he would win through in the end. If God has faith in us, we can certainly have faith in Him. Faith in God — *emuna* — means trust in God, His promise and His Torah, even though His presence does not show itself in our experience. The Torah tells us that God is all-powerful, all-wise, all-just and all-beneficent. Yet if we seek His traces in the world and society we would seemingly find everything but God. We see the forces of nature with their random impact; we see the power, the cleverness, the caprice of the human mind seemingly in control; we see the righteous suffering and the men of evil triumphant; folly succeeding and wisdom put to shame; chance apparently making sport of human happiness; and sickness, need, war, hunger and vice wiping out whole generations. Yet *emuna* tells us that we have not seen the whole picture. We see as much of the true pattern of events as a mite crawling in the pile of a thick carpet is aware of the pattern of the carpet.

THE EMERGING PATTERN

And yet, to the discerning eye a kind of pattern does emerge. Tyrants do not rule forever. In a process which may seem to us agonizingly slow, evil is brought low and right eventually triumphs. And the Jewish people — in accord with the ancient promise — still exists, against all odds. It has even returned to its ancient homeland. In fact it turns out that God's "withdrawal" from the world of man is more apparent than real.

Faith in Torah is vindicated by the fact that Torah communities today, in Israel and all over the world, are an oasis of optimism and sanity in a civilization which has lost its way.

Emuna is no "blind leap of faith." It has solid foundations in history, in the present and in pointers to the future. For us "faith" and "reason" do not oppose but complement one another.

76. Providence and Human Action

HUMAN-DIVINE INTERACTION / GOD'S MESSENGERS

GOD's plan stands forever,
His designs for all generations...
GOD looks down from heaven,
Seeing all the human race,
He observes from His abode
All the dwellers on earth.
He forms a unity from their desires,
Scrutinizing all their actions.

— PSALMS 33:11-15

(1) Human-Divine interaction

We saw in the last chapter that God's love and concern are never withdrawn from the world even for one instant.

On the other hand we have learned that we are obliged to take appropriate action to look after our health, to earn our livelihood, to defend ourselves if attacked, on the individual, communal and national levels.

There is no contradiction. God runs the world, but human action is part of the raw material with which He deals. We see from the Biblical narratives that there is a constant interaction between our activities and the acts and plans of God in the world. There is no ironclad "fate" which compels human beings to act in certain ways. But there are Divine plans and purposes to whose realization our actions contribute, whether we intend it or not. (We have met this idea before. See chapter 49(2).)

The Bible shows us many examples of this Divine-human co-operation. Foremost among these is the story of Joseph (Genesis 37-50).

HOW ISRAEL CAME TO EGYPT

Centuries earlier God had told Abraham that his descendants would become the people of God. In preparation for this they would undergo exile and persecution in a foreign land (Egypt). But Abraham's descendants — Jacob and his family — are not borne down to Egypt on angels' wings. Instead, jealousy breaks out between the brothers and Joseph. Unsuspecting, Joseph puts himself in their hands and they decide — a very "human" decision — to sell him as a slave to a passing caravan, which "happens" to be on its way to Egypt. After several reversals of fortune Joseph finds himself the virtual ruler of Egypt. When there "happens" to be a famine in Canaan, he brings his father and brothers and all their families to Egypt and by Pharaoh's consent settles them in the fertile Delta of the Nile. So the scene is set for the future persecution and Exodus, which launches Israel on its destiny as the nation of the Torah. As Joseph says to his brothers: "You thought you were doing me harm, but God thought otherwise. He used it to further His glorious and benevolent plans."

(2) God's messengers

We make use of this principle whenever we submit to medical treatment, start a new business venture or do any one of the innumerable things we do to further our interests on the personal, communal or national level. Healing comes from God, but the physician is His messenger. Success comes from God; the economic trends are His instruments. Victory is from God; He uses the God-given skill of the general and the heroism of the boys in the tanks in order to achieve His ends.

The Torah teaches that we live in a multidimensional world. Purely materialistic accounts of the world do not work. But neither do purely spiritualistic ones. We live in a world of dynamic interaction. The Torah does justice to all aspects of life.

77. Humility

TRUE GREATNESS/THE DEEPER NEED FOR HUMILITY

The man Moses was extremely humble; more than any
human being on the surface of the earth.　— NUMBERS 12:3

(1) True greatness

We usually think of "humble" people as hypocrites or else
as timid weaklings who are self-effacing because they
have nothing to show. This is not how the Torah under-
stands humility. On the contrary, humility is the greatest
crown of great men.

Moses knew more, saw more, did more than anyone else
in history. He possessed supernatural powers and stood
closer to God than any other human being. Yet his crown-
ing glory is humility. The humble man is fully aware of all
his powers and achievements. He is humble because he
knows that all he has comes not from himself but from
God.

Little men who are bound to "the surface of the earth"
and whose horizons are consequently limited, can have
illusions about their own importance. The closer one gets
to God, the wider the horizon, and one's feeling of self-
importance diminishes to zero. Seen from this vantage
point our personal achievements seem puny. Hence: humility is the mark of true greatness.

(2) The need for humility

Man's greatness lies in his ability to transcend his petty,
egoistic concerns and to redefine his goals in terms of
higher purposes. This is another reason why humility is so
fundamental.

321

   A person can only reach his full potential if his mind is open to influx from the higher levels of being. Egoism and arrogance block this flow. Humility makes the mind receptive to higher ideas. As the Rabbis say in their wisdom, "Just as water flows from the higher level to the lower, so Torah flows to the mind of the humblest."

THE LOST WAGER

A Jew once bet his friend 400 dinars that he could make Hillel lose his temper. (Hillel, the president of the Sanhedrin in Eretz Yisrael, 1st century B.C.E., was famous for his patience and humility.) One Friday when Hillel was taking a bath in preparation for Shabbat, the Jew went past Hillel's house calling out: "Where's Hillel? Where's Hillel?"

Hillel quickly dressed and went out to greet him. "My son," he said, "What can I do for you?"

"I have a question," said he.

"Ask, my son, ask."

"Why do Babylonians have round heads?"

"My son," replied Hillel, "you have asked an important question. The reason is that their midwives aren't well trained and don't handle the babies properly at childbirth."

He waited an hour and tried again, summoning Hillel in a loud voice. This time the "important" question had to do with the Palmyreans' squint. Hillel received him with the utmost friendliness and responded to his query to the best of his ability.

The third time he came up with a question about the Africans' flat feet and again met with a friendly response. It was already getting close to Shabbat, but the man had not yet finished.

"I have a lot more questions for you," he said, "but I'm afraid you'll get annoyed."

"Not at all, my son," replied the Sage. "Ask whatever questions you like. I am at your disposal."

"Are you Hillel, the one they call the President of Israel?" he asked. "In that case I hope there are not many like you around."

"Why not, my son?"

"Because through you I have lost 400 dinars."

"Take care, my son," said the Sage. "It's better that you should lose 400 dinars and another 400 dinars so long as Hillel does not lose his temper."

78. He Called Them "Adam"

MEANING OF EQUALITY/THE INNER AND THE OUTER/LIFE'S
VARIED OPPORTUNITIES

*He created them male and female and He blessed them. He
called them "Adam" on the day they were created.* — GENESIS 5:2

As Israel camped before Sinai...
God said to Moses:
"This is what you shall say to the house of Jacob
And declare to the sons of Israel..." (Exodus 19:3).
"The house of Jacob" means the women; "the sons of Israel"
means the men. — MECHILTA AD LOC.

(1) Sense of privilege

To be aware of one's true function in the Torah scheme is
certainly an important part of the inner life fostered by the
Torah. If we have inwardly digested the preceding chapters of this work we shall feel proud and privileged to have
been entrusted by God with a portion in His Torah. We can
be absolutely certain that the tasks He has set us are those
uniquely suited to us, to our character and capabilities,
whatever our sex, position or status in life. Since there is a
good deal of misunderstanding on this point in the modern
world, we shall try and clarify the matter in this chapter.

(2) Equality of value

Man and woman are equally valuable in the eyes of God.
At creation they stood shoulder to shoulder before their
Maker and together received their blessing as "Adam"
(Genesis 5:2 as quoted in the heading to this chapter).

And at the creation of the Jewish nation, at Sinai, the
women and men of Israel encountered God side by side.
Indeed, God gave precedence to the women (as our Sages
tell us) because of their eagerness to observe the mitzvot

and because of the all-important influence of the mother on the spiritual development of each new generation.

(3) Apparent anomalies

And yet there are some apparent anomalies in certain laws of the Torah and statements of our Sages in this area. For example:

• A woman's evidence is fully accepted in all matters relating to the prohibitions of the Torah, even of the gravest import. (For example, her statement that she has been to the *mikveh*; see chapter 23(6).)
Yet: the evidence of a woman is not accepted in court proceedings.
• The eagerness of women to do mitzvot is rated higher than that of men (see above).
Yet: women are exempt from some mitzvot which are bound to time.
• The women of Israel remained loyal to God when the men sinned in connection with the golden calf and again in their refusal to enter the promised land.
Yet: women may hold no position of authority in Torah society nor do they count in forming a *minyan*.
• A woman is endowed with superior understanding and can assess character better than a man.
Yet: a woman is exempt from the mitzva of high-level talmudic study.
• A married couple are as one person.
Yet: a man is commanded to found a family, a woman not.
• When a father dies and there is not sufficient income for both girls and boys, the girls have prior claim on the estate for maintenance and marriage expenses.
Yet: where there are male and female heirs, only males inherit the residual capital and real estate.

Let us see if we can resolve these difficulties.

(4) The inner and the outer

Human life in the eyes of the Torah resolves itself into two main areas: the nation and the family. Of the two, the Torah considers the family the more basic. A newly married man is free of all military service for one year "so that he can make his wife happy" (Deuteronomy 24:5). That first year lays the foundation of their future happy relationship, and we have already seen the important part this plays in the Torah's scheme. It is in the inner sphere of the family environment that the Torah's spiritual goals are nurtured and maintained. (See also chapters 22(1),33,34.) We understand why building a strong family takes precedence even over national needs.

On the other hand, the Torah's goals can be fully realized only in the public arena. This is the world in which one has to struggle to earn a living, to found and maintain a home, and to support the fabric and institutions of the Torah state. It is the world of commerce, industry and national and international relations, all of which must bear the strong imprint of the Torah's spiritual goals.

Family and society: one cannot exist without the other. But different and sometimes contrasting qualities are required for each. The family demands tenderness, affection and intuitive understanding. Action in society often needs toughness, analytic thinking, the ability to withstand great pressures and the courage to take a stand against evil forces.

(5) Innate qualities

All of us are endowed with all these qualities in varying degrees and they may all be needed by anyone at some time or other. And one can change. By great effort one can change oneself from a tenderhearted person to a tough one and vice versa. In principle it would be possible for any person, male or female, to work in either sphere, family or society at large. Each could develop the qualities he or she needs in each situation — tenderness for the family environment or toughness for the outside world. Indeed, we have to some extent seen this realized in our time. Many women run a home and at the same time make their way in the world of business and the professions, sometimes holding high executive positions.

But it requires exceptional talents to be able to do this successfully. The Torah does not demand of us such heroic efforts. It addresses its mitzvot to the normal run of humanity, and allocates each specific task to the sex whose innate qualities most suit it for that task. Women, who are naturally endowed with the requisite qualities, are entrusted with the most sensitive and most important of all tasks — the challenge of the family environment, the heart of Israel. Men, whose innate qualities normally tend to make them more suited for the world outside, find that their primary task lies in the public arena — the outer sphere of commerce, community and nation.

(6) Resolution

Once this principle has been grasped, the apparent anomalies we listed in paragraph (3) can immediately be resolved.

Evidence. In Torah law a witness in a *bet din*, whether in civil or criminal proceedings, is part of the legal system, and this belongs to the public arena. This accounts for the exclusion of the woman from the witness stand. Prohibited and permitted objects or acts come within the private sphere, and here a woman's evidence is fully accepted.

Mitzvot bound to time. A man engaged in the hurly-burly of life in the "outer" sphere needs mitzvot which occur at regular times to recall him to his Torah obligations. A woman whose life is lived largely in the "inner" sphere of the family needs these reminders less and is therefore exempt from a number of mitzvot bound to time. She may simply not need the periodic "prodding" as much as a man.

Positions of authority and counting in a minyan. Leadership in the community certainly lies in the public sphere. That this does not form part of a woman's task is therefore well understood. A *minyan* — a quorum of ten needed for public prayer (see chapter 65(5)) — represents the public face of the community of Israel. It is society in its public mode. It is clear therefore why it must be composed of males, whose main task lies in this sphere.

Talmudic study. High-level talmudic study involves analysis of the sources, and of the principles and reasoning which underlie the laws of the Torah. This in turn is needed to decide on new cases which may come up. This is something that affects Torah society at large. Our Sages tell us that women normally excel in intuitive understanding and character assessment rather than in analytic logic, and this seems to be consistent with recent psychological discoveries. Men are also encouraged to sublimate their aggressive instincts in the thrust and parry of talmudic argument — the hotter the battle, the greater the friendship in the end. (See chapter 64(4).) It will again be apparent why this is not usually the sphere of womanly activity.

The command to found a family. In the Torah's eyes, founding a family is a communal concern; it is building the community of Israel.

Inheritance. Maintenance from the income of an estate is a personal matter, and here girls have precedence. But when all matters of maintenance have been attended to, the residual estate is part of the nation's capital and the male heirs take precedence.

(7) The on-off switch

As we have seen in other contexts, the Torah prefers to operate what we have called an "on-off" switch rather than make its laws dependent on individual discretion or choice. We saw this, for example, in connection with self-incrimination (chapter 4(4)). Rather than giving the witness the right to refuse to give such evidence, the Torah prefers to rule it out of court completely. We saw it too in connection with the law of *yiḥud* (chapter 22(3)). The law which does not permit two persons of opposite sex to remain alone in an inaccessible place does not depend on the age, attractiveness or moral standards of the people concerned, giving scope for individual decisions in each case. "The law's the law" and no offense can possibly be taken.

Similarly, the Torah makes its laws concerning men and women completely independent of the individual qualities or attainments of the persons concerned. To do otherwise would only lead to invidious comparisons. The law is applied to men and women generally.

(8) Life's varied opportunities

People whose life presents them with a different challenge, for example a family without children or a woman who is not married, should never feel that they have no part to play in the Torah's plan. Any home can become a center of Torah and of concern for the physical and spiritual welfare of others. Biological children can be replaced by spiritual children. An unmarried woman can pursue the Torah's goal of being a blessing to others with as much zest as her married sister. There is a positive task for everyone if only one will take the trouble to look for it.

(9) Conclusion

Let us sum up our findings. The main differences in Torah law between man and woman confirm the idea that the Torah has given men the primary responsibility for developing society and the nation along Torah lines. Consequently it has given them the opportunities they need to foster those personal qualities specially suited to this goal. The Torah has entrusted women primarily with the task of fostering the family environment. It has therefore freed them as far as possible from other responsibilities (particularly the need to earn a living and to be involved in public affairs), so that they can develop the qualities essential for the successful accomplishment of this task.

79. Sanctifying God's Name

GOD'S "GOOD NAME"/WORTH DYING FOR/CURRENCY OF THE UNIVERSE

And you shall love God your God with all your heart and with all your soul... (Deuteronomy 6:5). — With all your soul: even if He takes your soul.   — SIFRE

You shall not desecrate My holy name; I shall be sanctified among the people of Israel. I am God Who sanctifies you.
                                        — LEVITICUS 22:32

(1) God's name

God's good name, so to speak, is in our hands. We are the people of God, the people of the Torah. How we behave in our everyday life, in our business dealings, in our human relations, will affect the honor and esteem in which God Himself is held by the people around us. God has sanctified us by giving us His Torah; it is up to us to sanctify Him in the eyes of the world.

This is not for His sake. He can do without our recognition. It is for our sake, since our whole being is bound up with the realization of God's purpose, and this can be successfully achieved only if we are able to maintain God's prestige at as high a level as possible. This is what we mean by "making God's name great" and "increasing God's glory."

DONKEY OR DIAMONDS

It is told of the Sage, Simon ben Shetaḥ (Eretz Yisrael, 2nd century B.C.E.), that he once purchased a donkey from an Arab. When he took it home he found in a pouch under its neck diamonds of great value. His disciples rejoiced: "See, Master, the blessing of God has made you rich."

"No," said the Sage, "I purchased a donkey, not diamonds. No blessing can be built on someone's loss." He went back to the Arab and found him sitting on the ground bewailing his great loss. "Here are your diamonds," said Simon. "My God has bidden me to return them." "Blessed be the God of the Jews!" cried the Arab. Simon said to his disciples: "Is it not worthwhile losing many diamonds to hear a non-Jew make this declaration?"

Every *mitzva* we do properly and sincerely increases God's glory in the world: first in our own mind and heart, secondly in our immediate circle, and finally in the world at large.

The Sages say: If a person has amassed a great knowledge of Torah, but his business dealings are not correct and he does not speak to people in a mild and friendly manner, what do people say? "We don't think much of all this Torah-learning if *this* is the result." This is a *ḥillul ha-shem* — a desecration of God's name. But if after studying much Torah a person is scrupulously correct in his dealings with people and speaks to them in a friendly manner, what do people say? "There must be something in this Torah learning; look at so-and-so — he learned Torah and see how he behaves!" This is a *kiddush ha-shem*, and God Himself says, "This is my people Israel in whom I can take pride."

THE INSURANCE CLAIM

In a North London suburb there lived a business-man who took his Torah seriously. He once had a burglary and filed an insurance claim. He was scrupulously careful to enter the precise current value of each article making due allowance for the number of years it had been used, defects etc. This claim form was eventually shown to the president of the insurance company. Some time later a large limousine could be seen making its way through the North London streets. The president wished to see what kind of person it was who could have submitted such an unusual claim. This was an example of business dealings being used to promote *kiddush ha-shem* in the world.

(2) Worth dying for

"If a man hasn't discovered something that he will die for, he isn't fit to live." So it has been said.

The mitzvot of the Torah are for the enhancement of life, and the saving of life takes precedence over all of them — except three. These are idolatry, sexual immorality and murder. One must be prepared to die rather than commit any one of these sins in any shape or form; they are touchstones of our loyalty to God in mind, emotions and body.

In the course of our history, countless thousands of our ancestors sacrificed their lives rather than give up their Judaism for another faith. By this they showed that Judaism meant more to them than life itself. They had "discovered something worth dying for."

(3) The currency of the universe

It is a tremendous concept, this "sanctifying of God's name." The Rabbis say that this was the purpose of the whole creation. Every individual who comes into the world has a specific task to perform, made up of all the moral challenges he has to meet during the course of his life. Each challenge successfully overcome creates a *kiddush ha-shem*. It demonstrates what kind of God he is serving, and also shows the power of that God. It is clear that he was able to overcome the challenge only because he drew on his hidden reservoir of spiritual strength — the power of the non-ego, which is the power of God. And so every family, every group, every nation has a task to perform, individually and collectively, just as *Klal Yisrael*, the community of Israel, has its task to perform. And not only horizontally, in the sense of all the people alive at any given time, but also vertically — all the people alive at all times throughout all the generations have a collective task to perform. Indeed the whole of mankind has its collective task to perform, its quota of *kiddush ha-shem* to provide to the spiritual treasury of the universe. And provided it will be, ultimately, despite all setbacks, all failures, all false starts, all wrong turnings.

The means of this final consummation will be considered in our next — and final — chapter: the Messianic age.

80. The Goal of Our Striving

MESSIANIC ERA — THREE STAGES/PURPOSE AND FEASIBILITY/A NEW BEGINNING

When all these things befall you, the blessing and the curse...
and you return to GOD your God, you and your children, with
all your heart and all your soul —
Then GOD will return your captivity and show you mercy, and
will gather you again from all the nations of your dispersal.
Though your outcasts may be at the uttermost ends of the
heavens, even from there will GOD gather you in.
He will bring you to the land your fathers inherited... and it
will be yours, and He will lavish on you more goodness and
abundance than your fathers ever had.
[Finally] He will circumcise your hearts... to love GOD with
all your heart and soul, and you will at last be truly alive.

— DEUTERONOMY 30:1-6

(1) The three stages

This is how Maimonides describes, in the final chapters of his great halachic code, the three stages he envisages in the coming of *mashiah*:

> [STAGE ONE.] If a king arises from the House of David, learned in Torah and devoted to mitzvot like David his ancestor...and he induces all Israel to follow [the Torah]...and he fights God's battles —
> *THEN IT MAY BE ASSUMED THAT HE IS THE MASHIAH.*
>
> [STAGE TWO.] If his efforts are crowned with success, and he proceeds to build the Temple on its site, and gather the dispersed of Israel —
> *THEN HE IS CERTAINLY THE MASHIAH.*
>
> [STAGE THREE.] He will then go on to influence the whole world to unite in the service of God, as it says: "Then I will make a revolution among the nations, so

that all of them, in clear speech, will call on God and serve Him with one will" (Zephania 3:9).

Although he describes him as "a king" it is clear that Maimonides sees *mashiah* primarily as a religious leader. "King" means a leader among men; "of the House of David" means in the Davidic tradition. Like David he will be a man of tremendous charisma, who by arguments and example and the power of his personality will be able to induce (or "compel" by the power of the spirit) all Israel to return to the Torah. (In this context "God's battles" probably refer to the spiritual battles involved in an educational effort of such magnitude, but it may also include repelling attacks by surrounding nations on the borders of Eretz Yisrael.)

At this stage there is still only an "assumption" that he is actually the hoped-for *mashiah*. Maimonides insists that his coming will not be accompanied by any miraculous signs; all that he does will be on the natural level. It is therefore legitimate to withhold judgment until the process is further advanced.

Once he demonstrates the Divine source of his power by fulfilling the prophetic promises of the ingathering of the exiles and the rebuilding of the national sanctuary, all doubts will be resolved and his acceptance will be complete.

Maimonides emphasizes that the Messianic rule will be accompanied by a willing acceptance on a national scale of *all* the laws of the Torah. As has been repeatedly pointed out in this work, when the laws of the Torah are put into practice on a comprehensive basis, the results are predictable. The fusion of spiritual values, justice, integrity and love will result in an ideal society which will be the wonder of the world.

From this secure base, the *mashiah* can then proceed to

336

the third stage — the winning of the world for the spiritual goals laid down for humanity as a whole.

(2) Purpose of Messianic era

In the concluding paragraphs of his code, Maimonides describes the purposes of the Messianic era as follows:

> The Sages and prophets of Israel ardently desired the coming of the *mashiah*. But they did not desire it so that they might rule over the whole world, nor in order to exact tribute from the nations, nor to gain prestige and honor from all people, nor to eat, drink and enjoy themselves. Their sole desire was to be free to devote themselves to the Torah and its wisdom without oppression or disturbance, so that they might attain the life of the World to Come.

How can we envisage that such goals can possibly be accepted by the Jewish nation, let alone by the generality of mankind?

Unquestionably a Copernican revolution of the mind will be required. Human beings will have to learn to substitute spiritual goals for the material goals they have been so avidly pursuing for so long. How can this come about?

Maimonides hints at a possible answer in the concluding paragraph of his code.

> In that epoch there will be no more famine, nor war, nor envy, nor strife. *All the good things of life will be bestowed in abundance and material treasures will be available like the dust of the earth.*

The pursuit of material goals has kept the vast majority of mankind occupied since the dawn of history. With the advance of modern technology the day can already be envisaged when Maimonides' prophecy will have come true. From one point of view this seems a grim prospect indeed. A life without challenge, without strife, without the spur to outdo one's neighbor? Is such a life worth living? Will mankind ever be satisfied with a life of games and sport — simulated strife? Is mass suicide the only solution?

No. There is an alternative — the Copernican revolution of the mind of which we were speaking. If there is a man, a leader, a nation, that can show the way, maybe the idea can catch on. The challenges of the mind, the challenges of the spirit, can be as zestful, as stimulating, as those of lust, envy, prestige, politics and war. No, when one gets involved in them, they can be incomparably more stimulating. The trouble with a material goal is that it is capable of fulfillment in a relatively short time. And once it has been achieved it turns out to have been hardly worth the effort. A group of people in a great and powerful nation set themselves the fantastic goal of putting a man on the moon within ten years. By enormous expenditure of effort and ingenuity and of twenty-four billion dollars in cash, the goal was achieved within the time set. Wonderful! But the excitement didn't last very long. People began to yawn and say, So what?

This does not happen with spiritual goals. The challenges present an unending series. Anyway, it seems clear that this is what Maimonides has in mind when he continues with the final, climactic paragraph of his great work:

> The sole goal of the world will then be to pursue the knowledge of God. It follows that Israel will then be great sages [because they have already been pursuing this goal for 4,000 years]. They will become aware of hidden matters and will attain the knowledge of their Creator to the utmost extent available to human beings, as it is said: "The earth will be filled with the knowledge of God as the waters cover the sea" (Isaiah 11:9).

(3) Is it feasible?

In our time we have seen tyrannies fall. Tyrannies of body and mind, dogmas which seemed entrenched and unassailable, backed by tremendous political and military power, have collapsed because they were seen to be rotten from within. We are not suggesting that these revolutionary changes have any Messianic import. They are clearly very far from the great revolution of the spirit of which we have been speaking. But they are suggestive. Materialistic dogmas which were supposed to have ushered in a paradise on earth have been shown to be hollow. They tend to show that ideologically mankind is in a state of flux, and no one knows what might happen next.

We cannot do better than to close with the words of Rabbi S. D. Sassoon, an original Torah thinker of our time:

> The Jewish people have in recent years produced men who have had a vision, and that vision has been accepted by millions of people. We had Marx whose ideas changed the face of the world and are still accepted by vast numbers of people. We have given the world Einstein whose vision of relativity is accepted by the scientific world. We have given the world Freud, whose ideas, whether we like them or not, have certainly changed the way people everywhere look at themselves. Who knows that we may not be able to produce a man who can give the world a real vision of brotherhood and peace, not the lip service which we've heard *ad nauseam* over the years, but a true feeling of brotherhood and spiritual insight which is not mere words but means the unlocking of the heart. When we produce such a genius, if we do, it will be easy to identify him with that figure for whom we have been praying these 2,000 years, the Messiah. This will mean a new beginning for mankind. In the words of the ancient prayer, with heightened anticipation, "May we merit to see this speedily and in our own lifetime."

Epilogue

This book is called "MASTERPLAN." Has a masterplan of Torah emerged from all that we have written in the previous pages?

We are all too prone to deal with the mitzvot of the Torah piecemeal, trying to understand each mitzva in its context but failing to see the vision of the whole. The prophet Isaiah complained long ago that this was the way the people of Israel of his day treated the mitzvot of the Torah.

> They treated the word of God (he says)
> As if each command
> Was a command for its own sake,
> Each guideline
> A guideline for its own sake;
> A little here,
> A little there...

They were unable or unwilling to comprehend what it was all about, what was the guiding principle or masterplan behind it all — with disastrous consequences (see Isaiah 28:11-13).

But what *is* the guiding principle? He hesitates to state it because he knows it will sound to them "like broken speech, like words in a foreign language." But he tells them anyway. These are his words:

> This is rest: Give rest to the weary!
> And this is tranquility.

And he adds despairingly:

> But they don't want to listen.

We may perhaps tend to sympathize with those in Isaiah's audience who failed to grasp the point of this remark. But we would be wrong. By now the point should be as clear as day.

The essence of Torah, Isaiah is telling us, is giving and not taking. Rest in this world is not gained by putting one's feet up and indulging oneself. The true spirit of man and of Israel will never be satisfied by a life of taking. Israel's spirit is at rest only when it is concerned with others. True rest consists in giving rest to the weary. This is the paradox which people don't want to understand. They have no ear for it so long as their spiritual potential remains undeveloped. The program of the Torah is designed to develop this potential.

"And this is tranquility." Tranquility is more than rest. "Rest" means to be in conformity with one's conscience. "Tranquility" means to be in conformity with the Spirit of the Universe.

We have seen that the function of the God-oriented mitzvot is to develop one's sensitivity to the needs of others. Is the goal of the Torah then the creation of a just and caring society, with the "holiness" mitzvot merely a means to that end?

But the ideal society provides an environment in which man's spirit can flower. Is the Torah society then merely a means towards that end?

The answer is that neither is an end in itself. The ideal society produces the flowering of the spirit. But the flowering of the individual spirit must be reinvested in society. This is a cyclic process. There is a dynamic interaction between the two, resulting in a kind of incandescence. The ultimate goal is that human life on earth will conform to a pattern laid down by the Divine Will and man will realize his full spiritual potential as "the image of God."

Appendix
Torah through the Ages

Throughout this work frequent reference is made to Torah, Mishna, Gemara, Talmud, Midrash, and post-talmudic authorities. It may be found useful therefore if we include here a brief summary of the development of Torah throughout the millennia.

For the sake of clarity it should be understood that the word "Torah" is used in two senses. In the restricted sense it refers to the Pentateuch, or Five Books of Moses. In the wider sense it embraces the whole corpus of law, practice, custom and concept which comprise authentic Judaism.

ORAL LAW

When the Torah was given in the Sinai Desert it comprised a written and an oral Torah. The written Torah which we have in the form of the Pentateuch, includes among many other things, an account of how the people of Israel came to be the bearers of a covenant with God, and an outline of the laws they undertook to observe. The details, in most cases, were left to be transmitted orally from generation to generation. This arrangement left scope for the ingenuity of Torah Sages to apply existing principles to new cases and changing circumstances as they arose — a process which continues to operate even in present times. *Halacha* is the name given to the definitive rulings on the practical requirements of the Torah.

PRE-MISHNAIC PERIOD

For almost 1500 years after the Torah was given, the traditions comprised in the Oral Law were not committed to writing. They could be learned only orally, by direct personal contact with a master of the Torah.

THE HEBREW BIBLE

During this period the prophetic works (*Nevi'im*) and the Holy Writings (*Ketuvim*) were recorded in writing and took their place beside — though subordinate to — the written Torah. These three together — Torah, Nevi'im, Ketuvim — form the **TaNaKh**, or Hebrew Bible.

The prophetic books include the recorded words of the prophets of Israel — a phenomenon unique in human history. Their passionate appeals in the name of God and His Torah for justice and brotherly love thunder down the corridors of time, and find their echo, too — in however muted a form — in the present work. The Holy Writings which include Psalms, Proverbs and Job, form the response of the great masters of the Holy Spirit to the spiritual challenges of Torah.

THE MISHNA

Towards the end of the 2nd century C.E., Rabbi Judah the Prince, foreseeing the long exile and dispersion of the Jewish people, presided over the recension and codification of all the main traditions of the Sages of the Oral Law up to his time. This was committed to writing and published as "the Mishna," meaning "Repetition" or "Transmission." A Sage of the Mishna is called *Shoneh* (in Hebrew) or *Tanna* (in Aramaic), and this period is known as the age of the *Tannaim*.

THE TALMUD

The Mishna immediately became the subject of new discussions. In the Babylonian yeshivot these discussions continued over a period of three centuries, and were summarized and edited with consummate skill by Rav Ashi and Ravina II at the close of the 5th century. These recorded discussions are called *Gemara* (Learning), and, together with the Mishna to which they refer, constitute the *Talmud*. By general consensus the conclusions of the Talmud were accepted as binding by all Jews loyal to the Sinaitic tradition. The Sages of the Talmud are called *Amoraim* ("Interpreters").

In Eretz Yisrael the yeshivot were forced to close in the middle of the 4th century as a result of Christian persecution. The discussions of the Palestinian *Amoraim* were edited at the same time to form the Palestinian (or as it is commonly called, the Jerusalem) Talmud. Close contact was maintained throughout this period between the two main centers of Jewish life, the Babylonian and the Palestinian.

SABORAIM

In the half-century following the completion of the Babylonian Talmud its contents were further considered by the successors of the Amoraim known as *Saboraim* ("Ponderers"), who added certain finishing touches to the text.

POST-TALMUDIC PERIOD

Although the text of the Talmud was now closed, discussion of its contents never closed. The work of the Amoraim and Saboraim was continued by the Babylonian *Geonim* ("Excellencies") during the period 540-1040 C.E. They initiated the *responsa* literature, in which authoritative replies are given to queries addressed to them by individuals or communities.

RISHONIM

With the expansion of the Jewish Diaspora, Torah centers grew up in Western Europe (Spain, France and Germany) and also in North Africa. In general, Jews under Moslem rule became known as *Sephardim* and those under Christian rule, *Ashkenazim*. There were — and are — differences of custom — mostly minor — between them. The Torah leaders of this time are known as *Rishonim* ("early authorities"), and their era extends from ca. 1000 — ca. 1500 C.E. Among the many great halachic works produced during this period, the outstanding one was the *Mishneh Torah* of Maimonides (1187).

AHARONIM

From circa 1500 onwards the masters of Torah are known as *Aharonim* ("later authorities"). The dominant halachic work in this present period was undoubtedly the *Shulhan Aruch* of Rabbi Joseph Karo, published in Eretz Yisrael in 1567. It eventually became a composite work, incorporating the glosses of Rabbi Moses Isserles of Cracow, Poland, representing the Ashkenazic view, superimposed on the text of the original author, who was a Sephardi. Many other great halachic works were produced, and, as in previous periods, responsa literature flourished.

As has been the case throughout Torah history, the discussions of the Aharonim center on the eminently practical task of applying the principles laid down in Torah and Talmud to all the differing social and economic conditions in which Jews find themselves in the course of the ages.

This process continues to the present day. If the present work, however inadequate, may be considered in some sense a further link in the great chain of Torah debate, the author will feel himself amply rewarded.

Sources and Notes

ABBREVIATIONS

H
: Rabbi S.R. Hirsch's *Horeb: essays on Israel's duties in the Diaspora* (1st ed. Altona 1837). The first number (in bold) after the H refers to the chapter and the second to the section (the sections run consecutively throughout the book). Thus "H45 332" means "*Horeb*, chapter 45, section 332".

H PENT. COMM.
: Rabbi S.R. Hirsch's Commentary on the Pentateuch (Frankfurt-on-Main, 1867-78).

SONCINO *HOREB*
: Dayan I. Grunfeld's English translation of *Horeb* (Soncino Press 1962).

TB
: Babylonian Talmud.

TJ
: Jerusalem Talmud.

MR
: *Midrash Rabba.*

MT
: Maimonides, *Mishneh Torah.*

ShA
: *Shulḥan Aruch.*

S.D.S.
: Rabbi Solomon David Sassoon (1915-1985). See biographical note, p.387

A.C.
: The author.

INTRODUCTION

p.ix
: THE WAYS OF PLEASANTNESS AND THE PATHS OF PEACE...: TB *Gittin* 59b based on Proverbs 3:17.
THE DIETARY LAWS WERE GIVEN TO REFINE...: See MR Leviticus 13:3.
THE ORDINANCES OF THE TORAH ARE...A MEANS OF ENSURING MERCY...: Maimonides MT "Laws of Sabbath" 2:3.

p.x
: ...'AS A NON-JEWISH HISTORIAN HAS PUT IT...': Paul Johnson, *A History of the Jews* (New York, 1987), p. 586.

p.xi
: "THE CONCEPT OF 'MITZVA' INTRODUCES A NEW MOTIVE INTO OUR LIVES...": This Torah concept of the supreme value of acting in accordance with a "mitzva" — a Divine command —

seems to stand in direct conflict with the Kantian doctrine of morality — a doctrine which has had great influence on Western thought. Immanuel Kant (1724-1804) maintained that in order to be moral a law must be self-imposed by one's own recognition of the moral imperative, and not imposed from without. According to Kant, if one obeys a law from fear of Divine punishment or hope of Divine reward or simply because it is the will of God, one's action is not moral. One has the choice of being either religious or moral, but not both.

Torah morality avoids this dilemma. When the people of Israel were confronted by the Divine Presence at Sinai they had the freedom to accept or reject the proposal made to them — to become the People of God. When, asking no questions, they replied "We will do and we will hear," they were not submitting to the dictate of an Outside Power. Their response came from the deepest levels of their Jewish soul and their acceptance was in the truest sense their own. The modern Jew, when confronted with a similar challenge, makes the highest form of moral choice when he decides to respond as his forefathers did.

p.xi ...'CREATED IN THE IMAGE OF GOD'...MEANS THAT...: Based on Rabbi E.E. Dessler, *Strive for Truth!* I p.119.

p.xiv TRADITIONALLY 613 MITZVOT...: TB *Makkot* 23b.

p.xv ...WITH SIXTY SUB-DIVISIONS, OR TRACTATES...: For the number "sixty," see MR Numbers 18:21. In our present division we have 63 tractates, however in Seder Nezikin the first three are one, and in ancient Ms. Sanhedrin and Makkot are treated as one tractate.

...WE FOLLOW, IN PRINCIPLE IF NOT IN DETAIL, THE INNOVATIVE CLASSIFICATION OF RABBI S.R. HIRSCH...: Rabbi Hirsch actually divided the mitzvot into six classes, in the following order:

1. TOROTH — Fundamental principles relating to mental and spiritual preparation for life.

2. EDOTH — Symbolic observances representing basic truths of Israel's life.

3. MISHPATIM — Declarations of justice towards human beings.

4. CHUKIM — Laws of righteousness towards beings subordinate to man: earth, plant, animal, towards one's own body, mind, spirit and word.

5. MITZVOTH — Commandments of love.

6. AVODA — Divine Service.

The considerations referred to at the beginning of this Introduction led us to place the Torah's social legislation — "Justice towards other people" — at the head of the book, followed by "Justice for the environment," another important contemporary concern. (Though the environmentalist may well find that the Torah's conception of the environment is much more comprehensive than his own!) As explained in the text, Group 3 and 4 are enrichments of Group 1 and 2 respectively. Thus the first four groups form an interlocking and self-reinforcing program. Group 5, "The Inner Life," comprising the faith, attitudes and character fostered by the Torah, is placed at the end because these spiritual attainments are in a sense the final goal and end-product of Torah life. But as pointed out in the Foreword to Group 5 they are not static. They form the impetus for a higher standard of commitment to the goals represented by Groups 1-4. The "Masterplan" is thus an unending process.

p.xviii   TORAH SYMBOLISM...: See Dayan Grunfeld's discussion of "Symbolism and Jewish law" in his Introduction to the English translation of *Horeb*, pp. cvii-cxx.

SOME MODERN PSYCHOLOGISTS...: See the work of C.G. Jung, with particular reference to his theory of "Archetypes."

WE HAVE FOLLOWED RAV HIRSCH IN OMITTING REFERENCES TO KABBALISTIC... INTERPRETATIONS...: See Dayan I. Grunfeld's Introduction to *Horeb*, pp. cxx-cxxix.

p.xix   ...KABBALA ITSELF IS ESSENTIALLY AN EXPLORATION OF THE INTERNAL WORLDS OF THE UNCONCIOUS MIND...: That the "worlds" of Kabbala are internal worlds was well understood by Rav Hirsch. He defines Kabbala as "inner vision and concept" rather than "external dream-worlds" that people mistake it for. (See *Nineteen Letters on Judaism*, Letter 18.) See also Rabbi E.E. Dessler, *Strive for Truth!* III p.221, and S.D.S. *The Sephardi Heritage*, London 1963.

p.xx   THE QUESTION RAISED...BY PROF. FREEMAN DYSON...: See F. Dyson, *Origins of Life* (Cambridge 1985), p.72.

p.xxi   MANY MORE THAN TEN BILLION NEURONS...: See, for example, John C. Eccles, *The Human Mystery* (Routledge & Kegan Paul 1984), p.148, who says that there are this number of neurons in the neo-cortex alone.

p.xxiii   EXCELLENT ENGLISH TRANSLATION OF HOREB...: Samson Raphael Hirsch: *Horeb, a philosophy of Jewish laws and observances*, transl. by Dayan Dr. I. Grunfeld (The Soncino Press, 1st edition 1962).

Group One :
Justice Towards All Human Beings

CHAPTER 1

p.2   (1) — (2) A.C. See also H **54** 393.

p.3   (2) LAW COURTS AND OFFICERS...: Deuteronomy 16:18-20. SANHEDRIN OR SUPREME COURT...: See Deuteronomy 17:8-12. ...EMPOWERED TO MAKE ORDINANCES...: *Ibid.* 17:10-11. See Maimonides MT "Laws of Rebels" 1:2: "'According to the Torah which they teach you' refers to the ordinances, decrees and customs which they introduce into society for the strengthening of the law and welfare of the public."
...THE DECISION TO GO WAR...: Mishna *Sanhedrin* 1:5.
BUT, ABOVE ALL, THE ROLE OF THE JUDGE...: Attributed to R. Hayyim of Brisk (1853-1918).
(3) Based on H54 394.

p.4   IF ANY...WRONGDOING IS PROVED...: Mishna *Sanhedrin* 3:3.
A JUDGE MAY NOT SPEAK IN A MORE FRIENDLY WAY...: *Ibid.* "Laws of Sanhedrin," ch.21.
(4) A.C.
HE WHO IS KIND TO THE CRUEL...: MR *Kohelet* 7:16.

p.5   (5) "WORK AMONG THE PRISON POPULATION OF ISRAEL...": See U. Timor, *Commitment to the Jewish religion as a Factor in Delinquent Rehabilitation*, (Doctoral Thesis, Hebrew University, Jerusalem, 1989).
HALACHA
IF ONE LIVES IN AN UNJUST...SOCIETY...: MT. "Laws of Behavior" (*De'ot*), 6:1.
THE TAKING OF BRIBES...: TB. *Ketubot* 105b.
PAID TESTIMONY...: TB *Ketubot* 105a.

p.6   A BASKET OF FRUIT...: Based on TB *Ketubot* 105b.

CHAPTER 2

p.7   (1) A.C. with reference to H 45 330-331. See also A.S. Abraham, *Comprehensive guide to medical halachah* (Jerusalem 1990), p. 177.
GOD'S IMAGE...: See above, Notes on Introduction, p.xi.
(2) A.C.
"Others will 'understand' their behavior." — Whenever a segment of the population is consistently dehumanized by a deliberate large-scale media campaign, as happened in Nazi Germany, all atrocities become "understandable." We must

beware that the same thing does not happen to us in our own home. The long-term media campaign against a certain segment of the population has already resulted in a leading artistic figure confessing that when he sees these black-coated figures and "the children they spawn" he can "understand the Holocaust" (Jerusalem Post, Nov. 16, 1990).

p.8   HALACHA
FROM A MAN'S BROTHER I SHALL DEMAND THE LIFE OF A MAN...: Genesis 9:5. "Even from one who loves him like a brother." (Rashi) This could be interpreted as a direct prohibition of euthanasia.
EVEN ONE WHO IS COMPLETELY COMATOSE...: A.S. Abraham, *op. cit.*, p. 180.
IT IS NOT PERMISSIBLE TO REMOVE ANY ORGAN...: A.S. Abraham, *op. cit.*, p. 173.
KILLING IN SELF-DEFENSE...: TB Sanhedrin 74a.
ONE MAY — AND SHOULD — KILL SOMEONE...: *Ibid.*
THE WAGING OF WAR...: ShA *Orah Hayim* 329:6-7.

CHAPTER 3

p.9   HALACHA
...IF CORPORAL PUNISHMENT IS USED...: ShA *Yoreh De'a* 245:10. Based on H **45** 332.

CHAPTER 4

p.10   (1) — (2) A.C.
p.11   (3) IF A NEIGHBORING HOUSEOWNER...: Mishna *Bava Batra* 1:4; TB *ibid.* 3a.
THE PRIVACY OF PERSONAL CORRESPONDENCE...: The ordinances of Rabbenu Gershom (10th cent.).
(4) A.C. See also N.Lamm, *Faith and Doubt* (New York, 1971), pp.271-289.

CHAPTER 5

p.13   (1) A.C.
...IT IS NOT THE CONCEPT 'MAN'... IT IS MAN IN GOD'S IMAGE...: A.C.
...THE LOVE OF GOD REVEALS ITSELF...: E.Levinas, "Nine talmudic readings," (Indiana U.P. 1990), p.xxvii.
p.14   THE DIGNITY OF THE LABORER...: Based on Mishna *Bava Metzia*, 7:1.

Sources and Notes

HALACHA

...WORKERS ARE ENTITLED TO FORM A UNION...: See Rabbi M. Feinstein, *Iggrot Mosheh, Hoshen Mishpat*(1)59.

(2) A.C.

p.14 THE MISHNA STATES...: *Bava Metzia* 9:12, Gemara 112b.

p.15 ...THE GENERAL RULE...: Mishna *Bava Kama* 3:11.

THE PATHS OF THE JUST...: Based on TB *Bava Metzia* 83a.

FOLLOW THE WAYS OF GOOD MEN...: Proverbs 2:20.

p.16 (3) A.C.

THE SAINTLY HAFETZ HAYIM...: In *Ahavat Hesed*, pp 34-42.

AVOIDING TROUBLE...: Based on *op. cit.* p.42.

p.17 (4) A.C.

...ONE MUST NOT ENGAGE IN ANY OTHER ACTIVITY...: Based on H **47** 354.

...EXTORTED FROM HIM BY LABAN BY A TRICK...: Genesis 29:22-24.

p.18 ...THE TITLE OF 'THE MAN OF TRUTH'...: Based on the verse "You allot 'truth' to Jacob, 'lovingkindness' to Abraham...," Michah 7:20.

WHEN THERE IS NO TIME FOR CONVERSATION...: Based on TB *Ta'anit* 23b.

CHAPTER 6

p.19 (1) — (4) Based on H **46**.

p.20 THE SILVER CUP...: Based on TB *Bava Metzia* 24a.

p.21 BORROWING AN OBJECT WITHOUT THE OWNER'S CONSENT...: MT "Laws of Robbery and Loss" 3:15.

...IT IS IMMATERIAL FROM WHOM YOU STEAL...: MT *ibid.* 1:2.

TAX EVASION...: MT *ibid.* 5:11.

BUYING GOODS WHICH YOU...SUSPECT ARE STOLEN...: MT "Laws of Theft," 5:1.

IF COATS...HAVE BEEN EXCHANGED...: MT "Laws of Robbery etc." 6:6.

CHAPTER 7

p.22 (1) Based on H **47** 345.

(2) A.C.

p.23 (3) ...MUST NOT TAKE ADVANTAGE...: H **47** 351.

DISHONESTY AGAINST A CORPORATION...: L. Levi, *Talks on Judaism*, p. 23.

p.24 HE WHO PUNISHED...: Based on H **47** 349. TB *Bava Metzia* 44a.

(4) ...A MAN WHO DOES NOT STAND BY HIS WORD...: TB *Bava Metzia* 49a.

...A STILL HIGHER LEVEL... See next note.

TRUTH IN THE HEART...: TB *Makkot* 24a, see Rashi s.v. *Rav Safra*.

p.25 (5) DO NOT BE MISLED... A.C.

WHAT MAKES HIM TICK?: Based on *Emuna U-bitahon* by Rabbi A.Y. Karelitz (*Hazon Ish*), 4:5-6.

p.26 (6) Based on H **47** 353.

p.27 (7) A.C.

YOUR FRIEND'S PROPERTY SHOULD BE AS DEAR TO YOU AS YOUR OWN...: Mishna *Avot* 2:12.

THE QUESTION OF LEGAL LIABILITY...: Explanation and Table — A.C.

CHAPTER 8

p.29 (1) Based on H **49** 360.

(2) IN A WORD, YOU ARE RESPONSIBLE...: A.C.

p.30 IF ANY PERSON OR FIRM...: A.C.

THIS PRINCIPLE IS PARTICULARLY IMPORTANT...: A.C.

(3) Based on H **49** 367.

REMEMBER: THE TALMUD JUDGES...: A.C. based on TB *Bava Kamma* 30a.

HALACHA

ANY ACTIVITY RESULTING IN SMOKE...: MT "Laws of Neighborly Relations" 11:4.

p.31 WE ARE THE PUBLIC...: A.C. based on TB *Bava Kamma* 50b. On this subject, see "Judaism and the quality of the environment," in A. Carmell and C. Domb (eds.), *Challenge* (Feldheim, 1976).

CHAPTER 9

p.32 (1) — (4) Based on H **50** 368-374. Partly taken from Soncino *Horeb*.

p.33 THE POWER OF TRUTH...: A.C. based on hassidic source.

p.35 (5) A.C., based on TB *Ketubot* 17a.

(6) Based on H **50** 375.

CHAPTER 10

p.36 (1) — (2) Based on H **51** 377-380.

p.37 WE WHO ARE THE HEIRS... A.C.

p.38 (3) Based on H **52** 381-385.

HALACHA

All these laws are based on the principle that it is forbidden to assist anyone in any kind of wrongdoing. See MT "Laws of murder and preservation of life," 12:12-15.

CHAPTER 11

p.40-42   Based on H 53 386-391.

Group Two :
Justice for the Environment

CHAPTER 12

p.45-49   (1) — (2) A.C.

(1) "GOD GAVE THE TORAH TO A NATION...": See Hirsch, Pent. Comm., Exodus 6:7-8.

...WAS TO LIVE IN A SPECIALLY SELECTED LAND...: Based on R. Solomon D. Sassoon, *Nathan Ḥochma Li-shlomo* (5749), "Why the Torah needs Eretz Yisrael," pp.14-27.

p.46   THIS WAS THE PLAN...: A.C.

p.47   THIS IS A SIGNIFICANT EVENT IN OUR HISTORY...: In Kislev 5708 (December 1948) Rabbi E.E. Dessler wrote:

"...in that hour of confusion...in that ocean of hatred...out of all this was born the precise opposite: they themselves [the nations of the world] decide to establish Israel in the Holy Land. Is this the way of the world? Is this a natural course of events?" (*Michtav Me-Eliyahu* III, p.350).

Other great rabbinic authorities, such as R. Yosef Ḥaim Sonnenfeld of Jerusalem and R. Meir Simḥa of Dvinsk also saw the finger of God in the changed attitude of the nations to renewed Jewish settlement in Eretz Yisrael.

MITZVOT PRACTICED OUTSIDE ERETZ YISRAEL...: Nahmanides Comm. to Leviticus 18:25. Also: *Midrash Lekaḥ Tov, Va-ethanan,* p. 14.

p.48   (2) See A. Carmell and C. Domb (eds.) *Challenge: Torah views on science and its problems,* pp.507-509.

p.49   HALACHA

THE MITZVA OF LIVING IN ERETZ YISRAEL...: See ShA *Even Ha'ezer* 75:5 and *Pit'ḥe Teshuva* ad loc. See also H.C. Schimmel and A. Carmell (eds.), *Encounter* (AOJS/Feldheim 1989), A. Carmell, "The mitzva of living in Eretz Yisrael: a halachic survey," pp.292-310.

HOWEVER ONE CANNOT BE SAID TO BE TRULY LIVING...: See above article in *Encounter*, pp.300-301.

CHAPTER 13

p.50   (1) Based on H 56 396-397.
p.51   (2) Based on H 56 398.

(3) THE MISER...: Based on H **56** 400.
IN THE HOLY LANGUAGE...: Hirsch, Pent. Comm., Genesis 11:1.
...AS MANY MITZVA-FULFILLMENTS AS POSSIBLE...: Based on H **56** 401.
HALACHA
WASTING FOOD...: TB *Shabbat* 67b.
EVEN FUEL IS TO BE USED IN THE MOST EFFICIENT MANNER...: TB *ibid.*
IT IS PERMITTED TO CUT DOWN...: Maimonides, MT "Laws of Kings and War," 6:9.

CHAPTER 14

p.52   (1) Based on H42 303 and H Pent. Comm., Levit. 19:23-24.
p.53   THE PLANET IS NOT OURS TO PLUNDER...: A.C.
THE OLD MAN AND HIS TREES...: Based on TB *Ta'anit* 23a.
WITH THE REVIVAL OF AGRICULTURE...: A.C.
(2) A.C.

p.54   HALACHA
The first four halachot may be found in Maimonides MT "Laws of the Second Tithe," ch.10.
NOWADAYS...: ShA *Yoreh De'a*, 294:6.

CHAPTER 15

p.55-60   (1) — (6) Based mainly on H **57**, and H. Pent. Comm. Leviticus 19:19.
The laws concerning the mixing of meat and milk were included by Rav Hirsch, with some support from Kabbala, in the class of mitzvot dealing with separation of species. We had some difficulties with this view and in the present volume we have transferred these laws to the next chapter: "Respecting motherhood in the animal kingdom."

p.57   (4) (c) THE REASON FOR THE SPECIAL SEVERITY OF THIS LAW...: A.C.

p.58   THE LOW INCIDENCE OF ALCOHOLISM IN TORAH-OBSERVANT COMMUNITIES...: See for example: C.R. Snyder, *Alcohol and the Jews* (Arcturus books 1977; orig. publ. 1958); M. Keller, "The great Jewish drink mystery," in *Br. J. Addict.* Vol. 64 (1970), 287-296.

p.60   HALACHA
EVEN A SINGLE THREAD...: ShA *Yoreh De'a* 299:1.

CHAPTER 16

p.61   MOTHERHOOD IS ONE POINT...: Based on H. Pent. Comm. Leviticus 22:28.

(1) H. Pent. *ibid.*

p.62 WHEN OUR FATHER JACOB...: See MR Genesis, 76:6.

(3) Based on H58. See also MR Deuteronomy 6:5 and Maimonides "Laws of Slaughtering" 13:7.

p.63 (4) ...THE SIGNIFICANCE MUST CERTAINLY LIE IN THE EXPRESSION...: A.C., based on Nachmanides Pent. Comm. Deut. 14:21.

p.65 WHERE ARE THE POLICE?...: Traditional.

CHAPTER 17

p.67 (1) — (2) Based on H **60** 415-416.

(1) ANIMALS ARE A RESPONSIBILITY...: TB *Brachot* 40a.

A CASE WITH HORSES...: Traditional.

p.68 (3) — (4) A.C.

p.69 (3) WE ARE NOT ALLOWED TO CASTRATE...: Levit. 22:24. ShA *Even Ha'ezer* 5:11.

WHEN WE READ OF MEDIEVAL POPES...: A.C.

CHAPTER 18

p.70 (1) — (2) Based on H **61** 419.

HALACHA

See ShA *Yoreh De'a* 343-368.

p.71 SCIENTIFIC EXPERIMENTS...: See, for example M.H. Pappworth, *Human Guinea Pigs*, Routledge, London, 1967.

(3) A.C. Based partly on H43.

TO SEE A HUMAN BEING BREATHE HIS LAST...: TB *Shabbat* 105b.

...SEVEN DAYS OF MOURNING...: See verse cited at head of chapter.

...RENDING GARMENTS...: Genesis 37:34.

...NEGLECT OF PERSONAL APPEARANCE...: Compare II Samuel 19:25.

p.72 THE FOUR STAGES...: A.C. Based on ShA *Yoreh De'a* 341,378-395 and on Rabbi Y.M. Tukachinski, *Gesher Ha-ḥayim* (Jerusalem 5720).

DO NOT ATTEMPT TO CONSOLE...: Mishna, *Avot* 4:17.

p.73 THE PROCESS AND THE AIM — THIS CAREFULLY GRADUATED PROCESS...: Based on Rabbi M. Lamm, *The Jewish Way in Death and Mourning*, (N.Y.1969), p.77.

THE DISCOVERIES OF PSYCHIATRY...: Quoted from J.L. Lieberman, *Peace of Mind*, in M. Lamm, *op.cit.*

SECONDLY THESE OBSERVANCES ENSURE...: A.C.

p.74 (4) A.C.

ONLY HE CAN ASSURE YOU THAT YOUR LOVED ONE IS NOT LOST...: From an idea of Rabbi M. Miller, Gateshead,

England.

p.75   (5) A.C. See also chapter 42.

CHAPTER 19

p.76   (1) — (2) Based on H **62** 426-428.

p.77   (3) Based on H **62** 429.

ONE WHO RENOUNCES EVERY BODILY PLEASURE...: TB *Nedarim* 10a.

p.78   (4) Mishna *Avot* 2:2. See also L. Levi "Talks on Judaism" no.34.

HALACHA

PRESERVATION OF LIFE...: TB *Yoma* 85.

...TO RISK ONE'S LIFE TO SAVE ANOTHER'S...: See TB *Bava Batra* 10b.

IT IS A MITZVA TO RISK ONE'S LIFE IN A WAR...: Maimonides "Laws of Kings and War," 5:1;7:15.

ABORTION...: See Rabbi M. Feinstein, *Ḥoshen Mishpat* (2) 69 etc.

CHAPTER 20

p.79   (1) — (2) Based on H **63** 430.

p.80   DOING A MITZVA...: MR Leviticus 34:3.

(3) Based on H **64** 431-432.

p.81   IN THE ADULT MALE... Based on H Pent. Comm. Levit. 19:27.

CHAPTER 21

p.82   (1) Based on H **70**.

p.83   THE LADY AND THE BRIDGE...: Related by Rabbi E.E. Dessler.

(2) A.C.

p.84   ADAM'S DONATION...: From Midrash *Bereshit Rabbati* on Genesis 5:1.

CHAPTER 22

p.86   (1) A.C. Compare Rabbi E.E. Dessler, *Strive for Truth! I* (Feldheim 1978), pp.118,131.

...TO ENSURE UNENDING VARIETY...: By the combination of half the father's genes and half the mother's genes in the gamete.

p.87   THIS IS THE TRUE SOURCE OF THE SHAME...: A.C.

EVERY UNION OF THE SEXES...: Based on H**65**.

SEX BECOMES TRIVIALIZED...: A.C.

p.88   (2) A.C.

YOU SHALL NOT FOLLOW THE NORMS...: See quotation from Leviticus 18:3-5 at head of chapter.
THE TORAH REQUIRES A MARRIED WOMAN TO COVER HER HAIR...: TB Ketubot 72a; Maimonides, MT "Laws of Marriage," 24:11.
...THE SEXES TO BE CLEARLY DISTINGUISHED...: A.C. See Deut. 22:5 (in heading to this chapter).
DO NOT COME CLOSE...: Levit. 18:6. ShA *Even Ha'ezer* 21.
TWO PERSONS OF OPPOSITE SEX...: ShA *Even Ha'ezer* 22.

p.89 WHAT DID MAIMONIDES SAY?...: "Laws of Forbidden Unions" 23:21.

(4) H **67** 446(end).

...AGE 11 IS NOT TOO EARLY...: Note: These are the words of Rav Hirsch written in 1837!

...IT WAS THE VISION OF HIS FATHER THAT SAVED JOSEPH...: TB *Sota* 37a.

CHAPTER 23

p.90 (1) Based on H **66** 441.
(2) A.C.

p.91 IT HAS BEEN SUGGESTED THAT THIS MAY BE ONE OF THE FACTORS INVOLVED...: S.D.S. (Personal comm.)
(3) — (5). A.C.

p.92 (4) THE PEOPLE OF ISRAEL ARE NOT SUSPECTED...: TB *Kiddushin* 82a.
See also N. Lamm, "Judaism and the modern attitude toward homosexuality," in M.M. Kellner (ed.), *Contemporary Jewish Ethics* (New York 1978) and in *Jewish Bioethics*, Rosner and Bleich (eds.) New York 1979.

p.93 (5) On the theory of Chaos, see J. Gleick, *Chaos: making a new science* (Cardinal, 1988).
(6) THE ANIMAL WORLD...: A.C. based on an idea of S.D.S.
THE PHYSIOLOGICAL BASIS...: A.C.

p.94 RESTORATION IS EFFECTED...: A.C.
"LIKE A NEW BRIDE" TB *Nidda* 31b.

CHAPTER 24

p.95 (1) A.C.
DOES IT REALLY MAKE ANY DIFFERENCE TO GOD...: MR *Bereshit*, 44:1.

p.96 THE TORAH CLEARLY ANNOUNCES...: Based on H **68** 447.
THESE FOODS ARE *TAMEI* FOR YOU...: Leviticus 11:4-8.

DO NOT MAKE YOURSELVES *TAMEI* THROUGH THEM...: Leviticus
11:43-44; 20:25.
...*ANSHEI KODESH*, PEOPLE OF DEDICATION...: Exodus 22:30.
(2) Based on H **68** 448.

p.97 ONE KOSHER MEAL...: From H. Teller, *Pichifkes* (Feldheim
1989).

CHAPTER 25

p.99 (1) — (2) A.C. Based on H **68** 450.
(2) ...SPECIES WHICH ARE PREYED UPON...: MR Leviticus, 27:5.
A FURTHER CHARACTERISTIC...: TB *Hullin* 60a.

p.100 THEIR COMPLICATED DIGESTIVE APPARATUS...: A.C.
...TO LEAD US AWAY FROM AN AGGRESIVE LIFE STYLE...: A.C.
(3) ...THE MAIN CRITERION OF A FORBIDDEN SPECIES...: Mishna
Hullin 3:6.
(4) ...FINS AND SCALES...: Leviticus 11:9-10; Deut.14:9-10.
(5) ShA *Yoreh De'a* 84:8.

CHAPTER 26

p.101 Sources: ...THROW IT TO THE [SHEEP]DOG...: See commentary
Hiskuni ad loc.
...FLESH WHICH IS STILL ALIVE...: Rashi *ad loc.* Lit. "flesh
whose life is still in its blood."
(1) — (3) A.C.
(2) THE ORAL LAW TELLS US...: See Maimonides, MT "Laws of
Forbidden Foods," 4:8.

p.102 (3) TB *Sanhedrin* 57a.
...THE BASIC GUIDELINE OF MORALITY...: Maharal of Prague,
Gevurat Hashem chapter 66.
A FURTHER EXAMPLE OF THIS PRINCIPLE...: See TB *Betza* 25b.

CHAPTER 27

p.103 (1) — (3) A.C.
(1) ...FORTY YEARS EARLIER THAN THE WRITTEN LAW...: The bulk
of the Oral Law was given to Israel early in the 40-year desert
period, while the Written Torah was handed over only at the
end of this period. (See Deut. 31:9,24.)
THE SHARP CUT CAUSES NO PAIN...LOSS OF CONSCIOUSNESS
IN A MATTER OF SECONDS...: This has been demonstrated in
many experiments. See, for example, S.D. Sassoon, *A critical
study of electrical stunning and the Jewish method of
slaughter (shehita)*, (Letchworth, U.K., 1956).
...A FREELY WILLED AND INTENDED ACT...: Based on Hirsch,

Pent. Comm., on Exodus 22:30.

(2) Based on an idea of S.D.S.

p.104   THE SHOHET AND THE WIDOW...: Based on "A nightmare to remember," in P.J. Krohn, *The Maggid Speaks* (Mesorah, New York 1987) p.152.

CHAPTER 28

p.106   (1) Based on Hirsch Pent. Comm. Leviticus 7:26.

p.107   ...SYMBOLIZED IN DRAMATIC FASHION THE DEDICATION OF ALL OUR VITAL FORCES...: Based on Hirsch, Pent. Comm., on Leviticus 1:5 and *passim*.

(2) AS AN ADDITIONAL WARNING TO OUR SUBCONSCIOUS MIND ...: Based on Hirsch, ibid.17:13.

(3) *Helev.* Based on Hirsch, ibid 3:17.

p.108   (4) A.C.

p.109   HALACHA

SALTING...: See ShA *Yoreh De'a*, 69-78.

p.110   EGG WITH BLOODSPOT...: Ibid. 86.

p.111   BLOODSPOTS AND BLOOD LIBEL...: Traditional.

p.113   (5) A.C.

CHAPTER 29

p.114   (1) — (3) Based on H **69** 457-459.

p.115   (2) ...ANY SOLDIER... IS EXCLUDED FROM IT...: Based on Nachmanides' Commentary on Deut. 23:10, "According to the simple meaning...."

(4) *Ibid.* 461.

Group Three :
Love and Concern for Other People

CHAPTER 30

p.118   (1) — (3) A.C.

...WHICH IS WHAT THE TORAH WANTS...: See TB *Shabbat* 10b, Rashi s.v. *tzarich; Tanna de-bei Eliyah Rabba* 2b.

THE MIDNIGHT RESCUE...: A.C. Video Series "Living Judaism," Program 1. Based on *Strive for Truth* I, pp 126 — 130.

p.120   (2) WHY DID HILLEL...: A.C.

THIS IS THE WHOLE TORAH...: A.C.

p.121   (3) A.C.
(4) THERE NEVER WAS A TIME WHEN THERE WAS SO MUCH CONCERN...: Cf. Chief Rabbi Lord Jacobovits. "The role of religion in world affairs," in *Le'eyla* (Jews College Publ., 1989).
ON THE OTHER HAND, THE NUMBER OF HUMAN BEINGS KILLED...: S.D.S. *Natan Hochma Lishlomo*, p.25.

p.122   ...THE EXISTENCE OF NUCLEAR WEAPONS HAS DRASTICALLY REDUCED THE LIFE EXPECTANCY...: A.C.
THE EXPLANATION OF THESE ANOMALIES...: A.C.

CHAPTER 31

p.123   (1) Based on H **72** 480.
THREE PARTNERS...: TB *Kiddushin* 30b.
THIS IS THE BASIS FOR THE MITZVA...: See Rabbi E.E. Dessler, *Michtav Me'Eliyahu* III, p.95.
GOD HAS EQUATED THEIR HONOR...: TB *Kiddushin* 30b.
(2) A.C.

p.124   THE HOW AND WHY OF A MITZVA...: TB. *Kiddushin* 31a-b.
p.125   THE RIGHTEOUS GENTILE...: Ibid. 31a.
p.126   (3) Based on H **73** 487. Partly taken from Soncino *Horeb*.

CHAPTER 32

p.128   A CIVILIZATION OF THE MIND...: A.C. with reference to H **74** 490.
HOW FOOLISH...TO STAND UP BEFORE THE SEFER TORAH...AND NOT...BEFORE THE SAGE...: TB *Makkot* 22b.
WE HAVE TO RISE BEFORE EVERYONE DISTINGUISHED IN TORAH...: H **74** 490.
...SEEMS TO INDICATE SYMBOLICALLY OUR READINESS TO BE OF SERVICE...: *Ibid.* 490(end).

CHAPTER 33

p.130   (1) A.C. based on Rabbi E.E. Dessler *Strive for Truth!* I, p.131.
(2) — (3) A.C.
p.131   (4) Based on H **80** 528.
p.132   (5) A.C.
HALACHA
THERE ARE TWO STEPS...: Based on H **81** 531.
p.133   SINCE EVERY MARRIAGE...: Based on *ibid.* 532.
...IN THE PRESENCE OF A *MINYAN*...: Ketubot 8a. For concept of *minyan* see chapters 65(5) and 78(6).
BLESSINGS...: T.B *Ketubot* 8a.

CHAPTER 34

p.134   (1) — (2) Based on H **84** 548-9. Partly taken from Soncino *Horeb*.

CHAPTER 35

p.136   (1) Based on H **85** 557.

p.137   (2) IN THE OPENING SECTION OF THIS BOOK WE LEARNED...: Based on H **85** 558.

WE ARE MEMBERS OF ONE COVENANT...: Based on L. Levi, "Israel and the nations," p.146 in H.C. Schimmel and A. Carmell (eds.), *Encounter* (AOJS and Feldheim, 1989).

IF ONE FINDS PROPERTY...: Mishna *Bava Metzia*, ch.2.

p.138   THIS LAW OF THE TORAH...SEEMS STRANGE...: Based on Maharal of Prague, *Be'er Ha-gola* (London 1964) p.31 et seq.

p.139   ...IT IS A MITZVA OF LOVE TO RETURN IT TO HIM ALL THE SAME...: Maharal, *ibid.*, p.32.

(3) A.C. based on Leviticus 5:1. See also *Sefer Ha-ḥinuch*, mitzva 123.

(4) — (5) Based on H **85** 562.

p.140   EXTRAORDINARY!...: A.C. based on Midrash Tanḥuma Mishpatim.

CHAPTER 36

p.142   (1) Based on H **86** 563.

See R. Yisrael Meir Ha-Cohen (*Ḥafetz Ḥayim*), *Ahavat Ḥesed*, ch. 1.

p.143   (2) Based on H **86** 567-8.

HALACHA

p.144   ...JOINT BUSINESS VENTURE:::*HETTER 'ISKA*...: ShA, *Yoreh De'a* 177.

(3) Based on H **91** 585.

THE RABBIS DECIDED THERE IS NO TIME LIMIT...: TB *Bava Metzia* 35a.

p.145   NO SODOMITES HERE...: A.C. based on TB *Ketubot* 103a; ShA *Ḥoshen Mishpat* 318.

CHAPTER 37

p.146   (1) A.C.

p.147   NOBODY BECOMES POOR THROUGH TZEDAKA...: MT Gifts to the Poor Ch. 10.

TABLE 3. — PRIORITIES IN TSEDAKA...: A.C. with some reference to H **111** 677. See also C.Domb, *Maaser kesafim* (On giving a

tenth to charity), (AOJS, London, 1980) Ch.4.
(2) IN OTHER SOCIETIES...: A.C.

p.148 THE QUALITY OF A MITZVA: Based on H **88** 572.
BETTER GET BURNT THAN EMBARRASS YOUR FRIEND: From TB
Ketubot 67b.

p.149 BETTER TO GIVE A SMILE WITHOUT MILK...: TB *Ketubot* 111b.
IF YOU CANNOT ACCEDE...: Based on H **88** 572.

p.150 ...ALMS BEFORE...THE DAILY PRAYERS...: ShA *Oraḥ Ḥayim*
92:10.
...IN MEMORY OF PARENTS...: H **88** 571.
(3) Based on H **88** 575. Partly taken from Soncino *Horeb.*

p.151 (4) Based on H **88** 576.
BETWEEN LIFE AND DEATH...: TB *Nedarim* 40a.
(5) — (6) A.C. With reference to H **88** 578.

p.152 (7) — (8) Based on H **88** 579-80.

CHAPTER 38

p.154 (1) A.C.
WHY THREE DAYS...: Personal communication.

p.155 (2) Based on H **89** 581. Partly taken from Soncino *Horeb.*

p.156 HE WHO SUFFERS WRONG AND DOES NO WRONG IN RETURN...: TB
Shabbat 88b.
PRESCRIPTION FOR CONQUERING RESENTMENT: R. Dov Katz,
*Tenuat Ha-Mussar,*Vol.1, p.379.

CHAPTER 39

p.158 (1) Based on H **90** 582.
WHEN LIGHTING THE MENORAH IN THE TEMPLE...: Based on H
Pent. Comm. Exodus 27:20.
(2) Based on H **90** 583.

p.159 (3) Based on H **90** 584.
(1) — (3) Partly taken from Soncino *Horeb.*

CHAPTER 40

p.161 (1) Based on H **95** 597.
(2) Based on H **95** 598.

p.163 (3) Based on H **95** 605.
(4) — (5) A.C.

Group Four :
Enrichment of the Environment

CHAPTER 41

p.167   (1) — (2) Based on H **21** 139-142.

p.168   (1) ...AS MAHARAL OF PRAGUE TELLS US...: See *Tiferet Yisrael* Chapter 40. (A.C.)

...INDICATIONS IN OUR SOURCES...: *Pesikta Rabbati* ch.23. See Dayan Grunfeld's Additional Note C in Soncino *Horeb*, pp. 271-272.

IN ANCIENT BABYLON...: See *Encycl. Ha-ivrit*, vol. 31, p. 423.

p.169   (2) ...WHEREVER WE SEE A GREAT CONCENTRATION OF POWER...: S.D.S., "Judaism: its challenge to science," in *Jewish Studies* (1990), p.20.

p.170   (3) Based on H **21** 144. Partly taken from Soncino *Horeb*.

p.171   (4) Based on H **21** 143.

p.172-6   (5) — (8) A.C.

p.172   ...EMPLOYER-EMPLOYEE RELATIONS...: A.C.

...ONLY FROM THIS VANTAGE POINT...: A.C.

p.173   THE SABBATH HAS GUARDED ISRAEL MORE...: The Rabbi of Gur, *Sefat Emet, Ki Tissa* [5633].

THE DISTURBED SABBATH...: Traditional.

CHAPTER 42

p.177   (1) A.C.

THE HAIRY AND THE BALD...: MR Genesis 65:15.

p.178   THE SECRET OF ISRAEL'S ABILITY...: Based on Maharal of Prague, *Discourse on Shabbat Teshuva* (London 1964) p.83. See also Rabbi E.E. Dessler, *Michtav Me-Eliyahu* II, pp. 98-100.

(2) — (3) Based on H **22** 155-157.

p.179   (4) *Ibid.* 157.

APART FROM THIS, EATING AND DRINKING ON YOM KIPPUR EVE HAS THREE FUNCTIONS...: Based on Rabbenu Yona, *Gates of Repentance*, 4:8-10.

(5) Based on H **22** 160.

p.180   ...TO HERALD THE ADVENT OF THE DAY OF ATONEMENT...: See Ramban, Torah Commentary, on Levit. 23:24.

p.181   HALACHA

THE FAST OF YOM KIPPUR...: Levit. 23:32.

NO REFRESHMENT...: ShA *Orah Hayim*, 612.

IN ADDITION WASHING...: *Ibid.* 613-615.

SICK PEOPLE...: *Ibid.* 617-618.

CHAPTER 43

p.182-7 (1) — (4) Based on H **23** 161-170.

p.183 (2) PESAH...CORRESPONDS TO THE SPRING-TIME...: A.C.
...THE TORAH...THE "FIRST FRUITS" OF THE EXODUS...: A.C.

p.185 (3) Based on H23 169.

p.186 SHEMINI ATZERET...THE AMAZING REGENERATION OF TORAH
LIFE...AFTER THE HOLOCAUST...: A.C.
(4) H **23** 171-2. Partly taken from Soncino *Horeb*.

p.188 Halacha Sh.A. Oraḥ Ḥayim 495.

CHAPTER 44

p.189 (1) A.C.

p.190-1 (2) — (3) Based on H **24** 178-181.

p.191 (2) A DIFFERENT PERSON...: Told by Rabbi S. Wolbe
(Jerusalem).

p.192 (4) Based on H **25** 186-192.

p.193 (5) Based on H **24** 184.
(6) A.C.
YOU SHALL EAT, DRINK AND ENJOY YOURSELVES...: This is a
paraphrase of Deuteronomy 14:23,26.

p.194 "FESTIVALS WERE GIVEN TO ISRAEL..." T.J. *Moed Katan.*
EXPENSES OF THE WEDDING...: The Maggid of Dubnow in *Ohel
Yaakov, P. Behar.*
...WILL BE REFUNDED BY GOD...: TB *Beytza* 16b.
...NOT GOD BUT OUR OWN BELLY...: MT "Laws of Festivals"
6:16.

CHAPTER 45

p.197 (1) Based mainly on H **26** 197-199.
AS SOON AS FLOUR IS KNEADED...: A.C.

p.198 IF WE DELIBERATELY FLOUT THE LAW...: Exodus 12:15.
IN OUR TIME, AFTER 2,000 YEARS...: A.C.
(2) A.C.

p.199 HALACHA
ḤAMETZ IS UNUSUAL...: TB *Pesaḥim* 11a.

p.200 ON THE NIGHT OF THE 13TH-14TH...: ShA *Oraḥ Ḥayim* 431-439.
...SYMBOLIC SIGNIFICANCE...: The candle symbolizes our con-
science which searches out the hidden recesses of the mind.
A.C.
...MAY NOT BE USED AFTER PESAH...: Ibid. 448.

CHAPTER 46

p.201 (1) A.C.
THE LAMB...SYMBOLIZED THE UNITY OF THE HOUSE OF ISRAEL...:

Sources and Notes

p.202 Based on Maharal of Prague, *Gevurat Ha-Shem* ch. 60.
(2) Based on H **28** 209.
TELLING THE STORY...: Traditional.

CHAPTER 47

p.204 (1) — (2) A.C.
...ONE *OMER*...ONE DAY'S FOOD SUPPLY...: *Exodus* 16:18.

p.205 BARLEY IS MAINLY FOOD FOR ANIMALS...: *Maharal of Prague, Tiferet Yisrael*, ch.25.
THIS IS WHY SHAVUOT IS SEPARATED...BY 49 DAYS...: A.C.

p.206 (3) Based on H **29** 215.
THIS IS SPECIALLY RELEVANT IN OUR TIME...: A.C.

CHAPTER 48

p.207 THE MESSAGE OF THE SHOFAR...: Based partly on H **32** 226-229.
...THE WILD CRY FROM THE HEART...: A.C.
THE TORAH'S SYMBOLISM REMAINS FOREVER RELEVANT...: A.C.

CHAPTER 49

p.209 (1) — (3) Based mainly on H **30** 216-221.

p.210 (2) EVEN WHEN HUMAN BEINGS THINK...: A.C.
(3) ...A COPERNICAN REVOLUTION OF THE SPIRIT...: A.C.

CHAPTER 50

p.212 (1) — (2) Based on H **31** 222B — 223.

p.213 Table 8. — Based on H *ibid.*
(3) A.C.
MAIMONIDES LINKED THESE SPECIES...: *Guide for the Perplexed*, III, ch.43.

p.214 HALACHA
ONE SHOULD TAKE ONE *ETROG* ETC....: ShA *Oraḥ Ḥayim* 651:1.
(IT WILL BE SEEN FROM THE TABLE ABOVE)...: Based partly on H *Pent. Comm.* Leviticus 23:40.
(TO MAKE A CIRCUIT AROUND AN OBJECT..)...: Based on H **31** 225.

p.215 AT CERTAIN POINTS IN THE SERVICE...: ShA *Ibid.* 651:9.
(...THAT HIS GIFTS FLOW IN ON US...): H **31** *ibid.*

CHAPTER 51

p.216 (1) — (3) A.C.

p.218 (4) THESE TWO EVENTS...UP TO THE PRESENT DAY...: A.C.

WE CAN NOW COMPLETE THE SCHEME...: Based on H **34** 249.
HALACHA
PURIM...: ShA *Oraḥ Ḥayim* 686-697.
NO HALLEL...: TB *Megilla* 14a.

p.219 (A TORAH FESTIVAL ENGENDERS ITS OWN HOLINESS...): A.C.
ḤANUKKA...: ShA *Oraḥ Ḥayim* 670-684.
THERE IS NO OBLIGATION TO HAVE A FESTIVE MEAL...: Based
on *ibid.* 670 *Mishna Berura* No. 6. "However it is customary...." — *Ibid.* 670:2.

CHAPTER 52

p.220 (1) — (3). A.C. with some reference to H **33**.
(2) A.C.
(THE FESTIVALS OF THE TORAH FALL IN THE EQUABLE
WEATHER...): From Maharal, *Netzaḥ Yisrael* ch. 8.
p.220 GEDALIA, A RIGHTEOUS MAN...: Jeremiah 40:7-41:18.
p.221 (2) Table 7. — A.C.
...THE DEATH OF THE RIGHTEOUS...: TB *Rosh Hashana* 18b.
WE MIGHT ADD...: A.C.
p.222 (3) ACCORDING TO OUR SAGES...: TB *Yoma* 9b.
THE REASON IS THAT A PERSON WHO FALLS INTO OPEN AND
OBVIOUS CRIMES...: See Rabbi E.E. Dessler, *Strive for Truth!* II
p.200.
FASTING IS A SIGN OF CONTRITION...: Based on H **33** 240.
(4) A.C. THE FAST OF ESTHER...: ShA *Oraḥ Ḥayim* 686.
THE FAST OF THE FIRSTBORN...: *Ibid.* 470.
HALACHA
ShA *ibid.* 549-559.

CHAPTER 53

p.224 (1) and Table 8 — based on ShA *ibid.* 428.
p.225 (2) Based on Hirsch *Pent. Comm.* Exodus 12:2.
(3) Based on TB *Rosh Hashana* 20a: ...BECAUSE OF THE
VEGETABLES...: Rashi: "So that the vegetables should not
wither [because no fresh supplies available for 48 hours]."
(4) Based on Hirsch *Pent. Comm. ibid.*
p.227 (5) A.C.

CHAPTER 54

p.228 (1) — (3) A.C. with some reference to H **36**.
p.229 (2) THIS IS THE SYMBOLISM OF CIRCUMCISION...: A.C.
p.230 (4) — (5) A.C.
p.231 GOD'S WORKS AND MAN'S WORKS...: Midrash Tanḥuma, *Tazria,*

No. 5.

p.232 HALACHA

ShA *Yoreh De'a* 260-264.

CHAPTER 55

p.233 (1) A.C.

...FROM THE HEBREW *PALLAL*, 'THINK'...: Cf. Rashi on Genesis 48:11.

p.234 (2) Based on H **38** 271 (much abbreviated).

...TORAH IN MINIATURE,"...: Hirsch, *Collected Writings*, III, "Jewish Symbolism," iii, 3B.

(3) Based on H **38** 274.

(...THE FRONTAL LOBE...CONTROLS VISION AND SEEMS INVOLVED IN DECISION MAKING...): See Sally P. Springer and Deutsch, *Left Brain, Right Brain* (rev. ed. 1985) p.282.

p.235 ...THE ACT OF BINDING...BY THE STRONGER HAND...: Cf. Mechilta on Exodus 13:9.

(4) (a) Based on *Collected Writings*, as above.

(b) ...OUR COMMITMENT MUST BE FIRMLY BASED...: A.C.

p.236 ...THE *SHIN* ON THE LEFT HAS FOUR ARMS...: A.C. based on a kabbalistic source.

(c) ...THE ONLY WAY TO BIND ONESELF TO THE ALMIGHTY...: A.C.

p.237 (d) ...THE MEANING RESIDES IN THE FACT THAT BLACK ABSORBS ALL THE LIGHT...: A.C.

ABSORBING AND RADIATING...: Based on article in *Yom Ha-shishi*, Jerusalem, 27.4.90, p. 24.

CHAPTER 56

p.238 (1) A.C.

THE RABBIS HINT THAT A PSYCHOLOGICAL FACTOR IS INVOLVED...: See A. Carmell, "Demons: a post-modern view," in *Jewish Study Magazine*, Jerusalem, Sept. 5738 (1978).

p.239 HALACHA

THE RABBIS COMPARED OUR MEAL...: See TB *Hullin* 106a, also Tosefot *ad loc.* s.v. mitzva.

...IF POSSIBLE A FULL MEASURE...IF WATER IS SCARCE...: Sh.A. *Orah Hayim* 158:10.

AT WHOSE COST?...: R. Dov Katz, *Tenuat Ha-mussar*, Vol. 1.

p.240 (2) Based on H **69** 464.

p.241 (3) *Ibid.* 463.

CHAPTER 57

p.242-4 (1) WE HAVE ALL EXPERIENCED...: A.C.
THE PSYCHOLOGY OF CLOTHING...: Personal communication to
author.
(2) — (4) Based on Hirsch, *Pent.Comm.*, Numbers 15:38.

p.244 FIGURE 3. — A.C. Based on Sh.A. *Orah Ḥayim* 11, *Mishna
Berura* 70. The order 7,8,11 is preferred by Ashkenazim over
the direct representation of the letters of the Divine Name,
10,5,6,5, because an ascending series is considered preferable.
However the latter scheme is widely adopted by Sephardim.

p.245 THINGS AT THE LIMIT OF OUR HORIZON...: Prof. Yehuda Levi
(pers. comm.)
DURING THE COURSE OF TIME...: A.C.
HOWEVER THE VERY ABSENCE...: Based on Hirsch *ibid.*
(5) A.C.

CHAPTER 58

p.247 (1) — (2) A.C.

CHAPTER 59

p.248 (1) — (2) Based on H **40** 287-289.
p.249 (3) Based on MT "Laws of Tefillin, Mezuza etc.," 6:13.

CHAPTER 60

p.250 WHEN ONE ACQUIRES...: ShA *Yoreh De'a* 121,120.
THIS IS A SYMBOLIC ACT...: Based on H **69** 465.
WE MAY ASK WHY *METAL* VESSELS...: Based on Hirsch *Pent.
Comm.* Numbers 31:22.

p.251 HALACHA
ShA *ibid.* 120.

CHAPTER 61

p.252 (1) — (2) Based mainly on H **41** 291-295.
...THE POTENTIAL OF PRIESTHOOD REMAINS...: Compare Rad-
vaz, *Metzudat David*, Mitzva 276 and Rabbi E.E. Dessler
Michtav Me-Eliyahu IV p.178.

p.253 (2) NUMBERS IN MITZVOT ARE ALWAYS MEANINGFUL...: A.C.
HALACHA
SHA *Yoreh De'a* 305.

CHAPTER 62

p.254   (1) A.C.

p.255   (1) NO SOWING OR PLOWING...: Mishna, *Shevi'it* 1-4.

(2) THE LANDOWNER MUST RELINQUISH...: *Ibid.* 9:2-4.

(3) THE PRODUCE MAY BE USED...: *Ibid.* 7-8.

TRUE HEROISM...: See MR Leviticus, 1:1.

BY THESE LAWS...: Based on Hirsch *Pent. Comm.* Leviticus 25:5.

...THE EARTH AND ITS FULLNESS BELONG TO GOD...: Psalms 24:1.

...THE ANIMALS OF THE WILD...: A.C.

p.256   (2) A.C.

50,000 ORANGE TREES...: Related to the author by Rav Mendelson.

p.257   (3) LOANS WERE USUALLY TAKEN...: Based on Rabbi N.Z.Y. Berlin, *Ha'amek Davar*, on Deut. 15:2.

...AS THE COURT WILL USE ITS DISCRETION...: See *Ha'amek Davar*, on Deut. 15:4.

CHAPTER 63

p.258   (1) — (2) A.C.

(1) ...DESCRIBED IN THE TALMUD AS A MAN OF FAITH...: TB *Shabbat* 31a *Tosefot* s.v. *emunat.*

p.259   WHAT THEY TEACH...: Based to some extent on H **42** 305.

TABLE 10: A.C.

Group Five :
The Inner Life

CHAPTER 64

p.265   (1) — (2) A.C.

EVERYONE IS OBLIGED TO STUDY...: MT "Laws of Torah study" 1:8.

p.266   THE FOREST...: Based on TB *Sota* 21a.

p.267   (3) Based on H **75** 493-494.

ACCOMPANY THEM TO THEIR HOUSES OF STUDY, TAKE PART IN THEIR LIVELY DEBATES...: A.C.

p.268   THE MOUND, THE CAKE AND THE LEAKY PAIL: MR Leviticus 19:2.

p.270   (4) A.C.

p.271   FATHER AND SON, TEACHER AND STUDENT...: TB *Kiddushin* 30b.

...TORAH LEARNING CAN SUBLIMATE OUR SEXUAL ENERGIES...: TB *Rosh Hashana* 4a.

p.272 (5) — (6) Based on H *ibid.*
(7) — (8) A.C.

CHAPTER 65

p.274 (1) — (10) A.C., with reference to H **111**.
p.275 (1) YOU ARE A FOOL!...: Jerusalem Post article.
(2) THE MEN OF THE GREAT ASSEMBLY...: See Mishna *Avot* 1:2.
THE TORAH ALREADY REQUIRED...: As quoted at head of this chapter.
p.276 TO SEE INFINITY IN A GRAIN OF SAND...: W. Blake, *Intimations of Immortality*.
(3) See *Otzar ha-tefillot* prayer book (Vilna 1915) Fo.11.
p.277 (4) See TB *Berachot* 26b: "the Prayers were ordained to correspond to the daily offerings in the Temple."
CONTINUING AND EXPANDING A MUCH OLDER ORDINANCE...: TB *Bava Kamma* 82a; MT "Laws of Prayer" 12:1.
p.278 (IN FACT THE RABBIS CALL THE SYNAGOGUE "THE TEMPLE IN MINIATURE...") TB *Megilla* 29a, based on Ezekiel 11:16.
(5) THIS IS INTENDED TO MAKE US CONSTANTLY AWARE OF THE GREAT PRINCIPLE...: A.C. See H **661**.
p.279 THE DREAM...: Personal communication.
p.280 (6) ...THE CLIMAX OF EVERY SERVICE...: A.C.
...A KIND OF 'HEAVENLY ECHO'...: One can imagine the Reader as a kind of relay station, relaying our own words back to us after they have been received in Heaven. — A.C.
p.281 THE STRUCTURE OF THE *SHEMONEH ESSREH*...: A.C.
p.282 THE THREE SERVICES OF THE DAY...: Based on H **99** 628; **101** 643; **102** 645.
(7) THEY HAVE PUT BEFORE US FOUR BLESSINGS...: A.C. See TB *Berachot* 48b and MR Numbers 23:7.
(8) HALLEL COMPRISES...: TB *Pesahim* 117a.
p.283 IT MAY ALSO BE SAID PRIVATELY...: Halachically speaking, this is no more than the reading of certain chapters in the Book of Psalms, though its significance to the individual may be considerable.
...RECOGNIZE HIS SAVING HAND DURING THE LONG NIGHT OF EXILE...: After the fall of Betar and the bloody suppression of the Bar Kochba revolt (135 CE) the Romans forbade burial of the dead for many years. Miraculously the bodies did not decompose and when burial was eventually allowed the rabbis added this fourth blessing to the Grace after Meals (TB *Berachot* 48b). This was to acknowledge that God's sustaining power remains with us even in the depth of exile.

371

Table 12. — A.C.

ON ROSH ḤODESH...: Sh.A. *Oraḥ Ḥayim* 422:2.

THE SAME APPLIES...: *Ibid.* 490:4.

p.284   ON ROSH HASHANA...: TB *Rosh Hashana* 32b.

ON PURIM...: TB *Megilla* 17a.

GO AND SAY HALLEL...: Personal communication to the author.

(9) See H **108**

p.285   A STROKE OF GENIUS...: A.C.

p.286   ...*DAF HA-YOMI* PROJECT...: Introduced by R. Meir Shapiro at Agudat Israel conference, 1923.

THIS ANCIENT ORDINANCE...: The prophetic readings are referred to as an established custom in the Mishna (*Megilla* 4:3,5), the Talmud and the responsa of the Geonim. See also R. Tam, *Sefer Hayashar* No. 182.

(10) ...TO CONCLUDE THE PRAYERS ON A HIGH NOTE...: See *Tur, Oraḥ Ḥayim* 133, R. Joel Sirkes, *Bayit Ḥadash.*

READINGS FROM THE PROPHETS...: A.C.

p.287   PEOPLE CALLED UP TO THE TORAH...: Mishna *Megilla* 4:1.2.

CHAPTER 66

p.288   (1) Based largely on Dr. J.H. Hertz, *Authorised Daily Prayer Book* (London 1963) pp. 265-269.

p.289   ...THE UNITY OF THE COSMOS — THE FOUNDATION OF MODERN SCIENCE...: Various thinkers have suggested that it was the absence of the concept of a single rational creator of the cosmos that prevented the Chinese and the Greeks, in spite of their intellectual brilliance, from developing anything resembling modern science. The latest to write on these lines is J.D. Barrow in *The world within the world,* (OUP 1988) p. 35.

p.290   (2) ...PART OF THE TEMPLE SERVICE...: Mishna *Tamid* 5:1.

CHAPTER 67

p.291   (1) A.C.

(2) TO AVOID THE IMPRESSION THAT THIS IS SOME MAGICAL RITE...: Based on H Pent. Comm. Numbers 6:22 and H **112** 685-6.

p.292   ...WITH UPLIFTED ARMS...POINTING UPWARDS TO GOD...: H **112** 685.

(3) A.C. based partly on H **112** 686 and Pent. Comm. *ad loc.*

(4) — (6) A.C.

CHAPTER 68

p.295   (1) Based on H **1** 1-3.
p.296   (2) A.C.

CHAPTER 69

p.298   (1) — (2) A.C.
(1) ...THE SOULS OF ALL FUTURE GENERATIONS...: Based on
Deuteronomy 29:14.

CHAPTER 70

p.300   (1) — (2) Based on H **2** 6-7.
p.301   I AM ONE, THEREFORE ONE LOVE SHOULD DOMINATE YOUR
LIFE...: This is implied by the first two verses of the Shema,
Deut. 6:4-5. (See chapter 74.)
...TO LOVE THE SOURCE OF THAT ACHIEVEMENT...: See Deut.
8:19.

CHAPTER 71

p.302   Introductory verses:
...ALONGSIDE MY ALL-PERVADING DOMINION...: This is
Hirsch's translation of *al panai*, lit. "before My face."
(1) A.C. based partly on H **3** 8-9.
WE SEE "NATURE"...RAISED TO A POWER IN ITS OWN RIGHT...: See
Rabbi E.E. Dessler, "The nature of nature," in *Strive for
Truth!* II p. 252.
p.303   THOSE WHOSE BELLIES ARE THEIR GOD...: Rabbenu Baḥya
(11th cent. Spain), *Duties of the Heart*, 9:2.
p.304   (2) A.C.
WE GOT HERE PURELY BY ACCIDENT...: J. Monod, *Chance and
Necessity* (Collins, 1972).
...THAT THIS STURDY, LUSTY AND VIBRANT CHILD...: S.D.
Sassoon, *Reality Revisited* (Feldheim, 1991) p. 209.
WHEN I THINK OF THE EYE, I SHUDDER...: From the letters of
Charles Darwin, quoted by G.R. Taylor, *The great evolution
mystery*, (Secker & Warburg, 1983), p. 4.
WHAT IS THE MOTIVE THAT LEADS MEN TO IGNORE THE
EVIDENCE...: S.D. Sassoon, *op.cit.* p. 211.
p.305   EVOLUTION NEED NO LONGER BE A DESTINY IMPOSED FROM
WITHOUT...: T. Dobzhansky, *Mankind evolving* (Yale U.P.
1962), pp. 346-7.
THIS IS THE NEW MYTHOLOGY...: This and the following

paragraph are based on: Langdon Gilkey, "Biblical symbols in a scientific culture," in *Science and human values in the 21st century*, R.W. Burhoe (ed.), (Westminster Press, Philadelphia, 1971), p. 72.

CHAPTER 72

p.306   (1) — (7) Based on H 8 38-48. Taken in part from Soncino *Horeb*.

(1) *YIRAT SHAMAYIM*...: Lit. "fear of heaven."

p.308   (6) THERE IS NO DARKNESS THAT CAN CONCEAL US...: *Ibid.* 11-12.

...OUR VERY THOUGHTS ARE OPEN TO HIS SCRUTINY...: Psalms 94:11; I Chronicles, 8:9.

SOME MEN, GREAT PERHAPS IN INTELLECT BUT DEFICIENT IN UNDERSTANDING...: A.C.

GOD IS NOT AN ALIEN POWER....: A.C.

...THE MIND OF GOD WITH WHICH OUR HIGHER SELF IS IN SOME SENSE CONTINUOUS...: See S.D. Sassoon, *Reality Revisited* (Feldheim, 1991) pp. 177-181. When we say that our mind is "in some sense continuous with the mind of God" we do not mean God in His essence, but as S.D.S. puts it, "the realm of the Divine Will." God's will is revealed in the sphere of the non-ego area of the human psyche and it is with this sphere that certain layers of the human unconscious may be in contact.

p.309   (7) JUSTICE AND RIGHT ARE THE FOUNDATIONS OF HIS RULE...: Psalms 97:2.

CHAPTER 73

p.310   (1) — (3) Largely based on H 9 49-56. Taken in part from Soncino *Horeb*.

(1) HOW CAN ONE BE COMMANDED TO LOVE?...: A.C.

p.311   (2) ...THERE IS NO PURER LOVE THAN THE LOVE OF DEEP GRATITUDE...: A.C.

(3) WHATEVER MEASURE HE ALLOTS TO YOU ...: Mishna, *Berachot* 9:5.

REB ZUSHA'S SURPRISE: Traditional.

CHAPTER 74

p.313   (1) — (3) Based on H 72 481-482. Taken from Soncino *Horeb* with some changes.

TRY TO FOLLOW MY EXAMPLE — AND LOVE!...: This summarizes the mitzva "to walk in God's ways," as explained in the quotations at the head of this chapter.

GOD'S IMAGE IS THE CAPACITY FOR LOVE...: See Rabbi E.E. Dessler, *Strive for Truth!* I, p. 119. See also "The image of God," in the Introduction, and chapter 2(1).

CREATION IS AN ACT OF LOVE...: See Maimonides, *Guide*, III, 53, who writes: "Lovingkindness is benefaction to someone who has no claims on you at all...and so all good that comes from God is lovingkindness...Thus the bringing into being of all existence by God is an act of love...[this is why] He is described as 'abundant in love.'"

p.314   BUT WE MUST NOT FALL INTO THE TRAP...: A.C.

(2) GOD HAS NO PLEASURE IN THE PUNISHMENT OF THE WICKED...: Ezekiel 18:23.

(3) A SENSE OF GRATITUDE IS OUR MOST TREASURED POSSESSION...: Comp. Rabbi E.E. Dessler, *Michtav Me-Eliyahu* III pp. 99-100.

p.315   (4) — (5) A.C.

CHAPTER 75

p.316   A.C. with reference to H **10** 69-70.

"GOD OF FAITH"? ASK THE RABBIS...: *Sifre* on Deut. 32:4.

YET IF WE SEEK HIS TRACES IN THE WORLD AND SOCIETY...: H **10** 70.

WE SEE AS MUCH OF THE TRUE PATTERN...AS A MITE...: A.C.

AND YET TO THE DISCERNING EYE...: A.C.

p.317   FAITH IN TORAH IS VINDICATED...: A.C.

EMUNA IS NO "BLIND LEAP OF FAITH"...: A.C. The phrase in quotes is taken from Kirkegaard.

CHAPTER 76

p.318   (1) — (2) A.C.
p.319   (1) HOW ISRAEL CAME TO EGYPT...: Genesis 37-50.

YOU THOUGHT YOU WERE DOING ME HARM...: Genesis 45:4-8; 50:20.

(2) HEALING COMES FROM GOD BUT THE PHYSICIAN IS HIS MESSENGER...: Compare Rabbi E.E. Dessler, *Strive for Truth!* II p. 295.

CHAPTER 77

p.321   (1) — (2) A.C.

(1) ...THE GREATEST CROWN OF GREAT MEN...: TB *Avoda Zara* 20b; MR *Shir Ha-shirim* 1:9.

...LITTLE MEN WHO ARE BOUND TO 'THE SURFACE OF THE

EARTH'...: — Ḥassidic source.

p.322　(2) ...INFLUX FROM THE HIGHER LEVELS OF BEING...: See S.D.S. *Reality Revisited*, pp. 176-180.

JUST AS WATER FLOWS FROM THE HIGHER LEVEL...: *Derech Eretz Zuta* 8.

THE LOST WAGER...: From TB *Shabbat* 31a.

CHAPTER 78

p.324　The contents of this chapter are based (with permission) on the original treatment of this subject by Leo Levi in his "Talks on Judaism" 15-16 (Heb.) (unpubl.). The presentation however is the author's (A.C.). In a few places the author has deviated from or added to Prof. Levi's ideas, and these are indicated below.

(1) A.C.

(2) A.C.

AT CREATION THEY STOOD SHOULDER TO SHOULDER...: So also in Gen. 1:27-28.

AND AT THE CREATION OF THE JEWISH NATION...: A.C.

GOD GAVE PRECEDENCE TO THE WOMEN (AS OUR SAGES TELL US)...: See MR Exodus 28:2.

p.325　(3) A WOMAN'S EVIDENCE IS FULLY ACCEPTED...: TB *Gittin* 2b; ShA *Even Ha-ezer,* 17:3.

...NOT ACCEPTED IN COURT PROCEEDINGS...: TB *Shevuot* 30a.

...MITZVOT WHICH ARE BOUND TO TIME...: Mishna *Kiddushin* 1:7.

...IN CONNECTION WITH THE GOLDEN CALF AND THE REFUSAL TO ENTER THE PROMISED LAND...: MR Numbers 21:10.

...NO POSITION OF AUTHORITY...: MT "Laws of Kings..." 1:5.

...IN FORMING A *MINYAN*...: ShA *Oraḥ Ḥayim* 55:1.

ENDOWED WITH SUPERIOR UNDERSTANDING...: TB *Nidda* 45b.

...CAN ASSESS CHARACTER BETTER...: TB *Berachot* 10b.

...HIGH-LEVEL TALMUDIC STUDY...: ShA *Yoreh De'a* 246:6.

A MARRIED COUPLE ARE AS ONE PERSON...: Genesis 2:24. TB *Menaḥot* 93b.

A MAN IS COMMANDED TO FOUND A FAMILY...: Mishna *Yevamot* 6:6.

...THE GIRLS HAVE PRIOR CLAIM...: Mishna *Ketubot* 1:3.

...ONLY MALES INHERIT...: Numbers 27:8.

p.326　(4) ...WE HAVE ALREADY SEEN THE IMPORTANT PART [MARITAL HAPPINESS] PLAYS IN THE TORAH...: A.C.

p.327　(5) ...INDEED WE HAVE TO SOME EXTENT SEEN THIS REALIZED IN OUR TIME...: A.C.

p.328　(6) ...CONSISTENT WITH RECENT PSYCHOLOGICAL DISCOV-

ERIES...: A.C. See for example Sally P. Springer & G. Deutch, *Left Brain, Right Brain* (W.H. Freeman, N.Y. revised edition, 1985) ch. 8.

...SUBLIMATE THEIR AGGRESSIVE INSTINCTS IN THE THRUST AND PARRY OF TALMUDIC ARGUMENT...: A.C.

...FRIENDSHIP IN THE END...: A.C. See TB *Kiddushin* 30b.

p.329   (7) — (8) A.C.

CHAPTER 79

p.331   (1) A.C.

DONKEY OR DIAMONDS...: TJ *Bava Metzia* 2:5.

p.332   EVERY MITZVA WE DO PROPERLY AND SINCERELY...: See Rabbi E.E. Dessler *Michtav Me-Eliyahu* III p.118.

THE SAGES SAY: IF A PERSON HAS AMASSED A GREAT KNOWLEDGE OF TORAH...: T.B. *Yoma* 86a.

THIS IS MY PEOPLE ISRAEL...: Isaiah 49:3.

THE INSURANCE CLAIM...: Personal communication to the author.

p.333   (2) IF A MAN HASN'T DISCOVERED SOMETHING THAT HE WILL DIE FOR...: Attributed to Martin Luther King.

(3) IT IS A TREMENDOUS CONCEPT...: See Rabbi E.E. Dessler, *Strive for Truth! I*, p. 89; III, p. 231.

THE RABBIS SAY...: *Pirkei Avot* 6 (end).

p.334   ...THE POWER OF THE NON-EGO...: S.D.S *Reality Revisited* pp. 177-179.

AND SO EVERY FAMILY EVERY GROUP, EVERY NATION...: Rabbi E.E. Dessler *op. cit.* 231.

CHAPTER 80

p.335   (1) Maimonides MT LAWS OF KINGS...: 11:4.

p.336   ALTHOUGH HE DESCRIBES HIM AS A KING...: A.C.

p.337   (2) Maimonides MT 12:4.

HOW CAN WE ENVISAGE...: A.C.

UNQUESTIONABLY A COPERNICAN REVOLUTION OF THE MIND...: See A. Carmell "Judaism and the Quality of the Environment", in A. Carmell and C. Domb (eds.), *Challenge* (Feldheim 1976) p. 518.

MAIMONIDES HINTS AT A POSSIBLE ANSWER...: A.C.

p.338   (3) IN OUR TIME WE HAVE SEEN TYRANNIES FALL...: A.C.

p.339   ...AN ORIGINAL TORAH THINKER...: S.D.S., "Judaism's challenge to science," in *Jewish Studies* no. 34 (1990), p. 29.

Bibliography

BOOKS FOR FURTHER READING

All books listed here are published or distributed by
Feldheim, except those marked with an asterisk.

GROUP ONE

CHAPTERS 5-8 : Employer-employee Relations/ Property
Matters/ Environmental Concerns

TORAH GUIDE FOR THE BUSINESSMAN
Rabbi S. Wagschal

IN THE MARKETPLACE
Jewish business ethics
Meir Tamari

CHAPTERS 7 and 9 : Property Transfers and Obligations

* THE MAIN INSTITUTION OF JEWISH LAW 2 vols.
Chief Rabbi Dr. I. Herzog
London/New York: Soncino Press, 2nd ed. 1965.

JEWISH CIVIL LAW
Arnold Cohen

CHAPTER 11 : Respect for Reputation (Laws of *Lashon
Ha-ra*)

THE SANCTITY OF SPEECH
Y.K. Krohn and Y.M. Shain

* GUARD YOUR TONGUE
Z. Pliskin
Jerusalem: Yeshivat Aish ha-Torah.

GROUP TWO

CHAPTER 12 : Building Up Eretz Yisrael

LAND OF OUR HERITAGE
D. Rossof

Bibliography

* ZION TODAY
A Torah Perspective.
Rabbi Y. Schwartz (transl. R. Steinberg)
Jerusalem: Jerusalem Academy Publications.

TO DWELL IN THE PALACE
Perspectives on Eretz Yisrael
Tzvia Ehrlich-Klein

CHAPTER 15 : Respecting Divine Order in the World (Laws of *Shaatnez*)
Detailed halachic guidance

A GUIDE TO SHAATNEZ
The laws of shaatnez and their practical application

CHAPTER 18 : Respect for Human Beings after Death (Laws of Mourning)

* THE JEWISH WAY IN DEATH AND MOURNING
Rabbi Maurice Lamm
New York: Jonathan David, 1969.

CHAPTER 19 : Respect for One's Body

THE COMPREHENSIVE GUIDE TO MEDICAL HALACHAH
Prof. A.S. Abraham

SMOKING AND DAMAGE TO HEALTH IN THE HALACHAH
Rabbi M. Slae (transl. B. Slae)

CHAPTER 22 : Respect for Our Sexuality

THE ANTIDOTE
Human sexuality from a Torah perspective
S. Silverstein

THE WONDER OF BECOMING YOU
How a Jewish girl grows up
Dr. Miriam Grossman

CHAPTER 23 : Regulating our Sexual Relations (Periods of Separation)
Introductory

A HEDGE OF ROSES
Rabbi Dr. Norman Lamm

THE SECRET OF JEWISH FEMININITY
Tehilla Abramov

Detailed halachic guidance

DAUGHTER OF ISRAEL
Rabbi Dr. K. Kahana

HALACHOS OF NIDDAH
Rabbi S.D. Eider

TAHARAS AM YISRAEL (ISRAEL'S PURITY)
Rabbi S. Wagschal

CHAPTERS 24-28 : Food from the Animal Kingdom

* THE JEWISH DIETARY LAWS (Vol. 1)
Dayan Dr. I. Grunfeld
London / Jerusalem / New York: Soncino Press, 1972.

THE NEW PRACTICAL GUIDE TO KASHRUTH
Rabbi S. Wagschal

GROUP THREE

CHAPTER 30 : Loving Your Neighbor

* LOVE YOUR NEIGHBOR
Rabbi Zelig Pliskin
Jerusalem: Yeshivat Aish ha-Torah.

CHAPTER 33 : Jewish Marriage

THE RIVER, THE KETTLE AND THE BIRD
A Torah guide to successful marriage
Rabbi A. Feldman

AIZER K'NEGDO
The Jewish woman's guide to happiness in marriage
Sarah C. Radcliffe

CHAPTER 34 : Parenthood and Education

RAISING CHILDREN TO CARE
Miriam Adahan

EFFECTIVE JEWISH PARENTING
Miriam Levi

THE DELICATE BALANCE
Love and authority in Torah parenting
Sarah C. Radcliffe

GROWING WITH MY CHILDREN
Sarah Shapiro

SUCCESSFUL *CHINUCH*
A guide for parents and educators.
Rabbi S. Wagschal

Bibliography

CHAPTER 36 : Support of Neighbor

> *** WITH ALL YOUR POSSESSIONS**
> Jewish ethics and economic life
> Meir Tamari
> New York: The Free Press/Macmillan, 1987.

CHAPTER 37 : Charity and Good Deeds

> **AHAVATH CHESED**
> The love of kindness as required by God
> The Chafetz Chaim (transl. L. Oschry)
> *Detailed halachic guidance*

> **MAASER KESAFIM**
> Giving a tenth for charity
> Prof. C. Domb
> *Insights*

> **THE HEALING VISIT**
> Insights into the mitzva of *bikur cholim* (visiting the sick)
> C. Shofnos and B.T. Zwebner

GROUP FOUR

CHAPTERS 41-51 : Sabbath and Festivals

> *Introductory*

> **THE SABBATH**
> A guide to its understanding and observance
> Dayan Dr. I. Grunfeld

> **MENUCHA V'SIMCHA**
> Basic laws and themes of Shabbos and Yom Tov
> Rabbi Mordechai Katz

> **THE BOOK OF OUR HERITAGE**
> Ample source material and discussion of all aspects of the
> Jewish year
> Rabbi E. Kitov

> *Deeper philosophical level*

> **CITADEL AND TOWER: QUEST FOR JEWISH MAJESTY**
> Essays on the Festivals, based on writings of Rabbi Y.
> Hutner zt'l (2 vols.)
> Rabbi M. Belsky

> All the following until Chapter 52 provide detailed
> halachic guidance:

CHAPTER 41 : Observance of Shabbat

HALACHOS OF SHABBOS
Rabbi S.D. Eider

SHEMIRATH SHABBAT
A guide to the practical observance of Shabbath (Vol. 1)
Rabbi Y.Y. Neuwirth (transl. W. Grangewood)

CARE OF CHILDREN ON SHABBOS AND YOMTOV
Rabbi S. Wagschal

CHAPTER 43 : Pattern of Festivals
43(5) Second Day Yom Tov

Detailed halachic guidance

YOMTOV SHEINI KEHILCHASO
The second day of Yom Tov in Israel and abroad
Rabbi Y.D. Fried

CHAPTER 44 : Celebration of Shabbat and Festivals

SHEMIRATH SHABBATH
As above, vol. 2.
Rabbi Y.Y. Neuwirth

CHAPTERS 45-46 : Laws of Pesaḥ

HALACHOS OF PESACH
Rabbi S.D. Eider

CHAPTER 50 : The Four Species

**SUMMARY OF HALACHOS OF THE FOUR MINIM
(SPECIES)**
Rabbi S.D. Eider

CHAPTER 51 : Purim and Hanukka

HALACHOS OF CHANUKA
Rabbi S.D. Eider

CHAPTER 52 : Fast Days

SUMMARY OF HALACHOS OF THE THREE WEEKS
Rabbi S.D. Eider

All the above from chapter 41 provide detailed halachic
guidance.

Bibliography

CHAPTER 53 : The calendar

THE COMPREHENSIVE HEBREW CALENDAR
Arthur Speier

CHAPTER 54 : Circumcision

BRIS MILAH
The Jewish ritual of circumcision
Dr. Henry C. Romberg

CHAPTER 55 : Tefillin

Detailed halachic guidance

HALACHOS OF TEFILLIN (Illustrated)
Rabbi S.D. Eider

CHAPTER 60 : Immersion of vessels

Detailed halachic guidance

TEVILAS KELIM (Immersion of vessels)
136 utensils and the proper way to immerse them
Rabbi Z. Cohen

CHAPTER 63 : *Teruma, Maaser* and *Halla* (Separation of Gifts)

Detailed halachic guidance

THE PROCEDURE OF SETTING ASIDE T'RUMOT AND MA'ASROT
Rabbi S. Reichenberg (transl. A. Angstreich)

GROUP FIVE

CHAPTER 64 : Torah Study

THE BLUEPRINT OF CREATION
The Chofetz Chaim on Torah study
R. Blumberg

THE INFINITE CHAIN
Torah, Masorah and man
Rabbi N.T.L. Cardozo

TORAH STUDY
A survey of classic sources on timely issues
Yehudah Levi

THE ORAL LAW
The Rabbinic contribution to *Torah sheb'al peh*
H.C. Schimmel

384

CHAPTER 65 : Prayer and the Synagogue

Siddur (prayer book) translation and commentary

THE HIRSCH SIDDUR
Rabbi S.R. Hirsch

THE WORLD OF PRAYER
Rabbi E. Munk

*** ARTSCROLL MESORAH
SIDDUR/MACHZOR/TEHILLIM**
New York: Mesorah.

Detailed halachic guidance

THE HALACHOS OF BROCHOS (BLESSINGS)
Rabbi Y.P. Bodner

PRIORITY IN PRAYER
A practical guide to common halachic problems in prayer
Rabbi Y.P. Feinhandler

CHAPTER 71 : Idolatry — Ancient and Modern

Torah and Science

IN THE BEGINNING
Biblical creation and science
N. Aviezer

CHALLENGE
Torah views on science and its problems
A. Carmell and C. Domb (eds.)
Also available in Spanish.

* GENESIS AND THE BIG BANG
The discovery of harmony between modern science
and the Bible
G.L. Schroeder
New York: Bantam Books, 1990.

CHAPTER 75 : Faith in God

WHY?
Reflections on the loss of a loved one
Rabbi M.Y. Vorst

CHAPTER 78 : He called them 'Adam'

HALICHOS BAS YISROEL
A woman's guide to Jewish observance
Rabbi Y. Fuchs

IN SEARCH OF THE JEWISH WOMAN
Rabbi Y. Miller

* JEWISH WOMAN IN JEWISH LAW
Rabbi M. Meiselman
New York: Ktav Publishers

GENERAL TOPICS

Torah and Modern life

ENCOUNTER
Essays on Torah and modern life
H.C. Schimmel and A. Carmell (eds.)

FUSION
Absolute standards in a world of relativity
A. Gotfryd, H. Branover and S. Lipskar (eds.)

Insights into the World of Mussar (Jewish ethics)

STRIVE FOR TRUTH!
3 vols.
Rabbi E.E. Dessler (transl. A. Carmell)

ETHICS FROM SINAI
Commentary on Pirkey Avoth, 3 vols.
I.M. Bunim

THE PATH OF THE JUST
Rabbi M.C. Luzzatto (transl. S. Silverstein)

AUTHORS FREQUENTLY QUOTED
IN THIS WORK:
SOME BIOGRAPHICAL NOTES

RABBI ELIYAHU ELIEZER DESSLER

Rabbi E.E. Dessler (1892 — 1953) was a major exponent of *mussar*, the ethical movement founded by Rabbi Yisrael Salanter in 19th-century Lithuania. Rabbi Dessler was active in England (1927-1947) and in Israel (Ponevezh Yeshiva, Bnei Brak, 1947-1953). He founded the Institution of Higher Rabbinic Studies (*Kollel Rabbanim*) in Gateshead, England, in 1941 and under his guidance his disciples founded many other Torah institutions worldwide.

His profound and illuminating insights into Torah and the words of our Sages opened up new vistas on the goals and challenges of Torah life in our time. A selection of these, culled from lectures and writings covering a period of 20 years, were published posthumously by his disciples as *Michtav Me'Eliyahu* (4 volumes so far). The depth and clarity of his thought have influenced the thinking of a whole generation.

The first volume of that work has been rendered into English and published under the name "Strive for Truth!" (3 volumes, Feldheim, 1976-1989). This has been translated (in part) into French, Spanish and Russian.

RABBI SOLOMON DAVID SASSOON

Rabbi S.D. Sassoon (1915-1985) was born in London to a well-known Sephardi family. A disciple of Rabbi E.E. Dessler from early youth, Rabbi Sassoon was ordained a rabbi at the age of twenty. He was exceptional in combining breadth of Torah knowledge and deep religious commitment with close familiarity with the cutting edge of modern science. He saw science as developing in directions which were bringing it ever closer to recognition of spiritual reality. His book on this subject, *Reality Revisited,* was published posthumously (Feldheim, 1991).

He also devoted himself to biblical research and made many remarkable discoveries, not least in the sphere of hidden numerical structures in the biblical text. (Awaiting publication.)

Those familiar with his work in many spheres consider him to have been one of the most profound and original thinkers to have arisen in Torah Jewry in our time.

Himself a generous supporter of charitable causes, Rabbi Sassoon also made prodigious efforts, worldwide, to raise funds for the Torah education of Sephardi youth. These efforts were blessed with considerable success.

Glossary

The meaning of all Hebrew terms will be found under the appropriate entry in the Index.

Index

Index

Index

symbolism of, 197
prohibited on Pesah, why?, 197
Hanukka, 217
Havdala (prayer at end of Sabbath),
192
origin of, 276
Helev (certain fats), 107
Hellenism, 217
Hevra Kadisha, voluntary burial
society, 151
Hillel, advice to proselyte, 118, 120
model of humility, 322
obligations to our body, 80
Hirsch, Rabbi S.R., his classification
of mitzvot, xv, 348
his ideas in this work, xv
place in history, xvii
Hol Ha-mo'ed (intermediate days
of festival), 193
Holiness, and enjoyment, 53, 190, 255
and good food, 190
in army camp, 114
is "giving", 131
meaning of in Torah, 3, 46, 88, 96,
101, 190
of land, 255
training for, 113
true nature of, 3, 46, 255
Holocaust, martyrdom in, 206
God's apparent withdrawal, 316
people of Israel survives, 218
regeneration of Torah after, 186,
205
Holy Language, no verb "to have," 51,
138
"Holy nation," meaning of, 3
Homosexuality, 92
Honesty, being true to commitments,
22
in advising others, 38
in examinations, 33
in speech, 32
Housewife, rabbis' concern for, 225
Human being, "image of God." See
"Image of God"
responsibilities, 169
significance of, 7
treatment of remains after death, 70
Human body, care of, 79

disfigurement forbidden, 79
extremely complex system, xxi, 79
mitzvot relating to, 79, 81, 228-41
Human rights, freedom from
oppression, 36
liberty, 10
non-self-incrimination, 11
privacy, 11
protection of reputation, 40-42
Humanist paradox, 7, 121
Humility, 321-23
Hurting feelings, 37
Hypocrisy, 34

Image of God, central to Torah
scheme, 7,13
man as, ix, xi, 7, 13, 313, 342
manifest in labor relations, 13
meaning of, xi, 7
Incest, 90
Insurance claim, 332
Intermarriage, 132
Intermediate days. See *Hol Ha-mo'ed*
Isaiah, Epilogue, 341
Iska, risk-sharing agreement, 144
Israel, "holy nation," meaning of, 3
people of, x
pilot project for mankind, x
Israel, State of, challenge presented
by, xxiii
not (yet) a Torah state, 164
opportunity to work for Torah
goals, 47, 164
Shabbat, official day of rest in, 175

Jacob (patriarch), model employee, 17
Jacob / Israel, 108
Jerusalem, "holy city," 53, 259
Job, 268
Judah Maccabi, 217
Judaism, alienation from, xxiv
comprehensive program, ix
120, 342
relevance of, xiii
universalism in, x, 210,
286
Judge, duties of, in Torah law, 3
Justice, prior to love, 4

392

Index

Miser, 51
Mishna, origin of, 344
  studying, 268
Mitzva, and Kantian ethics, 347
  as motivation, xi
  mode and motive, 124
  multi-level effects, xi
Mitzvot, classifications of, xv
  enhancement of life, xvi and passim
  reasons for, xvi and passim
  symbolism in, xviii and passim
  why complex, xx
Moderation, 57, 79
Mo'ed. See Yom Tov
Moon, new. See Rosh Ḥodesh
  phases of, 224
Moral pollution, 114-15
Moral strength, 23
Morality, how measured, in Torah, 30
  Torah's higher standard of, 23, 26
Moratorium on loans, 257
Mordechai, 216
Mother and young, not slaughtering
  on same day, 62
Mother bird, in nest, mitzva
  concerning, 62-63
Motherhood, in animal kingdom, 61
Mourning, and psychiatry, 73
  stages of, 72
Multi-national conglomerates, 30
Murder, 7-8
Mussaf (additional service), 180, 280
  of Rosh Hashana, 180, 286

Nation, mitzvot related to, 2, 326
  Shabbat and the, 175
  Torah given to, 2
Natural selection, 304
Nefesh (vital force), 107
"Neighbor," referring to God, 121
Neshama Yetera (extra soul),
  on Sabbath, 173
"Nine days," national mourning
  period, 98, 223
Nissan, month of promise, 225
Non-ego, xix, 374

Ohel Mo'ed ("tent of meeting"), 182
Omer, barley offering, 204

counting the, 205
  mourning period, why, 206
"On-off switch," in Torah law, 12,
  89, 329
Oppression, 36
Organ transplants, from corpse, 71
  from dying donor, 8
  from living donor, 136
Orlah, foreskin, 229
  restricted fruit, 52
Ownership, in Torah, 51, 138

Parenthood, and education, 135
  helping children in moral struggle,
  89, 123
  significance, 135
Parents, honor and respect for, why?,
  123
  if not Torah observant, 126
Partner for life, choice of, 131
Paschal lamb. See Korban Pesaḥ
Passover. See Pesaḥ
Peace-making, supreme achievement,
  152
Pentecost. See Shavuot
Permissiveness, a success?, 87
  in sex, 230
Persian empire, 216
Pesaḥ (Passover), must fall in spring,
  224
  prohibition of hametz, 197-200
  teachings, 185
  what it represents, 183
Phone tapping, 11
Prayer, contact with God, 274
  forms of, 275
  from the heart, 274
  in synagogue, 277
  Kaddish, 278
  silent, 280
Pre-emptive strike, 8
Privacy, protection of, 11
  respect for, 42
Promises, to God, 82
  to fellowman, 24
Promoting wrongdoing, 38
Property, gift of God, 19
  purpose of, 51
Prophets, 268, 286

INVITATION

If any reader would like further information or clarification regarding any of the topics discussed in this book, he or she is welcome to write to the author:

P.O.B. 16100
Jerusalem 91160, Israel

ישיבת שעלבים

YESHIVAT SHA'ALVIM

בס״ד

31ˢᵗ Anniversary Dinner
of
Friends of Yeshivat Sha'alvim in Israel

Shimon and Debby Kwestel
Joseph K. Miller Achdut Yisrael Award

Yossi and Agi Fried
Guests of Honor

Rabbi Allen Schwartz
Rabbinic Leadership Award

Dr. Arthur and Rifki Helft
Parents Award

Shmuel and Terri Wagner '81
Alumnus Award

Sunday, March 1ˢᵗ, 1992
26 Adar I 5752

Sheraton Centre
53rd Street and Seventh Avenue
New York City

MESSAGE FROM THE ROSH HAYESHIVA

Heartfelt greetings to all attending the 31st Anniversary Dinner of Friends of Yeshivat Sha'alvim. Blessings to the Dinner Committee, and to our distinguished Guests of Honor and Awardees: Shimon and Debby Kwestel, Joseph and Agi Fried, Dr. Arthur and Rifki Helft, Rabbi Allen Schwartz and Stuart and Terri Wagner. May the Almighty's blessing from Zion rest upon all.

The Tabernacle represents the Universe, the ways of G-d, the great soul of the human and the structure of the People of Israel. Regarding the essence of the Tabernacle G-d said, "I concentrate My Providence within it." Thus anyone within this spiritual framework is privileged with G-d's omnipresence. The Yeshiva strives to build in your sons a miniature sanctuary—a *mikdash me-att*. You fulfill the obligation to offer your contributions for the maintenance of the Yeshiva and the *mishkan* of the soul.

We are proud of our work in Russia and Israel, with the singular support of Prof. Shimon Kwestel. Our students and alumni are offering invaluable Torah education, inspiration and guidance.

May the Almighty crown all endeavors with success.

With appreciation to each and every one, and affinity to all our students and alumni.

Rabbi Meir Schlesinger

MESSAGE FROM THE ROSH HAYESHIVA

ברכה לבבית למשתתפי הסעודה השנתית ה-31 של קרית חינוך שעלבים, למארגניה הנכבדים ואחרונים חביבים אורחי הכבוד שיחיו — ברכת ה' מציון על כולכם.

המשכן מסמל בתוכו עולם ומלואו. את דרכי האלוקות בעולם, את נפשו הגדולה של האדם, ואת מבנהו של כלל ישראל.

בתוך מערכת מרוכזת של סמלים אומר הקב"ה: „מצמצם אני את שכינתי בתוכו," פירוש מי שימצא שם בדרך, בכוונה ובתכלית הרצויה, יזכה להשראת השכינה וזו תכוון את דרכיו ומעשיו.

אם נבנה את מקדש מעט שלנו בכוונה ובתכלית הנכונה יהיה הוא המרכז המחיה והמכוון של כל דרכי תלמידינו, ועל כך כל מאמצינו ותפילותינו.

זכינו לגדל בנים יקרים שלכם, וכולכם נותנים למשכן שלנו את הלב ואת הזהב. „כל נדיב לב יביאה את תרומת ה' וכו'" (ויקהל), ולפי הסדר הנכון מתוך תרומת הלב יביאו האמצעים הדרושים לקיומה של ישיבת שעלבים.

אכן זכינו לסייעתא דשמיא בראש ובראשונה בפעילות התורנית היומיומית בישיבה על כל שלוחותיה, בכולל הרבנים ובהשתלמותם, עד לדיינות, ובליווי צמוד שלהם בעת פעולתם הרבנית בקהילותיהם.

עבודה נפלאה נעשית בקליטת יהודי ברית המועצות שם וכאן במדינת ישראל, בסיוע המיוחד של מכובדנו פרופ' שמעון קוסטל הי"ו ובכל יום ובכל שעה עסוקים תלמידינו ובוגרינו במשימות חינוכיות במוסדות החינוך ובישובי העולים.

„עד הנה עזרונו רחמיך ולא עזבונו חסדיך ואל תטשנו ה' אלוקינו לנצח." כן יתן ה' לכם הצלחה בכל מעשי ידיכם לוותיקים ולחדשים איש איש כברכתו ויחד נבנה את המשכן בדור הגדול הזה ויהי נעם ה' אלוקינו עלינו.

בברכה ידידותית לכל אחד ואחד ובקירוב הלב לכל תלמידינו — בוגרינו.

דוש"ט,

הרב מאיר שלזינגר

MESSAGE FROM THE PRESIDENT

Our Sages have taught — כל ישראל ערבים זה בזה — all of Jewry are guarantors—are held responsible—one for another.

Our Yeshivat Sha'alvim, through its distinguished and beloved Rosh HaYeshiva, Harav Meir Schlesinger שליט"א, and his dedicated staff is not only a superb teacher to over 1,000 students of the "theoretics" of Jewish knowledge, philosophy and ethics, but sets a practical example of how to be true "Areivim".

For some six years our Sha'al Institute has sent Rabbinic and Educational Leaders, after intensive training, to give spiritual nourishment to Jewish communities all over the globe—from North and South America to Europe, South Africa, Australia and the areas formerly known as the Soviet Union—true Areivim for our brethren.

This past summer saw over 200 Jewish children attend the Joseph K. Miller Torah Center in the Ukrainian city of Kharkov. This ongoing program has won many deserved accolades and is jointly run by Yeshivat Sha'alvim and the Orthodox Union, whose Board Chairman, Professor Sidney Kwestel, one of tonight's Awardess, has made this a special and personal project of the heart. Well over a dozen Sha'alvim students have been to Kharkov on rotating tours of duty as teachers, leaders and true role models—how better to teach Areivus?!

Tonight's honorees—every one of them—fit comfortably into this mold of Areivim. They are all leaders in their homes and local communities, they are concerned for the welfare of K'lal Yisroel, and their impact has been felt in the Jewish World at large. We salute our Guests of Honor Joseph and Agi Freed, the Joseph K. Miller Achdut Yisroel Awardees Shimon and Debby Kwestel, the Rabbinic Leadership Awardee Rabbi Allen Schwartz, the Parents Awardees Dr. Arthur and Rifki Helft, and the Alumni Awardees Shmuel and Terri Wagner.

May Hashem grant them the strength and good health to continue to be shining examples of כל ישראל ערבים זה בזה.

Werner Rosenbaum

SHIMON and DEBBY KWESTEL
Joseph K. Miller Achdut Yisrael Award

The Joseph K. Miller, whom we all knew and loved, had a primary mission in life of creating a sense of unity of purpose and direction for all of Klal Yisrael. In its effort to keep that vision alive, Yeshivat Sha'alvim has established the Joseph K. Miller Achdut Yisrael Award.

Debby and Shimon Kwestel were chosen as the recipients of this year's Joseph K. Miller Achdut Yisrael Award. Shimon, through his efforts, in the Orthodox Union and Yeshivat Sha'alvim has demonstrated visionary leadership in coping with individual needs in the global arena. To Soviet Jews, Professor Kwestel is synonymous with a Jew who doesn't give up a cause. To world leaders, he is a straight talking, articulate voice who demonstrates an incredible grasp of the most complex of issues. To his co-workers and associates, Shimon is the hard-driving conscience who is unrelenting in his pursuit of emet. To us and his many other friends, Shimmy is that dear friend who is always there when needed. Clearly, all of these achievements would have been unattainable were it not for Debby's calm, patience and tolerance. The Torah home that they have established is a model for us all.

Shimon is a professor of law at Touro Law School and former partner of the Kaye, Scholer, Fierman, Hays and Handler law firm. He was graduated from Yeshiva University and New York University Law School. He is a former President of COLPA, the national Jewish Commission on Law and Public Affairs, and served as vice president of the Queens Jewish Center. Professor Kwestel was most recently National President of the Union of Orthodox Jewish Congregations of America and now serves as its Chairman of the Board and as Chairman of the Soviet Jewry Commission.

He is a former member of the Board of Governors of the Jewish Agency, the Executive of the World Zionist Organization, Board of Directors of the Memorial Foundation for Jewish Culture, the Board of United Israel Appeal and the Executive Committee of AIPAC and NJCRAC.

Mr. Kwestel is the relentless driving force behind the Yeshivat Sha'alvim-UOJCA/NCSY joint project, the Joseph K. Miller Torah Center in Kharkov/Ukraine.

Shimon is the Vice President of American Friends of Yeshivat Sha'alvim and Debby is a valued member of its Board of Governors. They reside in Forest Hills and are the parents of Steven, married to Dassy Sohn, Marc and Elliot, all Sha'alvim Alumni.

JOSEPH and AGI FRIED
Guests of Honor

Yossi and Agi Fried, residents of Denver since 1975, are the proud parents of four children. Ehud, the oldest, is currently a student of Yeshivat Sha'alvim. Yossi and Agi have been involved intensively in the Jewish community in Denver and are staunch supporters of Torah education, both in the U.S. and Israel.

Yossi, a graduate of Yeshiva Tichonit (Midrashiat Noam) in Israel and Hebrew University Law School, served in the Israeli Defense Forces as Acting Chief Counsel for the Defense Air Force with the Office of the Judge Advocate General and was also a practicing attorney. Yossi was graduated from the University of Denver School of Law and received his master's degree in International Studies. He now is an attorney in private practice and also involved in real estate investments.

The Frieds are members of East Denver Orthodox Synagogue where Yossi served as President twice during the past ten years. He was also a member of the Board of Directors of several local Jewish educational institutions.

Agi, born in Hungary and raised in Europe, has devoted much of her time since moving to Denver to communal and charitable endeavors. She is very involved in the East Denver Orthodox Synagogue Ladies Auxiliary, Hillel Academy P.T.A., and is also busy taking care of Bat Sheva, currently enrolled in Beth Jacob of Denver, and Avi and Shlomo, who are students at Hillel Academy.

MESSAGE FROM
THE GUESTS OF HONOR

We are very proud and honored to be associated with and recognized as supporters of Yeshivat Sha'alvim.

To us, as parents of a student at the Yeshiva, this institution symbolizes all that is beautiful and positive about the Yeshiva learning experience. The ability of Yeshivat Sha'alvim, under the leadership of Rav Meir, to combine high level and intensive לימוד תורה with that special feeling for ארץ ישראל and the love for מדינת ישראל is indeed unique. Rav Shlesinger and the staff should be commended for being pioneers in creating the institution of ישיבות הסדר and promoting the concept of ספרא וסייפא, which has become a source of pride to every orthodox Jew who supports Zionism and the State of Israel.

Although we are thousands of miles away from our son, we have, nevertheless, grown even closer in many ways during the past several months. The positive feelings which אהוד transmits in his letters and the enthusiasm in his voice when describing his life in the Yeshiva over the phone to us, have served to confirm, each time anew, our feeling that this year in Sha'alvim will indeed turn our son into a בן תורה and leave a lasting impression on him, as well as his friends, for many years to come.

As we are geographically somewhat removed from the large Jewish communities of the East Coast, we feel that it is especially important to support Yeshivat Sha'alvim because of its extra efforts to recruit students from smaller cities across the U.S., instill in them the love for Torah and Israel, and in so doing help strengthen the infrastructure of their respective communities upon their return home. Indeed, we in Denver have a nice contingent of students at the Yeshiva at the present time, and have had an ongoing relationship with Sha'alvim in years past.

Once again, ישר כח to Rav Meir and the entire staff at the Yeshiva העוסקים במלאכת הקודש באמונה

May ה' grant you continued success in all your deeds.

יצליח ה' דרככם ופועל ידכם יבורך.

Yossi and Agi Fried

DR. ARTHUR and RIFKI HELFT
Parents Award

Arthur and Rifki Helft have been active members of the Englewood Jewish community since 1974. Their four children—Yosef, Steven, Shari and Susan—attended the Moriah Hebrew Day School and Frisch Yeshiva High School. Yosef is currently learning at Yeshivat Sha'alvim.

Arthur, a graduate of Etz Chaim and Yeshiva of Flatbush High School, Columbia, Downstate Medical Center, State University of New York and a Major in the U.S. Air Force Medical Corps, is a surgeon at Beth Israel and Beekman Hospitals. He was President of Congregation Ahavath Torah in Englewood and serves on the board of the *shul*, the Moriah school and the Englewood *mikva*.

Rifki studied at Yeshiva University's Stern College and Teachers Institute for Women and is a graduate of the City University. She is a reading teacher in the NYC Public Schools, and has been involved in every aspect of Jewish communal life. She has served as President of the Ahavath Torah Sisterhood and President of the Englewood Chapter of Amit.

In 1987, Rifki and Arthur travelled to the then Soviet Union on a Lubavitch mission to bring *Yiddishkeit* and encouragement to the *refusenik* community.

A MESSAGE FROM
THE PARENTS OF THE YEAR

We would like to take this opportunity to thank Yeshivat Sha'alvim for providing an enriching Torah environment in which our son Yosef has grown and matured. The strength of the Yeshiva emanates from its students, faculty and friends. The students are a wonderful group of young men—enthusiastic, bright, and anxious to immerse themselves in learning, and to prepare themselves to meet the challenges of life with the strength they receive at the Yeshiva. The faculty of Rebbeim are so well learned and highly regarded as Gedolai Torah. With their warmth and caring they serve to guide and inspire their students. Our sages tell us

„כל המלמד את בן חברו תורה כאילו ילדו"

"He who teaches his friend's son Torah, it is as if he bore him". We feel gratitude and kinship with the Rebbeim who play such a major role in our son's education.

As parents and friends, we are enriched by the experiences and accomplishments of our children. Although we have been selected as Parents of the Year, it is really the Yeshiva that is being honored tonight. We are happy to lend our support and to contribute in some small way to the continued growth and success of Yeshivat Sha'alvim.

Rifki and Arthur Helft

RABBI ALLEN SCHWARTZ
Rabbinic Leadership Award

Rabbi Allen Schwartz was graduated from Yeshiva University with a bachelor's degree in philosophy and in 1983 received his master's degree in Bible. In the spring of 1983 Rabbi Schwartz was invited to teach *Tanach* at Yeshiva University and, at the age of 21, was the youngest instructor in the school history. He is now in the process of completing his doctoral studies at Yeshiva.

In 1985, Rabbi Schwartz came to New York's Upper West Side as rabbi of Congregation Ohav Sholom and was appointed as rabbi of Congregation Ohab Zedek in May, 1988. Rabbi Schwartz has a wealth of educational experience, having taught elementary school, high school and college students. He has been extensively involved in adult education, served for three years as the spiritual leader of a geriatric day care center in the Bronx and is one of the most popular lecturers on Jewish education in New York and New Jersey. The rabbi is a member of the Rabbinical Council of America, the Midtown Va'ad, Board of Education of Manhattan Day School, and served on the Board of Directors of Project Dorot. Rabbi Schwartz is the chairman of UJA's Singles Task Force and is on the Executive Council of Rabbis at UJA.

Rabbi Schwartz and his wife, Alisa, have four children — Shonnie, Chani, Moshe Manis, and Elli.

STUART and TERRI WAGNER '81
Alumnus Award

Shmuel Wagner personifies the educational goals of Yeshivat Sha'alvim. He incorporated the Torah he learned into the life he leads. His concern for the Yeshiva and loyalty to his alma mater are exemplary and have earned for him and Terri the recognition bestowed upon them tonight.

Shmuel (Stuart) Wagner attended Yeshivat Sha'alvim for two years (1979-81). Thereafter, he attended Queens College and Mesivta Ohr Torah Bais Medresh. He was graduated from Fordham Law School in 1987 and is currently a trial attorney, a partner in the law firm of Morrison and Wagner.

His wife, Terri, is a graduate of Queens College and studied at Bar-Ilan University. She is a member of Amit and Emnuah Women and the sisterhood of Young Israel of Forest Hills.

They are the proud parents of Aviva Rivka, Elliot Aaron and Shoshana Raizel. Their parents are Mr. and Mrs. Max Wagner and Mr. and Mrs. Leonard Klestzick of Far Rockaway.

ALLEN I. FAGIN
Dinner Chairman

Allen is married to the former Judith Rosenberg. Their son Robert learned in Sha'alvim in 1990/91 and is currently at Yeshiva University. Their son Charles is a student at Ramaz.

Allen, a partner in the law firm Proskauer, Rose, Goetz, & Mendelsohn's Labor Department, has been active in communal activities, has served as Vice President of the New York Region of the Union of Orthodox Jewish Congregations of America, and is a member of the executive Committee of the Orthodox Union's Institute for Public Affairs. He is a Vice-President of the Central Queens YM-YWHA and a member of the Board of the American Friends of Yeshivat Sha'alvim. He is the former President and Chairman of the Board of the Queens Jewish Center.

MESSAGE FROM THE DINNER CHAIRMAN

I am delighted to welcome each of you to the Annual Dinner of American Friends of Yeshivat Sha'alvim. We gather to support an outstanding Torah institution which embodies the ideals and practices that we all hold dear. All of us—parents, alumni and friends of the Yeshiva—owe a deep debt of gratitude to our revered Rosh HaYeshiva, Rav Meir Schlesinger, and to our Dean of Overseas Students, Rav Mallen Galinsky.

On a personal note, my wife and I will always be grateful to the dedicated educational staff of Yeshivat Sha'alvim for the outstanding educational experience they provided to our son, Robert.

We pay tribute tonight to an outstanding array of honorees. Our Guests of Honor, Yossi and Agi Fried, are dedicated Sha'alvim parents and staunch supporters of Torah education both in their Denver community and in Israel.

Our Rabbinic Leadership Award is presented this year to an outstanding teacher and scholar, Rabbi Allen Schwartz, Rabbi of Congregation Oheb Zedek. Stuart Wagner, our alumni awardee, studied for two years at Sha'alvim, and, together with his wife, is actively involved in the Queens community. Our Parents of the Year, Arthur and Rifki Helft, are pillars of the Englewood community and are involved in every aspect of Jewish communal life.

Finally, it is particularly gratifying to honor our friends and neighbors, Shimon and Debby Kwestel, recipients of the Joseph K. Miller Achudt Yisrael Award. I can think of no couple more dedicated to Torah and Klal Yisrael and who personify the ideals and goals that Joe Miller, ע"ה, stood for.

This Dinner would not have been possible without the dedicated work of Rabbi Philip Singer, Mrs. Sarah Hans, and our Israel leadership Rabbi Mallen Galinsky and Don Kates. My thanks to the entire committee and all the volunteers who worked so hard to make tonight's Dinner a success.

I hope that tonight's program will inspire each of us to redouble our efforts on behalf of the vital work of the institution that we all hold so dear.

Allen Fagin

MESSAGE FROM THE CHAIRMAN
OF FRIENDS OF YESHIVAT SHA'ALVIM

The 31st Anniversary is celebrated in a unique year. It is a leap year. It is a year of financial stress. Just at a time when communism in Russia crumbled, when democracy and capitalism are vindicated and victorious, we are experiencing problems. This would impose difficulties for the support of yeshivot, institutions and Israel.

But Jews are noble, kind, compassionate and generous. The recognition of the immigration into Israel of 400,000 from Russia and Ethiopia, and the realization of the vital role of Torah, impel Jews to uphold the mitzvah of helping with dedication and magnanimity.

We salute the Honorees of this Dinner: Shimon and Debby Kwestel, Yossi and Agi Fried, Stuart and Terri Wagner, Dr. Arthur and Rivky Helft and Rabbi Allen Schwartz. Thanks to the Dinner Chairman, Allen Fagin. My deep appreciation to the energetic Rabbi Mallen Galinsky. Thanks to Don Kates, Sarah Hans and Rochie Harari.

Accolades to the Rosh Yeshiva, Rav Meir Schlesinger, for his steadfastness, faith and dedication. His teaching and guidance are inspirations to the alumni, parents and friends of Yeshivat Sha'alvim. His influence is felt from the Yeshiva to Bet Shemesh, from Kharkov to Texas, from Vancouver to Melbourne and Perth in Australia.

May the Almighty bless all who contributed to the success of the Dinner, and lend their support to the Friends of Yeshivat Sha'alvim.

Rabbi Philip Harris Singer

MESSAGE OF THE DEAN
Man Does Count

For seventy years Communism claimed that man is nothing more than a number. Very striking to me, on a mission to Moscow, Leningrad and Riga nine years ago, was that no man revealed his identity. Names did not appear on the mail box, and telephone books were not available. You were told to come to a certain address, and look for Block x, Apt. y. In *shule*, people gave only their first names.

Judaism proved for over 3,000 years that man is **not** a number. He rates. He can be an עולם מלא, an "entire world". He should not and, indeed, cannot be reduced to a number, אשר לא ימד ולא יספר. We count sheep, we count money, we count objects—material things—which do not possess a personality. Man, however has a נשמה, a soul, the distinctive traits of mind, heart and behavior. Man should be measured in terms of quality, and not quantity. Truth does not lie in numbers.

Chazal in Tractate *Yoma* (22) have differentiated between two seemingly contradictory phrases in one verse: והיי מספר בני ישראל כחול הים אשר לא ימד ולא יספר (הושע ב) by saying: "When the Children of Israel fulfill G-d's bidding they cannot be counted. When they refrain from discharging their duties, they are as the sand of the sea."

People of quality are those who hear G-d's voice, follow His directives, and do His bidding. They are the people who are to be considered, even if they are few and humble. They are His emissaries in this world. One plus G-d makes a majority.

All of our honorees have distinguished themselves in this manner, and represent the backbone of Torah, Yiddishkeit and Eretz Yisrael. We proudly salute Shimon and Debby Kwestel, Yossi and Agi Fried, Rabbi Allen Schwartz, Arthur and Rifki Helft and Shmuel and Terri Wagner. We are confident that we shall continue to merit their friendship and yours as Sha'alvim enters its fourth decade with our face to Klal Yisrael the world over. Truth shall prevail.

Mallen Galinsky

MESSAGE FROM
THE DIRECTOR OF COMMUNITY RELATIONS

On a visit to an army base in the north of Israel, I met a group of our Hesder students. It is difficult to describe the Kiddush Hashem these young men represent. They rise early for tefila, and fill any free moment with Torah study, while fulfilling all the responsibilities of an Israeli soldier in a tough combat unit. They are known to all as Torah Jews, and are respected for their special spirit.

This spirit, combined with the family atmosphere at Sha'alvim, makes for a unique institution. It emanates from the Rosh Yeshiva, Rav Meir Schlesinger, and filters down through the rebbeim to the students.

This spirit will come through to you in the video you will view tonight. You will feel it when you view Sha'alvim's special project in Kharkov and its activities with recent Russian immigrants. Sha'alvim is not a yeshiva that makes "Shabbat for Itself." It is an educational institution that is dedicated, not only to its students and to Israel, but to all of Klal Yisrael.

Yossi and Agi Fried, Shimon and Debby Kwestel, Rabbi Allen Schwartz, Dr. Arthur and Rifki Helft, and Stuart and Terri Wagner have all shown this same spirit and dedication. Tonight we proudly pay tribute to them and offer our best wishes.

Don Kates

DINNER COMMITTEE

Chairman
Allen I. Fagin

Co-Chairman

Terry Aranoff   Alan Miller '80

Honorary Chairmen

Dr. Ira H. Friedman   Arnold Olshin
Gabriel Kaszovitz   Donald Press
Ira Kellman   Henry Wimpfheimer
Lawrence A. Kobrin   Michael C. Wimpfheimer

Joseph K. Miller הי"ד

Dinner Committee

June Aranoff   Walter Kahn
David Berkowitz '81   Alan Kestenbaum '80
Julius Berman   David Kupchik '86
Zev Berman '80   Marc Kwestel '85
Joseph S. Bodner '78   Steven Kwestel '82
Chaim Book '84   Esther Lerer
Avy Buchen '78   Dr. Paul Lerer
Dr. Warren Enker   Rabbi Howard Messinger
William Feller   Aliza Miller
Raphael Fink '81   Rhoda Miller
Gary Fragin   Steven Orlow
Cheryl Friedman   Esther Press
Erika Friedman   Daniel Quint '86
Dr. Richard Friedman '81   Iser Roller
Elliot Gibber   Sheldon Rudoff
David Goldberg   Rabbi Herschel Schacter
David Goldsmith   Rabbi Dr. Jacob J. Schacter
Dr. Gabriel Gurell   Herbert Schuster '79
Leonard Holler '84   Elliot Small '80
Alex Hornstein   David Sondheim '77
Vera Hornstein   Heinz Sondheim
Bezalel Jacobowitz '81   Rabbi Pinchos Stolper
Gustave Jacobs   Burton Weinstein '81

David Zharnest '81

Rabbi Meir Schlesinger   Rabbi Mallen Galinsky
Rosh Hayeshiva   *Dean*

Werner Rosenbaum   Alan Miller '80
President   *Alumni President*

Rabbi Philip H. Singer   Don Kates '71
Chairman   *Director, Community Relations*

DANIEL P. MOYNIHAN
NEW YORK

405 LEXINGTON AVENUE
SUITE 4101
NEW YORK, NY 10174-4101

United States Senate
WASHINGTON, DC 20510-3201

February 5, 1992

Dear Allen:

I am delighted to learn that Shimon and Debby Kwestel will be honored with the Joseph K. Miller Achdut Yisrael Award on Sunday evening, March 1, 1992.

I have long believed that Israeli Yeshivat servicing American students render an invaluable contribution to American society. Yeshivat Sha'alvim should be appreciated by all who cherish our national heritage of respect for religious freedom and educational excellence.

There could be no more appropriate recipients than Shimon and Debby Kwestel of an award named in memory of their good friend Joseph K. Miller. Joe would be deeply moved by this most appropriate tribute.

Please convey to Shimon and Debby my great congratulations and best wishes to those who have gathered on this festive occasion.

Sincerely,

Daniel Patrick Moynihan

Mr. Allen I. Fagin
Friends of Yeshivat Sha'alvim
5015 Fifteenth Avenue
Brooklyn, New York 11219

קרית חינוך שעלבים
SHA'ALVIM EDUCATION CENTER
Fact Sheet

INTRODUCTION:

A dynamic comprehensive educational center, Israel's **Yeshivat Sha'alvim** imbues its 1,407 students with unwavering dedication to Torah learning and observance and develops future spiritual and lay leaders committed to the People and the State of Israel.

This unique endeavor encompasses ten educational divisions, as well as residential facilities for students, teachers and staff. During the school year, some 1,650 people study and live at Sha'alvim, including the permanent population of 77 families numbering about 300 people. The Yeshiva provides the full range of municipal and social services, including housing, medical clinic, market, roadworks, water supply, electrical generators, sewage, sanitation collection, gardening, community institutions, etc.

Pre-School:
Day Care, Nurseries, Kindergartens .... 110 children

Elementary School:
Yeshiva, Kibbutz Sha'alvim and neighboring
    religious settlements .... 410 pupils

Junior and Senior Yeshiva High Schools:
Grades 7-12 .... 426 pupils

Yeshiva Gevoha:
Yeshivat Hesder, Overseas Division,
    Teachers College .... 391 students

Postgraduate Division:
Kolel, Sha'al Torah Corps .... 70 fellows

1987

Mr. and Mrs. Walter Kahn
Mr. and Mrs. Eli Schlossberg
Mrs. Mollie Frank Marks
Mr. Alan Kestenbaum

Chairman:
Mr. Joseph K. Miller ז״ל

1986

Rav Meir Schlesinger
Mr. and Mrs. Leon Nechamkin
Mr. Kalman Staiman
Mr. and Mrs. Maurice Ehrlich
Mr. Josef Chaim Teitler

Chairman:
Mr. Arnold Olshin

1985

Mr. Joseph ז״ל and Mrs. Rhoda Miller
Dr. and Mrs. Allen Goldtein
Mr. Leonard Warburg

Chairman:
Mr. Donald Press

1984

Mr. Leon Mayer ע״ה and Sarah Mayer Hammerman
Mr. and Mrs. Mayer Sutton
Mr. and Mrs. Donald Press
Dr. Jay Cinnamon

Chairmen:
Mr. Werner Rosenbaum and Mr. Henry Wimpfheimer

1983

Mr. Isidor M. Roffer
Mr. and Mrs. Iser Roller
Rabbi and Mrs. Meyer Fendel
Mr. Avy Buchen

Chairman:
Mr. Sidney Kwestel

1982

Mr. and Mrs. Werner Rosenbaum
Yeshiva Class of 5733

Chairmen:
Dr. Ira and Erika Friedman

Yeshivat Sha'alvim
salutes our previous awardees:
in appreciation
of their continued friendship and support

1991
Vera and Alex Hornstein and Avi
Rabbi Herschel Schacter
June and Terry Aranoff
Raphael Fink
Rhoda Miller
Chairman:
Michael C. Wimpfheimer

1990
Murray and Sara Leifer
Gustave and Henriette Jacobs
Rabbi Hershel Schachter
Rabbi Kenneth Brander
Chairman:
Ira Kellman

1989
Dr. Ira and Erika Friedman
Heinz and Ina Sondheim
Morty and Roslyn Feder
Alan and Aliza Miller
Chairman:
Gabriel Kaszovitz

1988
Dr. and Mrs. Shalom Abboudi
Dr. and Mrs. Yehudi Felman
Mr. and Mrs. Aryeh Jeselsohn
Dr. and Mrs. Sidney Stern
Mr. and Mrs. Mordecai Weinstein
Mr. and Mrs. Joel Zimmerman
Congregation Sharei Zedek, Coney Island
Chairman:
Lawrence A. Kobrin

1981
Mr. Jacob עייה and Mrs. Edith Reich
Mr. and Mrs. David Mitzner
Mr. and Mrs. Seymour Fenichel
Rabbi and Mrs. Leon Machlis
Yeshiva Classes of 5731 and 5732
Chairmen:
Dr. Ira and Erika Friedman

Endowments and Dedications at Yeshivat Sha'alvim

The Joseph Tanenbaum Campus

Buildings
JOSEPH K. MILLER HALL

Divisions
MORDECHAI HORNSTEIN INSTITUTE FOR OVERSEAS STUDENTS
KOLLEL KETER YEHOSHUA
LANDER TEACHERS COLLEGE

Synagogues
BLASBALG HALL
Charles and Els Bendheim

CONGREGATION SONS OF ISRAEL
Long Island City

OHEL RACHEL
Rachel Lowenstein, z"l

MEDICAL CLINIC
Dr. Falk and Chana Schlesinger and Yehudit, z"l

Synagogue Interiors
SIFREI TORAH
Congregation Shaarei Zedek, Coney Island
Dr. Moshe, z"l
Avner Michaeli, z"l
Rabbi Shaya Lebor
Rabbi Leon Machlis, z"l
Fogel Family

ARON KODESH
Samuel and Hena Kahn, z"l
Charles and Els Bendheim

NER TAMID
Bilha Haberman

BIMA
Dr. Ira and Erika Friedman

AMUD HATEFILA
Werner and Shelly Rosenbaum

Endowments and Dedications at Yeshivat Sha'alvim

FURNITURE
Israeli Hesder Alumni

TORAH ORNAMENTS
Dr. Michael and Ruth Matar

LIBRARY SECTIONS
Chaim Geiger, z"l
Josef Chaim and Sarah Teitler
Joseph and Pauline Silber
Rabbi Leon Machlis, z"l

HEATING AND AIR CONDITIONING
Mr. and Mrs. David Mitzner
Mr. and Mrs. Asher Schoenkopf
Israeli Hesder Alumni

Central Library

YOM KIPPUR WAR MARTYRS MEMORIAL
Moshe Yehiel Cohen
Moshe Yoram Isak
Menachem Mendel Shitzer

MIRSKY LIBRARY
Adele D. Gilbert and Betty Dorenter, z"l

RAV. D. ELI MUNK LIBRARY

AVRAM CHAIM MOTZEN LIBRARY

FURNISHINGS
Israeli Hesder Alumni
Guillaume and Rachel Friedman
Frieda Himelblau
Mrs. Rochel Seid
David Rosenberg, z"l

Dining Halls

Iser and Anna Roller
Rose Friedman

ACOUSTIC CEILINGS
Israeli Hesder

Endowments and Dedications at Yeshivat Sha'alvim

Faculty and Kolel Residences

Dr. Moshe Wallach, z"l, Quarter
Rav Zadok Tal, z"l
Rabbinical Alliance of America
Ludwig and Erica Jesselson

Computer Science Laboratory

Joseph K., z"l, and Rhoda Miller

OBSERVATION CENTER
Rudy Stern, z"l

Lecture Halls

S. Daniel Abraham
Jacob and Hinda Goldstein, z"l
Syrian Jewish Community of Brooklyn, NY and Deal, NJ
Isidor Roffer, z"l
Joseph and Meta Heiman, z"l
Maurice and Shoshana Ehrlich
Leon Meyer, z"l
Josef Teitler
The Nacham Family
Bessie Feller, z"l

Rosh Yeshiva's Study

Walter and Grace Kahn

REFERENCE LIBRARY
Yaakov Reich, z"l

RECEPTION HALL
Howard D. and Rita Geller
Marc and Debbi Geller
and Families

Endowments and Dedications at Yeshivat Sha'alvim

Faculty Studies

S. Daniel Abraham
Moshe Zalman Birnbaum, z"l
Abraham Levinsky, z"l
Willy and Bertha Schwab, z"l
Mary and Rose Jacobson, z"l
Great Neck Synagogue
Mr. and Mrs. Isadore Serelson
Dr. Chaim and Joy Mond, '79

Atrium

Edith Reich in memory of Yaakov Reich, z"l

Baruch Gopman, z"l,
by Seymour Fenichel, Elias Lauer, Rabbi Philip H. Singer

Dormitory Rooms

Isaiah and Sarah Stiglitz
Esther Ema Hauser, z"l
Elka Feist-Lerner, z"l
Abraham and Chaya Weinstock
Menashe and Bracha Frankel, z"l
Beatrice Smith
Boxenhorn-Tobias Family
Isaac Shalom, z"l
Marcus Oppenheimer
Rabbi Eli, z"l, and Sonia Rosman
Max Yablick, z"l
David H. Gluck Foundation
Riva Mustman, z"l
Mr. and Mrs. Samuel Black, z"l

Endowments and Dedications at Yeshivat Sha'alvim

Social Hall

Frieda Himelblau

Congregational Memorial Tablets

Congregation Sharei Zedek, Coney Island
Congregation Sons of Israel, Long Island City
Congregation Adath Jeshurun, Bronx

Endowments and Funds

Maurice and Shoshana Ehrlich
Bilha Haberman
Mollie Frank Marks
Heinz and Ina Sondheim

Joseph K. Miller, z"l
Avraham Chaim Motzen, z"l

הישיבה זוכרת בגאון וביגון
את תלמידיה היקרים
אשר נפלו על קידוש ה׳

משה כהן הי״ד
מנחם שיצר הי״ד
יורם איזק הי״ד
במלחמת יום הכפורים

שלמה אומן הי״ד
אברהם מוצן הי״ד
אריה שטראוס הי״ד
במלחמת שלום הגליל

אבנר מיכאלי ז״ל
מתניה בר לב ז״ל
אהרון לור׳ה ז״ל
בעת מילוי תפקידם

ואת תלמידי׳ שנספו

ר׳ שמואל ברונר ז״ל
ר׳ ישראל מנחם פייג ז״ל
משה פרידמן ז״ל
מרדכי הורנשטיין ז״ל
הלל בקסט ז״ל

A TRIBUTE

יוסף בן אהרן שמואל הי״ד
JOSEPH K. MILLER

MOTY HORNSTEIN INSTITUTE
FOR OVERSEAS STUDENTS
In memory of
MORDECHAI "MOTY" HORNSTEIN

לזכר
מרדכי ז״ל בן משולם וחיה הי״ו
נפ׳ ערב יום כפור תש״ן

In Appreciation to
the Honorees
and Our Friends, Parents and Alumni
Whose Generosity and Cooperation
Have Facilitated the Success
of the Thirty-First Anniversary Dinner
of Yeshivat Sha'alvim

Tonight's dinner and journal are a tribute to this vibrant and dynamic Torah community in Israel. Yeshivat Sha'alvim imbues its 1350 students with unwavering dedication to Torah learning and observance, and develops future spiritual and lay leaders with a commitment to the Land and People of Israel.

Responsibility for one's fellowman, the unity of the Jewish People, and the centrality of Eretz Yisrael find expression in the "ingathering of exiles" that transpires at Sha'alvim. Students from across the globe live and learn together in a warm, family atmosphere. The verdant grounds in the picturesque Ayalon Valley provide the backdrop for a thriving Torah environment.

A special faculty of resident Rabbanim and teachers, together with a caring administrative staff, is always available to students seeking direction. Adult perception and personal guidance complement high caliber scholarship and challenging Jewish learning. The many Sha'alvim alumni in educational and administrative positions on campus lend an added dimension to the close student-teacher relationships.

In the Yeshivat Hesder, heart of the Sha'alvim complex, young men combine their rigorous study of Talmud, Tanach, Halacha, and Jewish philosophy with service in the Israel Defense Forces. Students distinguish themselves in the Bet Midrash and in the army, bringing honor to religious Jewry.

The Yeshiva Gevoha was established in 1961 by the visionary Rosh Hayeshiva, Rav Meir Schlesinger. It began with a small group of teenagers studying Torah while undergoing military training and defending the region, then just a few meters from the Jordanian border.

Scores of overseas students spend a year or more of intensive Torah study at Yeshivat Sha'alvim. They supplement their learning with organized field trips, Shabbatonim, and social activism in development towns and absorption centers during vacation periods and weekends.

Kolel Fellows and married senior students pursue advanced Torah study and prepare for leadership roles in the Rabbinate and the Religious Judicial System, fulfilling the ordination (Semicha) requirements of Israel's Chief Rabbinate. The presence of these mature and dedicated scholars on campus emphasizes the intrinsic value of continued Jewish learning.

The Shlomo Aumann Institute staff helps restore rare manuscripts to the Jewish People by publishing corrected and annotated versions of formerly unavailable Halachic works.

Sha'alvim faculty utilize the latest data and information processing techniques to produce learning aids as well as material for scholarly journals.

The Teachers College offers certification in the field of Jewish education. Senior students enhance their Jewish knowledge with courses in psychology, history and methodology of education, and language skills. Student-teachers practice and refine educational techniques in Sha'alvim's pedagogical laboratory with junior and senior high school students, and in the neighboring kibbutz and development towns.

Sha'al is developing a Torah Corps of desperately needed educators, Rabbis, youth workers, and campus advisors for Diaspora communities. Participants commit themselves to a minimum two-year tour of duty in their native lands.

The junior and senior Yeshiva high schools provide an outstanding curriculum of Jewish learning including Torah, Talmud, Prophets, Jewish law, ethics, and Jewish thought. The pre-academic general studies program leads to matriculation in the sciences (biology, chemistry, physics, computer) and humanities, as well as in Judaic studies. Students interested in agriculture study beekeeping, botany, gardening, and modern agronomy. The young men gain Torah scholarship under the able guidance of their Rabbanim and Rosh Yeshiva, Rav Ya'akov Zur, and view the Hesder and Kolel students as role models for their own growth and development.

The Shalhevet Regional Elementary and Middle School, located on Kibbutz Sha'alvim, is now under the auspices of the Yeshiva's Educational Center. Youngsters from area religious settlements, the neighboring kibbutz, and faculty families attain the crucial basis for love and knowledge of Torah here while starting their general education.

Amud Hayeshiva

Amud Hayeshiva

Our deepest appreciation to
Vera and Alex Hornstein
Allentown, Pennsylvania

Pillars of Yeshivat Sha'alvim
and founders of
The Moty Hornstein Institute
מכון מרדכי
for Overseas Students

American Friends of Yeshivat Sha'alvim

Amud Hayeshiva

Amud Hayeshiva

For Jewish parents, especially the Jewish Mother,
to send a child to Israel for a year in yeshiva
is an extremely emotional experience.

At Sha'alvim,
the Administration, Rabbeim, and Madrichim
became surrogate parents to our three sons,
for a total of six years.

A year is only a year.
A year is just a fleeting moment.
But in a religious and spiritual sense,
a year at Sha'alvim
will be remembered for a lifetime.

Debby

We express
our deepest appreciation and Hakoras HaTov to
Rav Meir, Rabbi Galinsky
and the entire Sha'alvim family
for the shining example
they set as role models for our sons.
May
Itamar, Menachem and Eli
always reflect honor upon the Yeshiva
and continue to bring us nachas.
הי ישלח ברכה והצלחה בכל מעשה ידיכם.

Debby and Shimon Kwestel

Amud Hayeshiva

Dear
Shimon and Debby

You have taken Joe's dream and made it a reality.

Thank you.

Love,

Rhoda

Scholarship

In Honor of
Shimon and Debby Kwestel
role models and leaders for world Jewry

Mazel Tov on this deserved honor

Elliot and Debbie Gibber

Scholarship

In honor of our dear son
Yosef Helft

May he continue to grow
in Torah, Midot, and Ma'asim Tovim!

Love,

Mom and Dad

Scholarship

The Jewish Center

is very proud to honor its distinguished neighbor
Rabbi Allen Schwartz
who has made
such a tremendous impact
on our entire community
and
all the other Honorees

May they and their families
go from strength to strength

Dr. Jacob J. Schacter
Rabbi

Mr. Arthur G. Degen
President

Benefactor

In Honor of
the Rosh HaYeshiva,
Harav Meir Schlesinger
and
Rav Mallen Galinsky
for all their efforts on behalf
of our sons, the Yeshiva and Klal Yisroel.

**Gary, Patrice, Michael, Greg, Jessica and Samuel
Fragin**

Benefactor

Our gratitude to
Heinz and Ina Sondheim
for their continuous generous support
to
Yeshivat Sha'alvim

Benefactor

To
Mr. and Mrs. Ludwig Jesselson

In Deep Appreciation

Yeshivat Sha'alvim

ישיבת שעלבים

The Kharkov Great Synagogue

Patron

כל המכבד את התורה
גופו מכובד על הבריות

In Admiration
—with Honor and Respect—
to those who give honor to Torah
Joseph and Agi Fried
Shimon and Debby Kwestel
Rabbi Allen Schwartz
Dr. Arthur and Rivki Helft
Shmuel and Terri Wagner

Shelly and Werner Rosenbaum

Patron

In Honor of
the Rosh Hayeshiva,
Rav Meir Schlesinger, Shlita

Kol Hakovod to
the Guests of Honor

Arnold and Miriam Olshin
Ira Olshin 85-86
Michael Olshin 87-89, 91-92
Hillel 91-92

Patron

In Cherished Memory
of
Max and Ilse Rosenbaum
ז״ל

Shelly and Werner Rosenbaum
Linda and Jay Goldmintz and Family
Carol and Steven Rosenbaum and Family

Patron

In Honor of
Shimon and Debby Kwestel
Shmuel and Terri Wagner

Mrs. Gertrude Goldberg
Dassy and Marvin Bienenfeld

Patron

In Honor of
our distinguished מרא דאתרא
Rabbi Allen Schwartz
and our dear Rebbitzen
Alisa Schwartz
who have spread
תורה, אהבה, אחוה, שלום, ורעות
and created a sense of communal אחריות
in our West Side community

In Appreciation,

Shelly and Werner Rosenbaum

Sponsor

In honor of
the Rosh Yeshiva
Reb Meir Schlesinger
who has enriched the life
of our son, **Daniel,**
and, in turn, our entire family

Elliot and Debbie Gibber

Sponsor

Best Wishes to
Rav Meir Schlesinger
for Hatzlocha in his holy work

Hermann and Ulla Merkin

ישיבת שעלבים

Hadlakat Neirot in Kharkov

Tribute

We join in honoring
the Yeshiva,
its leader and faculty,
its students,
and
its honorees

Lawrence and Ruth Kobrin

Tribute

In Tribute to
Sha'alvim students
serving in the Israeli Army

Mr. and Mrs. Alfred Dessau

Tribute

We are proud to join those honoring
Shimon and Debby
in recognition of their outstanding leadership
in the Jewish community.

With warmest wishes

Liz and Marty Nachimson
North Hollywood, CA

Tribute

In honor of our special friends
consummate community askanim
Mr. Shimon and Mrs. Debby Kwestel
who will receive
the Achdut Yisrael Award
in the name of our mutual dear friend
Mr. Joseph K. Miller, O.B.M.
and carry it with great distinction

Isidore Feldman
Joseph Feldman
Sol Werdiger
Jonah Blumenfrucht
The Isfel Group

Tribute

Mazal Tov to Our Grandchildren
Shmuel and Terri Wagner
on this most memorable occasion

From your grandparents

Julius and Tessie Bienenfeld

Chai Page

In Loving Memory
of My Grandparents
Joseph and Rose Holler ז״ל
Isaac and Helen Gold ז״ל

Leonard Holler

ישיבת שעלבים

The Yeshiva in Kharkov

Gold Page

To
Shimon and Debby

With all your love
you have taught us the Derech Hashem.
Although no one will ever replace our father, ז״ל,
you and our remarkable mother
are models for us to emulate
as you continue to bring
Daddy's dream to fruition.

כל מי שעוסקים בצרכי ציבור באמונה
הקודש ברוך הוא ישלם שכרם.

**Alan, Aliza
Talia and Yosef**

Silver Page

In Tribute to

Our dear cousins
Shimon and Debby Kwestel
whose communal activities are legend

Our good friends
Arthur and Rifki Helft
Parents of the Year

Rabbi Allen Schwartz
Rabbinic Leadership Awardee

and all distinguished Honorees
and supporters of Yeshivat Sha'alvim

Dr. and Mrs. Ira H. Friedman
Joanne Friedman

Dr. and Mrs. Richard L. Friedman
Shoshana Miriam and Elana Esther

Silver Page

To the Honorees
Rabbi Allen Schwartz
Shimon and Debby Kwestel
Joseph and Agi Fried
Dr. Arthur and Rifki Helft
Stuart and Terri Wagner

Our heartiest Congratulations
and to
the Yeshiva and their faculty
A Yasher Koach
Michayil El Chayil

Gerald E. Feldhamer   **Jack Gross**

Silver Page

Rav Meir and Esther הי״ו

Mazal Tov upon the forthcoming marriage of
יסכה ובני
עמו״ש
בשעה טובה ומוצלחת

Rhoda
Alan, Aliza, Talia, Yosef
Gary, Karla, Zeke, Loren
Sharon
Geoffrey

Silver Page

In Honor of our children
Aliza and Alan Miller
and our grandchildren
Talia and Yosef

Rabbi and Mrs. Arnold B. Marans

Silver Page

מזל טוב

to

the Honorees

for their selfless devotion to Yeshivat Sha'alvim

כל הכבוד

to

Rav Schlesinger   Rav Galinsky

for creating an enriched atmosphere
where our children are motivated to learn Torah
in a supportive and meaningful manner
under the guidance of a devoted faculty.

Marvin and Rosalie Waltuch
Benjamin, Joshua and Deborah

Silver Page

Mazal Tov and Best Wishes
to our revered friends
Shimmy and Debby Kwestel
and
Dr. Arthur and Rifki Helft
and special recognition
to an outstanding young couple
Shmuel and Terri Wagner

Sara and Moishe Leifer

Silver Page

Silver Page

Silver Page

Greetings to
Rabbi and Mrs. Herschel Schacter

Reb Herschel and Penina,
our wonderful friends

Pinchos and Zirel Singer and Family
David and Elana Singer and Family

◆   ◆   ◆   ◆   ◆

Greetings to our great spiritual leader
Rabbi Herschel Schacter
and
Rebbetzin Penina

Mosholu Jewish Center

Silver Page

Congratulations to
Rabbi Allen Schwartz
for the spiritual revival of the West Side

Debby and Sidney Kwestel
Dear friends dedicated to communal affairs

Allen Fagin
Our partner in the New York Region OU

Susan and Avery Neumark

Silver Page

We salute
Alan Fagin
Your indefatigable Chairman
and
his Committee
on this important evening.

Phylis and Jack Gross

Silver Page

In Honor of
Rabbi Pinchos Singer
My Rebbe for more years than I care to admit.

Jerry Feldhamer

Silver Page

In Honor of a truly outstanding askan
of our generation,
Alan Fagin, Esq.
who combines professional excellence
in the field of Law
with an unparallelled dedication
to the ideals of Jewish Public Service.

Karen and Jerry Feldhamer

Silver Page

Mazal Tov to
the distinguished Honorees
and to
the Yeshivat Sha'alvim,
the outstanding learning center
that our son, **Jeffrey,** is attending.

Aaron, Carol, Jamie and Jeffrey Greenwald

Silver Page

In Memory of
the Gluck Family
Zev, Esther, George, David, Emanuel, Samuel, Henry, Lee, Mae Gluck Saks

In Honor of
Steven M. Schwartz
Sha'alvim '89

The Emanuel M. Gluck Foundation

Silver Page

In Honor of
the Rosh Yeshiva
Rav Meir Schlesinger שליט״א
and our son Elie's rebbe,
Rav Amital שליט״א

Dr. and Mrs. Joseph G. Tuchman

Silver Page

To
Debby and Shimon,

We congratulate Debby and Shimon
on this wonderful and well deserved honor
which enhances the esteem in which
the Jewish community holds them.

It is a fitting tribute to people whose lives
have been devoted to philanthropy,
advancement of Jewish education
and the furtherance of orthodox ideals.

Best Wishes,

Sylvia K. Friedman
Mannes, Helen, Daniel, Lisa and Andy Friedman
Allen, Mimi, Bennett and Jonathan Schachter

Silver Page

Mazel Tov to our Mechutonim
Debby and Shimon Kwestel
Your sincere devotion to all Torah causes
is an inspiration to us all.

Lorraine and Mordy Sohn and Family

Silver Page

Dear
Shimon and Debby

Your selfless dedication
to all aspects of Jewish life
has had a tremendous impact on our lives.
We look up to you with great respect and love.
May Hashem continue to give you
the strength to go מחיל אל חיל.

Love,

Leah and Danny Taragin

Silver Page

In Honor of
Shimon and Debby Kwestel

Alvin and Jane Feder

Silver Page

In Honor of
Rosh Hayeshiva Rav Meir Schlesinger,
Rabbi Galinsky,
The Rabbeim, Administrators,
and the entire staff
of Yeshivat Sha'alvim
for their dedication and devotion
to the task of teaching Torah to our children

Mazel Tov to the 1992 Dinner Honorees
Shimon and Debby Kwestel
Rabbi Allen Schwartz
Dr. Arthur and Rifki Helft
Stuart and Terri Wagner

Yossi and Agi Fried

Silver Page

In Honor of our son
Udi, ג"יּ,
his classmates at the Yeshiva,
and especially the Denver boys,
Joshua Jacobs and Avi Heller

We wish all of you much success in your studies
and hope that you will return home
enriched in Torah and love for Israel.

Special Thanks to our son's wonderful Rabbi
Rabbi Michael Yammer

Yossi and Agi Fried

Silver Page

To our dear
Yossi and Agi

יישר כחכם עלו והצליחו
May you see much nachas
from all of your children

**Ima, Teena, Menachem, David,
Rachel, Tehila and Gitel Shlomit**

Silver Page

We proudly pay tribute
to our cousins
Agi and Yossi

May they be zocheh to continue
their dedication and support of Torah causes.

Karen and Jerry

Silver Page

From a thrilled Congregation
who delight in joining you in Tribute
to our Beloved Rabbi and Rebbitzen
Rabbi Allen and Alisa Schwartz

May ה' grant them אריכת ימים,
נחת from their charming family
and the privilege to continue
their wonderful work
בגלוי וביחידות

Congregation Ohab Zedek
118 West 95 Street
New York

Murray Zucker
President

Milton Tomber
Chairman

Silver Page

In Honor of our dear friends
Rabbi Allen and Alisa Schwartz
Shonnie, Chani, Moshe Monis and Elli

Ruthy and Joey Bodner
and David Z. Bodner

Silver Page

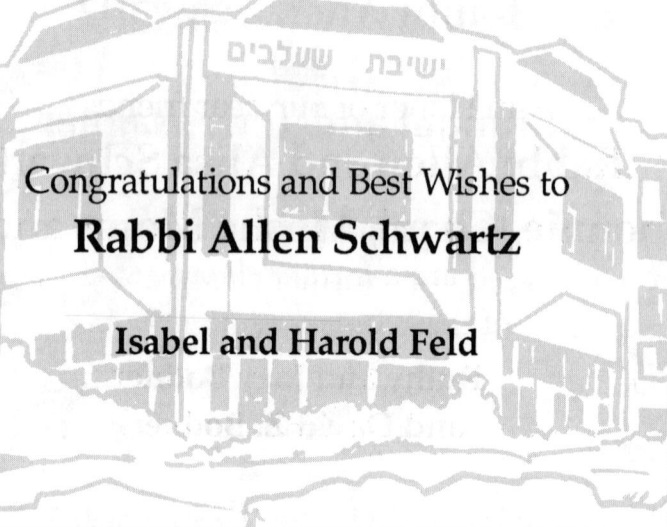

Congratulations and Best Wishes to
Rabbi Allen Schwartz

Isabel and Harold Feld

Silver Page

In Honor of
Rabbi Allen Schwartz
and
Shmuel and Terri Wagner

I am proud to be able to say
I am a former classmate
of these outstanding people.

From

Alan and Debbie Kestenbaum
Jordan and Arielle

Silver Page

Shmuel

We've come a long way together
from nursery through Sha'alvim
and are still the best of friends.

Terri and Aliza and our children
share our friendship.

Together we shall continue to serve Klal Yisroel.

מזל טוב

Alan

Silver Page

Mazal Tov to our dear children
Shmuel and Terri Wagner
We are very proud of you

Mom, Dad, and Grandpa Fischel

ישיבת שעלבים

Silver Page

To Our Dear Brother and Sister
Shmuel and Terri Wagner

Congratulations on receiving
this most prestigious award

Susan and Alan Klinger
Tammy and Steven Wagner
Barbara and Gary Simon

The Ulpana — Girls' Yeshiva in Kharkov

In Memory of
Joseph K. Miller הי״ד
במעלות קדושים וטהורים מזהיר

His friendship in lifetime a precious gift
His cherished memory a beacon of light.

Debby and Shimon Kwestel

כבד את אביך ואת אמך
Honor thy Father and thy Mother......

It is a true pleasure for us
to join with Yeshivat Sha'alvim
in honoring you for all you do for
the Jewish community world wide.

May Hashem grant the two of you אריכת ימים
and nachas from us
עד מאה ועשרים שנה

Love,

Dassy and Steven
Marc
Elliot

In Honor of
Debby and Shimon

Our friends for 42 years
who have dedicated their lives
for Torah and Jewish survival
throughout the world

Sheila and Mendy Ganchrow

Dear Menacham!

Thank you very much for your great help for us and for all young jewish people of Kharkov. Your work changed a lot in our life. This seminar became one of the most important points of our existance. Here we began to feel taste of, what it means to be jewish, what is jewish life, we began to understand that we are part of a great nation.

Thank you very much for your lectures.

We hope we'll meet again, and if you decide to visit Kharkov we hope to see you in our home.

Thank you! Thank you!
Thank you!
Lena, Lusha

Zabrodskaya L.
Fou x L
18 Uborevich str., apt. 188
Kharkov 310144, Ukraine   (0572)651-349

Украина, г. Харьков 310144
ул. Уборевича 18, кв 188.
Завродская Л.
Фукс Л.

שיר המעלות
In Honor of
Rabbi Mallen Galinsky
כמה מעלות טובות

We appreciate the multiple talents,
the wisdom, the sincerity,
the dedication, the diligence
in his leadership at Yeshivat Sha'alvim
and his invaluable inspiration,
guidance and assistance
in our pioneering holy work
to bring Torah and Judaism in Kharkov, Russia.

Our thanks to the Rosh Yeshiva,
Rav Meir,
who sparked and supported all endeavors
of Rabbi Galinsky
and
all noble volunteers and participants

Большои спасибо

Shimon and Debby Kwestel

In Honor of
our dear friends
Shimon and Deborah Kwestel

Their dedication to Klal Yisrael
is an inspiration to us all

Yaakov and Loni Melohn

In Memory of
Joe Miller ע״ה

Arlene and Bernie Silverstein

In Honor of
Shimon and Debby Kwestel

Arlene and Bernie Silverstein

ישיבת שעלבים

To
our dear cousins
Shimon and Debby
for their wonderful work

Harold and Marilyn Schwartz

Mazal Tov to
our dear friends
Shimon and Debby
who exemplify אהבת ה׳
and commitment to כלל ישראל
בלב שלם

Marcel and Paula Weber

In Gratitude
for all that Sha'alvim and its Rebbeyim
have meant for our son
Ari

Rabbi Benjamin and Elaine Blech

Mazel Tov and הצלחה רבה
for a very deserving couple
and
In Memory of a very wonderful person.

Your friends

Laurie and Debbie Cherniak

We salute ישיבות

Shimon and Debby Kwestel

עוסקים בצרכי צבור באמונה True

G-d bless you

Fifth Avenue Synagogue
New York City

To our dear friends
Shimon and Debby Kwestel
Two great human beings with
wisdom
dedication
and courage

George and Ilse Falk

We join in honoring
Debby and Shimon
Models of Love, Devotion, and Dedication

for אחינו בני ישראל

Your integrity and commitment
are an inspiration to us all

Pessy and Rafi Butler
Suri and Menachem Genack

In honor of two wonderful people
Shimon and Debby Kwestel
recipients of
the Joseph K. Miller A"H Achdut Yisrael Award.

We are happy to be able to join
in this most appropriate tribute.

Dennis and Shifra Rapps

ישיבת מזל טוב
to
Debby and Shimon
and to
Rifki and Arthur
from

Nicky and Morty

In Honor of
Shimon and Debby Kwestel
Rabbi Allen Schwartz
True leaders of our community

Cheryl and Elliot Small
David Saul, Daniel Ian, Andrew Marc

Mazel Tov to
Shimon and Debby

Your dedication to Jewish causes
is a true testimonial to our mentor
Joe Miller

Esther and Donald Press

In Honor of
Shimon and Debby Kwestel

ישיבת שעלבים

Their selfless devotion to Klal Yisrael
in the United States
and throughout the world
makes them exemplary recipients of
an award named for
Joe Miller,
whom we will always remember.

Judy and Harvey Blitz

With Respect to
Rabbi Schlesinger

With Gratitude to
Rabbi Yammer

In Honor of
Shimon and Debby Kwestel

Steven and Susan Orlow and family

and
From the
**Law Offices of
STEVEN S. ORLOW, P.C.**

*Practice Limited Exclusively to
Personal Injury Negligence*

Main Office
75-20 Vleigh Place, Flushing, NY 11367
(718) 544-4100

In Honor of
Debby and Shimon

Grace and Walter Kahn

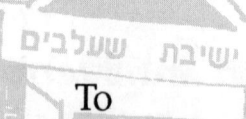

To
Shimon and Debby Kwestel
A team devoted to
Achdut Yisroel

Mr. and Mrs. Harvey Wolinetz

In Honor of
Shimon and Debby Kwestel
a couple whose support for Torah causes
is legendary.
They are role models to us all.
May they continue their good work
for the klal for many years to come.

Tzvi and Chaya Friedman
Baltimore, MD

In Honor of our friends
Shimon and Debby Kwestel
whom we greatly admire

And in reverence to the sacred Memory of
Joseph K. Miller ז״ל
whose undaunted labor
towards the goal of Achdut Yisrael
continues to inspire our Honorees and all of us.

Elliot and Ruth Stavsky

In Honor of
Debby and Shimon Kwestel
and
Allen I. Fagin

Julius and Dorothy Berman
Zev and Judy Berman

In Honor of
Mr. and Mrs. Shimmy Kwestel
With admiration for all the work you have done

In Honor of
Mrs. Joseph Miller

In the z'chus that you share
in all of your husband's great deeds
which affect all of us until today,
may you know of only נחת and שמחות
from your children, grandchildren,
and אי״ה, great-grandchildren.

Abraham Fruchthandler

In Honor of
Mr. and Mrs. Sidney Kwestel

Dr. and Mrs. Reuben Rudman

ישיבת שעלבים

Congratulations to
the Honorees
Shimon and Debby Kwestel

ישיבת שעלבים

Best Wishes
for a huge success
to the dedicated chairman
Allen Fagin

May you all continue
in your wonderful work and myriad
accomplishments on behalf of
Klal Yisrael ad meah v'esrim shana

Mr. and Mrs. Eugen Gluck

In Honor of
Shimon and Debby Kwestel
Recipients of the Joseph K. Miller Award

**Miriam and George Saks
and Sons**

ישיבת שעלבים

מרכז היהודי דקווינס

QUEENS JEWISH CENTER
& TALMUD TORAH

66-05 108TH STREET, FOREST HILLS, N. Y. 11375
Tel. (718) 459-8432 • Fax (718) 459-8495

February 18, 1992

Mr. Allen I. Fagin
Journal Chairman
American Friends of Yeshivat Sha'alvim

Dear Mr. Fagin:

It is with great pride and pleasure that we congratulate Yeshivat Sha'alvim for bestowing its Joseph Miller Achdus Israel Award on our good friends, Shimon and Debbie Kwestel, who have been loyal and devoted members of our congregation for many years.

Shimon and Debbie have made communal service a dominant focal point of their lives, and by their dedication have inspired many others to follow in their path. Shimon's active leadership within the Orthodox Union and his efforts to develop its programs to promote the spiritual redemption of Russian Jewry have struck a responsive chord within our community. In her own quiet and unassuming manner, Debbie has made an equally significant impact on our community through her tireless dedication to acts of chesed for the needy, the elderly, the sick and the bereaved.

We also have shared with Shimon and Debbie the pride and joy of watching their beautiful children grow and develop as Bnei Torah in the tradition of their parents and Yeshivat Sha'alvim. Steven, Marc and Eliot already have served our community in many capacities, including as youth leaders, Hatzolah volunteers and magidei shiur.

It is our pleasure to join Shimon and Debbie's many friends in celebrating this happy occasion. We pray that they may be granted the strength and inspiration to continue their dedicated and creative efforts upon behalf of Klal Yisrael for many years to come.

Sincerely,

Jonathan Shor
President

Benjamin Lopata
Chairman of the Board

MEMBER OF THE UNION OF ORTHODOX JEWISH CONGREGATIONS OF AMERICA

To
Joseph and Agi Fried

Congratulations and Best Wishes
for this honor

Mr. and Mrs. J. Jakabovits

ישיבת שעלבים

Mazel Tov to

Agi and Yossi Fried,

who are known far and wide
as the best cholent makers in Denver.

From their friends,

Jack and Barbara Greenwald

To our dear friends
Agi and Yossi Fried
Mazel Tov

Special Mazel Tov to
Mrs. Magda Rosenthal

**Jacob and Rebecca Rosenbaum
and Family**

In Honor of
Yossi and Agi Fried

May you have much הצלחה
in all your efforts on behalf of
תורה and כלל ישראל.

Tommy and Judy Rosenthal

CONGRATULATIONS

Commercial Bank of New York
is pleased to join in
this evening's tribute to

Dr. Arthur & Rifki Helft
along with
Shimon & Debby Kwestel

Their dedication and commitment
have served the entire Jewish
Community. We are proud to
honor them for all their efforts
and extend our best wishes and
deepest appreciation.

Commercial Bank of New York

A Safdié Bank

301 Park Avenue
Waldorf-Astoria Building
New York, NY 10022
(212) 735-0010

404 Fifth Avenue
at Thirty Seventh Street
New York, NY 10018
(212) 967-9400

"רבי חנינא בן דוסא אומר
כל שרוח הבריות נוחה הימנו
רוח המקום נוחה הימנו"
"He who is pleasing to his fellow men
is pleasing also to G-d."

To

Rifki and Arthur Helft,
two great, wonderful, human beings

Moish and Shirley Stein and family
Dena and Ephy Brilliant and family
of Raanana, Israel

„נבחר שם מעשר רב"
(משלי כ"ב:א)
"A good name is preferable to great riches"
(Proverbs 22:1)

We know first-hand that the good name of
Rifki and Arthur Helft
has been earned
by their lives of untiring devotion
to community service, Tzedakah, Chesed,
Torah values, friends and family.

The Yeshiva could not have chosen
more appropriate honorees.

Mazel Tov to
Rifki and Arthur Helft

Mindy, Muttie, Shira, Elana, Michael and Arielle Stein

To
**Rifki and Arthur
and family**

With love and admiration

Evy, Shimmy, Sari, Josh and Seth Stein

ישיבת שעלבים

In Honor of
Yosef Helft
We are so proud of you
and your parents
Rifki and Arthur Helft
for your devotion to Torah and Israel

Mildred and William Helft

Mazal Tov
Allen

We applaud you
for your dedication to Torah education;
We praise you for your devotion to your Kehillah;

We salute you tonight and always,
our brother and uncle;

We wish you continued success and nachas
with your Eishet Chayil, Alisa, and
your children, Shonnie, Chani, Moshe and Elli

Michael and Michelle Schwartz
Rena, Sralli and Ari

To
our wonderful parents
Rifki and Arthur Helft
We are so proud of you always.

To our brother
Yosef
Keep up the good work.
You have shown us the way.

Steven, Shari and Susie Helft

In Honor of Our Colleague
Rabbi Allen Schwartz

Mrs. Shirley R. Auslander
Rabbi Louis Bernstein
Rabbi Binyamin Blech
Rabbi Shmuel Borenstein
Rabbi Zevulun Charlop
Rabbi Herbert C. Dobrinsky
Rabbi Label Dulitz
Rabbi Steven Dworken
Rabbi Gedalia Finkelstein
Rabbi Shmuel Goldin
Rabbi Morris Gorelick
Rabbi Simcha Krauss
Rabbi Shlomo Krupka
Dr. Mitchell Orlean
Rabbi Jacob Rabinowitz
Rabbi Bernard Rosenzweig
Dr. Samuel Schneider
Rabbi Yaakov Schwartz
Rabbi Aaron Selevan
Rabbi Yeshaya Siff
Rabbi Moshe Tendler
Rabbi Binyamin Yudin

at Yeshiva University

In honor of
Rabbi Allen Schwartz
whose dedication, concern and creativity
have helped to revitalize
the West Side Jewish Community.

Mrs. Elias Hausman

In Honor of
Rabbi Allen Schwartz
our
מרא דאתרא

Kenneth and Jenny Michael

ॐ

In Honor of
Shimon and Debby Kwestel

Kenneth and Jenny Michael

In Honor of
Rabbi Allen Schwartz

Mr. and Mrs. Walter Lowenthal

Dear
Allen

שעלבים has brought us together again.
מזל טוב on an honor well deserved.

Alan Miller

Shmuel and Terri

All Good Wishes

מזל טוב

Rhoda Miller

Mazel Tov to
Shmuel Wagner
on your deserving award

ישיבת שעלבים

Your friends at
EXCALIBUR LAND SERVICES INC.
For All Your Title Needs

55 Northern Boulevard-Suite 205
Great Neck, NY 11021
Tel: (516) 466-0080   Fax: (516) 466-0170

President
KARLA MILLER, ESQ.

Vice President
GEOFFREY MILLER

Vice President, Sales
BRUCE PRIVETERRE

Customer Service Rep.
PHYLLIS CURTIN

To our good friends
Shmuel and Terri Wagner

Terri and Andrew Herenstein

ישיבת שעלבים

Congratulations to
Shmuel and Terri Wagner
and
Shimon and Debby Kwestel
and thank you for all you have done for our Yeshiva

Ruth and Jason Jacobowitz
Gladys and Matthew Maryles
Robin and Bezalel Jacobowitz

Mazel Tov and Best Wishes to
Shmuel and Terri,
on a well deserved honor.

May you continue to inspire us all.

Lisa and Tzvi Rubin

Mazel Tov to
our good friends
Terri and Shmuel Wagner

May you continue
to do more good work for Sha'alvim.

Naomi, David and Alex Kaszovitz

Mazel Tov to

Shmuel and Terri Wagner

We are proud to see you
following in the footsteps of
your parents and grandparents.

Lorraine and Mordy Sohn

ישיבת שעלבים

Mazel Tov to
Shmuel

We are so proud of you
and everything you stand for

Love,

Terri, Aviva, Eli and Shana

שפע ברכות לבביות
לכבוד מורנו ורבנו
הרב ר׳ מאיר שלזינגר שליט״א

ישראל ומאירה לויץ
Dr. and Mrs. Yisrael Levitz

In Memory of
Max Stern

Max Stern Foundation, Inc.

„אשריכם שנתמניתם פרנסים על בניו של מקום"
(רש"י במדבר יא:טז)

In Honor of
Rabbi Hershel Schachter

May He grant you
renewed strength, energy and wisdom
to protect His honor,
and
ongoing enthusiasm, humor and patience
to embrace His people.

Rabbi and Mrs. David Zharnest
Dr. and Mrs. Daniel Fink
Mr. and Mrs. Raphael Fink

To
Yeshivat Sha'alvim

Moshe Weglein	1982-83
Sholom Weglein	1983-84, 1986
Yaakov Weglein	1985-86
	1986-87
Shmuel Weglein	1989-90
	1990-91

Helen and Ernst Weglein

"ישמח משה במתנת חלקו"

Our thanks to our dear friends
Mr. and Mrs. Maurice Ehrlich
for their devotion, generosity
and loyalty to Sha'alvim

”תנו כבוד לתורה“

Our appreciation to

Rabbi and Mrs. Nachman Nacham

for their generous dedication of the

Kollel Keter Yehoshua כולל כתר יהושע

at Sha'alvim

In honor of
Dr. Herman Geo. Kaiser
Tulsa, Oklahoma

Rabbi Arthur Kahn

Best Wishes to
Rav Meir Schlesinger
Rav Pinchas Singer
Rabbi Mallen Galinsky

Iser and Anna Roller

In Honor of

Rabbi Meir Schlesinger

Rabbi Mallen Galinsky

Zvi Caspi

Rabbi Aaron and Dr. Marta Shapiro

Rashie, Saadie and Shem Tov —

Sha'alvim students

We Salute the Congregation

משאת בנימין אנשי פאדהייצע

and offer our appreciation to our friends

Mr. and Mrs. Marcus Schulman
Mr. and Mrs. Iser Roller

Our warmest congratulations to
all of our honorees.

Your dedication to Torah and Yiddishkeit
serves as an inspiration to us all.

May השי״ת grant you
strength and perserverance
to continue your work for Klal Yisroel.

Judy and Allen Fagin
Robert Fagin '91
Charles Fagin

Greetings and Blessings to

Dr. and Mrs. Nathan Averick
Guests of Honor

Dr. and Mrs. Sy Greenfield
Parents of the Year

Marc Geller
Alumnus of the Year

at the

Second Annual Chicago Dinner
of Friends of Yeshivat Sha'alvim

Saturday night, March 7, 1992

Rabbi Harvey and Vivien Well
Dr. Stephen and Cheryl Karesh
Chairpersons

Compliments of

Barron Consulting Group, Ltd.
Accounting Tax, and Financial Advisory Services

Terry D. Aranoff
9 East 40th Street
New York, NY 10016
(212) 679-7778 • FAX (212) 779-7148

Our heartiest Mazel-Tov Wishes to
everyone at Yeshivat Sha'alvim
and to
all of tonight's Honorees

June and Terry Aranoff
Ronnie '89, Barry and Alana

Best Wishes to

**Rav Meir Schlesinger
and Yeshivat Sha'alvim**

Mr. and Mrs. Shelley Goren

ישיבת שעלבים

Bracha V'Hatzlacha
David Wiseman (1990)

Reda Ruth and Alan Wiseman

ישיבת שעלבים

In Honor of
Alex and Vera Hornstein

The D'ver Family

Our Best Wishes to
our dear friends
Debby and Shimmy Kwestel
and
Terri and Shmuel Wagner
on these most deserved honors

Bonnie and Gabe Kaszovitz
Deena and Saul Kaszovitz
Jonah Kaszovitz
Daniel Kaszovitz
Naomi, David and Alex Kaszovitz

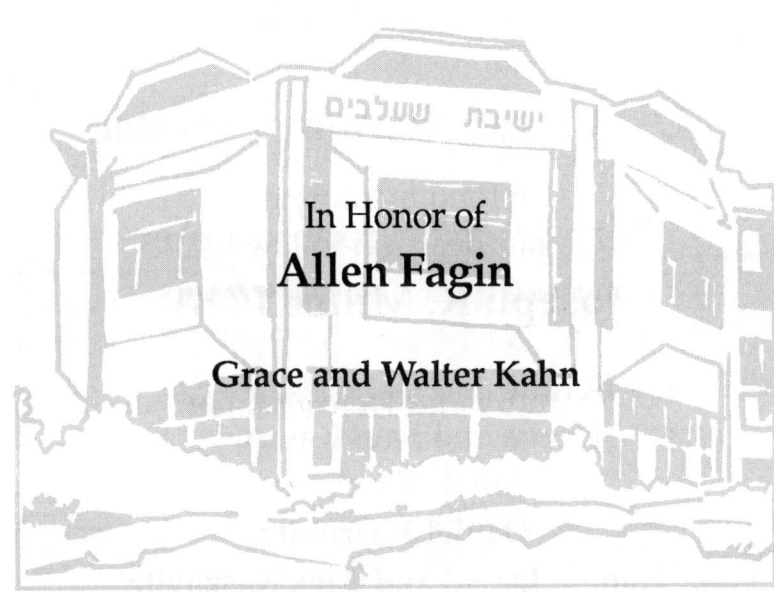

In Honor of
Allen Fagin

Grace and Walter Kahn

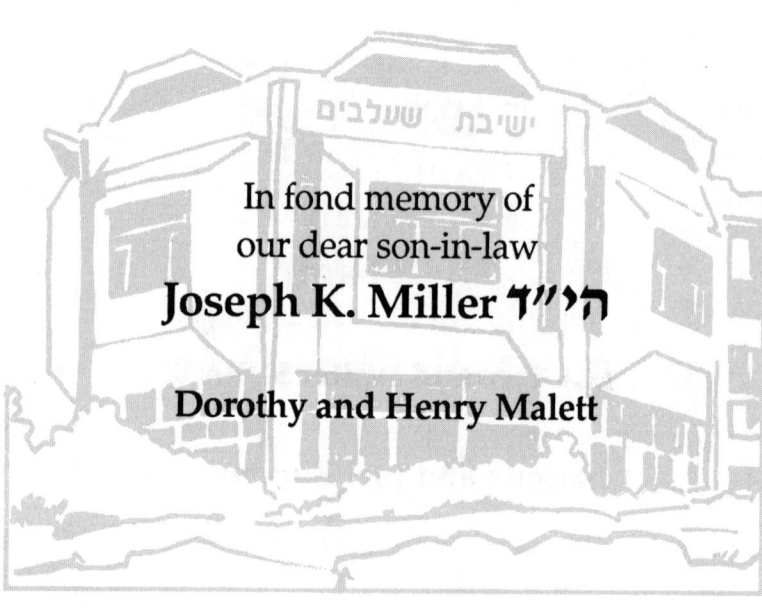

In fond memory of
our dear son-in-law
Joseph K. Miller הי״ד

Dorothy and Henry Malett

In Appreciation of
Yeshivat Sha'alvim
and
In Gratitude to
its eminent Rosh HaYeshiva
Rav Meir Schlesinger

Charlotte and Joel Zimmerman

In Honor of
Orly and Yakov Zimmerman

Aliza
Menashe
Efraim

at Sha'alvim

לז״נ

הרב יוסף טוביה
ב״ר דוב בער ז״ל

Founder of
the Rudman Foundation
and
the Torah Microfiche Library

In Honor of
the Rosh HaYeshiva
הרב מאיר שלזינגר שליט"א
and
the Dean of the Yeshiva
Rabbi Mallen Galinsky שליט"א

Mrs. Deborah Rudman

In Memory of
Joseph K. Miller הי״ד

Rabbi and Mrs. Alvin Marcus

In Honor of

the Honorees
and the Rosh HaYeshiva
Harav Schlesinger

The Scheinfeld Family
Herb and Esther
Benzion and Hillel

HERBERT I. SCHEINFELD
SENIOR VICE PRESIDENT /
FINANCIAL CONSULTANT
CHAIRMAN'S COUNCIL

1465 BROADWAY
HEWLETT, NEW YORK 11557

516 791 4300   800 248 2566 NY
800 635 0013 US
516 791 1669 FAX

We wish to thank
Rabbi Meir Schlesinger,
Rabbi Yammer,
and all the Rabbeim of
Yeshivat Sha'alvim
for making this year a wonderful experience
for their talmidim

From

Dr. and Mrs. Jacob Ackerman

Warmest Wishes to
Judd and his chaverim

from

S.W.
Doc
Happy
Sleepy
Sneezy
Bashful
Dopey
Grumpy

ישיבת שעלבים

In Memory of
our dear Parents

Dr. Jack I. and Mrs. Mae Saks ע״ה
Mr. Elie Neustadter ע״ה

Miriam and George Saks

In Honor of
Rav Meir Schlesinger
and
Rabbi Mallen Galinsky

Mr. and Mrs. David Goldsmith

Congregation Sharei Zedek
Sea Gate Sisterhood
and Talmud Torah
Coney Island, N.Y.

Rabbi Judah B. Galinsky
of blessed memory
Our Rabbi from 1944 to 1956

Our esteemed
Leaders and Founders of Yeshiva Sharei Zedek
Rabbi Galinsky and Rebbitzen Leah
of sainted memory, have passed on,
but their spirit lives with us
in our holy work
of spreading Torah and Traditional Judaism.
May their memory serve as a blessing and an inspiration.

Congregation Sharei Zedek
Sea Gate Sisterhood and Talmud Torah
Coney Island, N.Y.

salutes
Rabbi Meir Schlesinger
Rabbi Philip Harris Singer

and our own distinguished
Rabbi Mallen Galinsky

and

Yeshivat Sha'alvim

William Feller, *President*
Lottie Rosenkrancz, *President, Ladies Auxiliary*

Best Wishes to
Shimon and Debby Kwestel

Rabbi and Mrs. Fabian Schonfeld

To
Debby and Shimon
רדף צדקה וחסד ימצא חיים צדקה וכבוד
(משלי כא: כא)

From

Chemia and Vivien Kleinman

To
Shimon and Debby Kwestel
whose selfless dedication
does honor to Joe's memory

Sheldon and Hedda Rudoff

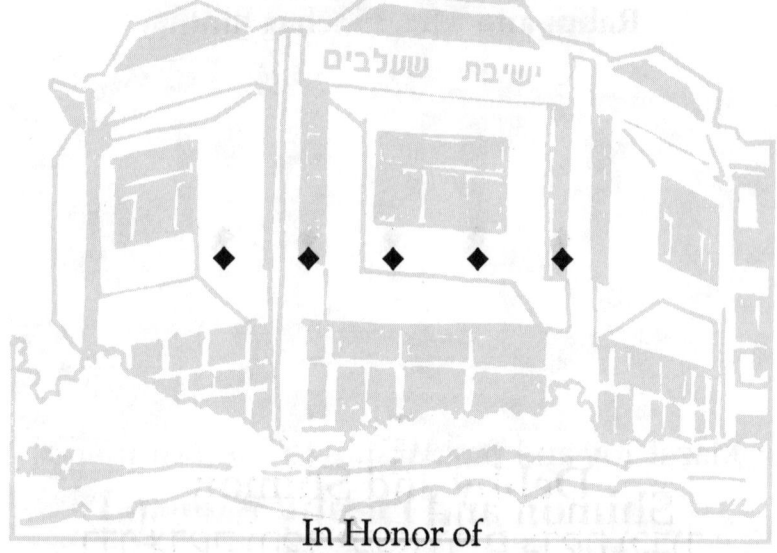

In Honor of
Shimon and Debby Kwestel

Mr. and Mrs. Joseph Shaw

In honor of our friends
Shimmy and Debby Kwestel
An outstanding Torah Leader
Champion of Soviet Jewry
Man of principal, vision and determination

Rabbi and Mrs. Pinchas Stolper

◆ ◆ ◆ ◆ ◆

Mazal Tov and Best Wishes to our dear friends
Shimon and Debby Kwestel
May G-d grant you good health and much נחת
so that you may continue performing acts of חסד
for כלל ישראל

Nettie and Joe Ellenberg

In Honor of
Shimon and Debby Kwestel
on receiving
the Joseph K. Miller Achdut Yisrael Award

In Memory of our beloved brother
Joseph K. Miller

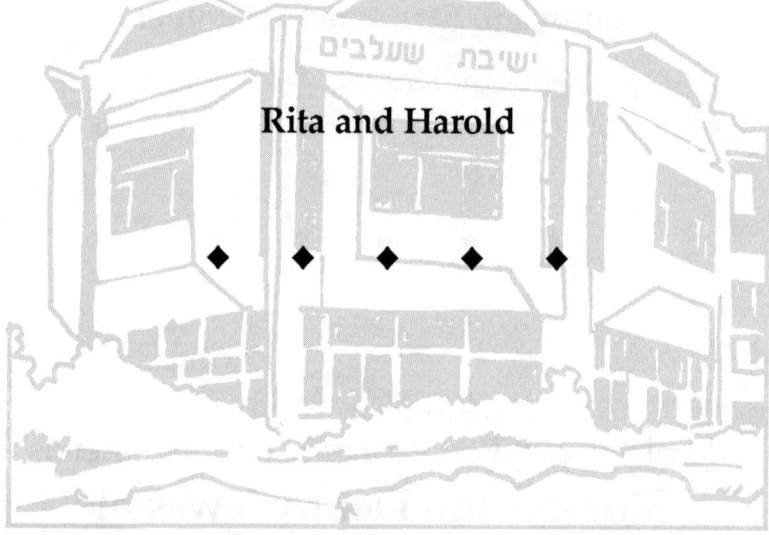

Rita and Harold

◆　◆　◆　◆　◆

Warm Mazel Tov wishes to our good friends
Debby and Shimon Kwestel

Lori and Bernard Levmore

Congratulations to
Shimon and Debby Kwestel
Your dedication
to community service and Gemilat Hasadim
have been an inspiration to all of us.

Ruth and Jonathan Shor
Deborah, Daniel and David

◆　　◆　　◆　　◆　　◆

To our dear friends
Debby and Shimon

We want to wish you Mazel Tov and Hatzlacha
in all your endeavors.
Much Nachas from your loving family.

Love,

Ann and Fred Frenkel and Family

To our cousins,

Shimon and Debby Kwestel

with affection and admiration
for all that they do for Klal Yisrael

Honey and Michael Rackman and Family

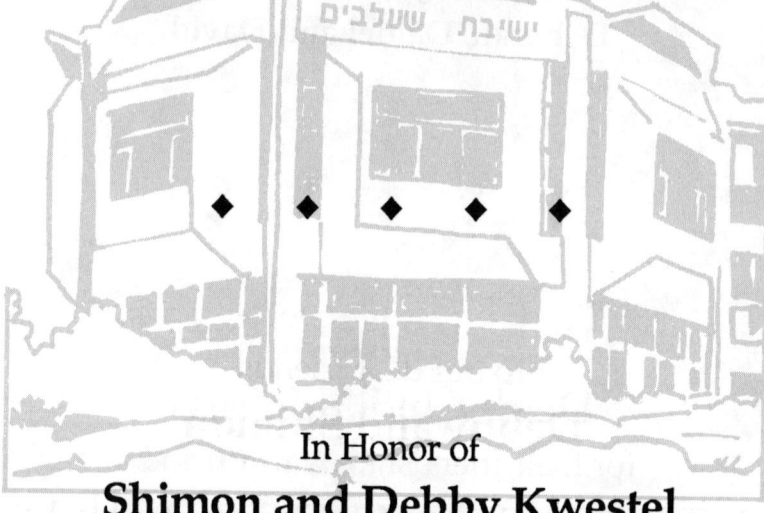

ישיבת שעלבים

In Honor of

Shimon and Debby Kwestel

and all the

Honorees

Rabbi and Mrs. Louis Leifer

Mazel Tov to
Shimon and Debby Kwestel

from

Heschel and Adinah Raskas
and family

◆   ◆   ◆   ◆   ◆

To
Debby and Shimmy
for their friendship, warmth and
commitment to the survival of our people,
all of which are unparallelled.

From their friends

Miriam and Howard Rhine

A Tribute of Honor and Affection to
Shimon and Debby Kwestel
and
Shmuel and Terri Wagner

Rabbi and Mrs. Manfred Gans
Congregation Machane Chodosh
Forest Hills, New York

◆　◆　◆　◆　◆

In Honor of
Shimon and Debby Kwestel

Dr. and Mrs. Herbert Taragin

Stuart and Terri
Mazel Tov to a most deserving couple

Beth and Josh Kalter

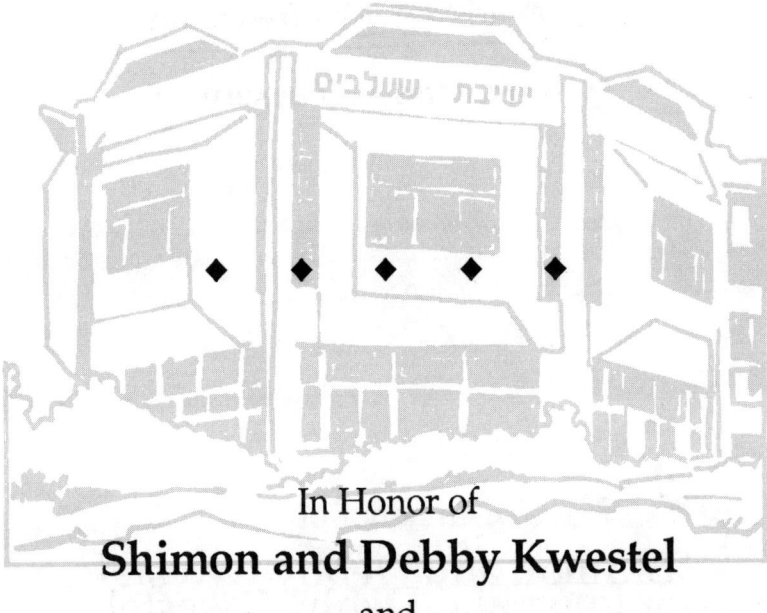

In Honor of
Shimon and Debby Kwestel
and
Stuart and Terri Wagner

Mr. and Mrs. Bezalel Jacobowitz

In honor of
Shimon and Debby Kwestel

A dedicated, dynamic couple
whose sincerity of purpose has been exemplary.
Their good deeds are an inspiration to all of us.

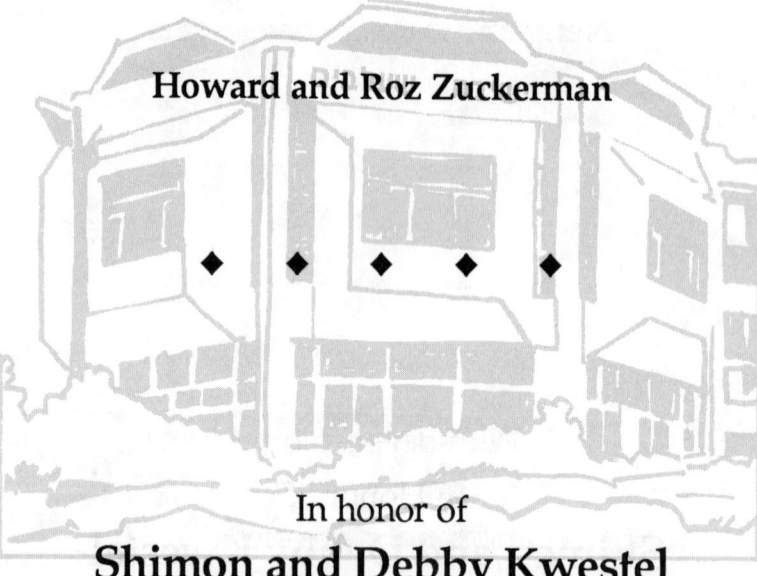

Howard and Roz Zuckerman

◆ ◆ ◆ ◆ ◆

In honor of
Shimon and Debby Kwestel
whose commitment to Torah causes
is an inspiration to all

Rosalyn and Franklyn Snitow

In Honor of
Yossi and Agi Fried

In friendship,

Netty and Aryeh Rosenbaum

ישיבת שעלבים

◆ ◆ ◆ ◆ ◆

With deepest love,
tremendous pride,
and fond memories,
we honor our dearest friends,
Agi and Yossi Fried

Kol Hakavod!

**The Gellers
Barbara and Ivan
Mike, Julie and Lauren**

Congratulations to
Yossi and Agi Fried

From

Leonard and Irma Strear

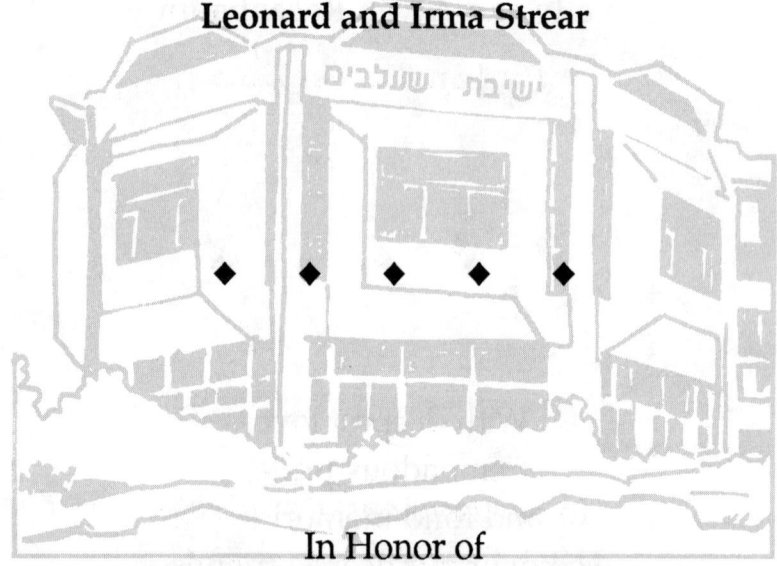

In Honor of
Joseph and Agi Fried

Mr. and Mrs. Albert Kahn

In Honor of our Uncle,
Rabbi Pinchas Singer,
truly devoted to the Yeshiva
and
Congratulations to
Rivky and Arthur Helft
Our dear neighbors and friends

Paul and Esther Lerer

◆ ◆ ◆ ◆ ◆

In Honor of our dear friends
Rivki and Arthur Helft

Malka and Paul Herman

Best Wishes to
Rifki and Arthur Helft

Dr. and Mrs. Albert Hornblass

Greetings to
Rifki and Arthur Helft

Dr. and Mrs. Walter Berkowitz

In honor of our good friends
Rifki and Arthur Helft

Laurie and Barry Badner

Mazel Tov
Rifki and Arthur

We honor you for being
loving parents and loyal friends.
You involve yourselves in every good cause,
always helping those in need.

Love,

Meilech and Renee Klaristenfeld

In Honor of our dear friends
Rifki and Arthur

Seena and Trudy

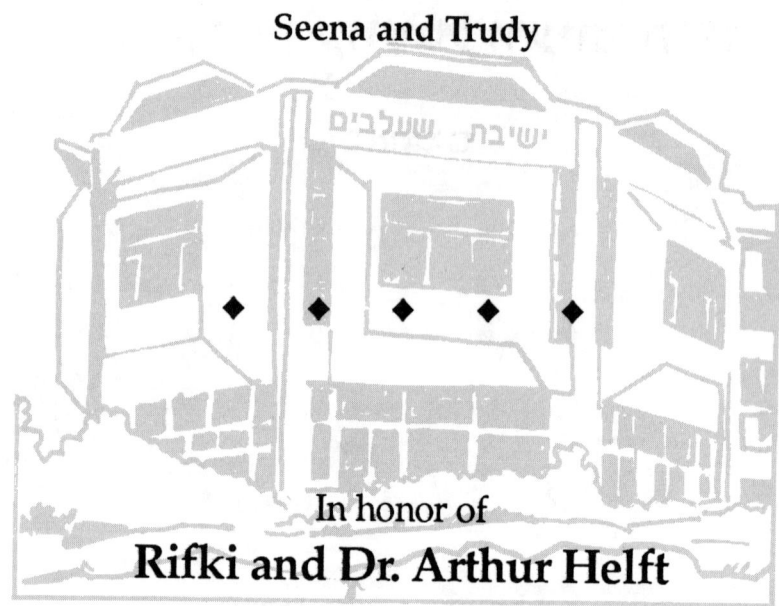

In honor of
Rifki and Dr. Arthur Helft

We value their ongoing efforts in meeting
the needs of the Jewish community.

Naomi and Louis Feder

ברכותינו המאליפות שלוחות לידידינו הדגולים מאד
מיסד וראש ישיבת שעלבים
הרה"ג ר' מאיר שלזינגר שליט"א
ולרב ר' מעלה גלינסקי שליט"א
ולידידינו הנעלים מאד
הרב אליעזר מאיר שוורץ ורעיתו שליט"א
ולר' שמעון קוסטל ורעיתו הי"ו

מאחלים

זבולון ויהודית חרל"פ

In honor of
Rabbi Allen Schwartz

Paul and Pia Rubin

Congratulations and Best Wishes to our loving son,
Rabbi Allen Schwartz
and his lovely wife,
Alisa, and adorable family.
May he continue his sacred mitzvah work
with bracha and hatzlacha always.

From

your loving parents
Sarah and Milton Schwartz
and loving sisters
Judy and Marlene
and niece **Chana Laya**

◆　◆　◆　◆　◆

In Honor of our beloved Rabbi and Rebbitzen
Rabbi Allen and Alisa Schwartz

Murray and Veronica Zucker

In Honor of
Rabbi and Mrs. Allen Schwartz

Marc and Micheline Ratzersdorfer

„מלוה ה׳ חונן דל וגמלו ישלם לו״

*"He who is gracious to those in need of help:
Lends to G-d, and G-d will repay his good deed to him."*
(Proverbs 19:17)

To
Rabbi Allen Schwartz
A man who lives to help others

Marisa and Richard Stadtmauer

Mazel Tov to
Terri and Stuart Wagner
Alumni of the Year

May you continue to be exemplary role models
to all alumni and future talmidim.

Esther and Baruch Weinstein
Rebecca Beth and Tova Gabrielle

◆   ◆   ◆   ◆   ◆

Our compliments to
Yeshivat Sha'alvim
for selecting a true Torah committed couple,
Stuart and Terri Wagner
as Honorees at this year's Dinner

Rabbi Jack and Marilyn Roth
Dr. Howard and Tova Roth
Michael and Sara Litton
Robert and Beth Shubowitz
Marc Roth

Mazel Tov to our good friends
Shmuel and Terri Wagner
who truly exemplify

עבודת תורה, גמילות חסד, ואהבת ישראל

Ricki and Joey Genachowski
Lauren, Steven and Evan

◆　◆　◆　◆　◆

Mazel Tov to
Shmuel and Terri

Elisa, Steven and Yishai Kadish

Mazel Tov
Shmuel and Terri

From all those who love you

**Mom, Dad, Hal, Noa
Ariel, Tovi, Aviva, Avrahmi
Yitzi, Evan, Sharon, Yonni, Yehudah
Moshe, Shani and Chaya
Aviva, Elli, Shana**

◆   ◆   ◆   ◆   ◆

In Honor of
Terri and Stuart Wagner

Mr. and Mrs. Moshe Orenbuch

In Honor of
Shimon and Debby Kwestel
Allen Fagin
Rabbi Meir Schlesinger
Werner Rosenbaum
Rabbi Mallen Galinsky
and
all of the Magidei Shiur at the Yeshiva

Susanne and Michael Wimpfheimer
Jan, Orit, Barry and Ahuva

◆　　◆　　◆　　◆　　◆

With gratitude to
Yeshivat Sha'alvim
חזקו ואמצו
and in honor of our children at Sha'alvim
Rabbi Ari and Sandy (Gila) Waxman
שואבים מים בששון ומשקים צאן קדשים

Chaim I. and Chaya Waxman

In honor of
Rav Meir Schlesinger שליט״א
and
Yeshivat Sha'alvim

Rabbi Dr. Joseph Ozarowski
Elmont Jewish Center

♦   ♦   ♦   ♦   ♦

Mazel Tov to
the Honorees!

A special Yasher Koach to:
Rav Schlesinger and Rav Yamer
who made David's year at Sha'alvim so productive,
teaching him skills that will allow David
to pursue Torah study for a lifetime!

To
Rav and Mrs. Ari Waxman
who opened up their home to David
so he could continue practicing piano.

To
all of David's Rabbaim, Chavrusot and Friends
who made the Sha'alvim experience so special.

Marilyn and Joseph Bench

BEST WISHES FROM

BankLeumi
TRUST COMPANY OF NEW YORK
Member FDIC

4410 13th AVENUE, BROOKLYN, N. Y. 11219
Telephone (718) 854-1800

◆ ◆ ◆ ◆ ◆

Compliments of

**Dr. and Mrs. Bernard D. Kosowsky
and Family**

The Mollie Franks Marks
Perpetual Scholarship Fund
In Sacred Memory of My Cherished Parents
Clara and Abram Frank

Mollie Frank Marks

◆　◆　◆　◆　◆

Greetings to My Esteemed Colleague
and Dear Friend
Rabbi Philip Harris Singer

Rabbi David Stavsky
Beth Jacob Congregation
Columbus, Ohio

Mazel Tov to our son and brother
Binyamin Zev Aronoff
on his very successful year at Yeshivat Sha'alvim.
May he rise ever higher in Torah and Mitzvot

אבא, אמא, Shifra, Miriam and Nehemia

With Appreciation for
the uplifting and inspiring month of learning—
January 1992

Daniel Schiffman, '89, '90

In memory of my beloved wife
Judith
Nov. 1, 1923 - Nov. 12, 1991

"She hath tasted and seen that her traffic is good:
Her lamp shall not be put out in the night."

Proverbs: Chapter 31, Verse 18

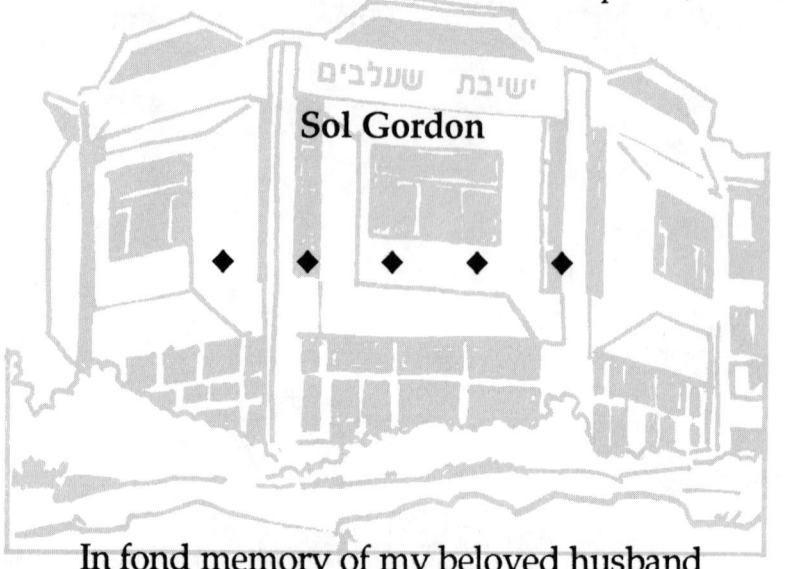

ישיבת שעלבים

Sol Gordon

◆　◆　◆　◆　◆

In fond memory of my beloved husband
Captain William W. Cohen

Eva Cohen

In Memory of
Morris M. Lewis

Lillian Lewis
and
Howard T. Lewis

ישיבת שעלבים

Best Wishes to
the Honorees

Solomon and Meira Max
David and Daniel

With much admiration to our children
Judy and Allen Fagin

Mom and Dad

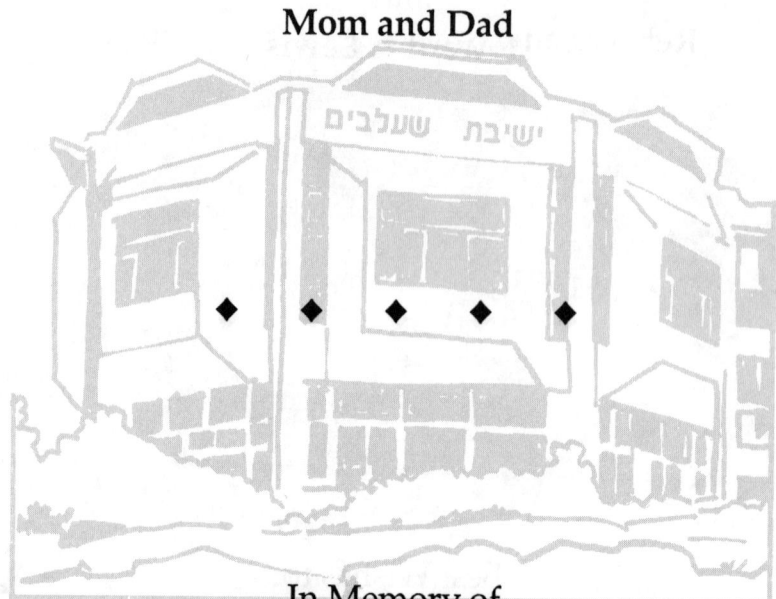

ישיבת שעלבים

In Memory of
Joseph Heller

Benjamin and Beth Heller and Family

Mazel Tov and Best Wishes to
all the Honorees.

Rebecca and Israel Rivkin and Family

In Appreciation for the wonderful job you are doing

Dr. and Mrs. Gabriel Gurell

Mazel Tov to
all the Honorees

Mr. and Mrs. Dovid Weinstein

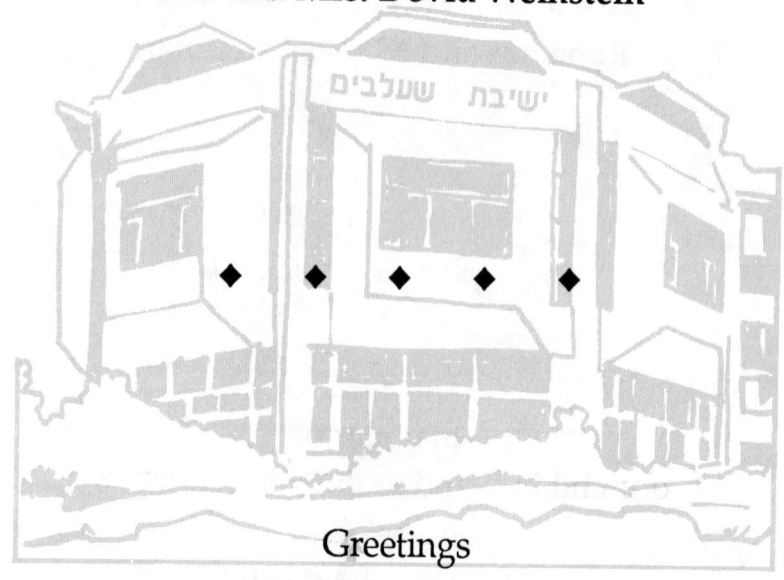

ישיבת שעלבים

◆ ◆ ◆ ◆ ◆

Greetings

from

Brenda and Albert Kalter

Best Wishes for continued success to
Rav Meir
and
the entire staff.

Rona, Ira and Michael Kellman

◆　◆　◆　◆　◆

In honor of
our children and grandchildren שיחיו
on Sha'alvim
Duv and Mechi
Gedalya Simcha
Yaakov Amitai
Elisheva Baila

Moishe and Feige Friederwitzer

In Honor of
Don and Susan Kates
for their hospitality to our son,
Ely Moshe,
during his stay at the Yeshiva

Rabbi Ira and Faigie Kronenberg

ישיבת שעלבים

◆　◆　◆　◆　◆

Rabbi and Mrs. Chaim Messinger
extend their Mazel Tov to their son
Shlomo
and to
Lisa Preis
upon their recent engagement

שמעון ודבי עמו"ש

רעים אהובים אתם לנו כאח ואחות
יתן לכם ה' ולנו את הכח להמשיך ולפעול
למענו ולמען תורתו, עמו וארצו

מעלה ושרה

◆ ◆ ◆ ◆ ◆

Congratulations to
Shimon and Debby Kwestel

Anne and Jerry Gontownik

◆ ◆ ◆ ◆

Mazel Tov to our dear friends
Shimon and Debby Kwestel
and our dear neighbors
Arthur and Rifki Helft

from

Judy and Stanley Rosenberg

◆ ◆ ◆ ◆ ◆

In Honor of a wonderful couple
Debby and Shimon Kwestel

Gloria Rosenstock

To
Shimon and Debby Kwestel
People of stature with great accomplishments for Klal Yisroel

Carmi and Pearl Schwartz

◆ ◆ ◆ ◆ ◆

In Honor of friends
Shimon and Debby Kwestel
who have earned their honor the hard way—they worked for it.

Dr. and Mrs. Leonard Shapiro

◆ ◆ ◆ ◆ ◆

Mazel Tov to
Shimon and Debby Kwestel
on a well deserved Honor

Phyllis and David Goldberg and family

◆ ◆ ◆ ◆ ◆

In Tribute and Appreciation to
Debby and Shimon Kwestel
הקב״יה ישלם שכרם

Chashie and Moshe Krupka

In Honor of
Debby and Shimon Kwestel
for their outstanding contributions to the Jewish community

Rachel and Israel Goldman

◆　◆　◆　◆　◆

To
Debby and Shimon,
מזל טוב on a well deserved honor.

Miriam and Ari Adler　　**Eva and Manny Sack**
Froma and Gerry Posner　　**Esther Weinstock**

◆　◆　◆　◆　◆

We are happy to honor our dear friends
Shimon and Debby Kwestel
May they be blessed to give of their manifold talents
to K'lal Yisroel for many years to come

From:
Mr. and Mrs. Jack Rottenberg
Mr. and Mrs. Mark Rottenberg
Mr. and Mrs. Sol Kanarek

◆　◆　◆　◆　◆

In Honor of
Shimon and Debby Kwestel
in recognition of their share
in the enhancement of Torah Judaism.

Chantze and Donald Butler
Pittsburgh, PA

In Honor of
Shimon and Debby Kwestel

Elaine Goldklang

◆　◆　◆　◆　◆

In Honor of
Allen Fagin and **Shimon and Debby Kwestel**
for their outstanding contributions to Klal Yisrael

**Mr. and Mrs. Norman Meskin
Dr. and Mrs. Allen Rubin
Dr. and Mrs. Nathan Wadler**

◆　◆　◆　◆　◆

Mazel Tov
Shimon and Debby
We're proud to join you in supporting this worthy institution

**Melanie and Mendy Kwestel
Adina Rachel and Paul Aaron**

◆　◆　◆　◆　◆

Congratulations and Best Wishes
to our dear friends and neighbors
Debby and Shimmy Kwestel

Tami and Nathan Braun

In Honor of
Debby and Shimon Kwestel

Lois and Avi Blumenfeld

◆　◆　◆　◆　◆

In Honor of
Shimon and Debby Kwestel
outstandingly devoted communal leaders
and
Rabbi Allen Schwartz
dedicated rabbi and educator

Henry and Golda Reena Rothman

◆　◆　◆　◆　◆

To a lovely couple who put all their efforts into Israel
Shimon and Debby Kwestel

Lenny and Molly Naider

◆　◆　◆　◆　◆

Best Wishes to
Shimon and Debby

Suzan and Fred Ehrman

To our dear friends,
Shimon and Debby
May you have the zchus to work on behalf
of Klal Yisroel for many years to come.
Thanks for everything.

Linda and Elly

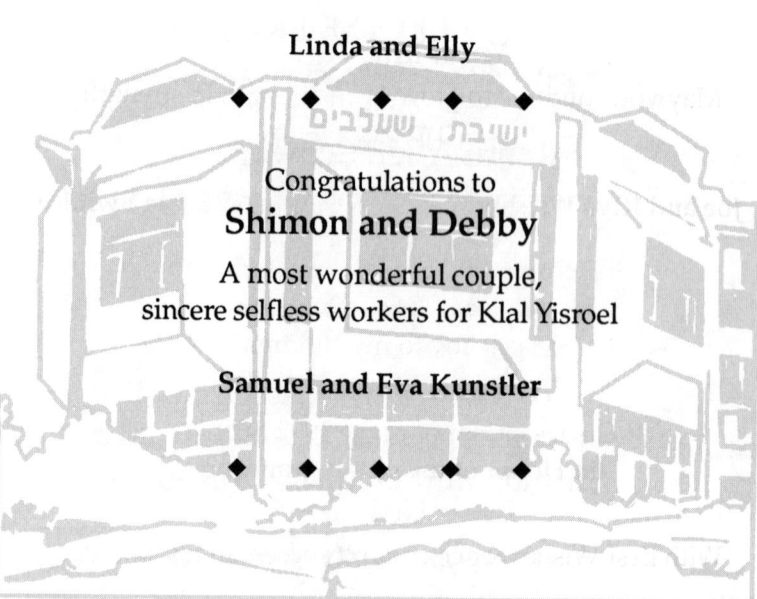

Congratulations to
Shimon and Debby
A most wonderful couple,
sincere selfless workers for Klal Yisroel

Samuel and Eva Kunstler

In honor of
Rifki and Arthur Helft

Carl and Sylvia Freyer

Mazel Tov to
Yossi and Agi Fried
May you go from strength to strength

From your "extended" family and friends of
East Denver Orthodox Synagogue
Denver, Colorado

◆　　◆　　◆　　◆　　◆

Yossi and Agi
May you continue to grow from strength to strength
מזל טוב

Joe and Riva Weissbrot　　　　**Nahum and Susie Swinkin**

◆　　◆　　◆　　◆　　◆

Mazal Tov to my children
Agi and Yossi Fried
Guests of Honor at the 1992 Dinner
In Honor of my oldest grandson
Udi
With Best Wishes for continued success in his studies

Magda Rosenthal

◆　　◆　　◆　　◆　　◆

In appreciation to the many sides of
Rabbi Allen Schwartz

The Genack Family

Our best wishes for continued Hatzlacha and good health to
the Rosh HaYeshiva שליט״א
and the Rabbeim of the Yeshiva

Dr. and Mrs. Fred Rosner

◆ ◆ ◆ ◆ ◆

Mazel Tov
Rifki and Arthur
We honor you for being loving parents and loyal friends.
You involve yourselves in every good cause,
always helping those in need.

Love,

Meilech and Renee Klaristenfeld

◆ ◆ ◆ ◆ ◆

Best Wishes to
Rabbi Allen Schwartz
on an honor well deserved.

Paulette Schauer   **Oscar Gottlieb**

To
Rabbi Schwartz
and his Aishes Chayil,
Alisa
who are wonderful spiritual leaders, people and friends
Thank you very much for all of your help in so many ways.

Love always,
Steven Fink and Mindy Toporovsky

◆ ◆ ◆ ◆ ◆

To our dear friend
Rabbi Allen Schwartz
for a well deserved Honor

Debra and Marvin Sternberg

◆ ◆ ◆ ◆ ◆

In Honor of
Rabbi Allen Schwartz

Warren Shimoff

◆ ◆ ◆ ◆ ◆

In Honor of
Rabbi Allen Schwartz

Sam Wind

Mazel Tov to
Terri and Stuart Wagner

Lynda and Ben Brafman
Jennifer and David

◆　◆　◆　◆　◆

In Honor of
Stuart and Terri Wagner

Denise and Alan Wildes

◆　◆　◆　◆　◆

Mazel Tov to
Stuart and Terri Wagner
on a well deserved honor.

Daniel, Miriam, and Sarah Herenstein

◆　◆　◆　◆　◆

Mazel Tov to our good friends
Shmuel and Terri Wagner
who have truly earned the title of Bnei Torah

Rabbi Feivel and Bina Wagner

In Honor of our good friends,
Shmuel and Terri Wagner
who set a shining example for their family and friends.
May you continue to go מחיל אל חיל.

Esthy and Elliot Hersch

◆　◆　◆　◆　◆

To our good friends
Shmuel and Terri
Mazel Tov for this honor you so richly deserve.
May Hashem grant you many more years
to continue your work for כלל ישראל.

Deborah and Alan Weichselbaum
Daniel and Jonathan

◆　◆　◆　◆　◆

Mazel Tov to
Shmuel and Terri Wagner
on a well deserved honor

Dr. David Hurwitz

Mazel Tov to
Shmuel and Terri Wagner

Rhoda and Daniel Zaslowsky
Shirley and Martin Kaye

◆　◆　◆

To
Reb Shmuel
and his אשת חיל
Mazel Tov and Congratulations
Your inclusion in our chevra has
placed us on a higher מדרגה.
We're proud of you.
Love,
Beth and Dovid Feldman
Danna and David Berk
Laurie and Robert Koppel

In Honor of
Lorraine and Mordy Sohn

Louis and Rachy Newman
Manny and Gloria Salomon

◆ ◆ ◆ ◆ ◆

In Memory of
Judith Gordon ע״ה

David, Pam, Moshe and Dena
Lehmann

◆ ◆ ◆ ◆ ◆

In Honor of
Rav Meir

Mr. and Mrs. Akevy Greenblatt

◆ ◆ ◆ ◆ ◆

Compliments of

Cheryl and Eddie Dauber
Jeremy Dauber 1990-91

Greetings to
Yeshivat Sha'alvim

Dr. and Mrs. Joseph Adler

◆　◆　◆　◆　◆

In Honor of
Rabbi Meir Schlesinger

Roslyn and Michael Feder and Mark

◆　◆　◆　◆　◆

מזל טוב and Best Wishes to our dear grandson and nephew
Binyamin Zev Aronoff
May you continue בדרך של תורה ומעשים טובים

Your loving Grandmother Mollie Chideckel
Uncle Dr. David Chideckel
Uncle and Aunt Norman and Rosa Chideckel

◆　◆　◆　◆　◆

Best Wishes

Renlyn Fashions, Inc.

Thank you to
my Rebbeim and friends at Sha'alvim

Ezra Shapiro
Teaneck, NJ

◆ ◆ ◆ ◆ ◆

To
the Rebbeim of Sha'alvim
In appreciation of the wonderful
values, midos, and learning you nurture.

Barbara and Stanley Shapiro
Teaneck, NJ

◆ ◆ ◆ ◆ ◆

Greetings to
Rav Meir Schlesinger and Rabbi Mallen Galinsky

From

Pauline and Joseph Silber

◆ ◆ ◆ ◆ ◆

Continued success in all your endeavors

Neil and Leah Israel

In Honor of
Rabbi Meir Schlesinger נ"י
Rosh HaYeshiva
and family

Dr. and Mrs. Walter Feder

◆   ◆   ◆   ◆   ◆

Shalom Uvracha!

Judy and André Ungar

◆   ◆   ◆   ◆   ◆

Greetings from
Matthew Herenstein, '84
and fiancée
Sharon Roth

◆   ◆   ◆   ◆   ◆

In Appreciation to
the Rosh HaYeshiva Harav Meir שליט"א
for all that he, together with the other Ra'mim,
has done to instill in our grandson
the love of Torah and Eretz Yisrael.

Lou and Lottie Herrmann

In Honor of
Rabbi Mallen Galinsky

Beatrice Smith

◆ ◆ ◆ ◆ ◆

Mazel Tov to
all of the Honorees

Pamela and Ari Hirt

◆ ◆ ◆ ◆ ◆

Greetings to
the Honorees

Morris J. Golombeck, Inc.
Importers
Spices,
Seeds,
and Herbs
Brooklyn, NY

◆ ◆ ◆ ◆ ◆

With Sincere Good Wishes to
all the Honorees

Moe D. and Ruth Karash

Congratulations to
**Shimon and Debby
Kwestel**
for their well-deserved award

William and Judy Rapfogel

♦ ♦ ♦

Best Wishes of Mazel Tov to
**Shimon and Debby
Kwestel**

Arthur and Carla Rand

♦ ♦ ♦

Congratulations and
Best Wishes of Mazel Tov to
**Debby and Shimon
Kwestel**
upon a well deserved honor.

**Rachelle and Israel
Schwechter**

♦ ♦ ♦

Mazel Tov to
our friends and neighbors
**Debby and Shimon
Kwestel**
on this well deserved honor

Carol and Hyam Reichel

In Honor of our dear friends
**Debra and Shimon
Kwestel**

Carol and Sheldon Borgen

♦ ♦ ♦

Mazel Tov to
**Shimon and Debby
Kwestel**

Harold and Marcelle Lowell

♦ ♦ ♦

To
**Shimmy and Debby
Kwestel**
A very caring couple who
give of themselves unstintingly
to Klal Yisroel, body and soul.
Congratulations
**Rabbi and Mrs.
Joseph Grunblatt**

♦ ♦ ♦

In Honor of
**Shimon and Debby
Kwestel**

Mr. and Mrs. Saul Quinn

Mazel Tov to
**Professor Shimon
and Debby Kwestel**
and to Alumnus of the Year
Shmuel Wagner

**Sheri and Richie
Judy and Yossi
Mimi and Ari
and families**

◆　　◆　　◆

Best Wishes to
**Shimon and Debby
Kwestel**

Boruch and Maria Goldring

◆　　◆　　◆

To
Shimon and Debby Kwestel
מרבה צדקה מרבה שלום
קנה שם טוב קנה לעצמו
קנה לו דברי תורה
קנה לו חיי עולם הבא
(אבות ב:ז)
In recognition, admiration
and friendship

Larry and Lorraine Brown
Memphis, Tennessee

◆　　◆　　◆

In honor of
Rifki and Arthur Helft

Carl and Sylvia Freyer

Our Best to
**Shimon and Debby
Kwestel**

Mr. and Mrs. Carl Hamada

◆　　◆　　◆

Mazel Tov to
**Shimon and Debby
Kwestel**
on this well-deserved honor

Leah and Avi Weinberg

◆　　◆　　◆

In Honor of
**Dr. Arthur and Rifki
Helft**

From

Ceil and Bernard Kabakow

◆　　◆　　◆

To
Rifki and Arthur

Mazel Tov

Ruth and Ted

In Honor of
Rifki and Arthur Helft

Freida and Michael B. Harris

◆ ◆ ◆

In Honor of
**Dr. and Mrs.
Arthur Helft**

**Friends at
Frisch Yeshiva H.S.**

◆ ◆ ◆

In Honor of
Rifki and Arthur Helft
a couple
whom we are privileged
to call our dear friends
אנשי חיל וגומלי חסד ואמת
Love,
Marion and Billy Weiss

◆ ◆ ◆

Mazel Tov to
Arthur and Rifki

Medinah and Charles Popper

In Honor of
the Helfts

**Dr. and Mrs. Saul G. Agus
and family**

◆ ◆ ◆

In Honor of
Rifki and Arthur Helft
Best Wishes and Mazel Tov

Karen and Alan Broderson

◆ ◆ ◆

Congratulations to
Arthur and Rifki Helft

Kenneth and Jeanne Prager

◆ ◆ ◆

Mazel Tov to
Arthur and Rifki Helft

Naomi and Robert Spira

Mazel Tov to our dear friends
Yossi and Agi Fried

From

Jay and Joyce Moskowitz
Denver, CO

◆　◆　◆

Congratulations to
Joseph and Agi Fried

From

Fred and Frieda Englard
Denver, Colorado

◆　◆　◆

In Honor of
Yossi and Agi Fried

Gary and Janice Feder
Denver, Colorao

◆　◆　◆

In Honor of our dear friends
Yossi and Agi Fried

Mazel Tov

Alex and Meryl Jacobs
Denver

Mazel Tov to
Joseph and Agi Fried

Zussman Family
Denver, CO

◆　◆　◆

Mazel Tov to
Agi and Yossi Fried

Your efforts on behalf of our
shule are greatly appreciated.

Ladies Auxiliary of EDOS

◆　◆　◆

Congratulations to
Yossi and Agi
on an honor well deserved

**Leah and Philip Mehler
and Family**
Denver

◆　◆　◆

Yasher Koach
Agi and Yossi

From

Fran and Dovey Heller

In Honor of
the Rosh Yeshiva

From a Talmid

Malkiel Nechamkin

◆　◆　◆

Best Wishes to
all the Honorees

**Dr. and Mrs.
Yashar Hirshaut**

◆　◆　◆

In honor of
**Rav Schlesinger
Rav Galinsky**
and
Don Kates

**Mory, Pearl, Sarah Sheindel
and Hinda Miriam Korenblit**

◆　◆　◆

To our dear friends
Agi and Yossi
Your energy and enthusiasm
for all Jewish causes
knows no bounds.
Mazel Tov
on this well deserved honor.

**Michelle and Yitzchak
Teitelbaum**

Compliments of

**Mr. and Mrs.
Morris L. Green**

◆　◆　◆

Greetings from

Richard A. Lopchinsky, M.D.
New York, New York

◆　◆　◆

In Honor of our children
Yossi and Agi Fried
Sorry we could not be
with you tonight
We are proud of you and **Udi**

Love

**Dina (Fried) and Avraham
Hershkovitz**

◆　◆　◆

Best Wishes to
Yossi and Agi Fried

From

Florence and Reuven Rosen

In Honor of
Rabbi Allen Schwartz
whose enthusiastic
dedication and committment
are truly exemplary.

**Andrew and Ronnie
Schonzeit**

◆　◆　◆

In Honor of
Rabbi Allen Schwartz

Dina Dyckman

◆　◆　◆

Congratulations to
Rabbi Allen Schwartz
עד מאה ועשרים שנה
on receiving
the Rabbinic Leadership Award.
Thank you for inspiring us
with your dynamic leadership.

Elliot Fuhrer

In Honor of
Rabbi Allen Schwartz

**Rabbi and Mrs.
Moshe S. Gorelick**
Young Israel of North Bellmore

◆　◆　◆

In Honor of
Rabbi Allen Schwartz

Reuben and Hindy Taub

◆　◆　◆

Congratulations to
Rabbi Schwartz
on an honor well deserved

Rabbi and Mrs. A.M. Farber

Best wishes to
Yeshivat Sha'alvim

Rabbi David Bergstein
Dr. and Mrs. Ernest Freeman
Morris Isaacs
Yaffa and Martin Katz
Mr. and Mrs. Lester Kaufman
Mr. and Mrs. Benjamin Rosenstark
Edward Zughaft

◆   ◆   ◆

In Honor of
Yossi and Agi Fried

Chaim and Susie Feder
Jay and Celia Feder
Dr. and Mrs. Philip J. Lightstone
Dorothy and Irving Lumerman
Miguel and Aniko Mogyoros
Maurene and Beryl Tesler

◆   ◆   ◆

In Honor of
Shimon and Debby Kwestel

Edith and Jack Feder
Rabbi and Mrs. Aaron Gewirtz
Toni and Nick Gordon
Rabbi and Mrs. Bertram Leff
Emma and Hy Mark
Rabbi and Mrs. Hershel Milner
Claire and Martin Psaty
Bernard and Esther Schrenzel
Rabbi Yitzchak Sladowsky

In Honor of
Rabbi Allen Schwartz

Bette Marie Barker
Saul Blau
Art Blazer
Blu and Irving Greenberg
Hildegarde Lasky
Mr. and Mrs. David Mason
Mr. and Mrs. Allen Rosenzweig
Judy Schneider
Martin Schwarzschild
Bernice Wallach

ישיבת שעלבים

◆　◆　◆

In Honor of
Dr. Arthur and Rifki Helft

Jerry and Sharon Hartstein
Alice Oppenheimer
Harriet and Heshie Seif
Dr. and Mrs. Ephraim Weinstein
Diane and Jerry Wolf

◆　◆　◆

In Honor of
Shmuel and Terri Wagner

Joel Blazer
R' Binyomin and Debbie Mittel
Elli and Lara and Kids

◆　◆　◆

M. Berlson, Ed.

Journal Typeset and Printed by
• **TOVA PRESS, INC.** •
945 - 39th Street, Brooklyn, NY 11219
718 - 438-8877 • Fax 718 - 871-0396